Rhetoric of Femininity

LEXINGTON STUDIES
IN CONTEMPORARY RHETORIC
Series Editor: Gary C. Woodward,
The College of New Jersey

This series provides thought-provoking and accessible analyses of the uses of language and media from the middle of the twentieth century to the present. In particular, this series examines how modern discourse is constructed and communicated in our distracted times. These books will provide depth and clarity about discourse more familiar than understood.

Titles in the Series

The Rhetorical Invention of America's National Security State, by Marouf Hasian, Sean Lawson, and Megan McFarlane

Rhetoric of Femininity: Female Body Image, Media, and Gender Role Stress/Conflict, by Donnalyn Pompper

Rhetoric of Femininity

*Female Body Image, Media,
and Gender Role Stress/Conflict*

Donnalyn Pompper

LEXINGTON BOOKS
Lanham • Boulder • New York • London

Published by Lexington Books
An imprint of The Rowman & Littlefield Publishing Group, Inc.
4501 Forbes Boulevard, Suite 200, Lanham, Maryland 20706
www.rowman.com

Unit A, Whitacre Mews, 26-34 Stannary Street, London SE11 4AB

British Library Cataloguing in Publication Information Available

Library of Congress Cataloging-in-Publication Data Available

ISBN 978-1-4985-1935-9 (cloth : alk. paper)
ISBN 978-1-4985-1936-6 (electronic)

∞™ The paper used in this publication meets the minimum requirements of American National Standard for Information Sciences Permanence of Paper for Printed Library Materials, ANSI/NISO Z39.48-1992.

Printed in the United States of America

Contents

Acknowledgements   vii

Introduction   ix

1   Femininity Matters   1

2   Ideal Femininity According to Family, Tradition, and Media   27

3   Female Gender Role Stress/Conflict: Learning about/from Femininity   53

4   Consumerist *Mis*representations: Rituals and Industries that Shape Femininity   75

5   Women's Femininity at Work   103

6   Women at Play: Sports and Femininity   123

7   Femininity as Shaped by Intersectionalities of Social Identity Dimensions   147

8   Sexuality, Masculine Femininity, and Feminine Masculinity   171

9   Age, Health, and Femininity   189

10   Femininity and Politics   207

11   Lessons and Moving Forward   227

Bibliography   239

Index   269

About the Author   279

Acknowledgements

I must thank a handful of people who were most supportive of this project. First, I am grateful to the numerous women who shared their stories and participated in the research that serves as the foundation for this book. Also, thanks to undergraduate student Lauren Apple, who enabled me to direct an independent study on this topic. We met many early Saturday mornings in Center City, Philadelphia, to take photographs of dusty women's magazine images. Lauren also worked with me to organize and conduct several of the focus groups with college women. Next, I acknowledge the support of undergraduates Lucy Cruz and Cat Deasis, who helped with other key tasks associated with data collection, analysis, and literature searches. Thanks, also, to graduate student Alanna Miller for some transcript typing assistance. In addition, I am grateful for use of the conference room in the Department of Strategic Communication in Weiss Hall at Temple University, sundry church and library assembly rooms, and resources at the Free Library of Philadelphia. I also thank Temple University's English and Communications Librarian, Kristina DeVoe. Special thanks to Nicolette Amstutz, James Hamill, and Gary Woodward at Lexington Books, an imprint of Rowman & Littlefield. Lastly, many thanks to my students who help me to remain curious.

Introduction

To explore the question, *What is femininity?*, the study reported in this book enjoins diverse women's definitions with a critique of ways girls and women are represented across media and popular culture and the stress/conflict they experience as a result. Theoretical underpinnings are borrowed from academic literatures of psychology, sociology, mass communication, and feminist/women's/girls' studies. Often researchers stick to one age group when studying issues relating to girls and women (e.g., teens, working women, seniors) or one ethnic group (e.g., inner city girls, immigrant women). In doing so, they may overlook the value of examining certain concepts or issues (e.g., childrearing, economic challenges, work-home life balance) across multiple perspectives. Curiously, *femininity* seems like one of those words that might (or, should) be easy to define. It's not. This book distills the essences of academic research which inspired me to launch this timely, innovative study. I have gathered new data among three age cohorts of women—college students and their aunts, mothers, and grandmothers—so that I might explore the basic question, *What is femininity?* Drawing upon the strengths of multiple perspectives offers the broadest lens possible for examining what femininity is and how it shapes the lived experiences of girls and women today. In the course of these multi-generational conversations, an overwhelming pattern of anxiety-conflict-pressure-stress emerged—with much of it linked to women's breasts and their wombs. Overall, women across age cohorts struggle to keep up with impossible-to-achieve standards simply for being female. To begin, I offer details about the research methods used for this study and the theoretical underpinnings which provided a foundation for the inquiry.

COLLECTING AND ANALYZING DATA USED TO EXPLORE THE QUESTION, *WHAT IS FEMININITY?*

Consistent with a larger feminist methodology, focus group and interview research methods were used to gather women's narratives. A hermeneutic phenomenological theme analysis technique was used to organize their voices and to rhetorically interrogate popular culture for the research question guiding this inquiry. I used a snowball sampling technique and collectively spoke with about fifty-five college-aged women and forty-five of their aunts, mothers, and grandmothers of diverse social identity dimensions, including age, ethnicity, faith/spirituality, and sexual orientation. We talked for hundreds of hours and considered forty-five images of women from 100 years of women's magazines (1910–2010) to stimulate discussions about *What does the word femininity mean to you?*

First things first. I gained approval for this study from Temple University's Human Research Protection Program. The study partially was funded through the Temple University Summer Grant-in-Aid program. College women were incentivized with a $5 coffee shop gift card and the opportunity to talk about an interesting topic to which they could relate. The same was true for their aunts, mothers, and grandmothers—whom I suspect were encouraged to talk with me because their niece, daughter, or granddaughter had done so. Geographically, the focus groups meetings took place at my home university in Philadelphia, but also in New York, Washington, DC, and near my residence in southern New Jersey. For research participants farther away on the West coast, Midwest, and across the South, I sent the stimulus materials (electronically and by U.S. mail) in advance of a telephone or Skype interview. So, women who participated represented multiple regions across the United States. As part of demographic information requested on pre-interview questionnaires, I asked about age and sexual orientation. I also asked about women's media usage. As promised, no real names are used in this book. I invited women to offer a pseudonym for use in publication of the study and I used websites for female names representative of ethnic groups for other pseudonyms, relying on self-identification women provided on the pre-interview questionnaires. I've only identified women according to sexual orientation if they pointed it out themselves in the course of interviews and focus groups—as it seemed relevant to a particular point they chose to make.

To stimulate discussions during interviews and focus groups, forty-five images were selected from the years of 1910–2010 on editorial pages of *Better Homes & Gardens, Good Housekeeping, Ladies Home Journal, McCall's,* and *Redbook.* The images were liberated (by myself and a female undergraduate student) from the Philadelphia Free Library archives via digital images captured on my camera. These magazines represent five of the "seven sisters" (inspired by the Greek myth, also known as the Pleiades), a group of the most popular magazines in the United States, historically, which have targeted female homemakers with husbands and children. Only *Woman's Day* and *Family Circle* were not consulted when I searched for images since the Library's holdings for these two magazines was incomplete for 1910–2010. Identifying a diverse set of visual representations to stimulate discussion about femininity was the goal, so choice of images was selective and not exhaustive. Images of women selected from the magazine pages represented diversity in women according to age, ethnicity, decade, each of the five magazines over ten decades, and public/private settings in the images. However, it must be noted that finding images of women of color among these magazines of the first half of the twentieth century was significantly more challenging than finding them in the latter decades. During focus groups and interviews, the forty-five images printed on 8.5 x 11 poster card were posted on walls around the room used for our meeting. When geography presented challenges to conducting interviews in person, I mailed the stimulus materials to women or sent them as an email attachment in advance of our discussion.

From the forty-five images, each research participant was asked to identify ten images she considered *most feminine* and ten she considered *least feminine*—and to explain each choice. Women also were asked to list words or phrases on the pre-interview questionnaire qualifying their own definition of femininity, which I collected at the end of focus group and interview meetings. The act of writing down key words/phrases, and discussing them with other women and/or me, enabled women who participated in focus groups and interviews to distill their thoughts about the deceptively simple word, *femininity*, in all its complexity. Findings are reported in chapter 2, with words/phrases used more than five times appearing in bold in Table 2.1. Noting the frequency of certain terms is relevant to illustrate comparison and contrast across age cohorts. Both exercises—examining 100 years' worth of magazine images and listing words/phrases defining femininity—served as meaningful exercises for the purpose of this book because women engaged with their own thoughts about *What is femininity?* and examined the term as a community of women during focus groups. Women reported that the opportunity to discuss femininity enabled them to focus on the concept more deeply than they ever had done before. Women told me during and after the focus group meetings and interviews that they appreciated the opportunity to relax for candid discussions about issues they celebrated, as well as those which troubled them. Degrees of bonding with one another in focus group settings clearly enriched data collection processes.

All conversations were recorded. To analyze transcript data, a hermeneutic phenomenological theme analysis was performed following Van Manen's (1990) technique. Women's voices, their perceptions and stories of their experiences in their own words, constituted the unit of analysis. Overall, the study's research question of *What is femininity?* served to navigate readings of transcripts, but not to the degree that larger issues (such as disdain for media representations of girls and women) became invisible. First, I and female graduate and undergraduate students read all transcripts several times to get a sense of the data—independently and together. Second, inspired by Glaser and Strauss's (1967) grounded theory approach to qualitative data, we then compared and contrasted research participants' voices, took notes and transferred them to index cards that were categorized in piles according to themes/patterns and reshuffled as needed, with anomalies noted. We also pondered statements and phrases throughout transcripts that seemed essential, or remarkable, and used colored highlighters to underscore key words and phrases.

THEORETICAL UNDERPINNINGS FOR THIS BOOK

To fully explore women's perceptions and stories, numerous theoretical foundations were summoned to bring clarity to understanding of the multi-faceted crystal of *femininity*. Theoretical underpinnings are introduced here and explored in greater depth in subsequent chapters, including: female gender role stress/conflict; feminist theory; intersectionality; and social constructionism, social comparison theory, and rhetorical critique. Various mass communication theory frameworks are summoned throughout the chapters that follow, as well.

Female gender role stress/conflict

Ways girls and women internalize traditional ideas about what it means to be feminine—being valued for beauty and passivity and rigid expectations for a restrictive gender role as mother and wife—may result in Gender Role Stress/Conflict (GRS/C). This is a psychological state wherein socialized gender roles have negative consequences for an individual or others (O'Neil, Good, & Holmes, 1995). An "aesthetic of femininity" (Bartky, 2010, p. 87) requires a female body that appears fragile and lacks muscular strength, making victimization by men's physical abuse a reality in many parts of the world. Theorizing about the stress and conflict women endure as part of their female gender role has been inspired by male gender role stress/conflict theory researchers' work published in the psychology and men's studies literatures. For feminist scholars, male gender role stress/conflict and masculinities research has had a corollary benefit of helping to expand understanding of issues that greatly affect women—such as domestic abuse, gendered salary disparity, and the organizational glass ceiling phenomenon, to name a few issues.

By contrast, there have been significantly fewer studies about female gender role stress/conflict and femininities to emerge amidst the psychology literature. Rather, researchers have devoted much attention to other important issues such as critiquing the *ideal images* to which women aspire and eating/health disorder effects. The current book project is designed to expand female/feminine gender role stress/conflict research, to incorporate femininities research from other fields, and to supplement it with empirical data about how today's women of multiple generations and social identities define *femininity*. By interrogating women's embodied experiences with the femininity construct, it is possible to advocate for resistance and change to social prescriptions about how women *should* live and be. Confusing perceptions about femininity among girls and women reflect internal stress/conflict they experience while navigating media-constructed signs and representations which become *normalized* in their minds. The way girls and women were raised, how they feel about their own body, and the images they experience in their everyday lives do not always match up.

Feminist theory

Scholarship about femininities, largely, has been explored by feminist researchers who offer critiques about power in a context of patriarchy. Some feminist scholars have debated about just what *femininity* is—perhaps united only by a charge for women to define it for themselves. Generational contestations between second-wave feminists and postmodern, or third-wave feminists, have escalated in recent years and manifested in *girl power* and *riot grrrl* movements. Numerous scholars have problematized the act of describing feminism using a wave metaphor, for to do so risks overlooking contributions made by women of color and women across sexual orientations who may have been excluded, historically. Like Orloff and Shiff (2016), I refer to waves of feminism throughout this book, but do so cautiously so as not to suggest that postfeminism or the third wave have been made multicultural merely by updating second-wave feminism which was rooted in middle-class Caucasian/White women's experiences. Each wave and perspective is unique and valuable in its own right, residing along a continuum rather than hierarchically rising above any other feminist position. Writings of Anzaldúa (1987), Baumgardner and Richards (2010), Collins (2005), Foucault (1980), hooks (2015), Tong (2009), and McRobbie (2009) have greatly influenced my perspectives about feminism and critique of power structures.

Rhetorical criticism, social constructionism, and social comparison theory

Rhetorical criticism is a process of systematically examining symbols and discovering how they play out in ways meaning is made. Rhetoric may be used to persuade, as an invitation to understanding, or as a way to discover or clarify how one feels about something. As Foss (1989) explained, "Every symbolic choice we make results in seeing the world in one way rather than in another" (p. 4). As a human construction, a symbol serves as a stand-in, or representation for something else in conjunction with some association, relationship, or convention (Foss, 1989). Girls and women consciously use symbols when communicating about a particular condition. For example, how often have you heard or said something like, "I'd like to go to the party, but I can't because I have nothing to

wear and my hair is a mess!" This type of *excuse* speaks volumes about
dissonance females experience with regard to a concept known as *emphasized femininity*. Looking one's best sometimes means emphasizing femininity through fashion and grooming. Isn't it sad that the above excuse
attempts to mask a girl or woman who really wants to go to the party?
She feels too stressed that she may not look her best, though. She chooses
to skip going to the party and will miss out on a fun time simply because
she does not feel confident about her appearance. Her conscious decision
not to go to the party—and the words she uses to express how she's
feeling—are symbols used to communicate her condition.

Like many other rhetoricians, I posit that social constructionism greatly informs our lived experiences. Who we are as human beings and how
we relate to others is shaped by the society in which we live. In turn, we
also shape that society. Social constructionism provides the backbone for
this book's attention to femininity. I subscribe to a womanist perspective
which, intrinsically, is humanistic and liberatory, fueled by a desire to
expose women's experiences as a means to build inclusive human communities. One means for accomplishing this goal is to recognize that
femininity ideology is a multidimensional construct; a *social* construct. So,
I designed the research project reported in this book as an examination of
how women's definitions of femininity may reflect social identity dimension intersectionalities. *Femininity* is not some objective word that exists
in a vacuum without context. It is a word socially constructed by other
people, and then embraced (or not) by individuals. Female gender roles
do not emerge from nature, but are products imprinted by socialization
patterns across generations (Zamarripa, Wampold, & Gregory, 2003).
Here's how feminist scholars posit that girls and women become socially
constructed. The human female, according to de Beauvoir (1968), is created by "civilization as a whole" (p. 249). Female gender is an *"interactional*
accomplishment" (Cerulo, 1997, p. 387, italics added) continually negotiated through relationships with others and with manufactured media
products. Hence, exploring subjective definitions of *femininity* means examining symbols and language that shapes and sustains meaning about
femininity. In this book, I interrogate the narratives of three generations
of women as they defined *femininity*. I closely examined the symbols they
invoked as part of their definition.

Through communication, rhetoric constructs a shared understanding
of the world—and rhetorical criticism enables us to interrogate questions
about power. Who has it? Who doesn't? How is that power used? Scrutinizing language usage and thought processes are activities central to rhetorical criticism. This means examining who constructs reality (especially
from a standpoint of privilege), why some particular constructions of
reality gain traction as opposed to others, and ways symbols shape our
perceptions. I subscribe to a *feminist reconstruction position* (Foss, Foss, &
Griffin, 1997) which is energized by a goal of eradicating an ideology of

domination through patriarchy—wherein people believe that girls and women are second-class citizens. Incorporating social comparison theory in my work also promotes understanding of symbols promoted by the media—with effects of subordinating women in society. This approach is useful in predicting outcomes associated with comparing oneself with others (Helgeson & Taylor, 1993), a routine the advertising industry uses in order to sell fashion and beauty products and the media industry promotes.

During focus group meetings and interviews, particular attention was afforded ways women attended to symbols, rituals, and social norms that they believe shape ways they think about femininity for themselves and ways others' perceptions are *imposed upon* them. During nearly every focus group discussion and one-one-one interview, women enveloped their personal definition of femininity within some comparison of how they and other women measure up to mediated standards set by film actresses, reality TV celebrities, models, porn stars, photos posted on Facebook and Instagram, vocalists, and more. All of these media products are forms of rhetoric. Collectively, women's voices and examples underwent a hermeneutic phenomenological theme analysis described above as part of my rhetorical criticism about femininity and results are shared in this book's chapters.

Intersectionality

Simultaneously, my work is driven by the approach and concept known as *intersectionality*, which values each person's social identity dimensions (e.g., age, ethnicity, gender, sexual orientation) and embraces multidimensionality of people's lived experiences. We who respect multiple social identity dimensions as constituting an individual posit that *each dimension is not some layer that is piled or added on*. Rather, uneven power distribution in a society complicates situated identities by more firmly entrenching some people at the center and others in the margin. Consequently, using the intersectionality approach means extending respect to voices of people living in society's margins (Crenshaw, 1989). My perspective on intersectionality significantly has been impacted by the work of Allen (2011), Childs and Palmer (1999), Gunaratnam (2003), and hooks (2015). I strategically use the phrase *social identity dimensions* rather than just *identities* to emphasize the reality that no two girls or women are the same—even if they share the same age, ethnicity, gender, or sexual orientation, for example. Each facet or dimension of a female's social identity is unquantifiable, is intertwined with other dimensions, and often is intangible. It is unique because it is hers alone as shaped by her lived experiences.

NOW, A WORD ABOUT WORD CHOICES

As scholars of masculinity recommend a plural form—*masculinities*—to account for ways intersecting social identity dimensions shape individual realities, I, too, use the plural *femininities*. I pay respect to the diverse women of intersecting social identities who experience the phenomenon. Yet, in this book, sometimes I talk of femininity in its singular form and others in its plural form—depending on whether referring to other researchers' work or my own. By adopting plural forms of these concepts, researchers are more likely to accept possibilities for inter-group differences and to interrogate them amidst the same gender group. Doing so also opens space for identifying and understanding how and why some forms of femininity are prized and idealized (especially thin, young, Caucasian/White, middle-class, heterosexual) while other forms of femininity are marginalized and/or denounced. No category created for understanding femininity or masculinity should be considered fixed or exhaustive. It must remain flexible. Moreover, social identity dimensions may go beyond simple demographic categories. For example, among some women of color, hair texture is a meaningful and meaning-filled social identity dimension (e.g., Collins, 2005). Like all concepts, social identity dimensions are better examined in context and situationally embodied in social actions. So, I designed this study as an invitation for women to consider *their own* definition of femininity rather than asking them to consider mine or others' definitions. I place value on the *individual's self-concept*— women relating to femininity of their own bodies and experiences (or not)—rather than, for example, my strictly counting instances of when rhetorical constructions of femininity compare/contrast with others'.

Generally, I use *gender* when referring to a social construction and *sex* when referring to biology. Also, sometimes for readability and/or grammar purposes, I use *woman* and *female* (in both singular and plural forms) interchangeably. This may be because use of *females* provides a means for including both *girls* and *women* in a sentence and sometimes this is because I refer to other researchers' study findings. For example, when talking about sports, it is easier to sometimes speak of *females*, which encompasses *girls and women*. Finally, *femininity(ies)* and *feminism* are not used interchangeably. The former is a concept applied to people's bodies, behaviors, and experiences. The latter is a political movement and scholarly framework for rhetorical critique.

HOW THIS BOOK IS ORGANIZED

Throughout chapters, I use specific lenses through which to rhetorically examine femininity—using intersectionalities of social identity dimensions including age, ethnicity, and sexual orientation as context. I recognize feminine gender role stress/conflict as an outcome when women fail to meet ideal standards for femininity. I also explore media's shaping and perpetuation of these standards. Chapters explore these issues in depth. Attention to female gender role stress/conflict and attention to the role of media in these outcomes is incorporated across chapters. In some, readers shall find heavier concentrations of attention to some media—such as magazines, television, social media—while in other chapters, critique of media attention is combined to illustrate an example.

The book is organized according to eleven chapters that cover several interrelated contexts for facilitating understanding of femininity and how we make meaning about femininity—in terms of body image, media, and the gender role stress/conflict that may result. Voices of women who participated in focus groups and interviews are woven throughout the chapters and are used to underscore specific contexts and issues wherein female gender role stress/conflict was reported as particularly salient or challenging. Also, the theoretical underpinnings described above are more thoroughly interrogated in chapters that follow.

Chapter 1: *Femininity Matters* provides a foundation for the rest of the book, a heavy dose of scholarly attention to the *femininity* concept. This includes feminist critique of gendered power dynamics and patriarchy, links between femininity and traditional female gender roles, backlash experienced by women who are considered *un*feminine, contemporary women's movements based on their ideas about femininity, how femininity plays out with androgyny, and the rhetoric of femininity and its symbols.

Chapter 2: *Ideal Femininities According to Family, Tradition, and Media* introduces femininity standards for what women and society consider to be *ideal*—and ways this plays out in families, traditions, and media representations. Issues covered in this chapter provide an underpinning for exploring why women experience gender role stress/conflict as they internalize strict social standards about what it means to be a feminine girl or woman. Social comparison theory is introduced, as well as issues including female gender stereotyping, thinness and body weight, and the college experience.

Chapter 3: *Female Gender Role Stress/Conflict: Learning about/from Femininity*, explores female gender role stress/conflict in depth as an outcome of social standards shaping femininity. Relationships between femininity ideology and the gender role strain paradigm are covered, as well as outcomes of demands that girls and women experience as they ponder, *"Am I feminine enough?"* This bundle of issues is examined in terms of social identity intersectionalities, competition among women, and how stressors and conflicts associated with femininity break down in the public sphere at work and in the private sphere at home.

Chapter 4: *Consumerist Misrepresentations: Rituals and Industries that Shape Femininity* examines ways industries use consumerism to strategically represent femininity in order to sell girls and women products that suggest they are *not OK the way they are*. Moreover, certain rituals establish emphasized femininity norms and strategically represent women in limited ways—from the beauty-fashion complex, the advertising industry, and rituals such as bridal and baby showers that perpetuate certain ideals for feminine appearance and behavior.

Chapter 5: *Women's Femininities at Work* is about exploring implications of female-gender division of labor in the public and private spheres. Effects of inequitable and inhospitable gendered workplaces are discussed, as well as trends of working-momism and the third shift of body work for women, occupations historically unavailable to women, feminized occupational fields, and media workers' representations of femininities.

Chapter 6: *Women at Play: Sports and Femininities* provides a look at women at play in contexts of sports by exploring female athletics before and after Title IX, sports and femininity as explained by gender role stress/conflict theory, social expectations surrounding femininity and athleticism, sports industry and media representations of female athletes, and the making of female celebrity athletes.

Chapter 7: *Femininity as Shaped by Intersectionalities of Social Identity Dimensions* explores femininity and body shape/size, non-heteronormative and oppositional femininities, religion/spirituality and women's feminine role, women of color and femininity, femininity and physical disabilities, and femininity and socio-economic class.

Chapter 8: *Sexuality, Masculine Femininities, and Feminine Masculinities* is about reconciling these seeming disparities in terms of how femininity is defined, femininity-inspired microaggressions, how heteronormativity is used as a social control, drag queen and king culture for emphasized femininity and masculinity, and masculine women in the military.

Chapter 9: *Age, Health, and Femininities* interrogates ways girls and young women are socialized to normative emphasized femininity, how older women are represented as lacking feminine qualities, and ways beauty-fashion-media industries represent older women.

Chapter 10: *Femininities and Politics* offers attention to stereotyping of women in politics and examines generational differences among popular and third-wave feminism, girls' and women's activism, politicizing women's issues, and news media coverage of women in politics.

Chapter 11: *Lessons and Moving Forward* concludes the book by acknowledging what we know about femininity and calls for working to alleviate female gender role stress/conflict. One means for accomplishing this end is to root out ways people are socialized into constricting notions of femininity which fosters femininity expectancies that end up holding back girls and women. I theorize about considering femininities on a continuum, recommend against defining femininities by exclusion, and advocate for alleviating unequal power relations.

ONE

Femininity Matters

Sugar and spice,
And everything nice,
That's what little girls are made of.
—Nursery rhyme, author unknown

Examining the concept of femininity today is more important than ever. As we interrogate ways femininity is defined, we discover how the concept is made to mean in the lives of girls and women—sometimes empowering and other times used as a microaggression in subtle or unconscious verbal or nonverbal insults directed toward them. College women, their mothers, aunts, and grandmothers shared personal definitions of femininity in contexts of their age, culture, ethnicity, faith/spirituality, gender, sexual orientation, and other social identity dimensions. During focus groups and interviews, they spoke of enduring stereotypes and complexities of *how I am* versus *how I'm supposed to be* in various phases and domains of their life. Hearing about women's stresses in trying to negotiate both realities was not entirely unsurprising. The depth and breadth of the conflicts they experience was.

College student Grisella, 20, Puerto-Rican, for example, explained that femininity is defined for the girls and women in her family rather than enabling them to define femininity for themselves. Ways girls and women are taught to dress, walk, behave, and conform to cultural traditions in her family can prove confining when she might prefer to express her individuality. When asked to list the first words that come to mind when she thinks of the concept, *femininity*, Grisella said:

> *Girlie.* I just think of like pink and lavender and flowers and daisies. And *sophisticated.* I guess you have to carry yourself in a way that says "Yeah, I am a woman and I'm confident," as well. And *petite.* I don't know why I just think of a woman as a smaller person. . . . [I]n my

1

family you would literally get a beat down if you aren't put together. . . . Sometimes I would like to wear sweats, but I can't. . . . [I]t's hard.
I know how I'm supposed to be because my mama, and abuela, and
tias taught me. But, it's just too hard. I want to be me!

Grisella clarified that "beat down" meant being verbally embarrassed in
front of others for wearing slacks to a formal occasion, or it could mean
having her hair pulled, or possibly a "slap upside the head" by an elder
to emphasize the gravity of a fashion faux pas. Voices of women expressing feelings of dissonance and stories about conflict and stress when it
comes to negotiating femininity as defined by others—with one's individual interpretation—are shared throughout this book.

This chapter about femininity matters incorporates these important
areas: 1) What is femininity? (Depends whom you ask and when you
ask), 2) Making a distinction between *sex* and *gender* requires regular
updating, 3) Femininity as critiqued through a power relations lens, 4)
Traditional female gender roles: Ties that limit our definition of femininity, 5) Historical perspectives on femininity that have held women down
and back, 6) Femininity expectancies of women and backlash effects
when social norms are violated, 7) *Girl power* and *riot grrrl* movements'
redefining of girlie-girl femininity, 8) Androgyny and femininity are not
necessarily incongruous, 9) Sharpening a focus on the rhetoric of femininity and its symbols, and 10) Discussion.

WHAT IS FEMININITY?
(DEPENDS WHOM YOU ASK AND WHEN YOU ASK)

The concept of *femininity* has evolved over thousands of years. Its definition goes far beyond biological femaleness; that with which a woman is
born. *Gender* and its attributes are learned. It seems that all known societies differentiate between female and male—and offer models of behavior for each group (MacKinnon, 2003). In the United States, perhaps our
earliest instruction about gender difference comes from a nursery rhyme
explaining what little girls are made of, as shared at the beginning of this
chapter. Throughout the life course, females become acculturated to the
notion that *femininity* and *masculinity* are conceptualized as related and
opposite—with women being feminine and men being masculine. Such a
binary, taken-for-granted view of people being lumped into one category
or the other based on biological makeup is slowly evolving as it becomes
more accepted that individuals inhabit "constellations of traits, attitudes
and behaviors" (Kulis, Marsiglia, & Hecht, 2002, p. 443) that shape their
social identity.

Gender construction of femininity and masculinity is exceptionally
complex, dynamic, and the femininity-masculinity dualism is falling out
of fashion in some circles. It is inherently flawed and being outpaced by

social change. Today, there are people who eschew the binary dualism altogether and self-identify as *non-binary*. Feminist communication theory acknowledges that one's biological features of sex at birth are subject to change, as is a fluid socialized gender identification process and sexual orientation by self and others (Wackwitz & Rakow, 2007). MacInnes (1998) argued that the terms *femininity* and *masculinity* have perpetuated an ideology people rely upon to justify using sex differences between women and men when "in fact there are none" (p. 1). Otherwise, binary dualistic thinking means that females who display masculine attributes and males who display feminine attributes violate social expectancies for gender performance and, consequently, suffer retribution. In particular, bisexuals, transgendered people, and those whose gender identity seems fluid or ambiguous are disempowered and marginalized amid "the heterosexual matrix" (Charlebois, 2011, p. 138). Thus, Tong (2009) has argued that femininity must be understood without requiring a reference point "external to it"—such as masculinity (p. 3). Processes associated with dichotomizing the world according to feminine and masculine categories traditionally has been central to gender schema theory and has served as a foundation for investigating how individuals describe themselves accordingly (Bem, 1983). During college student focus groups conducted for this book, Nicole, 18, self-identified Black-Japanese, expressed concerns about defining femininity:

> I feel like the concept of femininity doesn't exist. It's a ghost. It's an empty word that doesn't have any substance. Because to be womanly, does that mean to embrace your biological characteristics as a female, your breasts, the fact that you can bear children? Or, is it the social aspects of being female? There is really no way to answer that because it is going to fluctuate depending on where you are, who you are, what time in history you're talking about. There is really no way to have a definition of something that is so not concrete. . . . [U]ltimately, I have learned that people are people, whether they're women or men. I think that femininity is starting to fade away as we move on. And there are still traces of heavy oppression that went on in the past. There is no such thing as femininity.

So, for young women like Nicole, femininity has become a relic of the past; a social construction that has overstayed its welcome. Instead, she said she chooses to regard friends and people she meets at face value and is careful to ask them how they self-identify in order to avoid disrespecting someone by using the wrong pronoun, for example.

Feminine and *masculine* are hierarchical and separated by gender according to power. In many developed nations, male privilege over females in terms of access to institutional power may be considered a "patriarchal dividend" (Connell, 2003, p. 142). So, defining *femininity* may be less important than scrutinizing ways femininity serves as an active system for pleasing men to make them "appear more masculine by contrast"

(Brownmiller, 1984, p. 16). As a socially built concept undergoing constant reconstruction, *femininity* is overdue for an overhaul (Wajcman, 1998). In particular, when certain values like intuition, nurturance, warmth, and admonitions to be nice, silent, deferent to men, and domestic are ascribed to femininity, girls and women are held back (Crawford & Unger, 2000). Such oppressive qualities are mired in women's historical subordination to men, and psychologists long have hypothesized that interpretations of gendered characteristics relative to one's body are central to personality development. Connections among one's body, gender performance, and psychological make-up remain salient today and these connections are explored throughout this book. Feminist scholars remind us that it is easy to see the power implications inherent in many research findings about men and boys in psychology, cultural studies, and many other fields when findings simply are applied to girls and women without carefully examining the female lived experience in context. Mass media and feminist researchers posit that dominant media, similarly, are guilty of failing to explore unique experiences of girls and women by appropriating their voices; speaking *about* and *for* them. An example of this dynamic includes debates about policymaking affecting women—such as female reproductive health—but none of the policymakers, reporters, or people interviewed are female.

Remarkably, the basic blueprint for emphasizing femininity has remained relatively constant for a long time and across geographic borders—due in large part to stereotyping. Women around the globe (with some cultural nuances, of course), learn that to be considered feminine, they must subscribe to heteronormativity by being physically attractive for men and nurturing husband, children, and extended family members. Girls and women are socialized to adapt to these social roles which are based on beauty, love, conservative sexuality, family, motherhood—and to use these as benchmarks for setting their own self-standards. During an interview for the current study, Debbie, 51, Caucasian/White, offered her retrospective view on being socialized into femininity and the female social role. Here's how she described *femininity*:

> Well, it's not doing domestic work. It's not necessarily woman's work to me. I mean it is my job, but I don't think it's who I am. I think caring for my kids and taking care of my home was a big part of my life, but it did not make me more of a woman—or more feminine. I had to work at that. . . . Looking back on my life, there were times I forgot I was a woman. I just thought I was a Mom or a housewife. Now I look at my two daughters and they are both very strong, confident young women, and they are beautiful. I hope for them that they will always still remember they are a woman. Because you think differently than men. And I hope they enjoy that more than I did.

Debbie explained that emphasizing her femininity through beauty maintenance activities was not always realistic given the amount of housekeeping and childrearing labor she performed every day. The former took a back seat to the latter. But, rather than enabling private sphere responsibilities to define her femininity or her female identity, Debbie qualified these tasks as a necessary job. When she said she "forgot [she] was a woman," she realized that often she lacked the time to emphasize and to enjoy her femininity in terms of outward appearance.

When pondering *What is femininity?*, it is relevant to consider stereotypical traits commonly associated with a female gender role that demands women be compliant, cooperative, dependent on others, submissive/passive homemakers, and emotionally easy to read. In conjunction with these traits, girls and women are socialized to express deep concern for others, provide relationship building, and put others' needs ahead of their own. *Femininity* is what society, stereotypically, expects of its women; the inverse of what it expects of its men. Stereotypes are outgrowths of the binary dualism discussed above; risky logic anytime two concepts are framed as opposites since one is always going to be considered superior (Grunig, Toth, & Hon, 2001). Simultaneously, women who subscribe to and enact this brand of traditional femininity are careful to avoid "outdo[ing] men" in their lives for fear of being perceived as competitive (Wood & Fixmer-Oraiz, 2015, p. 21). In return, women who openly express their femininity are extended "little courtesies and minor privilege" (Brownmiller, 1984, p. 15), so long as they enact heteronormative femininity. In other words, these small degrees of privilege are not extended to bisexual, lesbian, and celibate women. Moreover, any "minor privilege" may be less frequently extended to girls and women of color. Young women across ethnic groups who live in U.S. Southern states seem especially clinging to traditional emphasized femininity in fashion and desire for heterosexual marriage with children (Pompper & Crandall, 2014). Irony becomes self-evident when considering restrictions or limited rights some women accept by accentuating their own femininity; a trade-off men may be far less willing to make in order to accentuate their masculinity.

In recent years, critical questioning of gender-based systems of advantage and disadvantage has focused on situations where some women resist social meanings about and representations of femininity. Existing ideologies about femininity and masculinity are subject to change as women and men interact, produce, reproduce and distribute these ideologies. Some women accept them, while others try to modify social meanings, and others eschew them completely. Women who reject traditional notions of what makes a woman feminine tend to be advocates for social change (Bartky, 2010). Moreover, one model for femininity (or masculinity) is never neatly erased while another takes its place. As Bederman (1995) posited that masculinity is experienced and understood in flux through ongoing "contradiction, change, and renegotiation" (p. 11), I argue that processes are similar—albeit more resistant to change and perhaps slower—for women and femininity. While current notions of femininity may be more contested than ever, it serves us well to consider the value which the U.S. (in particular) places on certain forms of nostalgia and artifacts of Caucasian/White femininity: dresses, high heels, gloves, hats, pearls, pink, red, silk, satin, sequins, lace, long shiny hair. This *paraphernalia of femininity* is what women who participated in interviews and focus groups collectively pointed out as personifying femininity. Some feminist scholars have labeled such objects as "commodified and kitschified" (Brown, 2000, p. 40) as a means for linking femininity with the objèt d'art—or a longing for a past that never was. Women are held accountable to normative behaviors considered appropriate for their gender group and those who violate social expectations soon discover scorn and ridicule designed to *correct* them on the proper way to act like a lady. Anyone who doubts the veracity of these claims has only to consider public figures deemed *insufficiently feminine* and ways mass media frame them as failures as women—especially women who are prominent in business, politics, and sports. These issues are covered in detail in chapters 5, 6, and 10.

MAKING A DISTINCTION BETWEEN *SEX* AND *GENDER* REQUIRES REGULAR UPDATING

The femininity concept has been under-theorized and essentialist claims endure, including female gender biases that stifle social change for girls and women. Betz (1995) challenged researchers to update and expand ways femininity is defined, theorized, and measured. Many people think females are born to be feminine and males are born to be masculine. These mindsets have become deeply entrenched in how social institutions operate, how gender roles are interpreted and imposed, ways work is organized, and means by which labor is categorized into women's work and men's work. Collectively, these activities promote certain femininity and masculinity styles that produce profound behavioral, psychological, and social consequences which become manifest in structural arrangements. Social constructionist scholars posit that human behavior relative to gender is learned and not biological or innate. Craig (1992) pointed out that "biological theories that see gender differences as 'natural' are themselves considered to be the product of these cultural distinctions" (p. 1). Hence, the femininity concept offers a set of social expectations for women—and in the U.S., the sex vs. gender distinction is undergoing steady change as society comes to recognize how one is born need not dictate how one lives.

Helping to facilitate this change, social media tools are used to promote scrutiny of social conventions and to elevate public discussions about sex, gender, femininity and masculinity. For example, something as institutionalized and seemingly innocuous as a bathroom sign captured worldwide attention in 2015, garnering 18 million Twitter impressions. Project management software developers, Axosoft, launched the #ItWasNeverADress campaign, underscoring ubiquity of "the bathroom lady" as a symbol on public signs labeling women's restrooms around the world by showing the silhouetted figure wearing a cape rather than what previously was assumed to be a universal costume of femininity—a dress. According to *Time* magazine, the image "will change how you see bathroom signs" (Berenson, 2015). At the time of this writing, pressure to change bathroom signs to accommodate transgender people continues. At the heart of the debate is confusion and fear associated with abolishing gender binary dualisms. Because femininity is a gender identity variable wrapped up in gender belief systems (Powell & Greenhaus, 2010), distinctions between sex (as a biological phenomenon) and gender (as a social phenomenon) deserve to be frequently revisited and updated.

Embedded within a sex vs. gender distinction and the femininity concept are socialization procedures that communicate normativity. This means little girls and women are regularly and frequently told how they *should* behave and how they *should* appear. McPherson (2003) defined femininity as "a set of ideas about *appropriate* womanly behavior and feelings that are generally based on cultural assumptions about female nature" (p. 21, italics added). Heterosexual women are defined in terms of their sexuality and are expected to look and act feminine in order to acquire male attention. Social power among women and men is far out of balance, so it is unsurprising that research findings still overwhelmingly underscore negative impacts of women controlling their body through self-change projects in order to conform to traditional notions of femininity. Such "body projects" include attention to the shape, size, contours, and muscle tone of one's body which often results in an unhealthful drive for thinness, use of pharmaceuticals, and cosmetic surgery. Appearance norms demand women subscribe to the *cult of thinness* (Hesse-Biber, 2007) and be simultaneously thin, as well as muscular and buxom. These are qualities that only can occur in tandem if women invest significant time, emotional energy, and money on exercise, cosmetic surgery, and diet. Indeed, women work hard to appear "normal."

Both women and men, historically, have enacted qualities which may be considered as belonging to the opposite sex. Femininity and masculinity are "relational concepts" (Connell, 1995, p. 43), such that one does not exist without the other in a yin-yang interdependent way. While these collections of phenomena shall be discussed in greater depth in chapter 8, I mention them here as a reminder that readers must be ever vigilant to avoid falling into essentialist thinking that only women are feminine and that only men are masculine. For example, Halberstam (1998) operation-alized masculinity as a category of behaviors which may apply to women as well as men, but she does not reject a traditional taxonomy of feminin-ity and masculinity. Rather, she expands *gender variance* to include people representing multiple and overlapping social identity dimensions—and opens conversations about female masculinity in order to negate percep-tions that heterosexuality must be compulsory and to ensure that femi-ninity is respected as a valuable concept for understanding human be-haviors and social meaning. As Connell (1995) divided masculinity into a plurality (masculinities) to accommodate multiple, overlapping social identity dimensions, I, too, consider femininity in terms of age, culture, ethnicity, faith/spirituality, sexuality, and more—and hypothesize that femininities may be far more diverse than actual masculinities. Chapter 7 offers a deeper investigation of intersectionalities of social identity di-mensions shaping femininities.

FEMININITY AS CRITIQUED
THROUGH A POWER RELATIONS LENS

Gender is a matter of power relations according to French philosopher Michel Foucault, who explained how one develops a social identity in comparison to an opposite and emphasized how language shapes dis-course about and understanding of this construction. Sexuality and gen-der are entwined and mutually sustaining discourses for Foucault. For example, feminine is considered to be the opposite of masculine and acquiring a female identity involves women putting distance between their femininities—and males with their masculinities. Extending Fou-cault's (1980) ideas, Bartky (2010) explained that male power and domi-nation come into view when focusing on ways that women accept (as common sense) that they are designed to perform up to men's social expectations in terms of how to make their bodies behave and appear. For example, poststructuralist feminists identify such subtle practices of femininity performance as women's sitting with knees together, walking, dieting, comportment, and wearing makeup and high heels. Words, acts, and gestures compel girls and women to "enact cultural norms of femi-ninity" (Campbell, 1998, p. 2) and to idealize the heterosexual bond (But-ler, 1990). Parents, teachers, peers, and mass media socialize girls and women about how to be feminine. Ultimately, these imperatives instill women with negative feelings of anxiety, conflict, stress, and shame should they fail to meet social expectancies. The cycle keeps women in a less powerful situation and a constant state of subordination with bodies made more docile, weak, and small as compared to men. Hence, the female body is both a product and a process; indeed, a "locus of social control" (Trethewey, 2000, p. 113). Indeed, sexuality and gender are entwined and mutually sustaining discourses.

Hegemonic masculinity and *emphasized femininity* are phenomena that are complementary and perpetuate ongoing gender power imbalance. Power is predicated upon domination with masculinity over femininity through consent and not necessarily force. According to leading feminist scholars, patriarchal social structures are maintained by social conventions which have developed over time, have become institutionalized, and perpetually reinforce men's dominance over women and by ensuring women's compliance. Living up to and through stereotypes creates confusion and conflict for many women at different points along the life cycle. For example, emphasized femininity is the traditional female stereotype steeped in sexuality and submissiveness/dependence as the basis of a woman's value (Scharrer, 2004). Thus, by definition, no form of femininity exists for women that is comparable to hegemonic masculinity for men since men maintain the highest levels of social power. Femininities are subservient to masculinities in the U.S. and many other parts of the world. Because men are the recipients of female subservience, it is impractical to think femininities ever can be hegemonic. Rather, I prefer using the concept of *marginalization* rather than *hegemony* when describing ways some groups of women inject their privilege over othered subordinate women in particular social settings. Collins (2005) called middle-class, heterosexual, Caucasian/White femininity "a normative yardstick" by which all femininities are measured; processes that relegate African-American/Black women to "the bottom of the gender hierarchy" (p. 193). Similarly, femininity research findings among some Asian cultures suggest that second-generation girls and women aspire to Caucasian/White femininity standards. I revisit this issue in chapter 7 as I address the power of Caucasian/White representations when perceived by immigrant groups. Connell (1987) invoked additional examples of women using privilege and marginalizing others, such as when some women use religious ideology and political backing from conservative men to attack feminist women's groups. Also, in interpersonal face-to-face contexts such as mother-daughter relationships or in girls' schools with age/grade hierarchies, powerful females may exert their dominance over other less powerful females. Despite women's social advances in recent decades, intergenerational differences suggest that although younger women qualify femininity in terms of low self-esteem, emotional distress, and as restricted/oppressed, they paradoxically express more hopeful/optimistic attitudes about femininity than their older counterparts—as older women qualified traditional femininity in terms of concern with their appearance and requiring/seeking help from others (Robertson, Johnson, Benton, Janey, Carbral, & Woodford, 2002). Overall, as Charlebois (2011) explained, "Significantly, we see how women's power pales in comparison with men's and thus unequal gender relations remain normative" (p. 28). So, femininities cannot be hegemonic in the same way masculinities are hegemonic.

There are additional ways to examine and critique femininities through a power relations lens. For example, as women who identify as non-heterosexual become more politically active, assertive, aggressive, and open about their sexual preferences, their behaviors and social identities are perceived to threaten the traditional social order steeped in *hegemonic masculinity* with *emphasized femininity*. From such behaviors emerge the labels of *pariah femininities* (Schippers, 2007) and *oppositional femininities* (Charlebois, 2011). These women's biological sex category is perceived as being out of sync with their lived experiences, so routinely they are stigmatized as sexual deviants and labeled *bitch, slut,* and *dyke.* Women categorized as representing *pariah femininities* (Schippers, 2007) resist the imbalance in gender relations created by patriarchy through non-compliance with an active resistance to hegemonic masculinity (since these women enact aspects of hegemonic masculinity themselves). These include behaviors which Charlebois (2011) prefers to label *oppositional femininities* to avoid negative connotation of outcast status implied by the term *pariah* and to encompass a broader set of women beyond non-heterosexuals, including celibate women and single women. This latter group of women could contribute to destabilizing the binary dualistic gender hierarchy in general—and in particular, disrupt the dominant male gender order since some single women resist any assumption that men are required to financially support women. The lived experiences among many of today's single women in the United States offer reflections of a changing social order in the wake of the 1960s sexual revolution (Traister, 2016a). Lastly, *equality femininity* describes a specific type of oppositional femininity; women who advocate for egalitarian, democratic relationships among women and men. Beyond democratizing gender relations, *equality femininity* means resisting *emphasized femininity* which ultimately disempowers women (Charlebois, 2011). Furthermore, definitions of feminism which focus on an equality concept promote freedom from outdated "constraints of gender expectations" (Foss, Foss, & Griffin, p. 2).

Feminist scholars also have examined how *emphasized femininity* keeps women subservient, stressed, and conflicted. A sex versus gender distinction has inspired multiple social scientists to resolve that femininity, as associated with gender, is a discursive construction and a learned behavior. Hence, women *perform, display,* and *emphasize* their gender through femininity, with some putting on a *spectacle* or a *masquerade.* In fact, Butler (1985) has called femininity a "mode of enacting and reenacting received gender norms which surface as so many styles of flesh" (p. 11). For Goffman (1976), femininity "strikes at the most basic characterization of the individual" (p. 75) and as Bartky (2010) explained, "disciplinary practices . . . produce a body which in gesture and appearance is *recognizably feminine"* (p. 79, italics added). As femininity plays out across the life course, Connell (1987) suggested that women strategically are motivated to engage in a pattern of emphasized femininity in order to sexually please and to attract men (in youth) and to fulfill their motherhood gender role; outcomes endorsed and perpetuated by media as images of emphasized femininities routinely appear in women's fashion magazines and Hollywood films. Although a social construction, emphasized femininity's details more often play out in the private sphere of home—in the bedroom and the kitchen. In this way, femininities become gender role projects across a woman's life course.

TRADITIONAL FEMALE GENDER ROLES: TIES THAT LIMIT OUR DEFINITION OF FEMININITY

Since a public-private sphere demarcation persists in most developed nations and gender role divisions remain discrete, women still are confined to roles and jobs that are considered second-tier or support functions. This outcome limits ways we define femininity. When politics was the reserve of public life in the days of Aristotle and Plato, the Athenians developed the idea of public and private spheres. Women were relegated to domestic responsibilities including motherhood, household management, and domestic labor. Still, social expectations that women serve as main caretaker for children and family is deeply embedded in the social fabric of "the modern feminine role" (Levant, Richmond, Cook, House, & Aupont, 2007). Historically, biological difference has been used to distinguish between female labor and male labor, acts that are "exploitative" and subscribe to some "romance of authenticity" which ends up reproducing patriarchal ideology wherein women are idealized as passive and subordinate to men (MacInnes, 1998, p. 2). Hence, a woman's marriage to a man, bearing of his children, and tending to his home means family life is her primary occupation (Reynolds, 2008)—and definer of her role in life. Thus, women who fail to measure up to this traditional blueprint are considered, socially, to be failures and deviants. On the other hand, research findings suggest that when unpaid domestic labor is unmoored from a socialized female gender role, family life tasks can become more equitably distributed to the degree that "maternal thinking develops in fathers, too" (Coltrane, 1989, p. 489). Division of gender labor contributes to how we define femininity.

Over generations, femininity has been defined by ways women express their limited gender roles involving nurturing, kindness, compassion, loving, and sharing. Such a "quintessence of womanhood" is considered to illuminate some kind of "natural expressions of femininity" wherein domestic duties reaffirm women's "gendered relation to men and to the world" (Coltrane, 1989, p. 473). In the early nineteenth century in the U.S., a *Cult of True Womanhood* meant "piety, purity, submissiveness, and domesticity" (Welter, 1966, p. 59) which Coontz (1993) posited adds up to roles of mother, daughter, sister, and wife. Marriage itself has been considered "the most salient interpersonal context" for expressing feminine traits (Kasen, Chen, Sneed, Crawford, & Cohen, 2006, p. 945). Expecting women to enact these qualities and roles has a way of turning in upon girls and women in a patriarchal culture that masochistically binds them to a life of servitude for benefit of everyone but themselves. Something as seemingly innocuous and positive as *loving* has the potential under patriarchy to manifest into "total self-sacrifice or martyrdom" (Tong, 2009, p. 60). A division of labor according to gender and using this as a basis for defining femininity socializes girls and women to internalize subordination so that what results is a social order based on a male worldview.

When media resort to using female gender stereotypes as a shorthand tool for characterizing girls and women according to traditional female gender roles, girls and women get short shrift and definitions of femininity become stilted. In readers' and viewers' minds, girls and women become boxed in and represented in limited ways. Magazine pages are filled with caricatures of girls and women. For generations, women's magazines have been standard bearers for *proper* female behavior — which is code for *femininity*. For the current study, images of women from editorial pages of the past 100 years served as stimulus materials encouraging college women, their aunts, mothers, and grandmothers to talk about how they define femininity for themselves. The magazine images offered a source of joy as women considered women's images from days long ago and displeasure at ways some images reflected very little change at all over the course of 10 decades. For example, women oohed and aahed at images of glamorous gowns reminiscent of Hollywood's golden age while snickering at the comparatively fewer images there were of women of color wearing them. Women also negatively critiqued how images of women at work consistently had them confined to home or office settings.

Popular culture and media long have exploited women's emphasized femininity, creating ideal images that continue to pressure girls and women to focus on their outward appearance. Inspired by the Folies Bergère of Paris, early-twentieth-century American Broadway showman and producer, Florenz Edward Ziegfeld, Jr., perpetuated a beauty ideal of 5 feet, 5 ½ inches tall, 117 pounds, and size 5 shoe size (Behling, 2001) and possessing femininity in the form of "loveliness, grace and imagination" (The ideal, 1926, p. 53). Flashing forward to the 1968 Miss America Pageant in Atlantic City, N.J., an annual celebration of young feminine women offered a protest venue for activists to crown a sheep Miss America in their support for the women's liberation movement. The sheep-being-led-to-slaughter metaphor offered contemporary political commentary about the fifty young women contestants offering up their swimsuit-clad bodies for surveillance by judges and millions of television viewers. Further examination of links between the Miss America (Scholarship) Pageant and child beauty pageants as rituals promoting feminine ideals is explored in chapter 4. While mediated representations of 1960s-1970s women served as a flash point for women's movement protests (Sherrill, 1970), the spectacularization of women exposing their breasts, bottoms, and pregnant bellies provided a teachable moment about femininity—that the image of a "wrong or embarrassing femininity" could encourage women to accept "the transformative promise of feminism" (Hesford, 2013, p. 59).

Magazines teach us how feminine girls and women are supposed to look, cook, raise children, capture and satisfy a man—but second-wave feminist Betty Friedan fought back. Historians and critics long have argued that magazines' pages have advocated for women to conform to a nation ruled by and for men and to cater to their desires through emphasized femininity. While mass-circulation magazines like *Ladies Home Journal*, *McCall's*, *Mademoiselle*, and *Redbook* say they have empowered women to be independent, creative, and nonconformist (Meyerowitz, 1993) while navigating their family through world wars and economic downturns, what these magazines and other media representations *really* have taught women is how to be loyal and committed wives, mothers, and consumers. Friedan's (1963) manifesta, *The Feminine Mystique*, was excerpted in *McCall's* and *Ladies' Home Journal* and, ironically, she resolved that magazines propelled an image of passive American femininity that made women seem "frivolous, almost childlike; fluffy" (Friedan, 1963, p. 36). Friedan charged U.S. women to resist ideal femininity as promoted in women's magazines by more actively and independently leading lives for themselves. This revolutionary book incorporated ideas of nineteenth century liberal humanism—rhetoric of human potential—to inspire women. Hence, Friedan's book successfully abolished the idea of femininity as "a monolithic construct" (Stern, 2003, p. 215) by arguing for a myriad of women's issues which cut across social identity dimensions, including sexuality. Impossible-to-achieve ideals regularly are displayed on the pages of men's magazines, too. Since 1978, 70 percent of *Playboy* centerfold models significantly have been underweight (Katzmarzyk & Davis, 2001). Images of women in magazines that emphasize femininity severely constrict the range of representations for girls and women.

Beyond media attention, the concept of femininity has attracted significant focus among psychologists over the years that also has limited ways we think of femininity today. Sigmund Freud (1973) pondered the riddle of the nature of femininity nearly 100 years ago and drew an inconclusive, albeit cheeky, conclusion:

> Throughout history people have knocked their heads against the riddle
> of the nature of femininity. . . . Nor will you have escaped worrying
> over this problem—those of you who are men; to those of you who are
> women this will not apply—you yourselves are the problem (p. 146).

In his *Femininity* lecture, Freud admitted that merely being born female is
no guarantee that a woman shall embody femininity (Glover & Kaplan,
2009). In years to follow, elusiveness of and confusion about the femininity concept has complicated creation of valid measurement tools to accu-
rately gauge femininity (Hoffman, Borders, & Hattie, 2000). People seem
to possess deep-seated ideas about gender and from these, beliefs about
the degree to which someone possesses psychological traits associated
with female gender have taken shape. In formal research, *I know it when I
see it*, or *We all know what we mean* simply isn't enough. Because multiple
sources contribute to our definition of femininity, even well-educated
people may have a hard time articulating just what femininity means
(Spence & Buckner, 2000). In the psychology literature, femininity traditionally has been measured either as a *personality trait* or as being synonymous with a *female gender role*. In an attempt to avoid restrictions associated with defining femininity according to stereotypical gender roles, some
researchers rely on the broader concept of *gender identity*, which refers to
one's subjective feelings toward femaleness or maleness (Golombok &
Fivush, 1994). This gives people wider berth to define *What femininity
means to me* rather than simply relying on gender roles prescribed by
someone else (Hoffman et al., 2000). A framework borrowed from
psychology used to undergird the study reported in this book involves
theorizing about femininity in terms of gender role stress/conflict (GRS/
C) (e.g., O'Neil, Good, & Holmes, 1995). As explored in greater depth in
chapter 3, GRS/C research suggests that girls and women may encounter
significant challenges in trying to adhere to or to measure up to social
standards attached to femininity.

HISTORICAL PERSPECTIVES ON FEMININITY
THAT HAVE HELD WOMEN DOWN AND BACK

Irrespective of definition, the concept of femininity has been used to diminish women's human rights in many parts of the world. Over the
course of modern history, great thinkers, events, and epochs have shaped
our meaning of femininity—including Aristotle, Charles Darwin's theory
of evolution based on survival of the fittest in 1872, the Victorian Era
(1837–1901) named for a British queen, the Industrial Revolution, and
states' perpetual failure to ratify the Equal Rights Amendment to the U.S.
Constitution (first introduced in 1923).

Women's second-class status has deep roots. The Babylonian Code of
Hammurabi served as the basis for the Western legal system, clearly

spelling out that a woman was a man's property; first her father's, then her husband's. Aristotle's fourth-century BC writings invoked "science" to explain how women are lesser than men—and many ideas founded on this view endured well into the 18th century. Weitz (2010) wrote: "According to Aristotle, only embryos that had sufficient heat could develop into fully human form. The rest became female. In other words, woman was, in Aristotle's view, a 'misbegotten man' and a 'monstrosity'—less than fully formed and literally half-baked" (p. 4). The Greek doctor, Galen, used this idea to explain why women's not-fully-developed reproductive organs are internal while men's fully-developed reproductive organs are external. Furthermore, according to some church doctrines, *uncontrolled feminine passions* were linked to witchcraft and used to justify cruel punishments (Ussher, 1991).

During the reign of Queen Victoria of Britain, Charles Darwin published *On the Origin of the Species* in 1872, which associated fragility with middle-class (Tuana, 1993) Caucasian/White women and did little to expand views on femininity. Historically, African-American women have not been considered fragile, but often less than human due to the color of their skin (Gilman, 1985), and to Darwin, all women were less evolved than men because finite energy is devoted to child bearing with little to spare for physical or mental development. Thus, Darwin rationalized that women are overly emotional, childlike, and dependent upon men for caretaking and rationality, a mindset that worked for Victorians who idealized middle-class Caucasian/White women as feminine, weak, helpless objects of male desire with no real ambitions or sexual desires of their own. In the nineteenth century, female sexuality officially was examined through a psychiatry lens and sex outside of marriage was pathologized (Ussher, 1991). Victorian society characterized femininity as "what a true woman wants" (Faludi, 1991, p. 71). By the 1900s, Victorian gender arrangements became less suitable for many women, so they launched resistance campaigns to gain entry into male-dominated public spaces and occupations (Cahn, 2010). The Industrial Revolution in the West preserved separation of private and public spheres, yet women were charged with using their domestic talents to make the home warm, personal, and private (Cancain, 1987). By the turn of the twentieth century in the West, with the introduction of bicycles for transportation and factory labor demanded for World War I efforts, women discovered how flexible their social roles could be. World War II needs later created factory jobs and women stepped up.

Social movements involving political activism for change in socio-economic conditions have helped to broaden the concept of femininity. Due to low socio-economic status, immigrant women of England's Victorian era could not afford to be *typically feminine* since they relied upon their physical strength and endurance (Kelinske, Mayer, & Chen, 2001). Reconciling post-war life and effects of the Great Depression in the United States meant rethinking traditional notions of femininity during the 1940s–1950s. By the 1960s, U.S. social movements shaped by activists' intersecting social identity dimensions demanded equality and freedom — such as Chicanas demanding better working conditions for field laborers. Also in the United States, an Equal Rights Amendment to the U.S. Constitution was resurrected from the early 1920s to ensure that *equality of rights under the law shall not be denied or abridged by the United States or any state on account of sex*. The ERA passed both houses of Congress in 1972, but an insufficient number of U.S. states failed to ratify it and the amendment expired in 1982 and never became law.

FEMININITY EXPECTANCIES OF WOMEN AND BACKLASH EFFECTS WHEN SOCIAL NORMS ARE VIOLATED

Today, perhaps more than ever before, confusion about what femininity means results in unmet expectations and backlash that threatens peace of mind among girls and women. Women are told that, on the one hand, they may strive to become whatever they choose. On the other hand, realities of accommodating (or not) what women perceive is expected of them may result in violations that lead to internal stress/conflict. Women who spoke with me during focus group discussions and interviews told of challenges they experience in "being *on*" in terms of emphasizing their femininity with dresses, full makeup, and high heels. As I collected women's perceptions about femininity and their stories about what femininity means to them, college student Kristyn, Caucasian/White, 19, commiserated with members of her focus group about how a busy schedule and the college lifestyle does not always lend itself to emphasizing one's femininity around the clock. Kristyn explained, referring to an image of a young Caucasian/White woman wearing stiletto heels and a short red figure-hugging sparkly sequined dress from the pages of *Ladies Home Journal* in the 1990s:

> No way am I getting up at 8 o'clock to do my hair every morning. I tried that during freshman year. And I don't even wear heels like that! It's too uncomfortable and I would never take my shoes off at a club. It's like if you're going to make appearances, if you're going to try to be a woman, stay that way the *whole time*. It's stuff like that makes you realize, it's *so hard*. For a lot of girls, being feminine all the time is, like, a full-time job.

Being expected to maintain a feminine appearance 24/7, agreed many college women sitting around the table, creates pressure that women with multiple responsibilities and too little time or money often feel unequipped to deal with.

As a result, girls and women who dress or behave in ways considered to be inconsistent with others' expectations for what a girl or woman *should be* may experience particularly harsh consequences. For example, language reinforces beliefs that women are less powerful than men—so that when they use more agentic or masculine linguistic modes, they still are refused access to power because they are perceived as violating expectations for appropriate female behavior, or femininity (Lackoff, 1975). Taking a que from Rowbotham's (1974) scrutiny of women's experiences that are "hidden from history," routinely ignored are the experiences of certain types of women—"spinsters, lesbians, unionists, prostitutes, madwomen, rebels and maiden aunts, manual workers, midwives and witches" (Connell, 1987, p. 188)—who are unlikely to be considered in terms of their femininity. Indeed, Johnson (2015) argued that some definitions of femininity are more valued than others. For example, in the United States and many other parts of the globe, the ideal feminine woman is supposed to be simultaneously painfully thin and muscular and buxom; qualities that Weitz (2010) argued are possible only when women have significant resources (time and money) to devote to achieving and maintaining them.

Critics of movies and the fashion and beauty industries—especially by feminist theorists—tend to universally challenge accepted ideas about women's bodies, power hierarchies that disenfranchise women, and ways the femininity concept turns in upon women. According to Faludi (1991), when "a society projects its fears onto a female form," a backlash reaction to feminism has resulted in deriding a century's worth of women's progress and a conscious effort to resurrect and reinforce traditional ideas about women in order to control them—while simultaneously making women's predicament appear to be their conscious choice:

> The demand that women "return to femininity" is a demand that the cultural gears shift into reverse, that we back off to a fabled time when everyone was richer, younger, more powerful. The "feminine" woman is forever static and childlike. She is like the ballerina in an old-fashioned music box, her unchanging features tiny and girlish, her voice tinkly, her body stuck on a pin, rotating in a spiral that will never grow (p. 70).

Since the 1960s, this backlash has emerged amidst women being pressured to control their body's shape, defining of post-menstrual women as sick, and rise of "fetal rights" and anti-abortion movements (Weitz, 2010, p. 9). Meanwhile, feminism (and feminists) have been over-simplified and caricatured in popular culture as "angry women—perhaps in combat boots, flannel shirts, and no makeup—who spout harsh, anti-male slogans or otherwise assert power over men" (Foss, Foss, & Griffin, p. 2). Caro (2016) posited that one reason feminism has been considered circumspectly by both men *and* women in the U.S. is because it is a philosophy "that puts women first. . . . [W]hy I will fight any attempt to rename feminism *equalism* or something similar. If we buy into that, we will just end up expected to put ourselves second yet again." Like feminists before me, I concur that not all feminists engage in man-hating and posit that femininities are far more complex than any one image might suggest. Postfeminism—sometimes termed *new sexism* and *retrosexism*—popularly suggests that feminism as a political movement is passé, no longer needed, and has left in its wake a world where young women may presume that they have rights equal to men. Braithwaite (2002), however, posited that third-wave feminists' embrace of their femininity through overt sexiness does not necessarily mean an apolitical throwback to traditional femininity. Undeniably, thinking about feminism in terms of waves underscores inadequacy of the metaphor (Baumgardner & Richards, 2004). I further explore in chapter 7 debates among feminist scholars about use of the wave metaphor.

GIRL POWER AND *RIOT GRRRL* MOVEMENTS' REDEFINING OF GIRLIE-GIRL FEMININITY

Young women define femininity in ways that reflect their sense of entitlement and in opposition to what they consider to be their mother's brand of feminism. Baumgardner and Richards (2004) found the girlie-girl concept and feminism most at odds among college-age women and young professional women. For them, patriarchy is not the enemy. Feminism is. Young women perceive unattractive and angry feminists to be a threat to their own individual expression. These are women who have traded in older women's negatively colored feminism—in exchange for bright pink freedom to enjoy sex and to consume and parade feminine products and services. This enthusiasm translates to a re-invigorated consumer culture which lays claim to an increasing number of young women who work and earn an income. Yet, women who position themselves among third-wave feminism feel neither subordinated nor duped by consumer culture (McRobbie, 2009, p. 157). Embracing the term *girlie-girl* means emerging from the shadow of older-generation feminists who felt compelled to downplay their femininity to prove their value in a male-dominated workplace. Among the young women who participated in my focus groups and interviews, a girlie-girl identity shapes their own personal brand of femininity. *Girlie* was one of the words college women often used to define femininity. Interviewed for this book, college student Jane, 20, Caucasian/White, explained what *girlie-girl* means to her:

> I'm in a sorority; we're the down-to-earth sorority. And, it's like we can get pretty and look nice and stuff, but it's like if I want to wear sweat pants and not put on any make-up, like, that's going to be okay. . . . I'm like really girlie and bubbly and enthusiastic. Like, I love headbands and bows and, like, wooo pink, but at the same time I'm smart. And,

because I'm bubbly and enthusiastic and stuff, people, like, assume that I'm dumb. Actually, no. My GPA is probably higher than yours.

College student Chloe, 22, Caucasian/White, said she feels as though she hasn't yet grown into her femininity:

> I wear make-up and I wear pink and stuff. But, at the same time, I don't wash my hair everyday and, like, my nail polish flakes off and sometimes . . . the make-up on my face is from yesterday. So, I guess I'm like a sloppy girlie-girl. . . . So, I think cleanliness or, like, neatness about your appearance is attributed to, like, supreme femininity. . . . In life, I do see myself as a woman, but I don't see myself as the woman I see my mom as or even my mom was when she got married. I think that has a lot to do with the instability or the transition period of my life. You know, I'm about to graduate college and it's almost this quarter-life crisis of, "Okay, I'm almost an adult," but I still kind of feel like I'm under my parents' supervision and because of that maybe I still don't see myself as a fully developed feminine woman. And so, I prefer to call myself a girlie-girl, instead. You know what I mean?

Stories like Jane's and Chloe's resonated across most of the focus group meetings I held among college students, suggesting young women think of the femininity concept the way they have since they were little girls, but have expanded the definition to include body adornment for emphasized femininity. These are young women enjoying the freedom of relying on their parents' financial support and the structure of college life.

For many girlie-girls, the global girl power phenomenon continues to find acceptance. Among one of the most successful and well-marketed global girl groups in history—earning up to $75 million per year (Svetkey, 1998) was the U.K.'s *Spice Girls*. They sang about what they *really, really want* across the 1990s and in a high-grossing feature film, *Spice World* in 1997 through playful characterizations of Baby Spice, Ginger Spice, Posh Spice, Scary Spice, and Sporty Spice. These discourses opened cultural spaces for girls and women to openly display agentic attitudes that were at the same time sexual (Dobson & Harris, 2015). At the height of their popularity, the *Spice Girls* had defenders among feminists who viewed the streetwise entrepreneurial women who knew how to grab what they want and embody "a new brand of feminism for the next generation" and a "confident display of high femininity" (Hinds & Stacey, 2001, p. 154), playfully asserting their sexual enjoyment and disassociating themselves from aging Caucasian/White, middle-class feminists (McRobbie, 1998). See Figure 1.1. In the decades since the *Spice Girls* have exited the pop culture scene, post-girlpower femininities have devolved into being less about power and more about the "sexualized girl" which easily is commodified as eye candy (Jackson & Goddard, 2015), girls who "have and spend money" (McRobie, 2000, p. 167).

In contrast to the girlie-girl image, young women enacting third-wave feminism also possess a fierceness, boldness, strength, and intelligence—especially the more radical members linked to the riotgrrl subculture. Orenstein (2011) opined that the extra r's in *riotgrrl* symbolized a rejection of consumer-fueled femininity. Activist, spoken word artist, and punk zine writer Kathleen Hanna, who fronted feminist punk bands including *Bikini Kill*, encouraged women to *dress like you're asking for it* to promote female confidence and individuality. Another pop culture bad girl in rock music, Courtney Love, was frontwoman for the alternative rock band, *Hole*, during the 1990s. She was accused of battling with Hanna backstage at Lollapalooza in 1995, chastised for abusing drugs while pregnant, and charged with attacking journalists. An all-women rock band that went on to influence several riotgrrl bands of the 1990s, *L7* also was no stranger to controversy—as when lead vocalist Donita Sparks responded to a rowdy crowd slinging mud onstage during technical difficulties by removing her tampon while on stage and throwing it into the crowd, yelling "Eat my used tampon, fuckers!" (Yarm, 2012, p. 369). These displays of a non-soft femininity suggest "woman as kitsch object [which] can be both illustrated and destroyed" (Brown, 2000, p. 40). Ways that consumerism and rituals shape the concept of femininity are explored in depth in chapter 4.

Figure 1.1.   Worldwide pop culture phenomenon, the Spice Girls, continue to express their emphasized femininity through public appearances, including the 12th Annual Victoria's Secret Fashion Show in 2007. Source: Ryan Born/ Depositphotos.com.

ANDROGYNY AND FEMININITY
ARE NOT NECESSARILY INCONGRUOUS

The *androgyny* concept, rooted in classical mythology and literature, does not necessarily equate with anti-femininity. Generally, androgyny represents a combination of personality characteristics typically associated with women (feminine), as well as those associated with men (masculine). Since the early 1970s, androgyny has captured the attention of psychology researchers motivated to explain similarities and differences among women and men. Here, the concept of androgyny had proved somewhat controversial as researchers have developed instruments and measures for assessing ways women and men may possess both feminine and masculine qualities—but critics have pointed out that the very act of dichotomizing and labeling femininity/feminine and masculinity/masculine as opposite traits further entrenches binary dualism thinking. Androgyny represents a combination of the expressive/communal (feminine) and instrumental/agentic (masculine) personality traits (Cook, 1987).

Among the women's magazine images examined during focus groups and interviews conducted for this book, some research participants were quick to point out images of androgyny that they admired for appearances of comfort and intelligence. A *Ladies Home Journal*, 1971, black and white image of a midlife-aged, short-haired Asian-American woman dressed in a white tunic and pants evoked positive responses from non-college research participants. Camila, 27, bisexual, Dominican aunt of a college woman who participated in a focus group for the study reported in this book had this to say about the image: "I like it a lot. Her posture, she's comfortable. It doesn't seem like she's been influenced by the media or what the world thinks women should look like. She's calm, cool, collected. She seems like she's aware." Similarly, Camila appreciated a *Good Housekeeping*, 1971, sepia-toned image of young woman dressed in a button-down-collared shirt, shorts, and black leggings, holding a pelican: "It feels like she might know a lot about the animal. She's educated. She's breaking the mold by not being at home—being out there researching. She looks comfortable with herself." Women like Camila argued for a new definition of femininity—one that diverges from the girlie-girl concept frequently invoked by college women. Defining femininity outside of patriarchy may seem impossible since male hegemony continues to persist. However, Tong (2009) recommended that each woman "renounce her false feminine self in favor of her true female self" (Tong, 2009, p. 3).

SHARPENING A FOCUS ON THE
RHETORIC OF FEMININITY AND ITS SYMBOLS

The concept of femininity, as it is represented in media and described by women of three age cohorts, is subjected to rhetorical criticism throughout this book. Long missing amidst the study of rhetoric, historically, have been women's perspectives. This is a shortcoming widely acknowledged by feminist scholars and embraced by them as a means for exploring "larger questions about the nature and functions of symbolocity" (Foss, Foss, & Griffin, 1999, p. 7) which prove useful in understanding precisely how people construct and (re)negotiate meanings. For example, during focus group meetings and interviews, women across age cohorts invoked feminist arguments (many without realizing it) that girls' and women's lives must not be reduced to a series of stereotypes. They consistently interrogated ways women's bodies and their femininities become mired in symbols which sexualize, and demoralize them—such as urgings to get ready to take their clothes off in summer to show off a bikini body and for girls to diet to lose their *baby fat*. Applying rhetorical critique to everyday texts that lend shape to how we define femininity is essential to rooting out ways women are objectified and treated as second-class citizens. More broadly, study of rhetoric promotes a shared understanding of the world. Being conscious of the ways texts, rituals, and symbols impact people's lives is an essential task of the rhetorician. Lending a feminist perspective to rhetorical criticism supports reconceptualization of concepts like *femininity* and advocates for communicating positive values without using negative means that may end up further contributing to female gender role stress/conflict.

Rhetorical analysis of popular culture as communicated via media products like television shows, movies, women's magazines, social media, and more reveals ways that femininity and its symbols are promoted—and provides clues about how girls and women may interpret them. Revealed during focus group discussions and interviews for this book were significant degrees of dissonance, or stress/conflict between what society deems as *normal* and how women interpret femininity for themselves. An "endearing femininity" (McRobbie, 2009, p. 12) which symbolizes women as scatterbrained but charming as in the *Bridget Jones's Diary* film trilogy—with a promise that subscribing to old-fashioned notions of femininity yields young women a marriage partner—offered mixed messages about workplace sexual harassment, sleeping with the boss, and objectifying oneself to secure employment. Several women interviewed for this book referenced Bridget Jones as a woman who struggled with her femininity. The adventurous romp of *Sex and the City* promoted consumer culture in the form of fashion, shoes, perfume, and more, promotes "rituals of enjoyable femininity" (McRobbie, 2009, p. 3). This cable television show and feature film reflected what McRobbie

(2009) characterized as young women worrying about being mistaken for a feminist and so instead adopted an "air of being girlishly distracted, slightly flustered, weighed down with bags, shoes, bracelets and other decorative candelabra items" (p. 67). In this media portrayal, femininity was greatly aligned with consumerism—and women interviewed for this book (especially college women) referenced the four women archetypes of *Sex and the City* when sharing their own definition of femininity.

By contrast, several decades earlier, symbols created to support World War II efforts in the United States reveal other ways the femininity concept was used as a tool of persuasion. War events interrupted traditional vestiges of femininity since women were required to work outside the home, engaging in volunteer work and paid factory jobs usually reserved for men. *Rosie the Riveter* symbolically played a patriotic role as part of a U.S. government propaganda campaign with the slogan *We Can Do It!* to convince women to join the World War II effort by working in munitions factories. Prior to World War II, only 1 percent of aircraft industry workers were women, but numbers climbed significantly to 65 percent during the war (Rosie the riveter, 2016), attributable in no small part to the propaganda campaign which symbolized a red bandana-wrapped head of a woman who proudly displays her bicep. The image remains an icon of working women in the United States. As in the earlier aftermath of World War I, women were told to return to the private sphere of unpaid domestic work when men returned from battle.

Women who served as research participants for the study reported in this book routinely mentioned both Princess Grace Kelly of Monaco and Princess Diana as symbolizing femininity. Princess Grace was an Oscar-winning American actress who married Prince Rainier III in 1956 and became Princess of Monaco. She died tragically in an automobile accident. During the late twentieth century, Diana Princess of Wales became a symbol of femininity representing the United Kingdom. Known as "the people's Princess," Diana married the heir to the British throne in 1981 and bore two sons. Called "a spectacularization of white femininity," Diana became an "idealized signifier of a modern woman of the millennium" and a perpetual object of media attention even fifteen years after her death (Shome, 2014, p. 2)—also in an automobile accident. Arguably, she has been sainted in global public opinion (Richards, Wilson, & Woodhead, 1999) and has come to symbolize global humanitarianism, multicultural fashion, motherhood, and femininity. Both Princess Grace and Princess Diana were blonde, Caucasian/White, and fashion icons.

Rhetorical critique of femininity, as defined by a diverse group of women interviewed for this book, as well as critique of popular culture representations of femininity across mass media platforms contributes to not only an understanding of how people make meaning about femininity, but should improve our ability as communicators and elevate our

Figure 1.2.   The "We Can Do It!" poster invited women to join the World War II war-time work force in the United States, particularly munitions factories and shipyards. The image, fondly, has become known as "Rosie the Riveter." Source: Rosie the Riveter Trust

awareness of and engagement with how and why society constructs the concept of femininity as it does.

DISCUSSION

As this chapter has explained, femininity matters remain highly complex. I problematize a seemingly simple concept by enjoining multiple sets of academic literature and rhetorically analyzing the texts of focus group discussions and interviews conducted among women representing three age cohorts. *Femininity matters* to all of us—no matter our gender or other dimensions of social identity intersectionalities, including age, class, culture, ethnicity, faith/spirituality, physical/psychological ability, and sexual orientation. What social conditions encourage all variety of women and men to consider femininity as a sense-making activity in their lives? To ponder this weighty matter, we need a broader view on *how femininities mean*.

This first chapter has provided a foundation for the rest of the book by introducing and defining key concepts and terms used throughout this book. It has explored femininity as a contextual concept (it depends whom you ask and when you ask), explained differences between sex and gender, explored how power relations in society significantly impact how femininity is defined, and addressed how traditional female gender roles may limit our definition of femininity. This chapter also offered historical perspectives on femininity that have held women down and back, explained how femininity expectancies of women may result in backlash effects when those social norms are violated, covered ways the *girl power* and *riot grrrl* movements redefine girlie-girl femininity, examined how androgyny and femininity are not necessarily incongruous, and sharpened a focus on the rhetoric of femininity and its symbols.

Some processes of emphasizing femininity through normalized, unhealthful, painful, and sadistic practices to shape women's appearance and to increase their value to men are abhorrent. In some parts of the world, practices of clitoridectomy, corseting, foot-binding, and scarification have given way to women imposing unhealthful practices on themselves that can lead to eating disorders and addiction to plastic surgery. Any time the life of a girl or woman is jeopardized in the practice of emphasized femininity, something is terribly wrong. Moreover, some of the practices listed above endure around the world, whether openly or subversively.

TWO

Ideal Femininity According to Family, Tradition, and Media

In urban modeling they don't mind if the tits are on more than a stick. So, you'll have all of the natural curves—not only in the breasts, but in the waist and in the hips, as well. It is a very cultivated, very calculated image. So they're going to put the most investment, and spend the most time on the girls who make money.

—Research participant Lorraine, 38, African-American/Black, heterosexual

Inviting women across three generations to peruse and chat about images published in women's magazines over the past 100 years (1910–2010) in conjunction with their own personal definition of *femininity* inspired a good deal of laughter, smiles, frowns, memories and stories, criticism, debate, and speculation for the future. Women's magazines' role in establishing normative codes of femininity over the decades is well established (Odland, 2009). Goffman (1976) even argued that women's magazines offer a *cult of femininity* and Lont (1995) described them as shaping and promoting *the ideal woman.* Collectively, dozens of college women and their mothers/aunts, grandmothers who participated in focus groups and interviews amplified their perceptions of *What is femininity?* as they compared/contrasted the magazine images used as stimulus materials (see Introduction for details). In the course of conversations, women expressed a good deal of internal stress/conflict suffered when they feel unable/unwilling to *live up to* what is expected of them in terms of pressures to be thin—which many associated with femininity. Overall, much dissonance and body esteem issues were shared when defining *femininity* for themselves—and for other women. The diversity of perspectives also revealed new information for many women, such as Lorraine's (above quote) shared behind-the-scenes experiences as an urban model.

As traditions evolve, women and their relationship with their body changes, too. Whereas women once were encouraged to maintain a modest appearance, they increasingly have experienced fewer restrictions on where they may go and what they may wear in many areas of the world. Attitudes toward women's "feminine destiny in maternity" (Bartky, 2010, p. 94) may not have changed that much, since many women who participated in the study for this book who are mothers defined *femininity* in terms of *ability to bear children*. Also, women universally still persist in a preoccupation with youth and beauty; an outcome easily blamed on daily barrages of ideal female images in magazines, feature films, television, the internet, video games, and more. To critical media scholars, these images have promoted a shift in thinking about femininity among women across social classes and age groups from being female-gender-role-specific (e.g., wife, mother, homemaker) to being female-body-centric (e.g., thin, curvy, sexy, smiling). As Bartky (2010) opined, "What was formerly the specialty of the aristocrat or courtesan is now the *routine obligation* of every woman, be she a grandmother or a barely pubescent girl" (p. 94, italics added). When sexualization is commercially driven, clothing companies target five-year-olds with thongs and T-shirts printed with slogans such as "When I'm bad I'm very, very bad, but when I'm in bed I'm better" (Gill, 2007a, p. 151). So, while some traditions and rituals have evolved to be more egalitarian toward women—others have developed which objectify the female form and further entrench girls and women in second-class status.

These issues are explored in greater detail throughout this chapter: 1) The ideal feminine woman: Lifetime of social comparisons; 2) Defining femininity in the new millennium; 3) Girls, women, family, and femininity; 4) Media images benchmark ideal, emphasized femininity; 5) Femininity and the college experience; and 6) Discussion.

THE IDEAL FEMININE WOMAN: LIFETIME OF SOCIAL COMPARISONS

From adolescence onward, girls and women experience pressure to conform to dominant femininity ideals and continually compare themselves to other women as an informal evaluation of self and/or to enhance their own self-perception; to feel better about themselves. This dynamic forms the basis for social comparison theory, used to understand effects and to predict outcomes associated with comparing oneself with others (Helgeson & Taylor, 1993). Gramsci's (1971) concept of hegemony explains how media representations are promoted as natural or common sense, reproducing dominant hegemonic meanings about heteronormative femininity and gender hierarchies. For example, mediated images establish templates for how women should look. Long ago, Festinger (1954) hypothesized that people instinctively are driven to compare themselves to others as a key step in self-improvement or self-enhancement processes—and Bandura (1977) suggested that individuals appreciate learning from a model who is more experienced or successful in a specific arena. Many researchers attribute these benchmarking behaviors—not to genetics, but to advertising-driven desires and consumption of media images of celebrities at red carpet events and fashion shows. For example, high school girls used media images of Beyoncé Knowles, Mo'Nique Hicks, and other celebrity entertainers for upward comparisons when selecting prom dresses, grooming hair, and strategically posing for photographs (Pompper & Crandall, 2014). Lorraine, a thirty-eight-year-old African-American/Black woman who participated in a focus group discussion for this book, shared behind-the-scenes experiences from her acting and modeling work. Her quote at the top of this chapter illustrates what she perceived to be ideal emphasized femininity norms for African-American/Black women, which include a fuller figure. Yet she said modeling agencies more often receive requests for "the standard industry, tiny waist and hips, big breasts, White girls."

Female breasts may be the most visible signifier of a woman's femininity and, thus, serve as a femininity ideal. Women's breasts may be among the most easily recognized symbols of femininity; one that women who participated in this study routinely mentioned. Young (2010) suggested that "breasts are the symbol of feminine sexuality, so the 'best' breasts are like the phallus: high, hard, and pointy" (p. 180). Under patriarchy, in the United States, girls and women perceive that their breasts are constantly under surveillance and judged according to their size and contours; a "tangible signifier of her womanliness" (Young, 2010, p. 180). In the United States and many other parts of the world, the quintessential sign of womanly value is breasts—growing them, hiding them, displaying them, and enhancing them—as adolescents "come to define their own value in terms of breast development" (Sotirin, 2004, p. 123). How symbolic is the training bra and its promise of femininity and womanhood; perhaps girls' first step in disciplining their body, forcing it to conform to the presentation expectations of male desire, and discovering mounting anxieties about their breasts' shape and size as they grow under society's watchful gaze. Media proliferation of large, enhanced female breast images sets an unattainable goal without surgical procedures, hence, fostering stress/conflict for many girls and young women early in their life cycle—and then negative scrutiny later on when their breasts lose their suppleness and elasticity. The topic of female breasts dominated many of the focus group and interview discussions conducted for this book. College student Ada, 21, Caucasian/White recalled how embarrassed she was to have large breasts:

I have the biggest boobs of my entire family. My mom doesn't have them, my grandma, I don't know where they are coming from. My friends don't have them, they are like a B-cup. I would wear sports bras—then two bras to flatten them so nobody could see them. Then a few years ago, I don't know why, but it changed and I'm glad I have them.

Martha, 20, Brazilian-Colombian, expressed mixed sentiments about her breasts, but agreed with other women in her focus group that breasts are a primary ingredient of a woman's femininity:

[M]y boobs started growing when I was like twelve and I was always the girl with bigger boobs. . . . I was really hating my boobs. . . . I would try to wear shirts that don't show my boobs at all or wear hoodies or stuff like that. It wasn't until probably like last year, probably college year [that] I started to wear tank tops, just not really caring.

Both Ada and Martha explained that, with maturity, they have come to be more comfortable with her own body—and to, perhaps, feel more comfortable with more closely matching with an ideal that has been established in the United States with regard to female breast size. This issue arose in another focus group session, too, with twenty-two-year-old Danielle, Latina, talking about her private school's "puberty closet" equipped with clothing used to help cover and to *constrain* girls' femininity:

If you come into class one day and your teacher notices that your shirt is too tight or whatever, they'll go in the back. Like you wore that shirt three months ago and it was fine, but now it's been a while and it shows some cleavage. They'll be like "Danielle, come to the back with me real quick. Here, give this sweater back to me later."

Danielle explained how her Catholic school upbringing made her feel negatively toward her body during puberty—as if her breasts were something to be hidden. The labeling of the area where sweaters were used to cover up girls' breasts—"puberty closet," suggests the school's uneasiness with femininity and girls' maturation.

Having large breasts has ethnicity dimensions and is not without discomfort for some girls and women. Several college women who participated in focus groups conducted for the study reported in this book mentioned *un*feminine bad posture that can result from having large breasts. Nicole, 18, self-identified as Black-Japanese, explained how ethnicity factors into breast size issues and complicates fashion decisions and ways others think of women:

I understand about the bad posture because my sister is a full D-cup and she's skinny, but she calls it *the White girl hunch* because Black women are so much more prouder of being curvy. They are not going to sit there and try to hide their boobs if they have big boobs. I don't know if it's the culture, but White women, in general, tend to try to put it away a little bit. . . . [A]nother thing is when you have big boobs and you have *good* posture, it looks like you're trying to stick them out when you're just being normal and you don't want to look arrogant. . . . You can't wear those little empire shirts or you'll get the quad boob where it splits them in half or if you pull it down all the way you'll show too much cleavage.

Clearly, as Nicole explained, there are implications of large breast size with regard to ethnic identity—with Caucasian/White women, perhaps, feeling more self-conscious about them than women of color. Too, women of color strategically think about how their breasts look when deciding what to wear. On the other hand, Kathleen, 54, Caucasian/White, told women in her focus group discussion that she grew up wishing she had larger breasts: "[N]ot huge, maybe a B would be ideal and that one day I might do something to have that happen. Now, I'm just lucky they don't sag." Interestingly, women complaining about their breasts during focus group meetings and interviews significantly outnumbered those expressing degrees of satisfaction about their breasts as some element they used to define femininity. It is difficult not to point to the role media play in establishing norms with regard to women's breasts. Unrealistic media images become internalized, making women's self-abasement inevitable and a normalized emotional state (Bartkey, 1988)—outcomes of social comparisons that have proliferated since the advent of social media. A study of MySpace profiles of young women over age eighteen revealed a plethora of images of lips, midriffs, and breasts (Dobson, 2011). Female breasts as objects for display have become normalized with photo-posting technologies used in social media.

Even before social media, selfies, and reality television, girls and women took their cues about femininity ideals from women's magazines—particularly with regard to undergarments supporting breasts. For example, the *Ladies Home Journal* in 1897 published advertisements for a corset that created a "bicycle waist" which qualified as the "epitome of femininity and good taste" (Kitch, 2001, p. 31) since the feminine form in its natural state without foundation was considered undignified by many female elders, as consistent with Puritan traditions of modesty and propriety. Kunzle (1982) characterized the corset as the most powerful symbol of nineteenth-century oppression of women within their own bodies; an undergarment that damaged internal organs and caused fainting and breathlessness. Davis (1992) speculated that the corset faded from daily-wear Victorian fashion when other means were found for women's sexual and self-expression. Today, hosiery-free legs and Spanx have replaced yesteryear's girdles for daily containment of female flesh, with corsets reserved for sexy lingerie and titillation.

Feature films and television programs serve up images which offer plenty of femininity cues, too. Ligon (2015) found "deep intergenerational friction and discord" (p. 56) between young brides and their female elders persists, however, on reality television shows such as *Say Yes to the Dress*, wherein brides negotiate a modesty-sexy divide in defining their own sense of femininity display with selection of a gown and what is worn beneath it. Interestingly, Rivière (1929/1986) collapsed *womanliness* and *masquerade* to underscore the social constructedness of emphasized femininity—which McRobbie (2009) posited as being aligned with consumer culture which promotes "pleasures and rituals of enjoyable femininity" (p. 3) while simultaneously serving as a signifier of female independence and empowerment. This dynamic has played out in popular culture feature film entertainment such as *Bridget Jones's Diary* on the big screen and *Sex and the City* on the small screen with characters and viewers who eschew feminism's critique of patriarchy while using their body to represent their femininity in terms of sexuality. Both narratives concurrently instill and resist traditional femininity; a tactic Charlebois (2011) suggested enables mediated representations to endure in a "postfeminist era of presupposed gender equality" (p. 109). The autonomous heterosexual young woman provides a powerful tool for modern femininity-as-linked-to-sexuality. Yet, the general principle of femininity discourse—for becoming a beautiful desired woman—can never be "perfectly realized" (Cranny-Francis, Waring, Stavropoulos, & Kirkby, 2003, p. 199) when advertising and the fashion-beauty complex tell girls and women they are in constant need of improvement, a dynamic that creates and perpetuates stress and conflict. These dynamics are explored in greater depth in chapter 4.

Conversations with research participants about 100 years' worth of magazines' female images inspired a myriad of conversations about femininity as a fluid, timeless, *I know it when I see it* concept—but one that revealed contradictory meanings associated with breasts and skin exposure. One of the most frequently selected images for representing *most feminine* was a soft focus, pale-pink-tinted photograph of a Grace Kelly-like female figure from a 1950s issue of *Good Housekeeping*. The model had her eyes cast down and wore a lacy corseted crinoline undergarment that exposed her bare shoulders and showed some cleavage. The image was very similar to the Figure 2.1.

Also frequently selected as representing *most feminine* was a 1930s *McCall's* sketched image of a tall, willowy thin Caucasian/White woman gazing at her image in a full-length mirror, admiring a floor-length bright red, fitting gown. Her back is completely exposed and the fabric tightly hugs her derriere. Women of all demographic groups enjoyed talking about how much they admired both images, suggesting a timeless quality to traditional femininity, with some even longing for a return to "classy," "retro" fashion. Indeed, fashion designers admit being attracted to femininity of yesteryear in the United States, as Faludi (1991) explained after interviewing Guess? Inc. co-founder Paul Marciano, who

Figure 2.1.   Research participants gravitated toward a 1950s magazine image of a woman wearing a corset as most feminine—not unlike this more modern version. Source: Iuliia Nemchinova/ Depositphotos.com.

explained, "Women want to look the way they did in the 1950s. They feel cheated by liberation" (p. 196). These two images of Caucasian/White women from decades ago—one wearing a lacy corset and crinoline and the other wearing a long, backless, red silk dress—perhaps derive their enduring power to personify femininity across age and ethnic social identities of women who participated in this study because of what McRobbie (2009) called the *postfeminist masquerade* rooted in Hollywood's heyday, as well as a "retro nostalgia for this kind of whiteness" (p. 71). Trying to emulate these representations of femininity comes at a cost for women of color—constituting a kind of racial violence—since these disaffirm beauty norms associated with their ethnicity and culture (Dyer, 1997).

In sum, my conversations with women across three age cohorts suggested that femininity is inscribed across a woman's entire body. Duke and Kreshel (1998) warned about such a mode of thinking tends to overemphasize a woman's body for its sexuality, rather than for its ability to perform labor. Ironically, women across age cohorts shunned a 1990s image from *Redbook* of a Caucasian/White woman wearing a navy-colored plush velour robe wide open at the front where her burgundy-colored push-up-bra-supported breasts were cradled in her folded arms. When asked why this particular image failed to meet their standard for *most feminine,* women explained that it "looked too slutty," "like she's trying too hard." Even college women like Amy, 21, Caucasian/White rejected this image, saying: "She can wear the bra, but she doesn't have to push all her stuff out. . . . She has that attitude that seems to be 'Look at me'!" Fay, 21, said: "Being feminine is leaving something to the imagination. Being feminine is empowering. *That woman,* she has no dignity." Even among older women, the image was negatively critiqued. Jacqueline, 52, Caucasian/White, explained: "Showing your breasts does not make you feminine. It's just a manipulation. . . . Feminine to me are the things that make you a woman, as opposed to being a man—and that can be a big variety of things. But baring your boobs doesn't make it. That's usin' it." Yifang, 52, Chinese-American, expressed a minority view on the image: "I guess it depends on what context, where she's at, and what she's doing that for. If she's at a cocktail party, that's slutty. If she's in the privacy of her bedroom with her husband, that's feminine." On the other hand, a 1980s *Redbook* image of a Caucasian/White woman with arms raised above her head and having her torso and breasts wrapped with a pink, gauzy tulle fabric was considered among the *most feminine* choices. Alejandra, 22, Dominican, described how she classified this image: "[I]t's just really soft and feminine. Like the pink fabric. And she's showing a lot of skin without being too, um, nasty. And she has long hair and pretty skin, too."

Perhaps some aspects of emphasized femininity may stray too far along the spectrum as to violate traditional norms of modesty. It could be that emphasizing femininity *with an intent to feminize femininity* is considered *too over the top to be feminine* among the women who served as research participants for this book.

Women's studies and feminist scholars widely have noted femininity can be ideal if a woman takes pleasure in it, although some have opined that a postfeminist shift from second-wave feminists' organizing and emphasizing social change—to narcissism—is counterintuitive for advancing women from second-class social status. Historically, women have enjoyed the "perks of being female" which include wearing make-up, jewelry, and other ornaments in their hair and on body parts (Sinkman, 2013, p. 130) because they take pleasure in their own bodies and have active libidos "whether or not another person judges her beautiful or ugly" (p. 129). Women of the 1950s in the United States who wanted to communicate femininity with refinement and upward mobility tradition-ally wore white gloves and a strand of cultured pearls (Brownmiller, 1984). Critics, however, have charged that popular culture offers images of grown women as "silly . . . self-absorbed girls" (Bellafante, 1998, pp. 57–58). Similarly, some feminists warn that merely wearing "spindly sti-lettos and pencil skirts" may not always signal "hyper-femininity of the masquerade" which could threaten to throw women back to traditional gender hierarchies—but instead reflect a "kind of feminism" since wom-en have a choice as to what to wear and how to adorn their body (McRob-bie, 2009, pp. 65–66). Brownmiller (1984) explained that each wave of feminism debates whether or not to recommend dress reform for women, but the question ultimately is withdrawn: "I suppose it is asking too much of women to give up their chief outward expression of the feminine difference, their continuing reassurance to men and to themselves that a male is a male because a female dresses and looks and acts like another sort of creature" (p. 79). Women shared many stories about how proud they are to express their femininity with fashion and confessions about how they watch other women to see how their own body compares.

Also widely known for comparing ideal femininity is a woman's at-tachment to mothering and housekeeping. Being a perfect mother—as the ultimate feminine accomplishment—historically represents a throw-back to Victorian ideals, Freudian psychology, a Roaring '20s that "trapped educated American women in their kitchen, babbling at babies and worrying about color combinations for the bathroom" (Cowan, 1983, p. 177), and 1950s television programs depicting some highly commer-cialized prototypical American family ideal. Indeed, some women saw housework as a means to express their femininity during the 1950s (Mat-thews, 1987). Several of the young women who participated in the study for this book defined femininity in terms of domestic chores, too. Second-wave feminists have critiqued ways media represent femininity in terms of a domestic role (Feasey, 2009). However, images relegating women to the domestic sphere restricts ways we think about how women may con-tribute to society. Moreover, it is a limited view since rarely considered are women's social identity intersections of gender along with age, eth-nicity, physical ability, socio-economic status, religion/spirituality, sexual orientation, and more (Pompper, 2014a). In the United States, military recruitment posters of World War I visually communicated an ideal femi-ninity that simultaneously drew from somewhat conflicting stereotypes glorifying women as angels and nurses—as well as warriors and con-querors (Banta, 1977). In years after that war, women's femininity, again, was dually represented in women's magazines as either the "devoted mother" or the "silly flapper" (Kitch, 2001, p. 140). In pre-World War II, motherhood was regarded as women's duty (Plant, 2010) and *Harper's Weekly* routinely connected femininity with working-class morality. The gendered nuclear family with public and private spheres was established as a cultural ideal in the late eighteenth century (Ehrenreich & English, 1978), one that during wartime firmly entrenched women as *natural* mothers and caregivers in magazine representations. Negotiating femininity as a concept which bridges the public and the private seems hypocritical to some. During the 1960s sexual revolution in the United States, anti-feminists like Phyllis Schafly, "preach[ed] the joys of home and hearth from her executive office" (Baumgardner & Richards, 2004, p. 61). Today, motherhood is a personal decision, a re-privatization of women's lives (Marsh, 1990). Yet, the old adage, *the more things change the more they stay the same*, underscored the salience of traditional female gender roles and stereotypes when a *Time* magazine reporter rejoiced in the late 1980s: "Feminine clothing is back; breasts are back; motherhood is in again" (Wallis, 1989, p. 81). Women's magazines, which McRobbie (2009) called a "hermetically sealed world of feminine escapist pleasures," have offered an unrealistic medium for feminist issues given their collusion with consumer culture and ultimately playing a role in the undoing of feminism. Yet, it must be recognized that women's magazines persist in communicating about femininity to women young and old. A focus group discussion among college women conducted for this book turned to influences of magazines in shaping their perceptions of femininity. Chelsea, 20, Caucasian/White described her seventeen-year-old sister as an avid reader of *Cosmopolitan* magazine:

> [S]he comes up with the craziest ideas. . . . Like, she tried this weird diet to "make him want you." You don't eat broccoli or celery. I'm like "What are you doing?" She has all these bizarre plans and reasons for doing things that she reads in *Cosmo*. I just sit her down and like "No. This is *not* what you're going to do anymore."

What Chelsea described was an opportunity to teach her sister about critically thinking about media and ways images and representations shape our way of thinking and how we use them to make social comparisons between ourselves and others.

DEFINING FEMININITY IN THE NEW MILLENNIUM

When interviewing college women, their aunts, mothers, and some grandmothers for this book, I was struck by high degrees of conformity in ways they defined femininity. In other words, age cohort (18–29, 30–49, 50+) did not seem to play a significant role since many of the same words and phrases were used to define femininity. Words and phrases used more than five times appear in bold. See Table 2.1.

Across three age cohorts, or generations, of women who served as research participants for this book, the words/phrases that most frequent-

Table 2.1.   Defining Femininity across Age Cohorts

Age 18-29	Age 30-49	Age 50+
Adventurous	**Balanced**	Ability to bear children
Beautiful	Confident	Capable
Can cook	Educated	**Caring**
Caring	Elegant	Clean
Classy	Gentle	**Comfortable**
Clean	Graceful	Compassionate
Comfortable	Grounded	**Confident**
Compassionate	Ladylike	Empowered
Confident	Non-competitive	**Empathetic**
Contented	Pretty	Enabling
Coy	Proper	Gentle
Curvy	**Smart**	Happy
Delicate	Soft	**Healthy**
Dependent	Toned	**Loving**
Docile	Traveled	Loves being a woman
Educated	**Well-kempt**	Medium height
Elegant		Muscular
Empathetic		**Neat**
Fair		**Nurturing**
Gentle		Pretending
Girlie		Reasonable
Goal-oriented		Secure
Graceful		Selfless
Happy		Self-reliant
Healthy		Smart
Honest		**Soft**
Independent		Strong
Kind		Sweet
Ladylike		**Thin**
Loving		Warm
Modest		Well-behaved
Nurturing		**Well-kempt**
Obedient		
Passive		

Poised

Polite

Powerful

Pretty

Pride

Restrained

Selfless

Sensual

Soft

Strong

Submissive

Supportive

Well-being

Well-dressed

Well-kempt

Bold = mentioned five times or more

ly resonated with their definition of femininity were *confident, gentle, soft,* and *well-kempt*. Other commonly used terms for defining femininity across two age cohorts were *caring, clean, comfortable, compassionate, educated, elegant, empathetic, graceful, happy, healthy, ladylike, loving, nurturing,* and *selfless*.

Of course, several of the words/phrases used to define femininity overlap somewhat and not all women in each age cohort used the same words/phrases, but comparing them reveals some meaningful patterns. For example, many women equated femininity with appearance—especially among women ages 18–29—with words such as *beautiful, curvy, elegant, medium height, muscular, poised, pretty, thin,* and *toned*. Words/phrases associated with behaviors included *ability to bear children, adventurous, balanced, can cook, coy, goal-oriented, grounded, independent, non-competitive, obedient, passive, polite, pretending, pride, proper, restrained,* and *traveled*. Also noted were several internal qualities/virtues: *caring, comfortable, compassionate, confident, contented, docile, empathetic, fair, gentle, girlie, grounded, honest, kind, ladylike, loving, modest, nurturing, proper, reasonable, secure, selfless, sensual, supportive, sweet,* and *warm*.

Contrasting femininity's defining words/phrases offered by three age cohorts of women interviewed for this book reveals a few paradoxes and potential contradictions; outcomes which may underscore the stress/conflict women experience in their daily lives and over the life course. For example, the age 18–29 cohort members defined femininity using words like *adventurous* and *independent*—which contrasts greatly with other words they used, like *dependent, passive, restrained,* and *submissive*. Women aged 30–49 used words like *confident* and *educated*—which contrasts with another word they used; *non-competitive*. Among women aged 50+, who may be considered as having lived longer and during earlier periods before women joined the paid-work-outside-the-home workforce en masse, their definition of femininity with words of *capable* and *self-reliant* contrasted sharply with younger women (many their granddaughters) who used words such as *passive* and *submissive*. In sum, findings of this word/term exercise suggested many paradoxes that lead me to conclude that no one definition of femininity could work in the United States. I am greatly troubled by findings which suggest an undercurrent of stress/conflict women experience today.

GIRLS, WOMEN, FAMILY, AND FEMININITY

Family behavior modeling and social norms serve as environmental factors which influence girls' general psycho-social health about the intertwined concepts of femininity, body, and weight. McRobbie (1978) reminded us that one's culture embodies group life across history such that girls are situated "within the pre-existent culture of femininity which they, as females in a patriarchal society, are born into and which is continually transmitted to them over the years by their mothers, sisters, aunts, grandmothers, neighbours and so on" (p. 97). In particular, thin ideal internalization is reinforced by family members, in addition to peers and the media (Thompson & Stice, 2001). A wide range of commentary underscores the importance of one's physical appearance and our propensity to draw comparisons of body shape and weight with others. Body image is measured by the difference between an individual's actual and ideal body size—with a focus on the drive for thinness and degrees of body dissatisfaction (Baugh & Barnes, 2015). Theories underpinning understanding of these phenomena include social cognitive theory (Bandura, 1994) and socialization theory (Thornton, Alwin, & Camburn, 1983). Both theory streams contribute to understanding of how people learn and the influences of peer groups in influencing behavior. Much of the literature on gender ideology construction has focused heavily on mothers and mother figures because there is a fundamental likeness that encourages close identification between a mother and daughter. Mothers offer intergenerational transmission of gender ideology and often fill roles of teacher, counselor, cheerleader, and provider of material and emotional support (Diggs, 1999). Indeed, the mother-daughter bond is fundamental to women's lives (Pipher, 1995) and their sense of femininity. Luciana, 20, identifies as a Latina and as a participant in a focus group discussion conducted for the study reported in this book, Luciana explained culture's influences in the way women behave in her family:

> [M]y mother she likes to get dressed up. She likes to wear makeup when she goes out. She puts on her little powder to go to work. Now, my grandmother, she's *really* about beauty. She is in the high sixties and she has her nails done all the time, dressed up all the time, and has a purse every day. If I go to her house in sweatpants, without my nails done, she will call me out on it, and make sure I get myself together.

Indeed, family matriarchs provide significant information and discipline to young women, in particular, with regard to feminine behavior and appearance. Many women noted that appearance for emphasizing femininity is important when women are young, but that women prioritize other things in their lives as they age. Several college women I interviewed shared stories about their mothers who are divorced or separated, struggling to renew a commitment to emphasized femininity and working to improve upon their appearance. Jennifer, 18, Caucasian/White, shared a story about how she tries to help her mother to feel better about her body image:

> My mom has four kids, and she had them in four years, so my youngest sibling is four years younger than me. I think that, in and of itself, is outrageous. And she still will complain, "This makes me look so fat." And, I'm like, "Hon, you have four kids!" Before the kids, she was a tiny 5'2," size zero. You're not going to get that back! It's, like, "I think you look fine. I think you look awesome."

Indeed, bearing children takes a toll on women's body and their body image perceptions. Among the older women who participated in my study, even those who said they "really don't care" how they look if they're overweight or have not visited a hair salon in a long time, it was clear that looking their best is a preferred alternative to appearing in public in an unkempt state.

In adolescence, females become more aware of gender expectations and grow increasingly concerned about what others think of them. Girls' socialization processes include negotiating inter-psychic tensions about role differentiation—as when they psychologically identify with and adopt their mother's ideals of femininity (Chodorow, 1978). Mothers teach daughters the cultural norms of beauty and ways to critique their own appearance (Clarke & Griffin, 2007), serving as a main source of body esteem for their daughters throughout adulthood. Findings of cross-generational negotiations of femaleness in the family underscores the primary role of grandmothers and mothers as "purveyors of beauty norms" among African-American/Black girls—as in "if they did not need make-up, why should their (grand)daughters?" (Duke, 2000, p. 384). In particular, early adolescence is when weight-related and body dissatisfaction concerns increase (Bucchianeri, Arikian, Hannan, Eisenberg, & Neumark-Sztainer, 2013). According to social learning theory, girls are conditioned through observing their role-model parents (McHale, Crouter, & Whiteman, 2003), a process which is supplemented by and offers a lens for broader cultural perspectives about gender (Bolzendahl & Myers, 2004). Two large literature streams, in particular, have deepened understanding of women and femininity—female gender stereotyping according to dress, and thinness and body weight.

Female gender stereotyping according to dress

Girls learn from an early age to focus on their appearance, often lessons they have learned via female gender stereotypes according to dress. Stereotypes are "shared cultural meanings" because they are simple, immediately recognizable, and imply consensus (Perkins, 1979, p. 141). Parents have shown gender stereotyping behaviors within the first twenty-four hours of their child's birth, describing girls as *feminine, delicate,* and *fine-featured* (Karraker, Vogel, & Lake, 1995). Some parents begin shaping their daughter's "understanding of her femininity, her sexuality, her self" long before she is born with their product purchases such as clothes, accessories, and furniture (Orenstein, 2011, p. 7). Over the life course, girls segregated into single-gender groups (such as at all-girls schools) are further encouraged to learn gender-stereotyped behavior (Marmion & Lundberg-Love, 2004). Obsessive thoughts about appearance and how to achieve some feminine ideal with regard to "faces, weight, breast size, clothing brands" (Douglas, 2010, p. 16) tend to follow women throughout their lives.

Social movements of the 1960s and 1970s in the United States seem to have provided mothers with mixed messages about how to dress their daughters. For a while, this played out with a "neutered femininity" inflicted on daughters through dressing them in "shapeless overalls" and encouraging them to embrace "the new postfeminist girlie-girl" (Orenstein, 2011, p. 58). The word *girlie* often is rejected by feminists who see it as disrespectful for reducing a *woman* to a *girl*; a throwback to "feminine trappings" against which they fought (Baumgardner & Richards, 2004, p. 61). As introduced in chapter 1, the term *girlie-girl* endures and sometimes is appropriated by groups of women who adopt it and make it their own. Today's postfeminist and third-wave feminists who embrace *girlie-girl* culture are just as adamant about resisting a too-serious, too-political stereotype as second-wave feminists were about being called *girl* in the office. Just because women oppose being sexually exploited does not mean they oppose being sexual, a position that Baumgardner and Richards (2004) argued wrongly "further concretizes the myth that older feminists hated sex and men" (p. 62). In fact, Goldman's (1992) *commodity feminism* concept is used to explain how feminist goals of independence, individuality, and control of one's life become subsumed by images of sexuality as communicated through dress. This outcome falsely promotes the idea that choosing to be seen as a sexual object equals an embrace of feminist ideology. Describing her own feminist metamorphosis from dresses to pants in the early 1970s, Brownmiller (1984) suggested that women of the 1980s and beyond might be considered "a stick-in-the-mud, a fashion reactionary with no sense of style" who returned to dresses to satisfy their desire for "some whimsical indulgence in the feminine esthetic" (p. 80). Female gender stereotyping according to dress has undergone ebbs and flows across the decades in the United States. Women who participated in focus group and interview discussions for this book unanimously agreed they appreciate the choice to wear what they want to wear.

Thinness, body weight, and ethnicity

Femininity and body weight norms often are differentiated along ethnicity lines. Femininity among Caucasian/White communities long has been associated with a slender build. Among African-American/Black communities, however, definitions of beauty and femininity are not tied to small body size (Franko & Roehrig, 2011). Research findings suggest that parental influence ranks among the most salient sociocultural factors associated with development of disordered eating in young adults (e.g., Rodgers, Faure, & Chabrol, 2009). More specifically, excessive talk about weight within families influences in adolescents harmful weight-related problems like body dissatisfaction and adoption of extreme weight-loss methods (Bauer, Bucchianeri & Neumark-Sztainer, 2013). Body dissatisfaction levels are related in mother-daughter dyads (Lacey & Price, 2004), often with the mother modeling weight-related norms (Pike & Rodin, 1991) through negative comments about weight, body shape and size, and dieting directed toward herself or her daughter (Chng & Fassnacht, 2015). Focus group discussions among college women conducted for this book included this story from Chloe, 22, Caucasian/White:

> Like, this whole insecurity about body thing, it's a *big* issue in my family. It's my mom and my sisters and I. My middle sister was anorexic. My older sister is pretty much a closet bulimic. She doesn't throw up, but she takes the diet pills and she watches how much she eats. And, you know, she's crazy, she is so thin! And, she's naturally thin. I'm the curviest out of my sisters and, I don't know, I feel like the minute that I started puberty, something, my size, my weight . . . I don't think I ever got mad at my sisters, but it's definitely something that, for a long time, consumed what I thought about. I think about it a lot.

Chloe explained how being feminine in her family is predicated upon thinness. Psychologically, the pressure girls feel to conform to ideal body norms via weight loss and unhealthy weight control behaviors has been linked to depressive symptoms across socioeconomic groups and racial-ly-ethnically diverse samples of adolescent girls and their mothers (e.g., Bauer, Bucchianeri & Neumark-Sztainer, 2013).

A drive for thinness and concerns about weight play out uniquely among girls and women of color. Because African-American/Black mothers may be more likely than Caucasian/White mothers to identify their daughters as best friends (Penington & Turner, 2004), they play a significant role in their daughters' body image (Baugh & Barnes, 2015) and communicate acceptance of a larger, curvier body (Overstreet, Quinn, & Agocha, 2010). Hence, African-American/Black women report receiving compliments and self-esteem boosting attention from their mothers (Hesse-Biber, Howling, Leavy, & Lovejoy, 2004), but negative attention if they *lose weight or seem too thin* (Wilson, Musham, & McLellan, 2004). On the downside, increased levels of body dissatisfaction (linked to a Caucasian/White slender ideal) are being reported by African-American/Black women across age groups (Latner & Wilson, 2011). Among women born outside the United States, identification with a slimmer personal body shape ideal can manifest in *acculturative stress* related to body dissatisfaction and unhealthy eating attitudes when they try to fit in and possibly resort to unhealthful weight regulation practices (Gordon, Castro, Sitnikov, Holm-Denoma, 2010). Among college women who shared narratives for this book, Nitya, 22, Indian, concurred with many other women of color about cultural differences in body size/shape:

> In my family, I'm Indian; they don't like girls who are really skinny. They don't find it appealing at all. Girls who have a little more meat on your skin look better. I guess maybe the clothes that we wear, they hug you very well and I guess if you're skinny, it kind of just drapes on you, whereas if you have curves it'll suit you better and it'll look a lot better. That's what they like. They don't like skinny people anymore.

In the same focus group, Lori, 21, African-American/Black, also emphasized cultural differences in shaping ideas about femininity and body size:

> I think for me, where I was born in Ethiopia, a lot of people who are skinny are still curvaceous. A lot of us are small boned but still curvy. People, being overweight, it's not that it was unacceptable, it's just really rare. It just wasn't even a frame of thought to be overweight. But in Kenya it was a little different. That's where I grew up. All my friends were from everywhere else. . . . In America the whole entertainment industry is like skinny; but then the average person as nowhere near that. It was this whole crazy catastrophe thing and everyone from home was like "When you get to America be careful and don't get sucked into that." People have to eat and when you eat you get a little bigger and people are fine with it, but you have to maintain health. Because nobody really gets that big, because the packaged food and processed food here [in U.S.] is very unhealthy. But everything at home is fresh so it's different.

Stories that Nitya and Lori shared are reminiscent of many others shared as I collected narratives for this book—especially among women who emigrated to the United States.

Females who strongly relate to cultural traditions involving food experience intense pressure. Latinas have reported feeling conflicted between their mother's advice to eat traditional meals of rice, beans, and tortillas while heeding the drive toward thinness that could give them a competitive edge in the workplace (Pompper & Koenig, 2004). During a focus group session for the current study, Valeria, a twenty-nine-year-old Latina, lamented a double standard across generations in her family: "Yeah, you know, most Puerto Rican people aren't thin. My mother, like, she's not small, but she thinks I'm supposed to be smaller. But the whole time she's feeding me arroz con gandulez, fried chicken, and this, that, and the third. I'm bigger so she says 'Oh, you need to lose weight.'" This double standard a mother imposes upon her daughter creates negative internal feelings for Valeria with regard to her own sense of femininity; feelings she said she has difficulty sharing with her mother. Debbie, 51, Caucasian/White, also spoke of cultural traditions in her family that encourage eating enjoyment, traditions that she has passed down to her children, too:

> I am Pennsylvania Dutch, and German, and everything we eat is bad—and delicious. You almost feel like you can't be a part of your culture or you can't enjoy certain things because it's really bad for you. My forefathers cooked with lard and it's a no-no. You know, I don't eat Pennsylvania Dutch food if I'm trying to lose weight.

For Debbie, self-denial of foods she enjoys and that celebrate her ethnic heritage creates dissonance. She said she feels conflicted and wrestles with internal dialog at every big family gathering. Similarly, Kierra, 23, African-American/Black college student shared her anxieties that build during the holidays:

> Thanksgiving is heaven and hell all at the same time. I can't cook those things, but when I go home for Thanksgiving, Christmas, New Year's, and then my birthday, it's just like a month straight of too much good food. I mean, I think that makes us a curvier people. But then again, not everyone has the weight land where you want it to land. So, for me, I don't feel like I'm very curvy. I'm very much like an up and down figure. Whereas, my mom is like small waist, big hips. . . . I call my mom a video ho. I call her this to her face, but it's because she has that, like, hourglass figure that I wish that I have, but I just don't and there's nothing I can do to change that, so. That's how my ethnicity works.

Kierra explained that even though she stresses about how body fat and family celebrations with food seem at odds for her, she explained how she's going to enjoy herself while young—and worry more as she gets older, when losing weight is more difficult. In the meantime, Kierra said she still feels feminine. Simply, she defines femininity using internal qualities/virtues such as *loving, proper,* and *warm.*

In families where mothers simply talk about dieting and body dissatisfaction, early-adolescent daughters have a greater likelihood for developing an eating disorder (Hillard, Gondoli, Corning, & Morrissey, 2016). Overall, the mother-daughter relationship remains persistently influential over the life span (Baugh & Barnes, 2015) and mothers' influence on daughters' body images and attitudes toward food is powerful (Davison & Birch, 2001). While parents may believe that commenting about weight (their child's or their own) could motivate them to lose weight, there is no evidence to support this. Investigating an adult woman's perception of the relationship with her mother is essential when studying body esteem. It stands to reason, then, that when girls and women hear their mother amplifying the same messages that they receive from larger social contexts about links between femininity and being slender that they could pursue extreme behaviors to achieve thin body ideals.

MEDIA IMAGES BENCHMARK
IDEAL, EMPHASIZED FEMININITY

Ways media construct and perpetuate certain feminine ideals through widely disseminated images which become integrated into our own definition of *what is femininity* is well-traveled terrain among gender and media researchers. Undeniably, media are significant purveyors of dominant, hegemonic, subordinate, and oppositional femininities (Litosseliti, 2006). Collectively, media serve as a powerful sociocultural agent in shaping women's self-perceptions (Linville, Stice, Gau, & O'Neil, 2014) since their images offer benchmarks for idealized notions of femininity, standards to which women are held accountable by themselves and others. This means media texts are more than innocuous entertainment vehicles and they must be critically examined. Many media representations of girls, women, and femininity are steeped in negative stereotypes which have been replicated in broadcast and print media for decades. Perhaps the *Gibson Girl,* a drawing made by illustrator Charles Dana Gibson in the late nineteenth and early twentieth centuries, was the first mass mediated visual stereotype of the American woman (Kitch, 2001), a personification of the feminine ideal of physical beauty featuring a corseted woman with an impossibly small waist. Joining female beauty ideals later on were mediated portrayals of the mother/homemaker role ideal (Pingree, Hawkins, Butler, & Paisley, 1976). African-American/Black women emphasize salience of media in representing Caucasian/White sexuality and femininity ideals (Baugh & Barnes, 2015). In fact, some African-American/ Black women's perceptions of ideal femininity are shaped by Caucasian/ White cultural definitions of beauty and femininity (Baugh, Mullis, Mullis, Hicks, & Peterson, 2010). This disconnect between *how I am* and *how I'm told I should be* play out in inner conflicts suffered by girls and women. Beverly, 59, an African-American/Black woman who identifies as lesbian told members of her focus group that she recalled growing up with confusing messages about femininity:

> [A]ll the pictures I saw were White women, so it didn't apply to me. Movies, magazine ads . . . they didn't look like me. And all the women that looked like me had breasts, had hips, and junk in the trunk. So, it was a disconnect for me because even though they kept saying "this is what you're supposed to look like," it didn't make any sense to me. It wasn't in my world.

Beverly and her partner, a Caucasian/White woman, both selected images of African-American/Black women from among the 100 years' worth of magazine images displayed to inspire focus group discussion about *most feminine* and *least feminine*. Both expressed joy at seeing diverse ethnic identities and body shapes among the images—even though there were fewer representing women of color and women of larger size.

In the United States and many other developed nations around the globe, media socially stigmatize fatness as a discrediting attribute and antithesis of the ideal feminine woman. Fat represents a character flaw, according to Goffman (1963); a "tribal stigma" for the United States as communicated in supposedly amusing advertisements and political cartoons (Farrell, 2011, p. 7). For women, the act of growing fat signifies an inferior body of one who has fallen from grace. These women, especially those in the public eye, are consistently ridiculed—not unlike actress Kirstie Alley's character in her *Fat Actress* television show which aired in the United States in 2005. Fat women are not represented as feminine women, but as second-class, inferior deviants to be ridiculed. Overweight women are perceived as not conforming to a feminine ideal and as violating the female sexual role (Hartley, 2001). To understand interlocking dimensions of femininity, fatness, Whiteness, middle-classness, and sexual desire, Gullage (2014) examined the narrative of the popular television program, *Friends*, wherein actress Courteney Cox put on a fat suit—also known as *Fat Monica*—to explore how popular culture normatively encourages girls and women to strive for an idealized svelte feminine physical form. Through flashbacks, the program showed audiences negative consequences of the character's life when she was fat and how it all could have turned out unhappily—as in no sex appeal and inability to find happiness with a husband had she not lost a significant amount of weight. Hence, heterosexual male desire offers both inspiration and reward for achieving a normative body for emphasized femininity.

Perhaps the most widely disseminated images of femininity for girls are blockbuster Walt Disney films' representations of princesses and damsels in distress. Even Disney films produced from the 1980s through

1990s offered physically attractive, sexually conservative, underconfident female characters of Ariel, Belle, Pocahontas, and Mulan with traditional notions of femininity, heteronormative narratives, and dominant stereotypical female gender roles which add up to the same moral that women's independent spirits are subservient to the completeness to be gained from long-term heterosexual romance (Charlebois, 2011). Indeed, emphasized femininity in the form of a narrow range of stereotypic and sexualized female roles is prevalent in the film industry.

Powerful hegemonic ideas about ruling class interests filter through unrealistic mediated representations to benchmark ideal femininity—often in ways that prove harmful to girls and young women. This cultural studies approach steeped in the writings of Gramsci (1971) provides a critical lens for examining ways dominant perspectives of femininity are shaped by fashion magazines, feature films, television programs, and the internet (Currie, 1999; Durham, 2001). Mediated texts also inform girls' reading of how they are *supposed to be feminine* like the female characters they see in the entertainment forms they consume. Perhaps more concerning, femininity constitutes bodily property in the form of playful sexuality, a shift from mere representational practice to one that is social and psychological (Gill, 2007a). Therefore, a postfeminist reading of the dynamic suggests a shift from objectification to subjectification wherein girls and women have an obsessive preoccupation with disciplining their body to make it conform to an ideal femininity. What a girl's or woman's body *should look like* is defined by "linguistic and imagistic repetition of ideals" (Cirksena & Cuklanz, 1992, p. 35). Examples include the body shaming television program genre in the United States dominated by shows like *What Not to Wear* and *10 Years Younger* which offer a conception of the female body against which real people measure themselves and others—especially by ridiculing non-celebrities and transitioning the woman being made over to embody aspirational lower-middle-class values associated with a more autonomously feminine ideal (McRobbie, 2004a). These comparisons are frequent fodder for before-and-after personal grooming makeover reality television shows because they enable people to feel better about themselves—as in, *Thank goodness I don't look that bad!* Television makeover shows have done more to "renew the hegemony of beauty culture as the apex of femininity" than perhaps any other media form (Tincknell, 2011, p. 83). Yet, continuing to look acceptable after the make-over requires maintenance. The new made-over woman must have the resources and willingness to actively engage in spending time and money on fashion and beauty products. Because sustained purchases for these products are impossible for the poor who struggle to pay for necessities like food and shelter, inner conflicts develop which may lead to depression. See chapter 3 for in-depth discussion of such outcomes.

Side effects of social learning processes include reaffirming one's views on femininity—or revealing how one fails to measure up to the ideal. For example, when a girl perceives that she cannot hit the mark, she may experience social disincentives when exhibiting behaviors that deviate from traditional social norms (Bussey & Bandura, 1992), and opt out of a social situation altogether to avoid potential humiliation (Sinkman, 2013). Processes of social learning from media images and popular culture also involve contact with reinforcing communications (Lazarsfeld, Bureleson, & Gaudet, 1944), or selective media exposure for maintaining a specific self-concept—including endorsement of one's views on femininity. Mediated representations of femininity highlight appearance as the most salient aspect of "performing femininity properly" (Thiel-Stern, 2014). Merskin (2005) found that while girls may incorporate hegemonic discourses about femininity into their online media products, such as selfies, they also engage in *culture jamming* by using blogging and other forms of technology production to challenge and resist dominant narratives about girlhood, body image, and ideal femininity.

Mass media also persist in representing women in the home as mother and homemaker, a context for reproducing gendered inequalities in the service of consumerism. Women's magazines offer an "authoritative grand narrative of reality" (McCracken, 1993, p. 2) and instruct women on how to embody femininity. Tracing history of the women's magazine, *Ladies Home Journal*, Odland (2009) found its pages required domesticity of all mothers. Karan (2008) argued that women's magazines directly engage with readers' lives and in doing so, shape women's feminine identity. However, most younger women I spoke with for the study reported in this book veered far away from integrating any aspects of house and home with their definition of femininity. Across age cohorts, however, women were receptive to characterizing three images relating to mother and wife roles among their choices of stimulus material images as *most feminine*. These included an image of a very pregnant woman wearing a black unitard which appeared in a 1990s issue of *Redbook*, a 1940s black and white image of a bride published in *McCall's*, and a 1980s *Good Housekeeping* photo of a Caucasian/White woman holding her baby in a rocking chair. Carla, 50, Caucasian/White, selected the latter photo as *most feminine*, equating motherhood with femininity:

> I'm looking at this woman and she's in a dress, she's got stockings, she's got jewelry on, hair is done. She's holding a beautiful baby. She's got this baby as an accessory almost. Taking everything that I thought of as feminine—and then adding the baby to it. That put her over the top.

Carla, a mother of three, explained that she identified with the image and considered it among those she selected as *most feminine* because the woman in the photo cared for a baby and also cared for herself through good grooming with styled hair, makeup, and manicure.

Yet, media audiences do more than serve as passive vessels when it comes to promoting images of ideal femininity. A vast body of literature has emerged to explain how media cultivate gender role learning and impact cognition; an association between exposure to media and effects on audience attitudes and behaviors (whether they realize it or not) (e.g., Perloff, 2002). Heavy television consumption, in particular, has been linked with viewers being socialized to gender and ethnic stereotyping and then acting on them when encountering challenging social situations in their life (e.g., Smith & Donnerstein, 1998). Stereotypical female images shaped by emphasized femininity extend beyond television programs to include video games, toy commercials, music videos, and more. Indeed, women still are confined to prime-time television roles based on idealized beauty standards (Scharrer, 2012) and ideal femininity even though Emmy-winning actress Julianna Margulies said television has entered a "new age" where "powerful female characters" are celebrated (Scott, 2014). Young women also learn about femininity away from the television screen, in college.

FEMININITY AND THE COLLEGE EXPERIENCE

Journalists, sociologists, psychologists, and social critics long have been fascinated with femininity and "college girls," a moniker which digital media scholar Turkle (2011) attributed to extended adolescence embraced as part of middle-class life on the internet. Undeniably, psychology researchers have been drawn to college life and its impact on women, in terms of body (dis)satisfaction and eating disorder risk. The proliferation of images of the ideal feminine woman may lead girls and women to be overly critical of themselves. If any good news has emerged among studies of these dynamics, some findings suggest that African-American/ Black girls have a wider interpretation of attractiveness than European-American girls (Parker, Nichter, Nichter, Vuckovic, Sims, & Ritenbaugh, 1995), and African-American/Black women rate their appearance more positively than their European-American and Latin-American counterparts (Aruguete, Nickleberry, & Yates, 2004).

Numerous study findings suggest that a drive for thinness accelerates during the transition to college (e.g., Linville, Stice, Gau, & O'Neil, 2014). Sorority membership on college campuses seems to amplify the thin-ideal (Rolnik, Engeln-Maddox, & Miller, 2010) and also offers the opportunity to examine ways femininities play out since Greek organizations generally focus on construction and maintenance of social status. Findings of one longitudinal study of college women's perceptions of their appearance were significantly lower than male counterparts across the college experience (Gillen & Lefkowitz, 2012). Farrell (2011) explored the 2006 Delta Zeta controversy at Indiana's DePauw University and critiqued the members' preference for women who were "white, thin, and 'American,'" so twenty-two women were "kicked out" for being "inadequately committed to the sorority" (p. 2), a euphemism for *fat*. More specifically, Farrell (2011) interrogated ways gender, fat, ethnicity, and class privilege intersected with popularity and femininity to determine who belongs and who does not on the road to college sorority membership and maintenance of its ideals. In sum, experiences and understandings attached to ideal femininity are highly complex in the United States—among college women and beyond.

DISCUSSION

Ideal femininity persists as an outcome of Caucasian/White, patriarchal, capitalist norms and this chapter is devoted to expanding understanding of how femininity is defined and how it plays out in family dynamics and is represented by media—and to what effect. Overall, undergirding themes of family and media representations are related theoretical concepts used to critique hegemony and consumerism. For, it is through saturation of images of a certain kind of femininity that some universally accepted ideal of what constitutes femininity has emerged and becomes entrenched in family teachings. Empirical research collected and analyzed for this book underscored the power of those ideals in shaping understandings, experiences, and resistances to them over the life course, no matter how young or how old a woman may be. For over a century, U.S. mass media have disseminated visual images representing femininity. In particular, fashion and beauty advertising encourages girls and women to equate dress and cosmetics with emphasizing their femininity. Women are socialized to use mediated images as guides for acceptable body masquerade which they internalize and use to compare themselves to other women. Even though girls and women in the United States today are considered as possessing greater freedoms than ever before, they remain tied to traditional ideas of femininity which may diminish their sense of empowerment. According to McRobbie (2004b), "The new female subject is, despite her freedom, called upon to be silent, to withhold critique, to count as a modern sophisticated girl, or indeed this withholding of critique is a condition of her freedom" (p. 260).

Other environmental factors shaping a woman's definition of femininity are infused family behaviors which also may reflect social norms shaped by popular culture media, as well as ethnic culture traditions, and college sorority communities. Two related concepts permeating familial relationships among daughters, mothers, aunts, and grandmothers which lend shape to femininity are body image, female gender stereotypes, and a drive for thinness. Certainly, mothers intergenerationally transmit ideas about femininity and pass on anxieties about body image and weight which negatively impact their daughter's self-image and her sense of femininity, too. Moreover, these anxieties can inspire unhealthful behaviors resulting from self-disciplining practices—and can turn women against one another, narrowing the "possibilities for women's embodied agency" (Trethewey, 2000, p. 115). No doubt, omnipresent feature films and their licensed products, women's magazines, social media, and other media varieties influence collective definitions of ideal femininity. In particular, fatness negatively correlates with femininity so that thinness and femininity are inextricably intertwined concepts which emerged in nearly every focus group discussion and interview conducted with women for this book project.

Sorting through women's inter-generational definitions of femininity and interrogating them in the context of femininity ideals promoted by media, it is clear that young women focused more on "sexiness" and "girlie-girlness" than their mothers, aunts and grandmothers. Appropriation of the *girlie-girl* concept as a distinct and empowering feminist identity was a theme connecting most focus group discussions conducted with college women, a word used only by their age cohort when defining femininity. To Baumgardner and Richards (2004), such a distinction clearly segregates third-wave from second-wave feminists, but to McRobbie (2009) any such dichotomy is distinctly anti-feminist, fails to account for self-reflexivity, and perpetuates flaws of second-wave feminists who glossed over experiences of non-Caucasian/White women whose own lived experiences play a significant role in how they define femininity and how others define it for them.

THREE

Female Gender Role Stress/Conflict

Learning about/from Femininity

My mother died of emotional and physical problems, and my grand-mother before me. My mother married during the war years . . . long auburn hair, nicely coifed . . . women paid attention to makeup and liked to dress up. Society's in extremes right now. We all run around in sweat clothes and then wear million-dollar gowns on the runways. I think women had nice Saturday night clothes when they went out. You didn't get on a train to go into the city if you didn't look proper. It wasn't a jeans culture. Maybe they felt proud of themselves because they often felt they made the effort to look nice and it paid off in their own minds. It paid off in the men that surrounded them and their female friends, maybe. . . . [W]e tend to be a very fractured society right now of extremes.

—Research participant Sally, 61, Caucasian/White, heterosexual

The restrictive nature of female gender-role socialization and ideals associated with the femininity concept means women throughout history have experienced social pressure to maintain a certain standard of appearance and to behave as nurturer and caretaker of others. Yet, as Sally described in the quote above, today's social norms have left older women feeling nostalgic for emphasized femininity of yesteryear. Gender is a social construct produced and performed in regulation with traditional norms—not some biological outcome dichotomizing humans according to female and male (Butler, 1990). Even though gender roles vary according to culture, Eagly and Wood (1999) posited that just about all societies are to some degree patriarchal and this forces girls and women to navigate a challenging set of expectations for performing the feminine role. Gender-based power structures end up benefitting men (Levant, 1996), so

53

that girls and women learn to perform their gender and to present femininity based on dominant cultural understandings of what it means to be subordinate to males. Women's successful femininity performance is the securing of a non-platonic heterosexual relationship (Charlebois, 2011)—even though social norms in the United States are changing slowly to accommodate women who eschew marriage and/or bearing children (Traister, 2016a), as well as those who choose a non-heterosexual lifestyle.

Thirty years after a pro-feminist influence in the United States, traditional emphasized femininity norms set up women for a life of uncertainty, conflict, and stress both at home and at work. McRobbie (2009) described this outcome as "an illusion of positivity and progress" that yields anxieties for women (p. 10). The gender-role stress/conflict paradigm explains ways restrictive gender roles limit women's human potential and cause psychological distress. Femininity fosters insecurity and instability among women and widely is endorsed by women themselves, as well as their partners, parents, siblings, friends, and media. *Emphasized femininity*, females' accentuated sexuality and submissiveness/dependence, corresponds with *hegemonic masculinity* norms (Connell, 1995). *Sexism* is "the social, political, economic, and personal expression of patriarchy in women's and men's lives" (O'Neil, 2008, p. 366). For girls and young women, emphasized femininity norms paradoxically urge them to be sexy and playful, yet not to go so far as to be characterized as *slutty* and risk becoming sexual harassed or raped. Categorically, older women are considered *un*feminine and invisible. Collectively, women internalize fear of consequences should they fail to meet others' expectations and struggle against paradoxes about femininity associated with their gender role. So, acceptance of traditional femininity ideology, combined with stress attached to failure to live up to the feminine role, results in anxiety symptoms and disorders among women (Richmond, Levant, Smalley, & Cook, 2015). According to Butler (1990), we "regularly punish those who fail to do their gender right" (p. 178). Indeed, internalizing all of these anxieties makes a woman's body a site of struggle; one she works on to achieve feminine ideals through sometimes harmful body control behaviors. For, women who do not adhere to prevailing myths about femininity run the risk of social ostracization, spinsterhood, or death.

Processes of discovering how women personally define *femininity* for the study shared in this book exposed just how complex and circuitous the road to pursuing ideal femininity standards can be over the life course for diverse groups of women. Women shared their stories about gender socialization practices—especially addressing others' expectations for their femininity—as well as external prompts and benchmarks promoted through mediated images, toys, relationship with the color pink, and other factors shown to contribute to body-related anxiety and stress. Findings generally concur with Connell's (1987) explanation of collusion between *hegemonic masculinity* and *emphasized femininity* wherein women in focus groups and interviews couched their definition of femininity within contexts of being "the opposite of masculine," finding a husband or partner, spicing up the bedroom, and motherhood.

This chapter explores these important areas of the gender role stress/conflict paradigm as it relates to femininity: 1) Femininity ideology and the gender role stress/conflict paradigm; 2) Girls and young women struggle with female gender role demands; 3) Stress attached to "Am I feminine enough?"; 4) Social identity intersectionalities may complicate gender role stress/conflict; 5) Female v. female competition and femininity; 6) Stress/conflict and the private/public spheres dichotomy; and 7) Discussion.

FEMININITY AND GENDER ROLE STRESS/CONFLICT

One's internalization of social beliefs about gender roles within the United States has been linked with anxiety, conflict, and stress—and is theorized by the Gender Role Stress/Conflict (GRS/C) paradigm which explores femininity as a core construct among lived experiences of girls and women. The GRS/C paradigm first emerged amidst psychology research to explain the *masculinity* concept and later has been modified to explain *femininity*. Findings suggest that endorsement of traditional gender roles for women and emphasized femininity behaviors have been associated with poor mental health outcomes for girls and women (Carter, Silverman, & Jaccard, 2011). Numerous research findings have suggested that socializing children into traditional gender role norms has negative psychological consequences which may manifest in gender role strain (e.g., Pleck, 1995). Peers, teachers, and parents reinforce in girls what they consider feminine and discourage behaviors and attitudes that they consider to be masculine (Wood & Fixmer-Oraiz, 2015). GRS/C theory predicts that traditional gender roles uphold gender-based power structures, which ultimately benefit men (Levant, 1996). For women, body objectification and inauthenticity of self in relationships have been associated with depression and lowered self-esteem (Tolman, Impett, Tracy, & Michael, 2006).

Female GRS/C theory explains that in trying to live up to social demands that they be feminine, thin, young, perky, and capable of *doing it all* creates anxiety, conflict, and stress for girls and women. For those who do not meet these ideal standards, media messages that they *should* can be stigmatizing, marginalizing, and demoralizing, symptoms rife for harmful psychological and behavioral outcomes (Crandall, Nierman, & Hebl, 2009). Because social pressures are so great, even women who may not consciously endorse traditional feminine ideals feel negative critique from others if they do not live up to feminine ideals, also known as *discrepancy strain* (Levant, 2011). FGRS/C manifests in cognitive, unconscious, or behavior problems caused by "socialized gender roles learned in sexist and patriarchal societies" (O'Neil, Good, & Holmes, 1995, p. 362).

Early on, psychologists encouraged respondents to use their own personal definitions of femininity and masculinity (Kelly, 1955), but numerous scales have been developed and tested to measure stress and conflict women experience in trying to achieve emphasized femininity's norms. Using the Femininity Ideology Scale (FIS), Richmond and her colleagues (2015) found an indirect relationship between endorsement of traditional femininity ideology and anxiety. An earlier study also discovered links between female GRS/C and elevated anxiety levels among women (Eisler & Skidmore, 1988). Similarly, the Female Gender Role Stress Scale (FGRSS) has been used to assess women's self-reports of depressive symptoms, low self-esteem, eating disorder behaviors, and shame-proneness (Efthim, Kenny, & Mahalik, 2001). Richmond and her colleagues (2015) supported therapy for women by framing their stress as contextual, or environmental, rather than some internal biological flaw.

Gender role conflict and the related concept of gender role strain also are useful in explaining males' fear of femininity. While theorizing about gender role stress and conflict experienced by girls and women represents a fairly recent inquiry, a "crisis of masculinity" (Bederman, 1995, p. 11) has been well documented among sociologists and critical scholars for years. The trend-setting research of James M. O'Neil and his colleagues begun in the mid-1990s has documented experiences of stress and conflict associated with men's sense of masculinity in the United States and United Kingdom. These effects are closely linked with gender role stressors and conflicts experienced by women, too. Collectively, men feel emasculated, unsure of themselves, and at odds with effects of the 1960s sexual revolution, a proposed Equal Rights Amendment to the U.S. Constitution, and changing gender norms. Hence, masculinities scholars have done much to document men's inner stresses and conflicts about what society expects of them and how to overcome a lifetime of being told to hide their emotions and to dominate in non-egalitarian households (e.g., Pompper, 2010). For boys and men, being negatively stereotyped for exhibiting feminine values, attitudes, and behaviors represents a threat to their masculinity (O'Neil, 2008). Early in life, being called "a girl" is insulting to boys, an outcome that contributes to a subconscious fear of femininity, as well as homophobia (O'Neil, 2008). Since the 1980s when women entered the paid work force in large numbers, men have experienced changes in the concept of *traditional masculinity* with the loss of a *man as breadwinner* identity, effects that have left men conflicted about their role in society. Findings of a multi-generational study across ethnic groups in the United States suggested that men experience anxiety, confusion, and frustration about the concept of *metrosexualism*—when image-conscious males invest considerable resources on appearance and

Figure 3.1. Worldwide, women experience stressors associated with navigating a female gender role of unpaid work in the private, or domestic sphere, with paid work outside the home in the public sphere. Source: Hongqi Zhang/ Depositphotos.com.

lifestyle—as a benchmark against which they feel pressured to emulate mass media–promoted male body images (Pompper, Soto, & Piel, 2007; Pompper, 2010). Implications of male GRS/C which involve fear of femininity not only include negative consequences for men's own mental well-being, but imply devaluation of women for their own femininity (e.g., Blazina & Watkins, 2000). These dynamics contribute to depression, anxiety, and marital dissatisfaction among women (e.g., Rochlen & Mahalik, 2004).

GIRLS AND YOUNG WOMEN STRUGGLE WITH FEMALE GENDER ROLE DEMANDS

Girls and young women are socialized to grow into a Procrustean vision of femininity which shapes their female gender role for life. Processes are not easy, expectations are high, and the rules are relatively inflexible. Because surveillance and self-discipline permeate every waking moment, gender role stress/conflict threatens girls' and young women's mental health and emotional well-being. Moreover, girls and adolescents routinely receive conflicting messages across media platforms and interpersonally — to be sexually attractive, but at the same time to act responsibly. Warnings and advice to be feminine while also aspiring to achieve their maximum potential can be confusing and difficult to sort through. Yet, an ability to measure up to emphasized femininity norms and body image bestows privilege, as Nicole, 18, Black-Japanese, explained:

> I spent my childhood in Japan and I go back every summer. The general population there is healthy and there are not as many people who are overweight or underweight. . . . I think that it depends on social hierarchy where beauty is considered the highest status. People say life is easier when you're pretty and I think that's so true nowadays — and that's so unfortunate.

Women who served as research participants for the study reported in this book were quick to point out their study abroad experiences, as well as opportunities to travel beyond U.S. shores, for points of comparison/contrast. Some women like Nicole lamented the emphasis placed on physical beauty as benchmarks for femininity in the United States. Instead, they equated femininity with internal qualities generally associated with female gender roles, including kindness, compassion, and sweetness.

Girls' studies scholars have noted deleterious effects of mass media images on ways girls and young women see themselves in terms of academic performance, body image, and self-esteem — with pressures experienced when girls and young women promote their own body as defining their identity. Harris (2004a) urged for care when operationalizing *girl*, since this category of young people is unknowable when they are universalized as one-dimensional. During a focus group discussion for this book, Caitlin, 22, Bhutanese-Jewish-American, advocated for broader interpretations of femininity, to *un*define it, and to tear down stereotypes:

> I think the word *feminine* has so many things that you immediately think — so many images that you see that've been labeled and defined over and over in lots of really wrong ways. You can't, it's so unfair, in general, to define a word that is supposed to pertain to billions of people. I think that's just silly. [W]hat we need to do is cling to our similarities and shine the light on those. If we're looking for equality, I think differences are the wrong way to go.

Caitlin referred to confining norms in her family and culture as she further explained that she feels offended by overgeneralizations of women of specific ethnic groups who are expected to dress and behave in certain ways. Indeed, effects of parental control over girls is a well-traveled research area among girls' studies scholarship.

Qualifying femininity of young girls by fetishizing their bodies contributes to heightened parental anxiety about girls' safety that requires regulation and control delivered in much higher degrees as compared to boys. For example, Best's (2006) fieldwork study of teen girls, driving, and parental protectionism revealed that girls have earlier curfew times than boys and are not permitted to use the family car as often as boys are, outcomes which limit girls' agency and individuality. Findings of studies about schoolgirls urge for revising narrowly defined constructions of girlhood which still rely on defining femininity as something synonymous with a need for protection. Psychology researchers have blamed increasingly restrictive gender role socialization processes that are "rigid, sexist . . . result in personal restriction, devaluation, or violation of others or self" for negative impacts on individuals' health and well-being (O'Neil, 1990, p. 25). Pipher (1995) simply referred to these negative dynamics as "a girl poisoning culture" (p. 12) wherein some girls succumb to eating disorders, depression, self-injury, attempted suicide, and sometimes death (e.g., Davies-Popelka, 2000). Research findings suggest that suicidal girls report gender role conflict at greater rates than do boys (Pinhas, Weaver, Bryden, Ghabbour, & Toner, 2002). In a study of femininity ideology and early adolescent girls' mental health, Tolman and her colleagues (2006) found that adolescent girls who internalize beliefs and behaviors about what it means to be appropriately feminine have lower self-esteem and higher depressed mood.

Protectionism based on limited ideas about femininity positions girls and women as weak and inferior. Girls are taught to control their body in terms of how to sit, stand, walk, talk, tilt their head, and comport themselves (Trethewey, 2000). Girls' physical maturation inflames parental fears and inspires restriction of girls' behavior (Pinhas, Weaver, Bryden, Ghabbour, & Toner, 2002). An ideal feminine appearance widely is esteemed as a central condition for achieving romantic success (Aubrey & Frisby, 2011), so maintaining a focus on controlling one's body is the only power many girls experience until they achieve adulthood. Young (1990) wrote of the "self-consciousness of the feminine" (p. 155) to the degree that in enacting femininity, girls actively constrain their body when thinking of themselves as fragile and immobile. More recent research findings about girls' lived experiences suggest a counter-ideal—girl as fighter—who is assertive, tough, intelligent, and physically strong (Brown, 2003). In a critique of mass media representations of teen girls and popularity of Facebook, Thiel-Stern (2014) found that journalists also perpetuate fears that girls need protection from juvenile delinquency and possibly a life of prostitution, lesbianism, inability to marry, being sold into slavery, or murder.

For girls, balancing a need to be sexually attractive against an imperative to be sexually responsible offers a setup for more regulation, control, and conflict. Girls' bodies are simultaneously fetishized as innocent and erotic (Walkerdine, 1997). Through pop music, hypersexualized images offer a cross between postfeminist empowerment discourse and a sexualized child discourse, a phenomenon which may prove confusing for girls (Jackson & Goddard, 2015). College women interviewed for the research reported in this book spoke out about degrading, sexually explicit lyrics in hip-hop songs. Mimi, 19, Asian-American, explained:

> I swear I think about that now every song I hear. Most of them talk about women and about their bodies. Now it's mainly about women, like, they're degrading them. . . . I'm subconsciously thinking *that*? I do think that music is huge, though, because if you really think about it, you know, it's just on. And then, you start singing along, and you're like, "What am I saying?" You know?

While some women in her focus group discussion brushed away Mimi's concern as just over-reaction, others agreed that popular music is obtrusive and seems innocuous, but worried that it could have subconscious effects that make young women want to measure up to sexualized images of women.

Adolescent girls receive conflicting messages to both cover up their bodies for modesty's sake, while also revealing their bodies with a thigh-high slit, bare back, and derriere-hugging prom dresses. Davis (1992) called this the "erotic-chaste dialectic" (p. 88) and explained its roots in a Judeo-Christian ethic praising modesty. Display and modesty are opposing concepts, an inherent conflict used by the fashion industry. According to Laver (1969), "fashion is the exploitation of immodesty," while modesty serves as a check on "the impulse to self-aggrandizement" (p. 97, p. 8). Anecdotal evidence of a particular brand of female gender role stress was reported among high school girls who attended a heterosexualized and emphasized-femininity event in the U.S. South—the high school prom. Girls experience an erotic-chaste dialectic enveloped in the New Southern Belle Code (NSBC) which draws upon old feminine traditions—making it difficult for them to walk a fine line between emphasizing femininity and looking *slutty* (Pompper & Crandall, 2014). The role of prom and other rituals in shaping femininity is explored further in chapter 4.

Becoming feminine is so entwined with the production of girlhood that girls receive a never-ending plethora of popular culture messages to consume reassuringly feminine products and services. Girls wade through a bombardment of contradictory messages for self-validation; what Rossie (2015) called "the new requirements for feminine visibility" (p. 232). Popular culture and mass media products persuade young women to adopt body maintenance imperatives as a "regime of self-perfectibility" and self-policing in response to internal panic and deep anxiety about "remain[ing] sexually desirable" (McRobbie, 2009, p. 67). Unrealistic body image ideals are synonymous with feminine identity and adolescent girls internalize to them, including maintenance of a sun tan and cosmetic surgery procedures (Crockett, Pruzinsky, & Persing,

2007). While teasing, flirting, and a promise of sexual accessibility often are considered acceptable behaviors for adolescent girls, they must maintain a reputation as a *good girl*, a dynamic which produces a significant source of anxiety and conflict for girls whose self-esteem demands being praised, liked, rewarded, and seen as attractive and/or romantically desirable (Levine & Harrison, 2009).

Sexting offers girls new performative pressures around displaying their bodies and feminine identities via social media. Findings of a study of teens' (ages thirteen to fifteen) sexting practices suggested that images of girls' bodies that they post are then used against them, to shame them online (Ringrose & Harvey, 2015). A study of comments posted below "Am I pretty or ugly?" YouTube videos exposed a feedback loop connecting content producers with consumers, revealing body pressures girls face and effects of limited definitions of femininity (Rossie, 2015). Negotiating with gender stereotypes on social networking sites reveals discriminatory gender standards with girls being called *slut* for having too many friends, having an open profile, or posting too much information, effects which threaten girls' ability to fully participate online and complicates potential willingness to "participate in defiant gender performances" (Bailey, Steeves, Burkell, & Regan, 2013, p. 91). Collectively, these social media study findings suggest social anxieties when teen girls deviate from dominant understandings of traditional emphasized femininity norms. Among social media content produced and consumed by girls and young women is no shortage of imagery involving breasts—and the proliferation of these images and emphases on their being perfect provides a source of consistent conflict and stress for women from early age through old age. As discussed in chapter 2, images of breasts provide benchmarks for comparison throughout women's lives. Feminine body parts (breasts and buttocks) become social media property of others to examine and regulate in complex ways (Springgay & Freedman, 2010). Teen girls asked to share images of their breasts through sexting with teen boys feel complimented, but they risk being categorically labeled a *slut* or as lacking in self-respect—effects of competitive, heterosexualized girl aggression (Ringrose, 2013).

STRESS ATTACHED TO *"AM I FEMININE ENOUGH?"*

A disconnect between *how I am* and *how I'm supposed to be* offers painful consequences for many women as they may resort to unhealthful behaviors in order to achieve some feminine ideal. Overall, women experience greater gender role conflict and suffer more anxiety disorders than men (Zalta & Chambless, 2012), with about twice as many women experiencing depression (Mayo Clinic Staff, 2016)—from childhood through puberty and menopause (Carter, Silverman, & Jaccard, 2011). Femininity is strongly bound to lesser gender power for women in the United States as they work to emphasize their femininity to appeal to men.

The femininity concept and the disconnect between reality and some ideal are enduring reminders that work of the feminist movement of the 1960s and 1970s in the United States is incomplete. Friedan's (1963) groundbreaking book, *The Feminine Mystique*, warned that trying to convince girls that their "highest value and the only commitment for women is the fulfillment of their own femininity" wholly undervalues women and subjects them to lives of conflict and stress in falsely believing they "can find fulfillment only in sexual passivity, male domination and nurturing maternal love" (p. 37). Conversely, women are cautioned to repudiate feminism or risk being perceived as "embodying bodily failure, hideousness or monstrosity" (McRobbie, 2009, pp. 61–62) should they fail to marry a man and bear children. Backlash against feminism today only increases pressures women feel to conform to normative emphasized femininity (Faludi, 1991). Wolf (1991) critiqued this as an unattainable ideal growing narrower and more limited over time. Some women resort to self-medication through overeating and drug and alcohol abuse (e.g., Greenglass, 1993).

While second-wave feminism has created many opportunities for women to expand definitions of femininity, such as gaining satisfaction from the paid-work force, social norms still dictate that women assume responsibility for creating comfort in the domestic sphere. Tasks associated with childrearing (Eagly & Mladinic, 1989) and other unpaid private domestic sphere work leaves women with fifteen hours less leisure time than their husbands each week (Hochschild & Machung, 2001). Hofstede (1998) used the masculinity/femininity dichotomy in an effort to reveal generalizations about the nature of cultures globally, discovering that women in most parts of the world place greater importance on quality of life and relationships with people than men do. In three decades since the women's social movement in the United States, young women have indicated that prototypical femininity's central features are low self-esteem, emotional distress, and (being) restricted/oppressed (Robertson, Johnson, Benton, Janey, & Cabral, 2002). Feminine ideologies enveloped within ongoing debates about working a second shift (Hochschild, 1997) and public-private sphere negotiations for women (Pompper & Jung, 2016) are reinforced by organizations' resistance to updating family leave policies and policymakers' arcane assumptions that domestic issues *should* rest predominantly on women's shoulders. For many women, a conventional path of "feminine adjustment" is offered up as natural and seduces women away from paths of independence "by marrying at eighteen, losing themselves in having babies and the details of housekeeping . . . simply refusing to grow up, to face the question of their own identity" (Friedan, 1963, p. 68). Single or married, when women encounter gender-related expectations that are inconsistent with their self-concept, they experience gender role stress/conflict when trying to conform.

Violence against women and blaming the victim discourses are dangerous, hurtful, redouble stress, and fail to expose or interrogate root causes of the violence. Contradictorily, women who dare to be sexy in their dress or behavior also live with fear that they are attracting unwanted attention and inviting invasion of their bodies through rape and possibly death. Socio-juridico discourses' default that women who dress scantily are inviting rape. Young women of lower SES who are non-Caucasian/White endure a particularly steep threshold for public approval/censure with regard to how they behave and display their bodies. Women's bodies are self-surveilled, disciplined, and controlled as part of contemporary femininity regimes which include routine diet, exercise, and makeup. Thiel-Stern (2014) called this a "never-ending feedback loop" (p. 3). The backdrop, of course, is a girl/woman's sense that her body, as is, is deficient or abnormal, a pervasive outcome of idealized femininity imposed upon both women and men in the service of gender power ideologies. Bartky (2010) characterized "the disciplinary project of femininity [as] . . . a setup" that just about every women is destined to fail in accomplishing and is socialized to feel shame for that failure (p. 86). Tolman and Porche (2000) concurred that femininity ideology is "an oppressive and hegemonic ideology" (p. 366). Coontz (1993) argued that the more femininity ideals are mythologized and held up to women as standards, the easier it is for men to either ignore or consciously abuse women who fail to measure up to those ideals.

For most girls and women—regardless of age—being considered *un*feminine is a harsh sentence. Indeed, failure in femininity carries "the charge of *mannish* or *neutered*" (Brownmiller, 1984, p. 235, italics added), negative consequences for women if they look or dress in ways that are considered masculine. Even though being thought of as a *butch lesbian* is not the stigma it once was due to changing social mores, girls and women who hope to be taken seriously in most workplaces know they cannot look or act too masculine. At the other end of the spectrum, girls and women who engage with hyperfeminine dress and behavior also worry about not being taken seriously. Women are pressured to *always* manage their femininity by wearing a constant smile. See chapter 8 for an extended discussion about women and smiling. Also, female athletes struggle with social norms for femininity, dynamics addressed in further detail in chapter 6.

Women who define femininity in ways inconsistent with Caucasian/White, heterosexual, middle-class norms soon discover conflict and social reprimand for either being *unfeminine* or *not being feminine enough*. Brown's (2003) findings in her study of *girl fighting* suggested that girls risk being categorized as troublemakers or stupid if they exhibit active and physical behaviors, or simply because of their ethnicity, sexual identity, or social class, and quickly are "put in their place" (p. 6) if they do not assimilate or pass. Amy, 21, Caucasian/White, told other college women during a focus group discussion for this book that she had experienced greater degrees of pressure to fit in—in high school than she does in college: "Like in college, you meet people because you have the same major or you have common interests. In high school, the group of people you want to be popular with . . . you care more about how you're dressing than you do in college." Amy, and several other college-aged women spoke of feeling more free to express and experience femininity in college since there are so many more students as compared to high school settings where femininity is more narrowly defined.

Compounding peer pressure that girls and young women experience to emphasize their femininity in school settings are demands of media film industries which advances images of feminine, ideal women for social comparison. During a focus group discussion conducted for this book, twenty-year-old Allison, a Caucasian/White student, expressed intense anxiety about not being able to measure up to porn star actresses: "There's just impossible standards that I just cannot meet. That's what guys expect, too." Some college women spoke of embarrassment they felt about their bodies during sex when pages torn from porn magazines decorating dorm room walls stared back at them. Women across age cohorts reported during interviews and focus groups just how difficult it is to tune out images and messages of how women are *supposed to look*.

Historically, media have communicated how women should look and the *lesbian* label—some antithesis of femininity and how women *should look*—has been used as a psychological weapon to create anxiety, depression, and discomfort among women. Political cartoons and poems represented suffragist leaders as mannish in their facial features, hairstyles, and dress styles—as if they were not women at all. Moreover, politically active women were characterized as unfit mothers and poor choices for wives, as explained by sexist male politicians in newspapers and magazines regularly throughout the late nineteenth and early twentieth centuries. Indeed, mass media used lesbianism to interpret the political movement as revolt against "the privileged domain of bourgeois femininity" (Hesford, 2013, p. 85). Similar representations were resurrected in the 1960s and 1970s civil rights era and women's liberation movement in the United States, to keep women within strictures of acceptable femininity as passive wives and mothers.

Today, women who desire careers wherein they work with and compete with men experience a paradox when it comes to their femininity in the workplace. Femininity must be carefully managed because perceptions about femininity play out in contradictory ways and may contribute to women's anxiety levels. Displaying one's femininity through fashion and makeup provides a "psychological grip on one's sexual identity" and can serve as "protective coloration in a man's world and as a means of survival" (Brownmiller, 1984, p. 236, p. 235), while displays of empha-sized femininity can end a woman's career aspirations since excesses fuel perceptions that such women are incompetent (Tavris, 1992). In addition to appearance, women must manage their speech and body language by adopting masculine values of control, determination, and emotional dis-cipline (Bordo, 1989). Meanwhile, acting and dressing too masculine has negative consequences—including stigma for exhibiting strong leader-ship ability and professional competence. Perceptions are that such wom-en overstep the boundaries of conventional femininity and are consid-ered *aggressive, bitch,* or *slut* (Schippers, 2007, p. 95). Those who fail to obey a narrow definition of feminine beauty become labeled and pun-ished with name calling and social ostracism. Body shaming and slut shaming, historically, have played significant roles in sexual regulation of femininity and girls' and women's bodies (Dobson, 2014a). Jamieson (1995) called these dynamics a *double bind* for women. Chapter 5 features an expanded discussion of issues associated with navigating femininity in a paid-work environment.

Theorizing about stress attached to *"Am I feminine enough?"* benefits by interrogating the construction of various femininities within the social institutions of school, work, organized sports, and the media. Concepts of *dominant, subordinate,* and *oppositional* femininities open spaces for legiti-mating femininities beyond traditional, normative emphasized feminin-ity ideology, which many feminists argue is Caucasian/White-, heterosex-ual-, and middle-class-oriented. *Oppositional femininities* refer to women who challenge the unequal relationship between hegemonic masculinity and femininity. These are girls and women who refuse to identify with constricting and idealized media images of femininity and consequently, are marginalized for it. Findings of a study about women who exhibit nontraditional sex-role aspirations—women who emphasize intelligence and professional success, but do not identify as wife or homemaker—suggested that they are nearly twice as likely as other women to engage in frequent binge eating uncontrollably at least once per week and/or try to control their weight by purging or using laxatives or diuretics (Silver-stein, Carpman, Perlick, & Perdue, 1990). These findings may mean that even though some women strive to carve their own independent defini-tion of femininity they still feel a need to conform to social pressures to maintain a thin, petite body. Debbie, 51, Caucasian/White, explained dur-ing an interview for this book how changing social norms have released a bit of pressure on women to display their femininity:

> In the fifties, my mother didn't vacuum in her pearls, but she'd dress up to go to the grocery store. I know things are different for me than they were for her and we are both housewives, but I think that things have changed so much. *We* are allowed to be women and still be a part of our society. I'm not going to tell you I dress up to go to the grocery store all the time, but I do find as I get older [that] I want to look nice. I

want to present myself as who I really feel I am. My mother would put on her heels to go to the grocery store. I mean it was different for her. This was the way women had to look. We don't have to look that way. I mean you can look feminine in a pair of jeans. . . . I like that we are able to be a woman and not feel bad about it. You don't have to feel like the only place you belong is at home and at the grocery store.

Debbie, a mother of one of the college women who participated in a focus group discussion for this book, explained during our interview that times have changed and that she feels increasingly comfortable and less pressured to emphasize a certain type of femininity than women of her mother's generation. She feels she has more choices and she is grateful.

Yet, some adolescent girls battle a damned-if-I-do and damned-if-I-don't paradox when it comes to emphasizing femininity. Findings of a study about ways U.S. media constructed narratives about teen girls and recreation over the past century suggested that girls too often are punished, victimized, or sexualized for portrayals as either too masculine/strong or too feminine/weak (Thiel-Stern, 2014). For girls, a need for peer group acceptance is strong. According to social learning theory, girls are rewarded when they act properly feminine—polite, quiet, and obedient. In addition, sex composition of school attended impacts girls' ongoing learning about femininity. Girls studying in co-educational settings tend to accentuate their feminine identity more than in single-sex schools, yet exhibit more inhibited classroom behavior (Brutsaert, 1999). In the college setting, young women who live in a dorm initially feel pressured to conform to the group but do not perceive a need to emphasize their femininity as their college experience advances. During a focus group conducted among college women for this book, Ally, 20, Caucasian/White, explained:

I remember freshman year in the dorm—you go down to breakfast on Saturday morning. I'd be with a bunch of my friends, we'd go down, pajamas, slippers. . . . No one cared; no one did their hair. . . . But, there were some girls on my floor that were like, "No I have to shower. I need to do my make up. I need to brush my hair." I was like, "Girl, I haven't brushed my hair in a week!" . . . When girls take it to those extremes, it's annoying and distracting. . . . I feel like there's other ways to be girlie and feminine without actually looking the part, like actually being bubbly. . . . I feel like being smart can be feminine, too. That goes back to being powerful and strong. . . . [T]hat's something I carry with me every single day. . . . I don't think that putting on make-up in the morning or like doing your hair in the morning really defines that femininity. . . . I'm lucky if I get three hours' sleep, okay? So, I wanna stay asleep. . . . [J]ust being confident and being a powerful woman and just carrying yourself is important.

Among many women who participate in either professional or recreational athletics activities, a need to manage femininity is strong. While these issues shall be interrogated in greater depth in chapter 6, stress/ conflict effects deserve mentioning here since the GRS/C paradigm explains how women negotiate both feminine and masculine gender roles by enacting opposite and conflicting behaviors (Bem, 1993). For example, women rugby players experience GRS/C and develop multiple strategies for managing it (Fallon & Jome, 2007). Among female athletes, even recreational activities can involve significant muscle development, an outcome which does not fit entirely with traditional emphasized femininity norms. So, some girls and women seek to regulate their eating behaviors through purging and binging in order to achieve or maintain a feminine physique. Beyond striving for a thin ideal, however, some female athletes seek to bulk up in body areas historically associated with masculinity, also a goal which may inspire unhealthful eating behaviors.

SOCIAL IDENTITY INTERSECTIONALITIES MAY COMPLICATE GENDER ROLE STRESS/CONFLICT

Gender role stress/conflict is intensified for many women of color in the United States—especially when social identity dimensions of socio-economic status and age are considered in conjunction with dimensions of female gender and ethnicity. Traditional ideals of femininity are steeped in youth, Caucasian/White ethnicities, and middle-class status, so it is important to not overlook the fact that there are many other femininities out there and degrees of GRS/C experienced is integrated and *not piled on*. Opening one's lens on femininity subverts dominant ideals of femininity—and for African-American/Black women, Asian-American women, Latinas, and many other women of color, lived experiences associated with femininity add up to more than the color of one's skin or the shape of one's body. These complexities shall be explored in depth in chapter 7, but it is important to mention them in this chapter with regard to femininities and GRS/C. Since mass media generally advance feminine ideals based on Caucasian/Whiteness, absence of girls/women *like me* causes anxiety and stress among girls and women of color. Without knowledge of social expectations associated with how females of ethnic minority groups should display their femininity, girls may experience high levels of GRS/C (Kulis, Marsiglia, & Hecht, 2002). In her focus group discussion, Margaret, 23, Asian-American, lauded the virtues of being of a mixed ethnic background and living in an urban neighborhood where she could see and interact with women like her: "I'm half Korean and half Chinese, and I grew up in a one red-light town in the middle of nowhere. . . . So, it was like a struggle because there was definitely a lot of insecurities that it took me a while to accept. Now, being in the city, it's so much easier to be accepted." Margaret explained that her early years growing up where she was the only girl who looked like her was difficult: "They didn't even think of me as one of the other girls." College life has helped Margaret to feel less stressed and to "feel feminine like other girls."

Historically, African-American/Black women have not been held to traditional emphasized femininity norms which are steeped in Caucasian/Whiteness. Moreover, use of Black women as slave labor on plantations in the South and use of their bodies for manual labor after emancipation has contributed to a racist history wherein African-American/Black girls and women are contradictorily perceived as simultaneously oversexed and *un*feminine (Collins, 2005). These stereotypes are particularly perplexing for girls sorting through sexualized imagery amidst teenage consumerism for beauty and fashion products (McRobbie, 1991). Teenaged African-American/Black girls occupy the ambiguous space between childhood and adolescence, and for them sexualized imagery offers a respectability-deviance tension between the two stereotypes (Weekes, 2002). The *Black lady* image was designed to counter claims of working-class African-American/Black women's promiscuity and "freaky sex" (Collins, 2005, p. 120), and subversion of dominant beauty definitions with regard to a larger body size (Noble, 2000). Rose (1994) argued that rappers and DJs who construct female gendered imagery around African-American/Black female bodies are redefining the notion of female beauty through a specific emphasis on their derriere.

For this book, interviews and focus group discussions with women across ethnic groups and generations suggested that skin color plays a significant role in women's definition of femininity. Although there were four women's magazine photographs of discernably African-American/Black women representing different age groups displayed to stimulate discussion in focus groups and interviews, only one of the forty-five images scored highly as representing women's personal definition of *most feminine*. It was a 1970s *Redbook* image of a smiling, thin African-American/Black woman wearing short, natural hair, a long pale pink dress, and holding a pink rose while standing atop a stair railing. Among the older women interviewed, Gloria, 58, African-American/Black, admired the *Redbook* image for recalling her sorority, Alpha Kappa Alpha, which promotes "acting and looking like a lady." Gloria said: "Magazines back then showed very few women like me. I didn't think those magazines were for me, anyway." Connie, 51, who identified as "mixed ethnicity" (African-American/Black and Caucasian/White), characterized femininity in terms of *softness*. She had this to say about the image: "This is that soft that I was telling you about. I think maybe it's the pink and the smile. I just like the photo. There's a flower. Even without the flower, there's a softness." Connie expanded on her definition of femininity in terms of *softness* as she admired a *Redbook* 1990s image of a blonde, Caucasian/White woman wearing an American Red Cross shirt: "I think she, too, has a very soft look. Totally different dress, very soft. Look how she holds her hands, her feet. Very feminine." Sally, 60, Caucasian/White, categorized this *Redbook* image as *most feminine*, too: "[I]t's her smile. I look at her and see a Peace Corps version of myself. She looks about a size 12. She's not striving to fulfill feminine archetypes. She's got the long hair and she looks just happy."

Mass media portrayals of African-American/Black women have been widely indicted for stigmatizing femininities among women of color. Collins (2005) posited that under "new racism," mass media portrayals perpetuate a gender role reversal with women who are "too strong" and men who are "too weak" (p. 184). Drawing upon Goffman (1963), Collins (2005) persuasively argued that Black femininity means managing a "spoiled identity" (p. 315) which contributes to stress/conflict. In the workplace, the *Black lady* image for middle-class women underscores contradictions of maneuvering through the old *Mammy* image while simultaneously maintaining an acceptable level of workplace aggressiveness for success and also being "appropriately subordinate" to Caucasian/White male authority (Collins, 2005, p. 40). At home, images of the *bitch* or the *bad Black mother* means working-class African-American/Black women lack the traditional feminine ideal of submissiveness (Collins, 2005, p. 197).

Sexism and racism also compound feminine identities and contribute to gender role stress/conflict for Asian-American women. While Asian cultures steeped in Confucian philosophy may be oppressive toward women, U.S. perceptions of Asian-American women stereotypically (and paradoxically) consider them to be wild, aggressive and seductive in terms of sexual labor—as well as submissive, passive, and domesticated. In Korea, Western beauty standards transmitted via globalization effects and advertising are considered superior to traditional Korean standards wherein traditional femininity places women in household settings or as decorations with no role in the paid-labor market (Kim & Shaw, 2008).

Girls and women broadly categorized as *Latinas* consist of numerous ethnic groups with multiple conceptions of what femininity means as they experience unique forms of gender role stress/conflict. Latinas' realities are shaped by centuries of imperialism and colonialism in Mexico, Latin America, Central America, South America and the Caribbean. According to *marianismo* norms, Latinas are expected to be virginal, submissive, passive, and maternal (Torres, 1998). An extended discussion about *marianismo* norms appears in chapter 7. Camila, 27, Dominican aunt of a college woman who participated in a focus group for the study reported in this book, critiqued ways economic conditions force women to use their bodies in *un*feminine ways:

> If we could separate the baggage of centuries of being concubines and only finding jobs in third world countries where you have to be a prostitute in order to get by because you can't receive a regular job or education, I wouldn't think that sexuality is such a bad or a negative

thing. I find myself to be a very sexual person. I also feel like women,
when they feel like they have no choice, [using their body] is just a very
easy route to take to escape. I know women in the Dominican Republic
who become prostitutes just to leave the country. This is the route they
would take in order to escape and to alter their reality.

As Camila explained, socio-economic status intersects with other gender
identity dimensions and can significantly impact how femininity is enacted and defined. In the U.S. workplace, Latinas may be encouraged to
use their femininity to dress seductively and to entertain clients as a
strategy for enhancing agency-client business relations (Pompper, 2007).
Also, motherhood is a respected gender role and symbol across many
Latin ethnic groups and a central component of femininity. According to
Geliga-Vargas (1996), the Puerto Rican mother image is one of suffering
and enjoying life only vicariously through her children.

FEMALE VERSUS FEMALE COMPETITION AND FEMININITY

Another outcome of life in a patriarchal society for girls and women is
intra-gender competition for two scarce resources—men and jobs—and
GRS/C manifests in nasty, catty, and mean (ab)uses of femininity when
channeling anger and aggression. Brownmiller (1984) explained that un-
certainties are embedded in roles women are socialized to play and the
likely victims are other women in the competition to win male approval
with outcomes that paint women with either/or brushstrokes: lady/
whore, provocative/chaste, and altruism/childlike dependency. When a
sexist ideology is used to stereotype and judge girls and women by denigrating qualities associated with femininity, females operating from a
standpoint of lesser power sometimes take out their fears and anxieties
by turning in upon themselves—and processes are not bound by age.
Brown (2003) posited that "manipulation and duplicity have been part
and parcel of the very definition of femininity" (p. 1). Hence, the stereotypes and caricatures of girls and women as jealous, complaining, back-
stabbing, and deceitful are better understood as *socialized* rather than
natural. Exacting anger, fears, and anxieties on other girls and women is
much easier than taking it out on males (for whom heterosexual females
compete) who perpetuate a sexist climate which "denigrates, idealizes, or
eroticizes qualities associated with femininity" (Brown, 2003, p. 6). College student Jennifer, 18, Caucasian/White described just how confusing
femininity can be and the conflict it causes in relationships with other
women:

I don't know if I've gotten over this because I'm older now. But, in high
school, sometimes you even hear women say, "Oh, I don't get along
with other women." And it's usually someone who's like extremely,
extremely, extremely attractive. They're like, "Oh, women are always

jealous of me." . . . I feel like we women care more about what the next woman thinks of us, than we do what a man thinks of us just because it's like we're almost basing how beautiful we are on whether or not another woman feels intimidated by us or welcomes us with open arms. "Oh, well, if I'm really friendly does that mean that I'm just not a threat to anyone because, you know, they just don't see me as competition so everyone can be my friend?" Or is it like, "Oh, maybe I'm just too beautiful, so nobody likes me?"

Jennifer and other women in the focus group engaged in a long discussion about ways that femininity can be a source of insecurity among women, as in constantly wondering, *Am I feminine enough?* She added: "I really wish it didn't matter, but it does. I know I'm feminine. I just don't like having to compete to prove it to other girls."

Peer bullying through verbal and physical abuse can occur among secondary school girls and later on among women in the workplace as a response to traditional, normative, emphasized femininity standards perpetuated by patriarchal systems. During a focus group meeting of college women, Advika, 23, Indian, explained how anxiety provoking peer pressure among girls can be:

> Eighth to twelfth grade . . . girls are mean. You try to fit in, but you can't because they won't let you. You know what I mean? I think it's just that age. . . . [Y]ou're not accepted, then you feel self-conscious about that. And then, when I left for college I think it was a totally different environment. It was, like, all open and stuff, and so I think about whether or not I'm *feminine enough* a lot less now.

Deeming another female to be *un*feminine means relegating her to the margins, as aberrant, or deviant and it occurs along age, class, and race lines (Messerschmitt, 2011). Social ostracization minefields await girls in schools where thinness, athleticism, and heterosexual desirability earmark emphasized femininity norms. Messerschmitt (2004) categorized violence among teen girls, adding additional layers to femininities with *preppy femininity* wherein academic achievement and conservative dress characterize some girls, while *badass femininity* associated with truancy, drug and alcohol abuse, and a sexualized style of dress earmark others. *Oppositional femininity* forms expressed by some adolescent girls offer a response to and form an unequal relationship with hegemonic masculinity. Some girls unintentionally sustain society's "largely negative views of girls' and women's relationships as untrustworthy, deceitful, and manipulative" (Brown, 2003, p. 5). Toward the end of adolescence, girls may tone down their closest relationships with other girls, for fear that complete honesty and shared secrets could be used against them in the event of conflict (Brown & Gilligan, 1992). Overall, femininity serves to reassure boys and men that they are important and needed; so much so that women are willing to fight over and compete with one another for their attention.

Beyond adolescence, women act out similar negative behaviors targeting other women in the workplace. Exhibiting femininity can be associated with weakness, inviting gossip, jealousy, and back-stabbing. Women can get caught up in assimilating Caucasian/White male models of behavior at work, becoming competitive, instrumental, and individualistic such that they engage in conflict with other women and sabotage likelihood for supportive connections with other women. Yet to maintain a façade of the ideal feminine self, women mask their competition, envy, jealousy, pettiness, rage, and scorn (Bell & Nkomo, 2001, p. 260). Among women with upper-level management aspirations, failure to support other women on their way up the career ladder and especially after breaking the glass ceiling—known as queen bee behaviors—are inspired by women's desire to maintain their place among dominant males without appearing to favor their own gender (Pompper, 2012).

STRESS/CONFLICT AND THE PRIVATE/PUBLIC SPHERES DICHOTOMY

Girls and women are socialized to be pretty and to take care of husband, children, and home. Women who must or have chosen a career of paid work outside the home have long felt conflicted, trying to negotiate the public and private spheres. Women's private life is steeped in interdependence and their public life on individual pursuit and self-interest. The problem of maintaining a proper balance between the two sometimes conflicting goals has plagued women especially since the 1980s when women entered the workforce in large numbers. The traditional feminine, care-giving norm for women is associated with the most significant amount of gender role stress/conflict (Richmond, Levant, Smalley, & Cook, 2015) and conflict between work and family is a major predictor of depression and anxiety for women (Zamarripa, Wampold, & Gregory, 2003).

One specific area of stress/conflict for women is negotiation of housework and childcare in the private sphere. Men have been socialized to consider household chores of cooking, cleaning, and childcare to be women's work. Women themselves feel more responsible for family commitments and home tasks than do men (Peake & Harris, 2002) because they have been raised to feel that way. However, with many women working full-time outside the home, too, negotiating with male spouses and partners to share the chores has been a significant source of domestic stress/conflict. Some research findings suggest that women reduce their paid work when household responsibilities escalate (Becker & Moen, 2002), thus crystallizing work-family conflict for women. Overall, women's lives are widely regarded as "time starved" because they are harassed, overworked, rushed, and bound by their biological clocks for childbearing—all of which defines female adulthood as "a state of chronic temporal crisis" (Tasker & Negra, 2007, p. 11). Kossek and Ozeki (1998) found that occupational well-being decreases with an increase in work-family conflict. On the other hand, some women may experience more conflict-reducing positive spillover, transfer of positive affect, values, skills, and behaviors from one domain to another than men, due to being conditioned to multitask (Powell & Greenhaus, 2010).

Much research has been conducted to investigate relationships between paid-work stress and women's health. Cultural acceptance of equating the feminine with the private sphere has proven a challenge for women who seek paid work in the public sphere and have been punished with harassment and made to feel like second-class citizens. Generally, women receive less pay for the same work, as compared to their male counterparts, a significant stressor for women which also decreases their job satisfaction levels (Eisenberg, Goodall, & Trethewey, 2010). Related negative outcomes experienced by women in the paid workplace include burnout and psychological and physical complaints (Frone, Russell, & Cooper, 1992). As compared to men, however, women are more likely to seek guidance for work stressors through advice, practical assistance, and emotional support, outcomes consistent with female gender role socialization, as women are taught to depend on others (Greenglass, 2002).

DISCUSSION

Girls and women are subject to strong social pressures to transform themselves into a properly feminine body and to live within the confines of the female gender role. Those who resist and try to negotiate contradictions run the risk of encountering stress/conflict that can exact negative consequences for a woman's quality of life. Roots of female gender role stress/conflict develop in families, schools, and interpersonal relationships—and may become exacerbated in the paid workplace. Moreover, balancing occupational and domestic demands—trying to have and do it all—forces many women to engage with self-surveillance and disciplinary practices to address anxieties, conflicts, fears, and stressors integral to the female gender role strain paradigm. This chapter has addressed how training of girls to be feminine has become a systemic outcome of patriarchy. Young women are encouraged to subscribe to heterosexual emphasized femininity norms by snagging a husband and having children before they grow too old. In addition to age, other social identity intersectionalities such as ethnicity and sexual orientation complicate complexities of embodying traditional emphasized femininity or finding

ways to negotiate norms. Along the way, girls and women endure competition with other girls and women, more outcomes inconsistent with
what femininity is *supposed to be* all about.

FOUR

Consumerist *Mis*representations

Rituals and Industries that Shape Femininity

[Y]ou always see these specific types, like lighter skin, or smoother skin. . . . [T]hey're basically Photoshopping images of women because they're not perfect, but they need to make them *seem* perfect so that people can buy these products . . . making them look thinner, smoothing out their skin, taking out any signs of imperfection that they may have.
    —Research participant, Isabella, 21, Dominican

Mass media play a salient and highly visible role in perpetuating fantasies about femininity since girls' and women's gender role identity and behaviors are remarkably influenced by commonly held beliefs about how a woman *should* look and behave. Popular culture, fashion, and advertising industries use market segmentation to inspire consumption among girls and women—and the effects, as Isabella lamented to her focus group members, set unrealistic expectations for girls and women. Collectively, these forces play a principal role in the construction, maintenance, and representation of female bodies and femininity. Advertising campaigns negatively affect women's self-esteem and produce stress and conflict because standards are nearly impossible to achieve. Indeed, numerous study findings have suggested that societal pressure to conform to femininity ideals is substantially greater for women than men.

Conversations about why *femininity* seems to be defined so narrowly and why messages about girls' and women's *need for perfection* are disseminated so widely thoroughly engaged college women, their aunts, mothers, and grandmothers who participated in the study reported in this book. They placed the responsibility for feeling constricted by emphasized femininity norms with cultural gatekeepers who serve as sources of authority. These are the people who make judgments for the fashion and cosmetics industries. Also deemed responsible are mass media decision makers who produce programming which fuels popular culture. Collectively, these dynamics propel consumption of products which promise to make girls and women *perfect*. The global "fashion-beauty complex" (Bartky, 1990, p. 39) loads popular culture with non-stop messages that offer young women "a modern kind of freedom" that McRobbie (2009) called "faux-feminism" (p. 9, p. 1) shaped by false consumerist promises that product and service purchases can make females glamorous and loveable. In fact, postfeminist culture commodifies feminism and represents it as a woman-as-empowered-consumer figure (Tasker & Negra, 2007). Postfeminism refers to an undoing of feminism that McRobbie (2004b) pegged as starting in the United Kingdom in 1990 when popular culture began routinely and uncritically sexualizing women's bodies on billboards and other advertising media. Many women interviewed for this book, like Isabella in her epigram at the top of this chapter, emphasized stressing about looking good for their partner (current or future) and told of how dressing up makes them "feel better." As Berger (1972) famously posited: "Men look at women. Women watch themselves being looked at" (p. 47). Feminist researchers consider fashion an important text for scrutinizing how culture constructs femininity and how signifying practices represent the female body. *Femininity* is defined narrowly and a drive for *perfection* permeates popular culture in most developed nations with media, fashion, and beauty industries.

Ideological at its core, clothing and its accoutrements are both a social practice and a system of signs ordered by a complex set of relations of domination earmarked by age, class, ethnicity, gender, and more. Yet, women who participated in the study reported in this book shared multiple stories about how femininity is *mis*represented (and exaggerated) across popular culture, social media, feature films, television, magazines, video games, and other media forms. Some women's definition of *femininity* was consistent with binary dualism biological markers—vagina, breasts, and femininity for women, with penis and masculinity for men; findings not entirely inconsistent with my earlier studies about men defining *masculinity* (Pompper, 2010; Pompper, Soto, & Piel, 2007). However, such an oversimplified gender differentiation based on biology gave way to frustration and sometimes anger that *femininity* really means so much more. Findings of at least one study suggested that despite powerful influences of mediated beauty and thinness images, women placed lesser emphasis on physical appearance than expected—by emphasizing expressive/relational components (Hoffman, Hattie, & Borders, 2005). In the course of my interviews and focus groups with women, conversations of contexts where femininities tend to play out turned to social and cultural rituals like weddings, baby showers, and proms which emphasize women's femininity framed in traditional ways as sex objects, homemakers, and mothers. This stereotyped iconography of femininity through mediated images may only partially represent women's femininity; ultimately perpetuating the incomplete idea that biological femaleness is enough to define femininity. Beyond rituals such as weddings, baby showers, and proms that many women in the United States experience over the life course, women who participated in focus group meetings and interviews also talked about beauty pageants as a normalized ritual. Women shared narratives about how they grew up watching the Miss America pageant on television and wanting to grow up to be beautiful and to wear a long, glamorous gown. As such, these mediated spectacles become just as real to women as attending a bridal or baby shower for a family member, friend, or next-door neighbor.

Postfeminist culture portrays feminine women as *empowered consumers* with choices and presumed full economic freedom. For many women in the United States, paid labor is a requirement for survival, not a *choice*. For young women, in particular, McRobbie (2007) wrote that the price of their compliance is "to be silent, to withhold critique, to count as a modern sophisticated girl" (p. 34). In return, girls and women are eligible to enjoy commercial beauty culture, consume it, and represent its contemporary pinup image—so long as they keep any negative or radical opinions to themselves. In this way, postfeminism forms a comfortable liaison with consumer culture's "emphasis on showplace domesticity, virtuoso parenting, and technologies mobilized in the name of family cohesion . . . and a moral discourse of virtuous familialism" (Tasker & Negra, 2007, p. 7). Overall, a postfeminism mindset tends to celebrate *mis*representations of women's femininity and supports perceptions of freedom and agency for women while simultaneously lampooning itself for being *too serious*.

This chapter expands upon important points about consumerist *mis*representations of femininity in terms of rituals and industries that shape femininity: 1) Beauty culture industry sets the femininity standard for perfection, 2) Fashion industry sets femininity trends, 3) Selling emphasized femininity across media platforms by creating anxiety, 4) Framing femininity as purity, innocence, and unattainable through rituals, and 5) Discussion.

BEAUTY CULTURE INDUSTRY SETS
THE FEMININITY STANDARD FOR PERFECTION

Perfection is not easy—mainly because standards for feminine beauty prove non-inclusive, inconsistent, and impossible for most women to accomplish. Still, women fight their own bodies to emphasize their femininity, purchase costly products and services, and engage in unhealthy practices attempting to achieve a certain appearance that, too often, falls short of stringent and culturally salient standards for perfect femininity. Bodily modification through consumerism (Nash & Grant, 2015) has been the accepted norm for girls and women for decades. For example, failure to emphasize youth and thinness images made omnipresent by the beauty, fashion and media industries, leaves women stressed and conflicted. Indeed, making oneself beautiful so as to be pleasing to others is no new phenomenon, a thread connecting narratives about Cinderella, Cleopatra, Helen of Troy, and other female figures real and imagined. The beauty, fashion, and diet industries long have enjoyed a comfortable arrangement in setting the pace for emphasized femininity norms of perfection.

Retail stores' sales personnel are hired for their appearance and by the 1980s, store mannequins had become impossibly thin as clothing size 2, 4, and 6 became ideal. Among focus group participants for this book, college student Carolyn, 20, Caucasian/White, talked about effects of such marketing routines: "[E]ven mannequins! Any time you see clothes modeled on someone, they're always going to be really tall and really skinny. So, that's how clothes are made to look. So, it puts pressure on you to be more like *that*." Alonda, a British exchange student born in Nigeria, 20, concurred that mannequins offer unrealistic representations:

> I went with my friend, who's a little bit of a big girl. [W]e went in, and she was saying "How is this a big girl's store?" And, I was like, "Oh, the mannequins aren't really that big. You're sure this is a big girl's store?" And, we looked around and they'd pinned back the clothes. And I thought, "You're in a store for clothes for your size and they can't even get mannequins that would represent your size!" It just seems like that's really stupid. What's the point?

Something as simple as a display created to hold up clothes being sold is anything but. Both Carolyn and Alonda talked about how "humiliating" and "depressing" the act of shopping can be as women are marginalized when they realize that the clothes and the *look* being sold are not intended for them. Overall, popular culture's feminine beauty ideal is curvaceously thin with bust-waist-hip proportion measurements of 36–24–36, as amplified in the 1977 popular song, *Brick House* by *The Commodores*. The inherent paradox is that these measurements represent three different women's clothing sizes of 10, 2, and 4 (Harrison, 2003). A woman with a very small waist and hips, but large bust, is atypical outside of cosmetic surgery circles. Little girls grow up knowing that to earn praise they must be cute, thin, and well dressed (Wood & Fixmer-Oraiz, 2015).

Fat as stigma has become an enduring cultural value in the United States, one that empowers manufacturing and service industries which support female body thinness norms and seek to bolster their financial investment by perpetuating a war on fat as both a personal and a social problem. Beyond describing flesh, fatness has come to mean "not controlled . . . immoral, lazy, and sinful" (Farrell, 2011, p. 10)—and in the United States there are products and services which money can buy to reduce or remove fat. Tavris (1992) reminded us that women's bodies are biologically designed to store fat reserves in hips, thighs, and derrieres—and it generally is not unhealthful. In sum, fat shaming divides women along lines of those who are feminine, privileged, and perfect—and those who are not. In the United States, reality show mother, June Shannon of TLC's *Here Comes Honey Boo Boo*, experienced fat shaming in addition to being chastised for being a bad, financially poor mother and failing to meet feminine ideals. This reality television program was the butt of numerous jokes perpetuated across social media platforms—with critique focused on Shannon's body size. Since cancellation of the show, attention has been turned to the body of her daughter with headlines like "Honey Boo Boo has grown up quite a bit." Fat shaming has become synonymous with *un*feminine and the majority of women who participated in interviews and focus group discussions said they had felt the negative effects in terms of reduced self esteem.

Playing on women's low self-esteem and anxieties about social acceptance has proven a winning sales strategy for the beauty industry. Women are persuaded to adopt self-loathing as their norm (Kilbourne, 2010; Wolf, 1991). In fact, beauty culture's success depends on femininity discourse and enabling women to see they could benefit from being *more* feminine (Cranny-Francis, Waring, Stavropoulos, & Kirkby, 2003). This trend has escalated since the 1980s when the pharmaceutical industry was permitted to engage with direct-to-consumer advertising. As Joyce and Mamo (2006) found, technoscience is used to enhance sales pitches—especially among aging women. Net results promote ageism. Older women rarely are represented or perceived as sexy and exuding emphasized femininity. Overall, women are characterized as fashion-and-beauty-industry victims who somehow come to believe advertising messages that tell them they are deficient and need to lose weight and purchase cosmetics, deodorant, face cream, depilatories, shampoo, and sundry other products that promise to repair them (Kilbourne, 1999). Social embodiment is essential to production of emphasized femininity. Following the women's liberationist movement of the 1960s, the beauty industry began promoting a "return to femininity" (Faludi, 1991, p. 201) and condemned women "unwilling to help themselves" by failing to purchase products and services (McRobbie, 2009, p. 73). Manufacturers of cosmetics and other beauty products successfully convince women that they must create their own beauty and repeat the process daily (if not several times throughout the day) in order to be perfect. Providers of hair care, manicures, and pedicures also set norms for feminine grooming. Fragrance manufacturers, too, use marketing insights to position "three stock feminine types" with their scents: "the upper-class lady of leisure," "the bride," and "the little girl" (Faludi, 1991, p. 206). Degrees to which these archetypes exclude most women become clear when considering intersectionality of female gender with age, ethnicity, and other social identity dimensions.

One space clearly marked as a site for perfection through beauty maintenance and femininity production is the hair salon. Over the years, hair has come to represent a woman's "display of femininity," and it is infused with meanings which shed light on a woman's life pressures and social forces, urging her to conform to emphasized femininity norms and idealized beauty (Gimlin, 1996, p. 518). Of course, the meaning of a woman's hair also is shaped by multiple social identity dimensions, including age, ethnicity, social class, and sexual orientation. For example, some working women may feel compelled to choose a low-maintenance hairstyle over another for the sake of convenience. Beauticians' low social status often translates to succumbing to pressures associated with promoting a female beauty myth (Gimlin, 1996). Even feminists recognize the cultural import of striving toward feminine perfection—or, at least others' perceptions of it. Second-wave feminist Betty Friedan was reported in the *New York Times* as keeping a hairdressing appointment before a 1970 Women's Strike for Equality protest with the headline, "Leading feminist puts hairdo before strike." The news story described Friedan's "emergency appointment with her hairdresser," the dress she was wearing on the day, "a raspberry colored shift," and her concern that people will think "Women's Lib girls don't care how they look" (Leading feminist, 1970, p. 30). Today, third-wave feminists consider makeup use less as evidence that they have been duped by the beauty industry and more as a plaything and symbol of their independence. Some feminists have argued that just because young women may appear *girlie*, wearing Gucci, miniskirts, and lipstick while espousing feminism, their voices should not be muffled underneath critique of their appearance (Baumbardner & Richards, 2004, p. 60). An in-depth exploration of the *girlie-girl* concept may be found in chapter 1.

While omnipresence of the fashion-beauty complex earmarks many developed nations around the globe, other industries which perpetuate femininity in terms of perfected physical appearance and ideal norms may seem less apparent. For example, the toy and comic book industries produce gendered products which play a significant role in shaping femininity and masculinity. Wonder Woman widely is considered a role model comic book and action figure encouraging both masculinity and femininity among girls and women. In addition, Wonder Woman has served as a feminist icon and symbolic of women's power and autonomy, gracing the cover of the inaugural July 1972 issue of *Ms.* magazine. Yet, Averett (2009) found no Wonder Woman action figures or any other strong, independent female role models for girls among the toy aisles—only "sexualized feminine objects" (p. 365). Beyond encouraging girls to play exclusively with toys gendered for boys, such as trucks, as recommended by "feminist rigidity" of the 1970s, Orenstein (2011, p. 22) posited that banning dolls would disparage the feminine and could suggest that toys traditionally reserved for boys are somehow *better* than those created for girls. Recently, LEGO has added more female characters who work in science, technology, engineering, and mathematics (STEM) professions, in addition to colorful fantasy playsets (Weinstock, 2015). Mattel's iconic thin, tall, buxom, and perfect Barbie has been marketed as a teenage fashion doll for generations in the United States. While critiqued by many as socializing girls to desire a limited view of idealized femininity, Barbie represents a "mode of becoming a girl/woman," an important "mass-cultural representation of femininity" (Driscoll, 2002, p. 97). It would seem that toy manufacturer Mattel either has cast a more progressive attitude toward femininity and body image—or pursued a marketing opportunity. Added to the product line in 2016 were three "real woman" figures that are curvy, tall, petite and of diverse skin tones, eye colors, and hair textures and colors (Kiser, 2016). Mattel's WNBA Barbie remains a buxom figure with arched feet and Anglo features, hardly representative of muscled women's basketball players—many of whom are African-American/Black. McPherson (2000) explained that the WNBA itself struggles to manage an image of team players as "both skilled and feminine" (p. 1850). Dynamics associated with femininity and athleticism among girls and women is the topic of chapter 6.

Toy manufacturers and members of the fashion-beauty complex have contributed to ensconcing Whiteness as the benchmark for perfect female femininity. A Caucasian/White, female-emphasized femininity norm has endured for many decades. Examining 1920s cosmetics and toiletries advertisements in newspapers and magazines, one research team identified a *modern girl* trope influenced by U.S. beauty product manufacturers and advertising agencies which was promoted across European and East Asian cultures and languages via the *flapper, neue frau, garconne, moga* and *modeng xiaojie* images (Barlow, Dong, Poiger, Ramamurthy, Thomas, & Weinbaum, 2005). The commodified bobbed-hair *modern girl* image— showing Caucasian/White skin, thin body shape, brows, and athleticism—transcended geographic boundaries and symbolized globalization and colonialist underpinnings, in effect, installing Caucasian/White femininity as the ideal by selling "products to cleanse and alter the colour of teeth and skin, and to change the shape and shade of eyes and lips" (Barlow, et al., 2005, p. 247). Advertising copy historically has linked vocabulary of alabaster and milkiness with purity, cleanliness, beauty, and civilized culture (Stacey, 1994) for an implicitly Caucasian/White feminine beauty ideal. Hence, emphasized femininity is not only racialized, but is "historically and geographically mobile" (Charlebois, 2011, p. 26). In a more contemporary context, perhaps nowhere has the celebration of femininity as Caucasian/White skin played out more transparently than with the passing of Britain's Princess Diana. Shome (2014) questioned how a privileged "white upper-class heterosexual British woman" that many never knew personally could so captivate the world and re-solved that her ethnicity played a primary role since, historically, "it is only white women who have risen to the level of a mythology" (p. 5). Princess Diana garnered unprecedented media representations as univer-sal "angel, good mother, global savior, icon of beauty, and the goddess" (p. 4). Even "black female icons" such as Naomi Campbell and Oprah Winfrey are represented "through scripts of privileged white femininity" (Shome, 2014, p. 6). Cherniavsky (2006) explained that consumerist pro-motion of Caucasian/White womanhood images are applied to all wom-en. Femininities as shaped by social identity intersectionalities, such as gender and ethnicity, are further explored in chapter 7.

FASHION INDUSTRY SETS FEMININITY TRENDS

Like the beauty industry, the fashion industry codifies femininity, sets body image standards, and has been critiqued for constraining women and limiting their roles in society. Davis (1992) posited that fashion emerged as a concept in the West 700 years ago. Because fashion is iden-tified with femininity put in the service of the heterosexual male gaze, many tend to overlook the fact that clothing designs are socially con-structed and that women have choices as to what to wear. Historically, women have served as decorative objects, an assumption built into many cultures. Women's formal wear is so associated with pleasing male de-sires that garments reflect "social expectations of femininity," conspicu-ously accent women's bodies, and are absent of useful pockets so as to avoid "distorting the line of the garment" (Wood & Fixmer-Oraiz, 2015, p. 127). As for shoes, comfort seems to be less important than flattering women's legs. Yet, McRobbie (2009) opined that patriarchy and hege-monic masculinities are less visible in recent years and that fashion and femininity in the quest for heterosexual male approval is more implied than explicit. This goal is so entirely subsumed by the female fashion system that it would *appear* that girls and women dress for themselves or one another.

Stress associated with simply covering one's body in order to secure femininity has become routine. Some women feel they must appear to be appropriately female gendered and feminine at all times so as to avoid others' negative judgments (Butler, 1990, 1993). Intellectual women seen as masculine feel compelled to "put on a mask of womanliness to avert anxiety and retribution feared from men" (Cranny-Francis, Waring, Stav-ropoulos, & Kirkby, 2003, p. 168). Fashion magazines such as *Elle, Marie Claire, Grazia*, and *Vogue* promote fashion in terms of a "globalized femi-ninity," with some feminist scholars critiquing ways these outcomes merely represent an enduring colonial force that perpetuates certain idealized styles of Caucasian/White emphasized femininity norms across space and time (McRobbie, 2009, p. 59). Hence, fashion for women offers an important text for examining how femininity is constructed and ways fashion serves as a field of representation for the female body.

The brassiere was championed by second-wave feminists as a symbol of how fashion can serve as an instrument of oppression. The brassiere simultaneously signifies femininity *and* women's liberation in terms of its absence. As discussed in chapter 1, female breasts long have been considered as personifying femininity. So, when second-wave feminists talked about burning their bra, this symbolized women's use of fashion to make a political statement in refusing to be uncomfortably constrained by patriarchal conventions. In protest during the 1968 Miss America Pageant, women were urged to deposit their bras and girdles into a Freedom Trash Can on the Atlantic City, NJ, boardwalk. Although no one did, the mass media widely covered the publicity stunt. Two years later, a powerful line drawing image of a stocky young, clearly bra-less Caucasian/ White woman standing erect, feet apart, and holding a burning bra was featured in *Time* magazine on December 14, 1970. It was captioned, *The Women's Liberationist*. About second-wave feminism, Hesford (2013) opined: "[T]he movement was engaged in an irreverent, disrespectful dismissal of normative femininity" (p. 30). So, the woman represented in the *Time* magazine line drawing was not constricted by fashion that requires undergarments like a bra and girdle, ergo, a woman demanding liberation to express femininity on her own terms.

The fashion industry long has framed femininity in terms of masculinity's opposite—so that any hints of masculinization in women's clothing has become fodder for political commentary about women and their role in society. Chanel's masculine-cut dresses and power suits were this designer's attempt at the turn of the twentietih century to level the playing field according to gender and to accommodate a changing social climate (Evans & Thornton, 1991). In the 1970s through 1980s, fashion designers saw shoulder pads and city suits as a means for women to gain credibility in a business world dominated by men as they sought to redress the gender-power imbalance in women's favor through clothing. Faludi (1991) opined that work suits of the 1970s were used by feminism's critics as a backlash symbol, that "women's liberation had denied women the right to feminine dressing" and "shackled the female spirit" (p. 173). She quoted fashion designer Bob Mackie who suggested that work suits for women "hurt their femininity," and fashion designer Arnold Scaasi agreed that women were "beginning to lose some of the feminine attributes" (Faludi, 1991, p. 173). Over time, women's fashion of that era that included shoulder pads has become the butt of jokes about women trying to be unfeminine, to be like men.

So fast-forwarding to the second decade of the twenty-first century when I interviewed women for this book about if/how they defined femininity in terms of fashion, I should not have been surprised when the overwhelming number across age cohorts equated *most feminine* with nostalgic images of emphasized femininity. As explained in chapter 2, these images included flowing gowns from the mid-twentieth-century. Conversely, nearly all images from women's fashion magazines that seemed gender neutral or somewhat masculinized with models wearing tailored suits, trousers, capri pants, blue jeans, and shorts summarily were placed in the *least feminine* pile by women interviewed. Among images unanimously categorized as *least feminine* were those of two Cau-casian/White women wearing denim and cowboy boots atop horses from *Redbook* in the 1970s, a reclining Caucasian/White woman wearing khaki trousers and a navy blue polo shirt from *Redbook* in the 1980s, and two images of women wearing a business suit and neck scarf (one African-American/Black, one Caucasian/White) from *Ladies Home Journal* in the 1980s and 1990s. Interestingly, women across age cohorts condemned a *Ladies Home Journal* 1990s image of a fashionably dressed, long-haired brunette Caucasian/White woman holding a handgun. Intensely negative were comments about how *un*feminine women considered the image. During our interview, Carla, 50, Caucasian/White, explained:

> I am not a gun person at all. I guess I associate femininity with life and I don't think it's feminine for a woman to have a gun. I don't care that she's dressed in her little yellow Chanel suit, little pastel pink bag, makeup, hair and nails done.

Even when I asked Carla if—without the gun—she might consider this image for her *most feminine* pile of images selected from among the stimulus materials used to provoke conversation about femininity, she said "no." Despite the woman's pastel suit with perfect accessories, hair, and makeup, Carla perceived the handgun as masculine and she could not remove the image of it from her mind's eye. Carla also considered tailoring of the suit to be "too masculine." It seems that suits for women tend to fall along a feminine-fashion continuum — with "severe suits . . . power dressing" at one end and "Laura Ashleyish *un*tailored floral, frilled and 'feminine' looks" at the other end (Evans & Thornton, 1991, p. 57). For women such as Carla, and others whom I interviewed for this book, it's the flowing silky and lacy fashions that they consider to be *most feminine* and useful in depicting how they, personally, define femininity.

Fashion also offers a means for young feminists to differentiate themselves from older feminists. Third-wave feminist Rebecca Walker (1992) — daughter of second-wave feminist activist, Alice Walker — explained in the 2013 feature film, *The Punk Singer* about Kathleen Hanna: "Third wave was founded in response to a feeling on college campuses in 1992 that feminism was in some ways dead, irrelevant, that women of my generation were apathetic, not desirous of working on behalf of women's empowerment" (Anderson, 2013). Third-wave feminists have sought a means to say, "We're different, but we're part of this history" (Anderson,

2013). At the height of the 1990s punk scene in the United States, young women "engaged *en masse* in the forbidden activity of confusing sexual messages" (Evans & Thornton, 1991, p. 58). As part of the movement, female bands like *Bikini Kill* featured ambivalence toward traditional femininity, smudged their makeup on purpose, and used their bodies to resist "artefacts of femininity" (Attwood, 2007, p. 240). Female friendship, fashion, and rebellion can fit hand in glove for a unique blend of agentic femininity. Fashion designer, Vivienne Westwood, worked through "a self-defined feminine libido . . . which communicates itself idiosyncratically through dress" (Evans & Thornton, 1992, p. 61) and explained the importance of feeling free to wear what feels sexy. This is an idea which resonates with third-wave feminism and one that McRobbie (2009) said represents a *"faux-feminism"* when women fail to see how objectification and sexualization of their body is not liberation or freedom at all (p. 1, italics included in original).

Representations of femininity as they relate to feminism and girl power have found a wider audience since 2003 as the fashion industry increasingly grew its news and information network across the blogosphere. Fashion bloggers use new media to forecast trends, spotlight what's cool, and promote fashion brands. Tools of user-friendly web design software for social media use have made it simple for fashion industry outsiders to use multi-media platforms and penetrate mainstream fashion media to connect fashion designers and brands with fashion consumers in a postmillennial digital economy, an outcome now widely respected among the fashion establishment (Sherman, 2010). Fashion blogging is an ephemeral form and the most successful bloggers update their work routinely—several times daily—to stay ahead of on-trend street fashions and to promote fashion even before retail stores make items available to the public. This has been called a form of "enterprising femininity" (Gray, 2003, p. 492). Although fashion bloggers are not considered full-fledged journalists, fashion magazines consult with them and spotlight them in editorial features. Emphasized femininity is promoted among top-ranked fashion bloggers who articulate a form of entrepreneurial femininity through a "having it all" ideal of "destiny of passionate work, staging of the glam life, and culturally curated social sharing," social media producer-brands constructed within capitalist frameworks (Duffy & Hund, 2015, p. 1). Female and male Asian fashion bloggers may be numerically dominant (Pham, 2013), but the most popular fashion bloggers are overwhelmingly young, thin, and Caucasian/White (Banet-Weiser, 2012, p. 89). In fact, African-American blogs have received significantly less support from powerhouses of the fashion media (Thomas, 2010), and fashion bloggers underrepresent women of color, LGBT, and plus-sized models (Duffy & Hund, 2015). Keller's (2015) case study of Tavi Gevinson, who started blogging about fashion at eleven years old and now edits the online magazine *Rookie*, underscores the porous nature of postfeminist media culture as she makes feminism relevant to teenage girls, not unlike *riot grrrl* activities. This dynamic enables girls to engage with their own sense of femininity and provides a "significant deviation from the apolitical media for girls primarily created by adults" (p. 274).

So, the concept of femininity long has been interwoven with the fashion-beauty complex, consumerism, media representations, and political movements. Even though the relationships women have had with these dynamics may not have been easy ones over the years, the links *are* illuminating as a means for understanding just how femininity is defined.

SELLING EMPHASIZED FEMININITY
ACROSS MEDIA PLATFORMS BY CREATING ANXIETY

Advertising images are cultural products created to sell branded goods and services. Consumer capitalism relies on this commerce. The advertising images sell through persuasion techniques designed to exploit women's anxieties about their femininity. Outcomes of these forces are neither straightforward, nor neutral. We already know that advertising affects our lived experience by imposing limited representations of gender identity (Goffman, 1979). Yet, how advertising images influence our ways of thinking about femininity is less understood, a goal embedded in the research conducted for this book.

Gender role stereotypes provide important context for examining how femininity is made to mean. Use of feminist rhetorical critique affords the opportunity to challenge misrepresentations of women and to explore implications for ways femininity is defined across socio-political dimensions. Ads involving food, housekeeping, and childcare stereotypically feature women more prominently, as if men are uninvolved in the domestic sphere (Wood & Fixmer-Oraiz, 2015). Masculinity theory reminds us that sexist media images sustain socially sanctioned standards of femininity and masculinity and dominance of men over women (Connell, 1987) in business, government, and bed (Dill & Thill, 2007). In a focus group discussion hosted as part of data gathering for this book, Cathy, 53, Caucasian/White, suggested that the advertising industry owes a debt of gratitude to women when she said: "Sex sells. They can make something more alluring and attractive by comparing it to a woman. Then it will sell the product better." Indeed, because masculinity and femininity are semiotically connected, juxtaposed against advertising images of masculine men driving fast cars are feminine visions of women "applying makeup, driving a minivan, eating 'light,' doing the laundry, and decorating houses" (Schroeder & Zwick, 2004, p. 22). Goffman's (1976) analysis of visual representations in advertisements emphasized the salience of popular culture in social construction of gender because people tend to mimic gender performances they see in advertising. In the 1950s, advertisers reported that women considered "housework a medium of expression for . . . [their] femininity and individuality" (Friedan, 1963, p. 204). Female gender identity and femininity continue to be shaped according to consumption promoted by the advertising industry and visual representations in ads still reinforce ways we think about girls, women, and their femininities.

Perhaps more than any other medium, magazines for girls and women have done more to confine femininity to limited/ing images and to support the beauty and fashion industries' narrow views about femininity as a single-dimension concept. Combined forces of markets and institutions perpetuate dated symbols which editors use to support their mission when visually defining femininity across magazine pages—both in print and online. In recent years, magazines do not shirk from simultaneously amplifying a stereotypical image of the 1950s Donna Reed television housewife in pearls as the epitome of femininity, as well today's sexualized version of femininity as personified by images featuring Kim Kardashian's derriere on the internet. The aunt of a college woman who participated in a focus group for the study reported here, Camila, 27, identifies as bisexual, Dominican, and criticized advertising's simultaneous normalizing and alienating functions:

> Everywhere you see the ideal woman in terms of body parts. I just saw an interesting documentary about vaginas and we never realized there are just so many different types. You don't realize that until you're in your late thirties or fifties. I feel like the media just gives you one image of what a woman should look like. If you go against that, you're a rebel, or a dyke, or a *feminist*. It's always an extreme. There isn't anything that allows you to be one or the other or both.

Camila explained how worried she feels that even today, young women like her niece are growing up in a world where femininity is both an ambiguous and a confusing concept. She added: "All my niece worries about is looking sexy. That's fine if that's what makes her happy, but that's not the only thing in life!"

The meaning of femininity in today's postfeminism era has been subsumed and commodified by media industries for strategic purposes rather than as a concept which has evolved as a product of historic, political processes. Postfeminist thinking today constructs feminism as "extreme, difficult, and unpleasurable" (Tasker & Negra, 2007, p. 4), outcomes that suggest negativity and contribute to anxiety, conflict, and stress. By amputating the political as change agent for achieving gender equality, femininity is redefined and feminism is made more palatable to young women as something synonymous with individualism steeped in using one's body to be sexy, independent, sophisticated—and feminine. These are attributes that fit comfortably with goals of media aimed at women wherein images offer representations which rely on emphasized femininity to sell products. When unmoored from its political roots, feminism has become a shadow of its earlier days and femininity is used as a tool to sell stress/conflict which can be resolved only through the purchase of the right fashions, products, and services. As addressed in chapter 3, girls and women continually are told they are not perfect as they are—with media images perpetuating girls' and women's inner stress/conflict.

If individualism is the goal of women today, accepting emphasized femininity ideals in order to appeal to a man proffers an irony too obvious to ignore. When feminism is linked to politics, it is considered a dirty word in many circles. In particular, women's magazines' commodified sexualization of the female form suggests an *aggressive* individualism that relies on consumption of products and services required for achieving perfection. The most popular women's magazines rarely offer a forum for political organizing and feminist critique about femininity or other concepts central to the female experience. Falling advertising revenues have forced significant restructurings at U.S. magazines targeted for women and girls that includes magazines reconsidering their own identity and shifting from a print culture to an online one where a magazine's brand is its primary concern (Duffy, 2013). That identity now is based on convincing girls and women that they are *not* perfect.

Feminism is entirely unwelcomed by many girls and young women today. In 2013, a social media trend launched by a Twitter hashtag, #WomenAgainstFeminism, morphed into a Tumblr blog, and social media campaign on Facebook and YouTube wherein girls and women took selfies holding up signs explaining why feminism is not for them. Chang (2015) wrote that reactions to the campaign have been global and varied, but argued that comments are "a reasonably fair description of a large, influential, highly visible segment of modern feminism." Part of Chang's (2015) online news article featured several of the poster signs women created for the #WomenAgainstFeminism hashtag string on Twitter. Several of the photographs suggested remarkably limited ideas about femininity. For example, as the concluding line after a list of reasons why she loves her BF, one young woman wrote: "When I dress feminine, it's for me." Contrastingly, another woman wrote: "I love to be sexy for my man and cook for him in the kitchen." Outcomes of this well-publicized hashtag campaign suggest that the media and beauty-fashion complex strategy of defining femininity in ways that create stress/conflict in order to get them to purchase and consume what they think they need to accomplish emphasized femininity norms in order to satisfy their significant other has proved quite successful. In the process, the political roots of feminism have been severed.

Processes for defining femininity among girls' media are not dissimilar from those used to define femininity among women's media. *Adolescent femininity* is characterized by an uncertain border separating girlhood from puberty (Driscoll, 2002), ambiguity capitalized upon through titillation and the erotic-chaste dialectic. Bodily display and modesty are opposing concepts and representative of a conflict exploited by the fashion industry and media who amplify it. A girl is a body/subject in process but requiring of discipline and appreciation. Woman's magazines are designed to "stimulate a desire for perfection through consumption" (Rakow & Wackwitz, 2004, p. 177) and magazine editors frame boundaries of adolescent femininity using similar techniques (Smith, 1990). U.S. magazines have thoroughly embraced the *teen girl* concept, a social construct for dependent young females constantly in need of supervision as they constantly are "lurching from one crisis to another" (Jackson & Goddard, 2015, p. 241)—whether it is the Ophelia crisis about girls' lost self (Pipher, 1995), mean girls (Ringrose, 2006), or sexualized tweens aged seven to fourteen (Cook & Kaiser, 2004). Mass media have maintained that teenaged girls are powerless against biological tendencies of their own, as well as those of teenaged boys and men—and, hence, must be controlled and protected. This impulse is rooted in patriarchy, a framework which constitutes girls as daughters and future heterosexual partners and mothers. In the process, femininity is sexualized and images are reflected back at teen girls, messages that increasingly are aimed at younger and younger girls (Durham, 2008). Findings of Currie's (1997) study suggested that fashion magazines hold appeal for ultimately helping teen girls feel better about themselves (after initially making them feel bad), but that teen zines' absence of commercial context offers an alternate medium to consider "realistic" (p. 470) negotiation of femininity as a key dimension in the maturation process.

Popular culture channels in both social and commercial mediascapes—especially magazines, music, and feature films—rhetorically amplify notions of youthful femininity as *empowerment*. Meanwhile, the global girl often represented in fashion magazines is sexualized, friendly, and intelligent—but low in self-esteem (McRobbie, 2009). Celebrating music and punk culture of the 1980s, girls and young women used fashion to subvert traditional female gender role images by wearing combat boots and piercing and tattooing their bodies to exercise their power and to signify with their own brand of "tarty" (Evans & Thornton, 1991, p. 58). Feature films rank among the most prolific media formats for representing youthful femininity. The *woman's film* or *chick flick* targets a female audience through story, female protagonists, and feminine themes. Several of the mothers, aunts, and grandmothers interviewed for this book reflected on the power of movies to shape perceptions of and to set standards for femininity. Connie, a fifty-one-year-old woman who identifies as "mixed ethnicity" (African-American/Black and Caucasian/White) explained during her interview for this book ways that media shaped how she defines femininity:

> I love back in the fifties, the thirties, the old black and white movies. . . .
> Even the full-sized ladies. . . . Always something unique about them . . .
> an elegant era. Whether they were wearing a dress or even if they were
> dressed to work in the yard. They always had the very cinched waist
> and neat look. Now [young] women are out there in the flip-flops and
> looking a hot mess some days.

Connie's sense of nostalgia framed by yesteryear was typical for her age cohort as I collected data for this research about defining femininity. However, it bears repeating that even younger age cohorts seemed transfixed by the glamour of mid-twentieth century women's fashion as an ideal for defining femininity. In a different focus group, Jane, 20, Caucasian/White, offered a more critical interpretation of the power of movies in representing women and their femininities: "I really get angry at movies now. . . . [W]henever I see pretty girls who find true love or whatever, I'm like "That is not real." . . . Just because you're cute and petite doesn't mean you always find love. . . . Like, it kinda pisses me off." Jane, like several other college women, did not hold back her passion for expressing dissatisfaction with media representations of women and their femininities in film and other media products. With regard to the film medium, even though female film characters may hold a privileged position in a storyline, they routinely represent eye candy and are denied a point of view. To explain this phenomenon, Doane (1982) argued that femininity is "produced very precisely as a position within a network of power relations" (p. 87). An iconic feminine representation of a woman, by many standards, was offered in *Gone With the Wind* (1939), a Hollywood film featuring a protagonist named Scarlett O'Hara. She was a beautiful U.S. Southern belle who shaped her own brand of femininity and amplified what Robison (2009) argued was a "scrappy feminism" (p. 1117). Fast forward to 2002, the feature film, *Divine Secrets of the Ya-Ya Sisterhood*, also set in the U.S. South, promotes a vision of strong femininity. In teen prom films like *She's All That* (1999) and *Never Been Kissed* (1999), a cross between the Cinderella tale and Scarlett O'Hara myth converge in narratives about how femininity can be enhanced with makeover consumerism in order to forge a heterosexual happy-ever-after ending. Film actress Angelina Jolie possesses "successful femininity" for her transnational adoption of children, involvement with the United Nations Refugee Agency, and her elective double mastectomy surgery (Favara, 2015). Linking femininity to girls' and women's *appearance* continues to limit representations of girls and women across media platforms.

The television medium and video gaming industry also perpetuate the femininity-through-sexualization pattern. The widely popular U.S. program, *Sex and the City*, represented four young women empowered by their sexuality, a show considered groundbreaking in giving voice to "frank, taboo-breaking discussions of sex and femininity" (Nash & Grant, 2015, p. 977), even though emphasized femininity shaped the narrative

(Arthurs, 2003). Reality television figure Kim Kardashian may be challenging femininity ideals as a woman of color who possesses an "atypical" fuller figure (Hare, 2015), but the focus remains on her appearance. In the video gaming world, aggressive female video game figures are also objectified, sexualized, glamorized, and trivialized—and are not "true figures of liberation" even though the majority of female characters (62.2 percent) may be represented as aggressive (Dill & Thill, 2007, p. 861). On the other hand, some current television dramas are featuring powerful women leads, such as on *The Good Wife*—a story about a politician's wife who resumes her career as a defense attorney after her husband lands in prison (Scott, 2016).

U.S. popular culture also sells femininity by using luminosity, or *sparklefication*, perhaps as an antidote for the anxiety, conflict, and stress girls and women may feel when they perceive their bodies as lacking, less than perfect, and unable to achieve ideal femininity. Conveniently, luminosity and sparklefication trends tap into femininity's mystery, elusiveness, and allure and provide immediate gratification for feeling happy. Objects that glow and sparkle in the natural world long have captured humans' fascination, including flickering candles, shooting stars, sunlight glistening on water, and fireflies (Kearney, 2009; Moseley, 2002)— and are revered as the manifestation of ancestral spirits or heavenly energies (Bille & Sørensen, 2007). Foucault's (1990) theorizing about the body, power, and visibility inspired Deleuze (1986) to write of ways light catches a "flash, sparkle or shimmer" (p. 52), forms of simulacra postmodern girls and young women use in glittery makeup, clothing, and accessories to affirm and amplify their femininity through creativity. Fashion blogs, like theglitterguide.com, and Glitter Girlz party organizing trends to get girls creating rather than watching television have capitalized on the trend, too. Unsurprisingly, an image of a young Caucasian/White woman wearing a short red figure-hugging sparkly sequined dress from the pages of *Ladies Home Journal* in the 1990s made the *most feminine* list for every woman who participated in this study's focus groups and interviews. Luminosity, sparkle, fantasy, and femininity have proved fertile territory for postfeminist sensibilities among YouTube do-it-yourselfers, as well as television and film producers of female-centered stories seasoned with sparkly, magical special effects. These include Disney's feature films *Fantasia*, *Cinderella*, *Brave*, and *Frozen*, and supernatural happenings on HBO's *True Blood* and Nickelodeon's *The Secret World of Alex Mack*. U.S. actress Claire Daines wore a fiber-optic-woven couture organza gown to the 2016 Met Gala, themed "Manus x Machina: Fashion in an Age of Technology," which lit up in the dark. Hindi films, increasingly popular internationally, long have promoted female fashions bejeweled with small mirrors, sequins, and beads (Maira, 2002). In 2007, the Disney Company launched wedding apparel inspired by fictional characters of

Ariel, Cinderella, and Snow White (Olson, 2007). Femininity and fantasy become synonymous in a world of luminosity sparklefication.

Perhaps femininity's most valuable sales tool is the color pink. Pink signifies youthful femininity and sexuality (especially in Victoria's Secret lingerie and accessories stores)—in addition to differentiating girl baby things from boy baby things. For decades, the color pink has symbolized femininity in U.S. culture (Picariello, Greenberg, & Pillemer, 1990). Popular culture and media proliferation of images swathed in pink, glitter, and princess glamor challenge mothers who may become overwhelmed by it all (Orenstein, 2011). *Girlie girls,* as discussed in chapter 1, have reclaimed the color pink as personification of girl culture and reclaimed makeup, nail polish, and fun (Baumgardner & Richards, 2010). These items are linked to feminine behaviors closely aligned with consumerism and the antithesis of "anti-feminine, anti-joy" second-wave feminism (Dejmanee, 2015, p. 463). U.S. actress Gwyneth Paltrow elevated the color pink when she wore a pink Ralph Lauren spaghetti-strap ball gown to the Oscars in 1999 and won Best Supporting Actress. Among the stimulus materials selected for women to discuss and critique in defining femininity for the study reported in this book, six featured women wearing pink and all but one made their way onto women's *most feminine* lists. Five images featured women wearing pink dresses during the 1920s, 1950s, 1960s, 1970s, and 1980s. The exception to making women's *most feminine* list was a 1990s *Better Homes & Gardens* image of a long-haired Caucasian/White brunette woman who wore a pink sweatshirt with blue jeans, and held a trowel with gardening gloves. Very few women across age cohorts seemed to give the image much consideration as either *most* or *least feminine.* They seemed turned off by the blue jeans and the idea of getting dirty—preferring instead to define femininity using the glamor of lace and gowns illustrated in other images. Women are socialized to equate pink with femininity, but cannot reconcile it with denim, getting dirty, or wearing gardening gloves. Research participants' lack of reaction to this image may reflect what Davis (1992) referred to as "certain strategic ambivalences" (p. 191)—women are hard-wired into perceptions about ways women *should* look to emphasize their femininity. College student Carol, 19, Caucasian/White, bisexual, told of her complicated relationship with the color pink:

> Yes, I do think pink is still the color most widely associated with femininity. When I was growing up my mom dyed all of my pink clothes red and painted all of my pink toys red. I was not allowed to have anything pink. I think she knew I was gay before I did. Like, I found out when I was two. So, I had this beautiful pink scooter, and she painted it red. And, I would chip at the red paint and she would paint over it red again. And, to this day, if people, like, give me pink things, I think "Why am I getting that?" And, I'm really feminine, but pink is just—ugh, it's pink.

Carol told other women in her focus group discussion that she worries that girls and women feel pressured to either like pink or to be identified with it: "There are so many colors under the rainbow! Femininity is all colors. Why limit yourself to one?!"

From a socio-political standpoint, postfeminist culture embraces contemporary luminosities as stand-ins for femininity. Glitter and pink associate fun and desirability with hyperfemininity (like emphasized femininity)—using the female body as a site of pleasure produced through (supposedly) agentic consumption and masquerade for self rather than to exclusively appeal to male desire. In recent years, campy theatrical spectacles involving glitter have provided subversive potential for members of queer communities to push back against heteronormativity with activist groups' glitter bombing of those who oppose same-sex marriage. In June 2011, Congresswoman Michele Bachmann from Minnesota was glitter bombed by an LGBT activist for supporting religious groups that oppose LGBT issues (Vinciguerra, 2011). Adopting a queer lens offers a broader view for postfeminist subversion of patriarchy (Doty, 1993) and new ways to define femininity in terms of agency, too.

FRAMING FEMININITY AS PURITY, INNOCENCE, AND UNATTAINABLE THROUGH RITUALS

Rituals, many organized by religion/faith systems, long have represented femininity in terms of purity, innocence, and virginity. Emphasized femininity among Latin/Hispanic communities is heightened and displayed during the traditional *coming of age* celebration of a fifteen-year-old girl's birthday party—the Sweet 15 Quinceañera. These parties often are rife with rhinestones, sequins, and glitter (Colloff, 2009), luminosities and sparklefication used to sell femininity (as discussed above). For girls, the Quinceañera ritual, not unlike the high school prom, serves as precursor to a fantasy wedding and realization of a feminine dream shrouded in celebrity culture which has grown in popularity since the early twentieth century (Pompper & Crandall, 2014). See Figure 4.1.

Rituals and traditions practiced by religious and cultural groups across the United States emphasize the importance of femininity and its underlying meaning as something to be protected. For example, the Sweet 15 Quinceañera also serves as a "talisman" against teen pregnancy (Stewart, 2004). Some other Christians in the United States also host purity balls, formal father-daughter dinner dances wherein girls take a ring and pledge abstinence from sex until marriage. Yet, purity pledge takers may be more likely to end up pregnant or to contract an STD than young people who did not take a sex abstinence pledge (Paik, Sanchagrin, & Heimer, 2016). Jewish tradition includes the bat-mitzvah where dressing formally contributes to a celebration of womanhood at age thirteen.

Figure 4.1.   As part of the Quinceañera ritual for Latinas celebrating their fif-
teenth birthday, emphasized femininity fantasies are made real with lavish productions and accessorizing suitable for a fairy tale princess. Pictured: Donnalyn
Borge. Photo by Roberto Borge.

Among Romani Gypsy and Traveller cultures, Jensen and Ringrose (2014) posited that the wedding ceremony—with girls sometimes as young as sixteen—blends fantasy and spectacle which subverts "tasteful, middle-class femininity" (p. 382). In the United Kingdom, these groups' fondness for hyperfeminine meringue wedding dresses and making an exhibition of a "white trash" or "not quite white" culture are lampooned on the U.K. realty television show, My Big Fat Gypsy Wedding (Wray, 2006). Weddings have proved romantic fodder for all manner of stories and today romanticize a bygone era when some women experienced compromised femininity and *had to get married* due to pregnancy because they did not have a myriad of choices (Beck & Beck-Gernsheim, 2001).

Wedding rituals are considered to be entirely the domain of girls and women. Feminists who critique power dynamics among gender relations find wedding rituals to be particularly paradoxical—as in *why study women's acquiescence to patriarchy through marriage* (Susong, 2016). The black and white *McCall's* 1940s magazine image of a Caucasian/White bride used to stimulate discussion about femininity for this study evinced a clear consensus among women interviewed as a *most feminine* image. Indeed, group discussions reflected middle-class women's "guilty desires for a meringue wedding dress," possibly a reaction to stress/conflict women experience about "impossible demands of contemporary femininity" (Jensen & Ringrose, 2014, p. 383) and reference to the Cinderella-style dress and fantasy pumpkin coach wedding as default which is engrained into women from childhood via mass media. Somehow, the wedding dress means a woman has made it—successfully emphasized her femininity and captured a man. Lola, a twenty-one-year old woman who identified as Dominican, was most enthusiastic about the 1940s McCall's, black and white image of the bride: "The lady in a wedding dress. . . . [M]aybe I see feminine as, I don't know, already established with like family." Lola explained that weddings are an important part of her culture and considered a natural extension of womanhood in her family. Nicole, 24, African-American agreed: "She's in a wedding dress! I mean, possibly, I guess I selected the two pivotal feminine moments of a woman's life: baby, wedding dress. I never realized I was so traditional." See Figure 4.2 for a likeness of the image shown to research participants. Both Lola and Nicole expressed perspectives of many of the young women who participated in focus group discussions for the study reported in this book. Clearly, the wedding industry and mass mediated representations are successfully communicating a woman's wedding as one of her lifetime's crowning achievements. On the other hand, the endurance of "marriage culture" (McRobbie, 2009, p. 62) as made visible across popular culture may be offset by growth in single women's culture (Traister, 2016) and women's decreased reliance on a husband or male partner breadwinner. Even so, representations of the wedding dress may just continue to endure as a personification of femininity—at least, if women who participated in the study reported in this book have anything to say about it.

In addition to the wedding traditions, prom represents rite-of-passage culture, royalty, and the Hollywood red carpet rolled into one. The high school prom ritual across the United States has become a focal point for emphasizing femininity and breaking out of institutional norms with regard to dress. Annually, U.S. high school girls transform their bodies and display their feminine identities at the prom for dates and other girls. According to Condé Nast, producer of teen prom magazines, the prom represents an estimated $2.7 billion industry. Advertisers target girls with annual prom-themed women's fashion magazines, as well as *Your*

Figure 4.2.   A black and white magazine photograph of a bride wearing a white gown captured the fascination of women who participated in interviews for this book as they qualified it as *most feminine*. Source: Manuscripts and Archives Division, The New York Public Library. (1935–1945). Fashion, World of - Models - Gowns - Model in wedding dress.

Prom and *Teen Prom*. Teen girls take scores of pictures for an "immortal gaze," forever preserving images of their young bodies (Pompper & Crandall, 2014, p. 945) and savoring a ritual of "enjoyable femininity" (McRobbie, 2009, p. 3). Girls living in the U.S. South report significant degrees of female gender role stress due to pressures to conform to a New Southern Belle Code (Lynxwiler & Wilson, 1988). For example, high school girls negotiate their fashion preference for hypersexualized dresses with parents who favor more modest dresses, struggle against low-SES when negotiating about "financing the fantasy," and perform body work such as when African-American/Black girls strive to achieve beauty ideals of lightened skin and straightened hair (Pompper & Crandall, 2014, p. 946). The prom dress or gown "induces the body to strut about in small, restrained yet show-offy ways" (Brownmiller, 1984, p. 79), not unlike Southern "Beauty Walk" pageants (Lalik & Oliver, 2005), formal Jack and Jill chapter events, and other elite groups' invitation-only debutante cotillions. An influential and inspirational ritual, the red carpet phenomenon which has been part of the Academy of Motion Picture Arts and Sciences' Oscars event since 1961, has spilled over into reality for high school women. Media celebrity interviewers such as the late Joan Rivers and her daughter, Melissa Rivers, used their Red Carpet interview gigs to promote "a glorified prom dress with a couture tag" (Mlotek, 2016).

The prom experience enables some young women to express alternate identities to what is expected of them. In recent years, some teens have resisted heteronormative proms with gay proms and scaled-down events. During data collection for our prom study we found two high school girls hoping to inspire new trends, such as wearing pants under a skirt or hosting a prom in a barn with country boots, jeans, barbeque, and fries theme (Pompper & Crandall, 2014). Also, dressing in uniforms for school or work takes its toll on individuality, as explained Alonda, 22, who identifies as West Indian/Caribbean. She told members of her focus group session for the current study that expressing herself with clothing has been a challenge: "[A]t my school we had a dress code, and you weren't allowed to wear certain things. And then I would wear a uniform at work. So I couldn't really dress how I wanted to and I kind of lost out on like how to come up with my own identity." Little girls' and teen girls' first experiences with fashion often are very intense and sexualized (Gullette, 1997) and dressing up empowers them with an occasion to express alternate identities (Best, 2000). See Figure 4.3. Reluctance to show a thigh or reveal a midriff may be old-fashioned and prudish to some (Brownmiller, 1984), but to others, an immodest dress can be made over by replacing spaghetti straps with sleeves and by covering low backs (Church of Jesus Christ of Latter Day Saints, 2004).

Beyond weddings and proms, ritualistic representations of ideal femininity play out across mass media replicating traditional versions of femi-

Figure 4.3.   Little girls often learn about emphasized femininity through play—trying on makeup, high-heel shoes, feathered boas, and long necklaces. Copyright: tcsaba. Source: Csaba Toth/ Depositphotos.com.

ninity and establishing them as norms for millions of viewers, regularly. These images and messages stress one point: Women who deviate from the norm are subject to shaming. Popular culture products like the Miss America pageant—where the average weight of winners has decreased while their average height has increased (Rubenstein & Caballero, 2000)—are comparable to Indian beauty queens who are complimented and rewarded for their devotion to fitness and grooming (Parameswaran, 2004). Mediated images of these women set patterns for how to define femininity. For example, the world of child beauty pageants has taken reality television in the United States by storm and the public imagination, perhaps ever since six-year-old child beauty pageant competitor JonBenét Ramsey was found murdered in her home in 1996. Child beauty pageants offer "hyperbolic femininity" that sexualizes and fetishizes little girls who wear cupcake dresses, while producers demonize stage mothers who ply their daughters with candy for a sugar high and bully them to perform on stage, as displayed in the TLC reality television show, *Toddlers and Tiaras* (Dejmanee, 2015, p. 460). Whereas girls on the *Toddlers and Tiaras* show are empowered for exemplifying successful femininity, three typologies of bad motherhood are represented through the mom who is vicarious, usurping, and/or neglectful, women who are depicted as struggling to vicariously hold on to youthful, sexualized femininity but become a scapegoat for their own failed femininity (Dejmanee, 2015). Rather than critiquing hegemonic patriarchy which perpetuates emphasized femininity, the mother-daughter dyad is attacked with mother shaming providing the entertainment in these and other reality television programs.

Some traditions and rituals frame femininity in terms of lifecycle transitions, events that socialize girls and women into new female roles of wife and mother. At such times, feminine performances are almost exclusively female domains and emphasize women's interdependence: bachelorette parties and wedding and baby showers organized and attended by female family members and friends. A ritual offers a lens through which to examine enactments of social norms and moral sentiments, and rituals lend meaning in a culture by "linking the past to the present and the present to the future" (Kertzer, 1988, pp. 9–10). Turner (1995) held that rituals mark social processes defining an individual undergoing a status passage. In the context of this book, rhetorically examining femininity in terms of rituals and traditions deepens our understanding of what femininity means and how it is defined among diverse groups of women.

Considered woman's rituals, wedding (or bridal) and baby showers reinforce female gender membership and share many similarities across the United States in terms of gifts, decorations, food, games, photographs, laughter—with primacy of the bride or mother-to-be often seated at the center of the room (Cheal, 1989). These are female-bonding, community-building exercises with established structures and scripted activities, fully feminine events. Shower gifts are selected to help the recipient with her new role as caregiver to a husband or baby and include food preparation and housekeeping items or baby care products, supporting the recipient in her new female gender role. The bridal shower is rooted in the sixteenth or seventeenth century when a poor Dutch girl without a dowry was embraced by friends who sought to ensure her happiness by providing material goods so she could marry (Clark, 2000). Today, the bridal shower event enables friends and family to symbolize and enforce "social rules associated with the role of the bride" and they attend bridal showers even if they may not want to do so but follow through because they feel an obligation (Montemurro, 2002, p. 70). See Figure 4.4.

Another female gender role event undergirded by femininity is the baby shower. Baby shower guests prefer to know the baby's gender in advance of the shower so they may decorate the event and bring appropriately colored items of pink for girls and blue for boys (Brubaker, 2007). Love, the ethic of care, empathy, and sentimentality are central elements of femininity (Brownmiller, 2000), so women engage with wedding and baby showers to affirm their status as good women. Wedding and baby showers reinforce traditional emphasized femininity gender norms of women as caregivers of men and children. A study of lesbian couples' baby showers revealed that traditional emphasized femininity norms and

Figure 4.4.   Wedding and baby shower parties are highly feminized, female-bonding rituals in the United States. The bride-to-be often is gifted with home-making items, lacy wedding night lingerie, and sex toys in support of her new female gender role. New mothers receive baby clothes and accessories. Copyright: londondeposit. Source: Craig Robinson/ Depositphotos.com.

gender role dynamics persist with one partner not being invited or not being permitted to fill in the baby book (Padavic & Butterfield, 2011). As discussed in chapter 2, women who participated in interviews and focus groups for this book frequently placed images of pregnant women and women with babies on their *most feminine* list. Childcare remains synonymous with definitions of femininity.

Even cosmetic surgery has become a ritualized routine for women of all ages. A rhetorical analysis of cosmetic surgery-themed, mass-produced greeting cards suggested that cosmetic surgery has become a normalized outcome of feminine body management (Naugler, 2010) and part and parcel to emphasized femininity. Feminist scholars have explored this trend (e.g., Bordo, 1995; Davis, 1997) about ways a preponderance of women using plastic surgeons' services enables them to come closer to unrealistic beauty ideals via breast enhancement surgery, rhinoplasty, labiaplasty, vaginoplasty, and more, to reproduce specific standards of emphasized femininity. Cosmetic surgery marketers capitalize upon the procedures' promise of normalcy and belonging as a side effect of recapturing one's youth (Gilman, 1999). In similar ways, women are pressured into subscribing to a "kind of body panic" by adopting post-pregnancy regimens to get bikini ready by using any means possible, a trend which emphasizes mothering and beauty as femininity's most important facets (O'Brien Hallstein, 2011, p. 113). This newest form of fat- and body-shaming behavior aimed at women rhetorically invokes the before-and-after format used so successfully in women's beauty magazines and online—so that the before (pregnant) form is bad and the after (quickly back to slim) form is good (Dworkin & Wachs, 2009). This issue is addressed in greater depth in chapter 5 in terms of new working-momism and third-shift body work.

DISCUSSION

Driven by capitalist directives, the beauty, fashion, mass media, and advertising industries run on images that do not always adequately represent girls and women, but significantly impact them, nevertheless. Individually and combined, these social forces set standards for how we perceive and internalize what perfection and femininity *should be* and then sell it back to us across multiple inter-connected platforms. Women across age groups who participated in the study conducted for this book project spoke of femininity as it is experienced, femininity as it is enacted, and femininity as it is represented. Due to these multiple contexts as shaped by women's intersecting social identity dimensions, no one definition of femininity is sufficient. In fact, this key finding is precisely why the concept of a single, fixed and unified femininity is indefensible, findings that mirror Beynon's (2002) argument that mapping multiple masculinities (as in plural) offers a solid route to exploring such a complex concept. MacInnes (1998) recommended that gender scholars shift from thinking about how masculinity might be abolished or reformed in order to end patriarchy for a new era of a politics of equal rights. In tandem, we must press forward with thinking of femininities beyond the service of capitalism and subservience in order for girls and women to play an agentic role where equal rights are practiced and celebrated. Such a vision is far removed from Kosinski's (1965) metaphor of a painted bird to illustrate his point that women stripped of their femininity would reveal some *true femaleness*. I argue that plain or painted, girls and women must be permitted to embrace their femininities in agentic ways without having to resist dominant/idealized/hegemonic forces bent on keeping them at subordinate, second-class citizen status.

Consumerist and corporate interests which fuel popular culture offer false promises to girls and women and use some universal notion of normative emphasized femininity to do it, playing on women's anxieties and conflicts strategically put in place by hegemonic patriarchal systems that include the advertising industry. A defining feature of femininity—as supported by the fashion industry—is maintenance of a certain look, "insofar as women wear the sorts of things that a society deems appropriate for them" (Barnard, 2001, p. 121). Undeniably, only certain feminine ideals are reproduced by the fashion industry and its media. Building up girls and young women with glamour- and glitter-filled fantasies that too often succeed in violating their expectations perpetually sets girls and women up for letdowns. This sidetracks them from questioning and participating in the dismantling of patriarchy.

FIVE

Women's Femininity at Work

I think independence is feminine and women making money for themselves proves they're feminine. I just think it's a really attractive quality.
—Research participant, Kathy, 21, Caucasian/White, heterosexual

Women may experience the greatest amount of stress and conflict associated with expressing their femininity when negotiating the non-paid domestic-private sphere—with their paid work outside the home in the public sphere. Women who participated in focus groups and interviews for this book shared stories about what to wear and how to behave at work in order to be comfortable and competent while still being feminine (but not *too* feminine). They discussed in great detail stress/conflict associated with gender-ratio imbalances attached to specific career fields, and anxieties about their own perceptions of femininity and what is expected of women working in certain fields. Women also shared anxieties about challenges attached to work in fields to which they may aspire, but the jobs may require something they are perceived as not possessing. On a positive note, women like Kathy (as cited in the above epigraph) also defined *femininity* as something that goes far beyond women's appearance alone. She qualified her own definition of *femininity* in terms of self-sufficiency and independence.

Today, women hold a U.S. workforce majority (but not among top-level managers), in colleges account for 57 percent of undergraduate and 62 percent of graduate students—and women represent the majority of law and medical school graduates (Kreamer, 2011). The rapid growth of women in the paid workplace in the United States over the past several decades has been attributed to Congress's passage of the Equal Pay Act in 1963, the Civil Rights and Economic Opportunity Act in 1964, as well as a report of the President's Commission on the Status of Women. Yet, a

Federal Glass Ceiling Commission was established under Title II of the Civil Rights Act of 1991 and reported that women were advancing toward highest pay and other rewards above the glass ceiling at exceptionally slow rates due to negative stereotypes of women in organizations (U.S. Department of Labor, 1995). Women perceived to be lacking in managerial preparedness exacerbate glass ceiling effects (Woo, 2000). Moreover, women's second-class status is steeped in their gender role assignment to private sphere domestic duties, reproductive role, and child rearing—as women around the world perform nearly two and a half times more unpaid care work than men (Puri, 2016). Overall, replicated patriarchal and racist patterns and traditions enable gender inequality to persist.

This chapter examines issues about femininity as it plays out in these areas: 1) Inequitable and inhospitable gendered workplaces, 2) Female-gender division of labor in the public and private spheres, 3) Media workers' representations of women and femininity, 4) Occupational fields with gender imbalance and what it means for femininity, and 5) Discussion.

INEQUITABLE AND INHOSPITABLE GENDERED WORKPLACES

Women's second-class status in the paid workplace has been exposed across numerous occupational fields. Not only are U.S. women paid less than men at every educational level and in every job category in the United States (Coontz, 2013), but they encounter every form of glass architectural metaphor (ceiling, walls, cliff) (Barreto, Ryan, & Schmitt, 2008) in trying to climb to and sustain in upper-level management occupied predominantly by Caucasian/White males. Moreover, U.S. workplaces offering family-friendly benefits or flexibility are in the minority and working mothers are more likely to experience prejudice on the job than working fathers (Coontz, 2013). Finally, in the United States, a *CNN Money* report pegged the wage gap at women earning 76 to 79 cents for every $1 men make (Sahadi, 2016). Globally, the wage gap is larger for women with children and gender gaps in pay and work opportunities for women mean they can earn up to 75 percent less than men over their lifetime (U.N. Women, 2016). The National Women's Law Center estimates that women lose an average of $430,480 over the course of a forty-year career; with losses for Latinas and African-American/Black women more than double that amount (The lifetime, 2016). Popular culture celebrity Jennifer Lopez released a 2016 music video called "Ain't your mama" (Walter & Gottwald, 2016), personifying stress and conflict many women experience daily in conjunction with their femininity and others' perceptions of the female role. The video features a hyperfeminine singing-and-dancing Lopez wearing 1950s style fashion while scrubbing a black and white chessboard kitchen floor, typing on a manual typewriter in a *Mad Men*-esque 1960s office with a Don Draper–like character, and shouting out an open window in a *Network* (1976) "I'm as mad as hell, and not going to take this anymore!" manner. The video's message urging women to consider ways they should be respected for balancing non-paid housework with paid work outside the home resonates with women confused about female gender roles and femininity.

Women are held responsible for managing their body and their femininity at work. Organizations try to control how people relate to one another, as well as how employees' bodies perform. In particular, organizations are arenas of men's sexual dominance and systematic "corporate patriarchy" shapes institutions, buildings, and bodies (Wajcman, 1998, p. 53), as men are stereotyped as analytical, rational, and focused on work. By contrast, women are considered as representing the opposite of these traits. Interviewed for this book, Yifang, 52, Chinese-American, described how femininity and perceptions of it play a significant role in women's growth in a corporate workplace. Yifang explained how she defines femininity as an inner quality which guides outward appearance and behaviors:

> Well, I'm on a lot of boards. I observe how fellow board members conduct themselves. I think no matter what your body weight is, no matter how old you are, it's just how you carry yourself—whether people listen to you, pay attention to you, or take note of you. It's how you carry yourself and conduct yourself, what you say and what you do.

Even though Yifang defined femininity in terms of women's internal qualities, it's femininity as defined by exterior qualities that many organizations seek to regulate through policies and unspoken censure of dress, emotions, pregnancy, breast-feeding, menstruation, and child care. These are issues that affect more women than men.

Historically, women have been required to deny their essential femininity in order to be successful in the paid workplace (Kreamer, 2011). Acker (1990) resolved that women's bodies are perpetually "suspect, stigmatized, and used as grounds for control and exclusion" (p. 152), with organizations branding them as inappropriate for certain types of paid work. Although women adorn themselves by accenting features that make women's sexuality visible, some women in the paid workplace feel compelled to de-emphasize their femininity. The institution of motherhood, in particular, is considered a feminine domain, one especially challenging for women who work outside the home when they become pregnant and worry about how and when to notify a supervisor who might interpret their pregnancy to mean disloyalty or lack of commitment to the workplace and employer (Clair, Beatty, & Maclean, 2005). Since contemporary social values have driven some gender prejudice underground, covert discrimination against women may involve outcomes such as lesser pay and support, lack of acceptance by colleagues and work groups, limited career advancement, difficulty in finding a mentor, and isolation at work.

Women experience conflict and stress related to their femininity in conjunction with across-gender encounters at work. For example, women who fail at practicing feminine qualities of passivity and subservience may be relegated to lowest status in organizations (Collinson & Collinson, 1996)—while men who perpetuate masculine qualities of aggression and leadership gain high status (Martin, 2003). Men are more likely to sexually harass women at work (more so than the other way around, although this is *not* unheard of) since men have the most organizational power (Fitzgerald, Magley, Drasgow, & Waldo, 1999). Full-blown sexual harassment is when a boss threatens to have an employee fired from her/ his job or refuses to give her/him a promotion if s/he refuses to have sex with her/him. Some lesser-workplace-status female employees adapt to subordination by trading power for patronage—as when female coal miners acquiesce to male coworkers' sexual harassment because doing so tends to affirm their femininity and because they gain degrees of protection in hyper-masculine environments (Yount, 1991). I return to issues of gender imbalance in the workplace later in this chapter. Many women have adopted coping strategies for self-preservation and to keep their job. Because U.S. courts have ruled that sex-based harassment is unlawful, fear of litigation has inspired some organizations to create policies prohibiting even consensual sexual relations between coworkers.

Ideas about *feminine styles* of leadership and management popularized in the United States in the 1980s are linked to this book's goal of defining the femininity concept. Researchers have discovered positive perceptions of *femininity* in organizations, as reflected in coalition building, cooperation, and listening behaviors which play out in terms of affection, kindness, interpersonal sensitivity, and nurturance (e.g., Eagly & Mitchell, 2004). Also, feminine values have been considered democratic and participatory with binary dualisms of feminine/masculine translating to soft/ hard and emotion/reason when characterizing leadership and management styles according to gender. However, female gender role traps set up impossible gauntlets for women with management aspirations, enduring stereotypes men use to negatively categorize women. These include mother/Madonna, seductress/whore/sex object, pet, and iron maiden. Falling into the first three submissive female gender role traps means a woman is unsuitable for leadership, while the last does, too, but for different reasons. The iron maiden stereotype represents a threat to male masculinity. Women who challenge male dominance on the job may experience harassment in the form of control through punishments or withdrawal of rewards.

Benefits of androgyny associated with individuals occupying both qualities of femininity and masculinity has been considered among organizational researchers as an opportunity to achieve universal equity and respect in the workplace. As more women enter the workforce, roles and values have become less gender specific (Nelson & Burke, 2002). For example, the service-provision nature of both home help services and hospital environments enhance the value of femininity's caretaking role regardless of workers' gender (Westerberg, 2001). Overall, employees in many organizations still feel uncomfortable with androgyny because they are unsure how to relate with/to people whom they do not perceive to be clearly either feminine or masculine.

FEMALE-GENDER DIVISION OF LABOR IN THE PUBLIC AND PRIVATE SPHERES

Women confront two sets of demanding expectations regarding their female gender role and this contributes to stress/conflict which complicates how they engage (or not) with their femininity. Conflicting social norms of working a first shift outside the home for pay and a second shift at home for no pay complicate the concept of femininity and ways it plays out in women's lives. In a patriarchal society such as the United States, women's interests shaped by their femininity are subordinated to men's interests. Under Victorian influences in the early twentieth century, it was widely held that a Caucasian/White woman who worked for wages outside the home threatened social stability—since women's independence and intellectual interests could mean women might no longer be dependent upon men. Meanwhile, women of color and many women of lower socio-economic status have been earning a living outside the home for generations. Some women settle for careers they hope will enable them to manage career with home life, where they anticipate serving as primary homemaker and child caretaker (Corning, 2000). This means they may land in paid-work careers outside the home that fail to fully satisfy or fulfill them intellectually, setting women up for a lifetime of anxiety and depression (McBride, 1990).

Women who do find satisfaction in both public and private spheres may discover they are required to lead a *double life*, maneuvers which expend much emotional energy. It is this type of strain that made *The Mary Tyler Moore Show* so entertaining on 1970s television in the United States as the fictional character, Mary Richards, emphasized her femininity as a fashionable young *career girl* with an active home and private life. Fashion designer Isaac Mizrahi spoke of the program's cultural import in the feature film, *Unzipped* (1995): "Basically, I think, between her and Jackie Kennedy, they shaped this country. . . . It's what shaped Americans' whole taste level" (Keeve, 1995). Postfeminist narratives decades later, however, evade public-private sphere tensions by representing joys of emphasized femininity rather than authentically characterizing women's lives as "a state of chronic temporal crisis" earmarked by overwork, rushing, harassment, and attention to their biological clock (Tasker & Negra, 2007, p. 10). Instead, many postfeminist narratives focus on women's sexual and economic freedom, as addressed in chapter 4.

During an interview for the study reported in this book, Jenni, 42, Korean-American, explained how she carefully negotiates her work in the public and private spheres:

> As a working mom, I think there is a sense of pride and there is this side of me that appreciates that I can be *all* those things. The fact that I'm able to juggle that and have this feminine quality—being ladylike the way I approach things, I think this is an important quality to have.

Women like Jenni defined femininity in terms of ability to manage their own lives and those of family members—and to do it flawlessly and seamlessly. So, again, the notion of striving for perfection raises a cautionary flag, a signifier that women may expend a good deal of emotional energy and experience high degrees of stress/conflict that their male counterparts do not. This is simply because women are socialized to female gender roles and encouraged to emphasize their femininity. During a different interview for this book, Debbie, 51, Caucasian/White, highlighted challenges associated with managing multiple female gender roles which leaves little time for enjoying one's femininity. Not unlike Jenni, who talked about managing tasks and pride associated with femininity, Debbie said she worried about losing her feminine identity in the process of negotiating her various roles:

> A woman needs to be thought of as a woman, not just Mom or what they may do at work. They want people to know they are a woman. . . . [I]t's important for your self-image. . . . I want people to look at me and see that I like being a woman. I think you are a strong person when you are a woman. You have to put up with men!

Work-home life conflict, as a constant stressor in women's lives, is a reality for many women who experience a complicated sense of femininity in both spheres. In the following sections, I closely examine femininity in a home-life context, femininity in a work-life context, and then a new trend called *the third shift*.

Working in the domestic private sphere, at home

The private sphere of home is where mothers raise their children and women serve as caregivers for their partners or husbands—and sometimes parents and in-laws. In the early 1960s, most Americans considered gender equality impossible or even undesirable (Coontz, 2013). Today, mothers still maintain primary responsibility for childcare, despite educational opportunities designed to level the economic and occupational playing fields for women and men in the wake of second-wave feminism. Femininity's links with caregiving and kindness are amplified in the private sphere. See Figure 5.1. This reality can complicate women's paid-work lives in the public sphere when they arrive late or leave early to tend to their children—and contribute significantly to their experiences of stress and conflict.

From a young age, women are socialized into female gender roles which are equated with the femininity concept. Girls learn about female gender roles by helping with household chores. In the West, motherhood is understood as a great responsibility but offers little by way of autonomy or flexibility, a negative condition experienced by women who also choose to build a paid career outside the home. While examining magazine images selected to stimulate women's discussion about perceptions of femininity for this book, Cathy, 53, Caucasian/White, chose a black and white 1960s *Redbook* image of a young woman wearing a housedress and folding clothes out of a dryer and included it on her *most feminine* list: "That's an image of a nurturing mother and wife and that, to me, is something that portrays femininity . . . that type of a feeling. Different from a man—not abrasive, not hard or stern—but more soft and subtle. Caring. I think feminine is synonymous with nurturing." Cathy is a mother of two young women, and explained that she still launders her college daughter's clothes, "It's my job. I like doing it," she said.

Comforts and pleasures of housekeeping and childrearing associated with female gender roles are perceived by some as a strategy for avoiding full-time work—while others who want to successfully manage non-paid work at home with a paying career outside the home feel conflicted and anxious about *trying to do it all*. Femininity can offer a "welcome retreat from the demands of ambition" (Brownmiller, 1984, p. 221) for some women and represent a response to "labor-market discrimination against women" (Connell, 1987, p. 187) for others. Women in the United States and other parts of the world also are expected to provide care for aging parents and in-laws. Called the *sandwich generation* because midlife-aged women are presumed to be primarily responsible for childcare as well as eldercare, stressors for them are exceptional if they also have paid work outside the home (Pompper, 2011). Regardless of one's standpoint, the potential for conflict and stress is omnipresent in women's lives.

Feminist writers are challenged to help women navigate stress and conflict associated with traditional female gender roles to which women are socialized. Young women, in particular, are anxious that they cannot take joy in family and fashion—and still maintain feminist sensibilities (Baumgardner & Richards, 2004). Some scholars have suggested that conventional femininity has the potential to disempower and marginalize women—while masculinity limits men's engagement with family life and confines them to labor outside the home (Nelson & Burke, 2002).

Figure 5.1.   Women perform much more of unpaid labor than their domestic partners. Outcomes include negative quality of life for women who choose to pursue careers outside the home and strive for perfection in both public and private spheres. Copyright: fotoksa. Source: Оксана Гильман/ Depositpho-tos.com.

Working in the public sphere, the paid-work environment

Sometimes, emphasized femininity and paid work co-exist like oil and vinegar. Or, back in 1928, a sewing metaphor was used by a *Woman's Journal* writer to describe the working woman as a "reversible wife" who was "pale pink clinging semi-transparent on one side (for evenings and Sundays) and sensible blue serge on the other for weekdays, nine to five" (Behling, 2001, p. 164). While motherhood persists today as a widely revered institution, women who are mothers receive little support in the United States as compared to many other parts of the world where employers sponsor workplace day-care centers and generous maternity leave (DeMarneffe, 2004). Women in the United States tend to get pregnant in their late twenties or early thirties, just after the entry-level stage in their career (Kreamer, 2011) and take an "off-ramp" to exit their career to have and raise their children and later take an "on ramp" return to work only to find that their decision to nurture a family has negatively affected salary and career growth opportunities (Hewlett, 2007).

Meanwhile, older women worry that they could be terminated or laid off because they are considered too old, *un*feminine, or too expensive due to a higher salary related to seniority and healthcare costs. Among college student focus group participants, Gertrude, 19, Caucasian/White, explained how her grandmother emphasizes her femininity at work to offset negative stereotypes that dwell there:

> [M]y grandma has been married for about fifty years now, and she still dyes her hair. . . . [S]he's still working. She is a real estate agent, and I think she feels she needs to uphold a certain appearance in order to still be in the workforce, being as old as she is. Like, I think she still needs to kind of put on that persona that, "Even though I'm seventy-five, I still work as hard as the forty-year-old or thirty-year-old." There are reasons why older generations have to still keep up a positive body image.

Among older women who participated in interviews for the study reported in this book, Amanda, 61, African-American/Black, explained why she still spends time enhancing her feminine appearance as a strategy for achieving her career goals:

> It might be sad, but true. People's impressions are shaped by their first visual impression. That might not be fair for people who look a certain way and are extremely brilliant. Because of that fact, I figure, I'm going to work with this body. . . . I like wearing makeup. I still like putting on a pretty face to look good or to enhance my looks. I spend the time every four weeks to get my hair dyed and fried and shaped. I buy clothes and I try to enhance how I look with colors and a coordinated palate. I still try to look nice to be attractive, I suppose, to the opposite sex—because I don't want to turn off the opposite sex. Sometimes I think that just looking good creates an aura that people want to talk to you or they want to know you. Who knows, it could be my next client.

It's important for the workplace, important for your own self-esteem —
if your desire is to remain attractive.

Undeniably, concerns about aging in the workplace add yet another psychological stressor to women's lives. Women like Amanda and Gertrude's grandmother feel compelled to continue emphasizing their femininity so that they will be accepted as valuable employees.

In the workplace, women seem stuck between a rock and a hard place when it comes to femininity. Those who are playful and cutesy are doomed to fail. Moreover, a large-breasted "ultra-feminine look" (Tavris, 1992, p. 31) is inconsistent with a professional business culture. Paradoxically, women perceived as too hard, who act tough, and swear are damned, too. In male-dominated management fields, women traditionally have experienced a need to prove they are *more effective* than men in order to secure and keep their job. In the inhospitable executive suite, women feel conflicted as to whether they should enact their feminine characteristics or adopt some masculine ones since executives stereotypically are defined by masculinity. In sum, women must be better than men and also better than the stereotypical view of women. These dynamics are rife with conflict. To illustrate the extremes women experience, partnership status in an accounting firm was denied to a woman named Ann Hopkins because she was considered "macho, harsh, and aggressive" and an attorney named Brenda Taylor was fired for being "too feminine" (Tavris, 1992, pp. 21–22). Having a feminine tone of voice and speaking style also negatively reflects on women in organizations. Men tend to establish dominance in conversation while women who speak clearly are ignored even when they repeat themselves — often hearing their ideas later articulated by a man who receives accolades in the same meeting (Pompper, 2011). Interrupting, over-talking, and *mansplaining* are socialized male speech dominance behaviors which overpower and outrank feminine speaking behaviors (Solnit, 2015).

During our interview for this book, Carla, 50, Caucasian/White, talked about the concept of femininity in her male-dominated workplace: "You don't really *focus* on being feminine. You hold on to your womanly traits because sometimes they can help you out — work through a situation. But I don't go out of my way to *be* feminine. You've got to use what God gave you, right? No matter what it is." Kathleen, 54, Caucasian/White, spoke in a focus group meeting about her identical twin sister who works as a mechanical engineer: "She's working with the EPA in a man's world, doing a man's job. Yet she's never sacrificed, hidden, or exploited her femininity." It is doubtful that Carla's and Kathleen's concerns about effects their femininity may have on their career occur to such an extent among men as they consider effects of their masculinity.

Some female gender role socialization processes tend to work against women who pursue a career outside the home. For example, women are socialized to "carry an extra burden of emotional labor" which stimulates crying at work when they are frustrated, stressed, and criticized (Elsbach, 2011). Rather than scrutinize systemic organizational practices at the root of sex discrimination and other negative outcomes, organizations are too quick to blame women for issues associated with their femininity—such as deeming women weak if they cry at work. Findings of Kreamer's (2011) emotion-in-the-workplace survey suggested that 41 percent of women (especially *young* women) and only 9 percent men reported crying at work during the previous year. Researchers have found anatomical differences between women's and men's tear ducts, with women crying more visibly and with a larger volume of tears (Bylsma, Croon, Vingerhoets, & Rottenberg, 2011). Paradoxically, female emotions are *expected* at home, but *not* at work outside the home (Thorne, 1982). Many girls are taught to display feminine emotions from a young age. They learn passive habits such as taking turns and not interrupting or cursing. These processes follow girls when they go to school where they find that teachers reinforce the behaviors while boys are encouraged to adopt agentic ways (Chemaly, 2015). In the end, even women who are qualified and successfully find some way to navigate conflicting or ambiguous expectations about female gender and femininity cannot expect to be treated on equal footing with men at work.

A cottage industry of self-help books and websites has thrived since the 1980s to help women cope with conflicts and stresses associated with navigating their femininity and/or others' perceptions of it. Such resources end up blaming the victim, skewering women for paradoxes inherent within inflexible ideals, double standards, and systemic, infrastructural discrimination against women which has persisted since U.S. civil rights movements of the 1960s. Friedan's (1963) international best seller, *The Feminine Mystique*, has been widely credited with empowering women to resist patriarchy and to find self-gratification beyond housework. More than fifty years later, however, I remain convinced that as a society, we have failed to fully embrace or even appreciate much of her message. I concur with Coontz (2013) when she wrote in the *New York Times*: "The gender revolution is not in a stall. It has hit a wall" (p. SR-1). Self-help books prey upon "women's alleged inner flaws and psychological deficiencies" (Tavris, 1992, p. 23) that make them feel like failures most of the time. Diet books are particularly harmful, driving a feminine ideal for thinness and offering advice that runs counter to a woman's biological composition. Fashion self-help media send women mixed messages about how they should dress and carry themselves in the workplace or emphasize their femininity.

Business suits that feature male-tailored jackets with miniskirts that reveal women's legs serve as painful reminders of the paradox under which women's femininity exists. During focus groups and interviews with women, lively discussions ensued about whether women should wear suits at all and whether they should be some pastel color or navy blue, gray, or black. A *Ladies Home Journal* 1990s image used to stimulate discussion featured an African-American woman wearing her hair in dreadlocks and a burgundy-colored suit with trousers. Women who participated in conversations about femininity for this book unanimously placed the image on their *least feminine* list. Perhaps one explanation for why the image of a women of color was relegated to *least feminine* could be because women who participated in the study were reacting to fewer representations of women of color in magazines prior to the late 1960s. Historically, magazines have preferred "light-skinned" African-American/Black and "respectably demure" Asian-American models—if non-Caucasian/White models are used at all. As pointed out in chapter 4, any business attire image may have violated research participants' expectancies since readers are socialized to expect "norms of dominant white glamorous and high maintenance femininity" (McRobbie, 2009, p. 71) among magazine images. In the 1980s, men's dress styles were appropriated for women's fashion and were considered *power dressing* for women who sought to compete in male-dominated workplaces (Pham, 2012). Accoutrements such as pearls, ruffles, and lace made such styles appear more feminine, a phenomenon Felshin (1974a) dubbed *feminine apologetic*.

New working-momism, the third shift, and celebrity culture's impact on defining femininity

In the private, domestic sphere, *new momism* suggests that motherhood and physical beauty are the epitome of women's femininity. Thus, it is women's third-shift responsibility to eradicate postpartum body acknowledgement of maternity as quickly as possible so they again may emphasize their femininity in public. New momism has added a third shift to the sum of women's first-shift paid work outside the home, second-shift unpaid work inside the home—and now additional unpaid *body work* required to appear appropriately feminine as soon as possible after giving birth. This third shift of body work is required for new mothers to quickly get back in shape and return to their slender, bikini-ready selves (if, indeed, this ever existed) and this imperative is amplified across popular culture and media products. New momism is a tough taskmaster, designed to address women's post-second wave crisis in femininity (O'Brien Hallstein, 2011).

Popular culture in the United States is rampant with examples of celebrities who engage with body work to return their bodies to pre-pregnancy state. Now iconic in this role are members of the Kardashian family as represented on the *Keeping Up With the Kardashians* reality television program. In a focus group discussion conducted for this book, Andrea, 19, Caucasian/White, referenced the Kardashian family when sharing her thoughts on ways magazines distort femininity and realities of a woman's postpartum body:

> The Kardashians are just airbrushed queens in magazines. I feel like every one of them who has a kid, like, three months later they're on a cover. Actually, Kourtney Kardashian, going back to the show after she had that baby . . . an insane amount of time later they had her on the cover of a magazine like, "Bounce Back from Baby," in this tiny little skinny thing. And, she actually came out with a statement that said, "That was before I got pregnant. Like, that picture isn't from now. Don't think I can bounce back from having a baby in, like, four weeks." What? Women are supposed to feel like a failure because you didn't bounce back in four weeks, which is completely just ridiculous!

These popular culture images keep women in a constant state of stress and conflict in feeling that no matter what they do, they cannot achieve ideal femininity and attain perfection. As part of another focus group discussion, twenty-one-year-old Mariana, Dominican, expressed a body image fear that she will be unable to measure up to the mediated images:

> [T]he epitome of being a woman, to a certain extent, is being able to have children, but . . . a lot of the women in my family, once they have babies, they *never* get that figure back. Like at *all*. And it's weird, you know, you see people bounce back and people like workout and whatever. But the women in *my* family *balloon*. Like my sister went from, I wore her prom dress when I was twelve. . . . [A]fter her first baby she went from like a size 2 to like 14.

In continued discussion with the other college women, Mariana confessed that she may choose not to have children: "Why risk getting all fat and not being able to get skinny again after having a baby?" A shift toward a neo-traditional family may be in effect with this trend. The private domestic sphere offers reinstallation of and justification for stereotypical gender division of household labor with women being primarily responsible for housekeeping and childrearing. Economic realities in the United States, however, often require that women must contribute to household breadwinning, too.

Pressures celebrity mothers such as the Kardashians, fashion models, and actresses experience to return to their pre-pregnancy figure before going back to work now spills over into the non-celebrity world through women's magazines, social media, websites, television, and feature films—complete with body shaming bullying backlash experienced by women who fail to lose weight quickly. Often, this is passed off as entertainment. Women who successfully complete this third-shift responsibility are rewarded with being labeled a "feminine, sexy mom," or a MILF (O'Brien Hallstein, 2011, p. 124). According to the online Urban Dictionary, the MILF [Mother I'd Like (to) Fuck] acronym represents a woman whom "a male individual sees as physically attractive enough to want to have sexual intercourse with them. . . . The ones in good shape have worked at regaining control over their vaginas" (J. R. J., 2016). Some women also strive to achieve third-shift goals for sexy femininity after childbirth through internal and external plastic surgery.

Occupations historically unavailable to women

Further emphasizing a public-private divide are occupational fields historically closed off to women due to their female identity and/or femininity. Despite gender-equality progress on certain legal, educational, and social fronts, some women remain barred from specific careers and this negatively impacts their ability to feel at ease with their femininity. In particular, many organized religions forbid women from becoming the premier spiritual leader, but women may attain other leadership positions in some organized religions. Women clergy are prohibited at the top-most positions among Roman Catholicism, Orthodox Christianity, Orthodox Judaism, Mormonism, Buddhism, and Evangelical Christianity (Mason, 2007). Also, STEM fields (sciences, technology, engineering, mathematics) have been notoriously unwelcoming to women and have been outed with negative publicity campaigns and positive efforts to boost numbers of women in these occupations in recent years. Until 2013, there were no female astronauts in the U.S. Sally Ride, PhD in Physics, made history when she climbed aboard the Space Shuttle Challenger. Yet, *Glamour* magazine, which targets a young female readership, framed its story with questions about Ride's bathroom habits in space, makeup, and underwear—and was asked if she cried in the simulator during malfunctions when training for the mission (Bobst, 2016). During a focus group discussion among college women for this book, Tanya, 20, Caucasian/White, a STEM (sciences, technology, engineering, mathematics) major, was aware that her gender could be a factor in holding her back in her chosen career: "I'm going into a very male-dominated field and there is so much more pressure to be more professional and almost masculine. So, I will still take on some of that so I can be successful in my career—but at the same time, I want to be who I am." For young women like Tanya, femininity is fraught with landmines and it is a matter of survival in certain public spheres like industries where the dominant employees are men.

Moreover, media framing of femininity as weakness, with limited ability, and unacceptability persists in shaping public attitudes; all contributors to girls' and women's second-class status in all spheres.

MEDIA WORKERS' REPRESENTATIONS
OF WOMEN AND FEMININITIES

Without doubt, journalism shapes our perceptions of women and their femininities—as evidenced by newsroom composition, what women are permitted to write about, and ways girls and women are represented. Collectively, the hard news style, preponderance of male news workers, and stereotypical framing of news involving women makes for news media products that offer limited representations of women. The journalistic paradigms of detachment and objectivity traditionally are associated with a masculine narrative style, one that negatively impacts newsworkers' ability to characterize femininity fairly. Numerous feminist media scholars have questioned whether storytelling in a masculine style truly can capture the female experience (e.g., Creedon, 1993) or adequately explore issues and topics associated with femininity.

Gendered production of news means that even when women journalists write stories, narratives conform to patriarchal ideas about femininity (Heilbrun, 1988) when editors are male and news managements are male-driven. News reportage long has been guilty of gender bias favoring men while representing women primarily in ways that emphasize femininity. Male dominance among global media outlets has been well documented for decades, with women serving as eye candy illustrating their femininity in images while males dominated copy (LaFrance, 2016). News media's focus on male power brokers means representation of women is low (Shor, van de Rijt, Miltsov, Kulkarni, & Skiena, 2015), with only 24 percent of international news featuring women as news subjects (Global Media Monitoring Project, 2010).

Across media fields, narrow ideas about women and their femininities persist. Among earliest documentation of women working at newspapers are records of women relegated to the women's or society page, where *girl reporters* were encouraged to apply their femininity by writing about women and babies. Wrote female reporter, India McIntosh, several decades ago, "The city desk, with all its democratic leanings, is wary of the woman reporter's emotional equipment and seldom dares to put these traditionally unstable factors to a test which might smear up the front page" (Herzberg, 1947, p. 29). Also, among both female and male novelists, it has been widely accepted that writing about sentiment is a feminine literary trait. So entrenched are beliefs that femininity and sentimentality are synonymous—and that women can write only about family or feelings—that a content analysis of 10,287 reviews from the Sunday Book Review of the *New York Times* published since 2000 confirmed that reviews were three-to-four times more likely to use words such as *husband*, *marriage*, and *mother* when describing books written by women. It is as if we are being "jettisoned back into a linguistic world that more nearly resembles our Victorian ancestors" (Piper & Jeanso, 2016).

In literature, wider gender representation does not necessarily equal less gender discrimination. Indeed, since the early 2000s, the U.S. culture industry (especially film) has become a space of protest with demands for better film roles for women beyond those typifying traditional femininity and respectful dialog with actresses on the Oscars red carpet beyond their clothes and families, as noted by the #AskHerMore hashtag Twitter campaign. Also, editors at two femininity-defining national girls' magazine organizations defended their representations of *real girls'* femininity. Rather than accepting full responsibility for defining femininity according to unrealistic body sizes for inauthentic images of women and girls, editors (several of whom were women) blamed inter-departmental conflicts, external industry forces, standards, and readers' expectations for fantasy over realism, resolving that "criticisms of media portrayals of femininity become struggles at the institutional level of cultural production" (Milkie, 2002, p. 856).

The journalism industry also plays a part in female gender role socialization dynamics when news narratives advance the idea that motherhood is a sacred institution—and is quick to shame women who display behaviors considered deviant. The ideal mother and wife is promoted among news narratives (Ruddick, 1995) and newsworkers routinely judge women. Research findings suggest that news narratives routinely offer moral lessons about mothers who stray from perfection by exhibiting inappropriate sexual or violent behaviors—especially those who kill their own children (Barnett, 2013). Many working mothers already feel guilty for leaving their children in daycare before reporting to work. In particular, mothers who self-identify as women of color, are unmarried, poor, or lesbians fall under greater scrutiny to follow some Caucasian/White heteronormative norm (Kinser, 2010) and routinely find themselves victims of *mother-blaming* by the media when their mothering skills are called into question (O'Reilly, 2010). News accounts of bad mothering routinely shame women.

The concept of *career girl* offers a powerful context for explaining how negative perceptions about women and their femininities endure in news products. *Career girl* dates back to the 1930s and grew in popularity during World War II when many women joined the paid workforce in the United States. By the 1960s, access to higher education and introduction of the birth control pill inspired young women to pursue white-collar jobs in unprecedented numbers (Johnson, 2011). Perhaps as a patriarchal protectionist response and/or outright racist rejoinder to civil rights and black militant speech, news media panic rhetoric of the 1960s warned mobile young Caucasian/White women to be safe whilst enjoying their new freedoms away from home in big cities. A series of bloody murders of young women during 1963–1964 were labeled by the New York *Daily News* as *Career Girl Murders*. One victim was the middle-class, Caucasian/White, twenty-one-year-old daughter of a television and advertising producer who later wrote a book, *Career Girl, Watch Your Step*, and cautioned about city living: "[N]ever grow to feel safe in it. Feel threatened. You *are* threatened. You are *never* safe" (Wylie, 1964, pp. 91–92, italics in original). Findings of Johnson's (2011) rhetorical analysis of the event suggested journalists' raced coverage, blaming of female victims for transgressing boundaries of traditional femininity, women's complicity in embodying provocative sexuality and femininity, backlash against liberal reforms associated with the civil rights movement, and authorities' wrongful blame of an African-American man.

OCCUPATIONAL FIELDS WITH GENDER IMBALANCE AND WHAT IT MEANS FOR FEMININITY

The ways women define femininity for themselves may not always correspond with others' definitions of femininity—and sometimes the gaps are made particularly salient in occupational fields where gender is not equitably distributed. In some careers, no doubt, women have rejected stereotypical female gender roles and enjoyed the freedom to choose their professional work lives without conflict between self-perception and others' expectations. As addressed above, increasing awareness of gender imbalance among STEM fields tends to be attracting women who are developing their own strategies for success.

Nevertheless, being comfortable with one's own femininity is not easy for women working in male-dominated fields. Among psychology research, findings suggest that women placed in jobs considered atypical for women experience increased stress levels linked to incongruity between assessment of self and others' perceptions of job performance. Women's choice of an occupation that is inconsistent with what society norms deem appropriate for women has had a significant relationship to levels of stress/conflict women experience (Luhaorg & Zivian, 1995). Mirroring men's masculine behaviors tends to challenge women's sense of femininity, placing them on shifting sands and possibly causing negative psychological effects (Marshall, 1984). Also, organizational socialization to conform may interfere with women's career development and inhibit their maximum potential-reaching ability (Metcalfe, 1989). Overall, a woman's internal psychological frictions may cause her to experience gender role stress/conflict with or without external pressures (Baucom, 1980).

Beyond individual psychological conflicts women may experience working in fields typically considered to be masculine, the actual occupations themselves have suffered diminished respectability when majority gender concentrations shift from predominantly male to predominantly female. When this happens, the particular field is said to have become *feminized*. In conjunction with feminization trends, fields of teaching, library science, psychology, and public relations have suffered a credibility problem with side effects of lower pay and status for women employed in those arenas (Grunig, Toth, & Hon, 2001). Feminization trends await many professions as more women join the public sphere (Sprowl, 1993). On the positive side, women's movement into stereotypically masculine career tracks has the potential to raise women's social status (Cejka & Eagly, 1999).

Indeed, femininity is one of those concepts which, when scrutinized, reveals the extent of power relations evident among gendered division of labor. Consequently, any definition of femininity must account for context and structure which lend meaning to ways the concept is used and understood.

DISCUSSION

Arenas where femininity and stress/conflict effect women's experience with pronounced consistency are home in the unpaid domestic-private sphere and outside the home amidst the paid work public sphere. Pretty much everywhere, right? Undeniably, women's femininities (and others' perceptions of them) are *at work* wherever women are present—and these dynamics persist whether or not women are shaping the definition of femininity for themselves. This chapter addressed inequitable and inhospitable gendered workplaces, female-gender division of labor in the public and private spheres, media workers' representations of femininity, and implications of gender imbalance among occupational fields.

Enacting masculine behaviors such as assertiveness and independence in the home, as well as the office or the shop floor, can prove challenging for women to negotiate with the emphasized femininity norms they have been socialized into since birth. What is more, the seeming paradox of women who enact both femininity and masculinity may be viewed as deviant or inappropriate by supervisors, co-workers, and direct reports. Traditional feminine stereotypes set up a paradox and foster conflict and stress for women because the widely held view is that private-public modes for women should be mutually exclusive—and that women should be able to do it all. Women push themselves to be perfect in every way, too. Yet, for women *in* or aspiring *to* management levels in the paid-work world, qualities and behaviors typically associated with masculinities in management roles may prove necessary or desirable for women. Several women who participated in interviews and focus group discussions for this book defined femininity in terms of self-sufficiency, as Kathy explained at the outset of this chapter. To succeed in being independent women, *femininity* must accommodate a wide variety of contexts and differences.

Any definition of *femininity* must be flexible enough to embrace across-gender behaviors and perspectives—and to accommodate the myriad social identity dimensions of women inhabiting their femininities. Gender-ratio qualifiers often are used to assess whether or not someone is *feminine enough* or *masculine enough* to succeed in a given field dominated by women or men regardless of the job's tasks. So scrutinizing whether or not people's beliefs about career fields and people occupying them are accurate is a necessary pursuit for gaining deeper understanding about how femininity, rhetorically, is made to mean.

Finally, examining how media promote certain limited frameworks shaping femininity provides insights into how media exposure constitutes a central factor influencing ways femininity is defined. When girls' and women's magazines advance predominantly idealized images of emphasized femininity, when book reviewers promote limited ideas about femininity in terms of stories women write, and when newspapers perpetuate fears about how femininity equals vulnerability requiring men's protection, women's own sense of femininity is incomplete and their educational and vocational aspirations are restricted.

SIX

Women at Play

Sports and Femininity

Like, I would never call an athlete a *girlie-girl*. Even if she was gorgeous
and cared a lot about her appearance. Someone who that's all they are
is what I consider a *girlie-girl*. They're usually pretty and they care a lot
about how they look and they put a lot of effort into themselves and
know a lot about fashion.
—Research participant, Amy, 21, Caucasian/White

Sport offers a complex setting for examining ways *femininity* is defined
and provides a window on social norms for femininity in a world dominated by masculinity. In particular, this chapter examines stress and conflict women suffer as a result of shortcomings and double standards associated with feminine/masculine binary dualism. Because sport is perceived as men's natural domain, the contrast of emphasized femininity
with realities of women athletes and hobbyists who sweat, develop muscles, play competitively, and express anger tends to be too great for some
spectators and journalists. Female athletes themselves experience difficulty in trying to reconcile what they have been taught about femininity
with what they have come to (or aspire to) embody as an athlete. Mediated representations of women who have climbed to the top of their game
as professional athletes offer up female forms considered deviant by
many, raising concerns about not only gender discrimination in the
world of sport which undergirds sex-testing trends, but deeply-en-
grained ethnic-, sexual orientation-, and class-based social biases, as well.
Historically, exclusion of women from certain sports has been justified by
perceptions that women have a biologically inferior body as compared to
men—and women who play masculine sports are deemed *un*feminine
(Trolan, 2013). During slavery, women of color were abused for their

physical labor and considered *un*feminine as compared to Caucasian/
White women. Also, boys and men equated with femininity in the sports
arena are stigmatized as weak and lacking in courage; often called *sissy*
(Kaskan & Ho, 2014) or *pussy* (Pompper, Soto, & Piel, 2007; Pompper,
2010).

Women who participated in interviews and focus groups for this book
project concurred that thinking about femininity in terms of a continuum
serves as a good first step to changing perceptions of what a full range of
femininities looks like. Accenting human difference according to *femininity or masculinity* is a firmly established norm around the world. Over
time, this dichotomy has proven useful for dividing labor according to
biological sex, as discussed in chapter 5. An aesthetic of Caucasian/White
femininity dictates that women must be fragile without significant muscular strength. From a feminist perspective, keeping women physically
weak means they offer little resistance during physical abuse at the hands
of men (Bartky, 2010). Albeit too infrequently, space opens for conversations about female athletes who demonstrate physical and mental ability
in zones typically dominated by men. This inspires discussion about the
epic failure of the socially constructed, heteronormative feminine/mascu-
line dichotomy. Sport is just one arena wherein women's biological difference (from men) may be minimized, and their socially inscribed subordinate position and dependency on men eliminated.

Some sports are perceived as producing the ideal feminine body (even
for females otherwise considered "ordinary")—while others are perceived as stigmatizing women with a masculine, muscular body, a signifier of deviance. Female athletes' performance and achievements in
individual athletic activities appear to conflict least with social definitions
of femininity. It is participation in *team* sports characterized by masculine
rituals that provoke the greatest amounts of negative social commentary
about female athletes who are said to eschew emphasized femininity
norms. This belief undergirds *sport typing*, which suggests that women
who play *feminine sports* (e.g., figure skating, swimming) are judged more
for their beauty and grace, but women who play *masculine sports* (e.g.,
basketball, soccer) are labeled by media as *lesbians, mannish, Amazons,
grotesque,* and *unnatural*. Sports which amplify emphasized femininity
ideals are popularly embraced and rewards are showered upon female
athletes who pursue them with advertising contracts and magazine covers designed to capitalize on feminine bodies well displayed. Olympic
Game events which bring together the world's very best athletes even
have resorted to sex-testing to allay fears about the *true identity* of female
athletes whose performance achievements mirror or exceed those of men.
Many people simply are in disbelief when female athletes outcompete
male athletes. It is as if medical science serves as a definitive tool for
keeping women at second-class status.

These issues are covered in greater detail throughout this chapter: 1) Female athletics before and after Title IX, 2) Sports, femininity, and gender role stress/conflict (GRS/C), 3) Sports industry and media representations of female athletes, 4) The making of tomboys and female celebrity athletes, and 5) Discussion.

FEMALE ATHLETICS BEFORE AND AFTER TITLE IX

Overall resistance to girls and women playing sports involving aggression, competition, physicality, and skill is linked to Victorian America's gender ideology about femininity and womanliness as being the opposite of masculinity and manliness. Differentiating female athletes and their gender roles—from male athletes and theirs—reveals the power of stereotypes and deeply entrenched discriminations against women which position them as second-class citizens. No gendered differences were found in a study designed to gauge perceptions of benefits associated with sport participation—but men may be more likely to follow society's definitions for femininity and masculinity when stereotyping sports (Kelinske, Mayer, & Chen, 2001). While some male athletes have been negatively stereotyped as *big and dumb*, they still are revered as talented men who conform to traditional masculine norms. However, a woman's athleticism can negate her essential womanliness and brand her as an outcast or undesirable anomaly simply because her muscular physical appearance, natural talents, or interests do not comfortably fit with emphasized femininity ideals. Indeed, late nineteenth-century attitudes toward girls' and women's involvement with sports reinforced norms about femininity and females' place in society for decades to come.

Athletics and fears about sex and pregnancy

During the early twentieth century, however, women began actively challenging gender binary dualisms in sports, politics, and paid work. By the 1930s, a rhetoric of female sexual inversion stigmatized girls and women who played sports as not-quite female if they had forsaken emphasized femininity through appearance, submissiveness, or domesticity in order to join the athletic playing fields considered men's domain. Critics of females playing sports worried that intensified levels of physical activity and emotional excitement would heighten women's sexual desires, not just for men. Some journalists of the late 1920s through early 1930s period went so far as to characterize muscular female athletes as "unattractive, failed heterosexuals" and used the slur *muscle moll* to describe female athletes (Cahn, 2010). Earlier, the negative term, *moll*, had been attached to gangsters' girlfriends and prostitutes, both groups signifying deviance from emphasized femininity norms.

Combined fears that sportswomen's inability to attract a man and warnings that sports activity could damage female reproductive capacity potentially threatened the larger social order in the United States. Among high school and college physical education curricula from 1900 to 1960, warnings about menstrual dysfunction and threats of sterility and birth defects suggested high degrees of protectionism for girls and the sanctity of heteronormativity. Intramural sports were promoted but extramurals were discouraged, consistent with what Fidler (2006) qualified as a "restrictive philosophy" for girls and women to not exert themselves in physical play, but to preserve their femininity and health in order to "be better citizens, wives and mothers" (p. 19). Publicity and spectators at high school and college games where women played were restricted, only women could coach girls and women, and any emphasis on *winning* in school physical education programs was discouraged (Sefton, 1941).

Critics in decision-making capacity responded to the female protectionism trend. The Amateur Athletic Union (AAU) countered claims about effects of sport by recommending rigorous activity for girls on the grounds that exercise could *enhance* the female reproductive systems for future mothers to produce hearty sons (Steers, 1932). Moreover, framing athletic high school girls as *beauty queens* representing feminine respectability inspired an ideal for girls based on the erotic-chaste dialectic — young women appearing sexually available, but still modest. For more discussion about *modesty* and the *erotic-chaste dialectic*, see chapter 3. By the 1930s, female athletes were represented as "lovely, feminine charming girls" whose fitness, suppleness, and grace merely made them "more beautiful on the dance floor that evening" (Mooney, 1937; Sefton, 1937). The *Woman Citizen* celebrated passing of the "beanpole type of beauty" in exchange for a feminine ideal emphasizing the beauty and curves "nature intended" (Return of curves, 1927, p. 29). The concept of fitness being fun in high school gym classes evolved by the 1950s to promote mild athleticism as a personal appearance strategy for waistline and complexion. The ideal of girl athlete as beauty queen resonated with the early twentieth century's playful tone expressed via commercial leisure culture (Friedman & D'Emilio, 1988).

The birth of professional women's sports

In the mid-twentieth century, female athletes enabled the United States to momentarily shift its collective thoughts away from the stressors of wartime to the all-American pastime of baseball. Professional men's sports were put on hold during World War II and Philip K. Wrigley, owner of the Chicago Cubs National League baseball team, originated the idea for professional *women's* baseball in 1942. Women recruited for the All-American Girls Professional Baseball League (AAGPBL) were accomplished athletes before joining and as many as seven hundred women played professional baseball during the 1940s and 1950s, with salaries somewhat higher than other jobs offered to women (Madden, 1997). How female players played the game, dressed, behaved—and even their nicknames of *Tiger*, *Sonny*, and *Tommy*—was perceived as emasculating (Kenosha, 1943). They were considered *tomboys*, "a new type of American girl, new not only physically, but mentally and morally," according to *Good Housekeeping* (de Koven, 1912, p. 150). Publicity efforts for driving spectators to AAGSBL/AAGPBL games evolved from Recreation for War Workers, Family Entertainment, and Community Welfare, to an overemphasis on femininity by focusing on players' feminine appearance and domestic skills, and by hosting publicity gimmicks such as *baseball finishing school* instructed by beauty salon owner Helena Rubinstein who offered feminine instruction in makeup and posture (Fidler, 2006). In addition, the uniform featured a skirt rather than pants, as worn by male players. What women athletes wore—shorts or pants versus skirts—was a significant source of controversy regarding degrees of femininity in uniform designs (Cozens & Stumpf, 1953). The AAGSBL uniform was a flared-skirt dress inspired by field hockey, figure skating, and tennis outfits, in pastel shades of peach, yellow, blue, and green. Also, women were contracted to serve as team chaperones, and players were schooled in *feminine charm* (Ladies, 1943) since both AAGSBL/AAGPBL and female college athletes were required to always appear in feminine attire when not playing and to avoid smoking and drinking alcohol. See Figure 6.1.

Emphasized femininity served as a prominent news angle for promoting women's baseball, softball, and basketball. The news value of *novelty* associated with promoting a men's sport filled by women in key roles attracted significant publicity in *Life* magazine, *Forbes Magazine of Business*, the *New York Times Magazine*, among other news outlets throughout the 1940s. Fidler (2006) found that publicity campaigns and media coverage of AAGSBL/AAGPBL players nearly always highlighted the most *feminine-looking* players in terms of their facial features and figures. Press releases explicitly explained *Tom Boy Tactics Out of Bounds in All-American Softball League*, and *Girls Softball Loop Favors Beauty, Grace as Essential Factors* (Kenosha, 1943). As part of focus groups and interviews hosted for this book, women acknowledged the beauty and talent of professional female athletes. However, when asked to consider what they define as *most feminine* and *least feminine* among the magazine images shared during discussions about defining femininity, not one woman selected a black and white image from a 1950s issue of *McCall's* featuring a young woman with muscular thighs dressed in a professional woman's baseball uniform (skirt) and cap, holding a baseball bat as *most feminine*, while several classified the image as *least feminine*. Some research participants recalled the feature film, *A League of Their Own* (1992) as part of interviews, noting how feminine the actresses like Madonna were in portraying professional baseball players. Yet the black and white magazine im-

**Figure 6.1.   The AAGSBL Kenosha Comets pitcher applying makeup, 1943.
Source: Bettmann/ Getty Images.**

age only attracted negative commentary about how *un*feminine the wom-
en looked. Amanda, 61, African-American/Black chuckled as she examined the image: "I remember when I first got to an all-girl high school.
Our gym outfits we used to have to wear with the flared leg. They were
the least feminine things that you could ever wear. It took me back."

Similarly, basketball was a sport with a masculine image and de-
pended on promoters to bring in audiences. So, representing female athletes as feminine and heterosexual drove basketball tournament Queen
and Court events photographed for media. Female basketball athletes
also were forbidden from wearing traditional men's clothing or sporting
"severe haircuts" (Cahn, 2010, p. 296). In the 1990s, two professional
women's basketball leagues were founded—the American Basketball
League (ABL) and the Women's National Basketball Association
(WNBA). Green and Alexander (2000) posited that these developments
were undergirded by capitalists who saw profitability in women's basketball. Overall, large-scale all-women sports teams have been slow to
emerge in the United States. Once, U.S. female college basketball players
had to relocate to Europe or Japan to continue playing professionally
after graduation.

Female athletes willing to inhabit and express a gendered social identity that seems out of step with heteronormative, emphasized femininity ideals do so at their own peril. Mainstream sports culture cannot seem to loosen its grip on old stereotypes which reflect societal expectations about the femininity and masculinity of athletes (Jones & Greer, 2011). Gender identities are relational and dichotomous, a framework of opposites promoting an *either/or* template which has proved resistant to change. Enduring are Caucasian/White supremacist constructions of African-American/Black masculinity—as applied to a man or a woman (Ferber, 2007). So, too, are notions of heteronormativity, with lesbianism among some female athletes used as a stigma to diminish girls' and women's athletic achievements. In chapter 8, I deepen the discussion about sexuality, masculine femininities, and feminine masculinities. In reaction to these negative stereotypes, some female athletes have adopted an apologetic stance toward their athleticism. During media interviews, female athletes combine talk of competitiveness with sharing about their traditional feminine hobbies (e.g., cooking), mention of boyfriends, and marriage aspirations (Del Rey, 1978). This pattern endures today as female athletes are entirely cognizant of media framing of those who do not conform to emphasized femininity ideals.

In the United States, no form of legislation has done more to make room for girls and women in organized sports in school than Title IX of the Educational Amendments to the 1964 Civil Rights Act to prohibit gender discrimination in federally funded educational facilities.

School sports for girls and Title IX

In the United States, public school and parks and recreation athletic program funding routinely has fluctuated with economic conditions—with cut programs during bad times. The Great Depression after the 1929 Wall Street crash meant significant government and corporate cuts. In particular, slashed were sports programs benefitting working-class urban girls who trained and competed in track events. During the 1930s, media, parents, and other cultural authorities advocated a femininity ideal for school girls in terms of a *modern girl* who should be healthy and fit without becoming masculine so as not to jeopardize girls' reproductive systems. This meant that basketball and track and field which involved greater physicality, strength, and endurance were downplayed for girls. Effects for high school girls' sports were significant with cancelled girls' track-and-field teams, suspension of varsity letters for girls in sports, easier play rules for girls to reduce strenuousness, and annulled state tournaments for girls' basketball. Consequences of these changes negatively impacted public perception about girls and sports for decades (Thiel-Stern, 2014). Even with passage of Title IX legislation, a dominant binary dualistic understanding of femininity as *weakness* in comparison to masculinity as *strength* persists and continues to shape ways girls in sport are limited and marginalized.

The U.S. Congress, in 1972, passed Title IX of the Educational Amendments to the 1964 Civil Rights Act to prohibit gender discrimination in educational facilities which receive federal funds. Title IX guarantees girls and women the right to equal participation in athletics. Researchers' findings suggested a 600 percent increase in girls' participation in sports during 1972–1978, health improvements in girls (Kaestner & Xu, 2010), and better education and employment opportunities for girls who participated early in sport (Stevenson, 2010). Lough (1998) reported that before Title IX, fewer than 300,000 females participated in interscholastic activities but by 1998, that number had climbed to 2.25 million. However, Title IX may not have turned out to be the panacea initially promised. Hegemonic masculinity persists in many schools, with limited definitions of masculinity and femininity rationalizing an unequal gender order wherein male-dominated sports are valued more than sports designated for girls and women (Charlebois, 2011). Benefits of sport participation—networking, competitive behavior, learning to be a team player—advantage people of all genders (Kelinske, Mayer, & Chen, 2001).

As addressed earlier in this chapter, *sport typing* makes girls' and women's participation in some sports easier than others. Activities labeled as *feminine sports* are not as negatively stereotyped as those labeled as *masculine sports*. Perhaps this is why one sport that has thrived for high school girls is cheerleading, an activity universally sexualized across popular culture and one that resonates with third-wave feminism. Yet, cheerleading suffered a popularity setback during the second-wave feminism, post–Title IX era, as cheerleaders were stereotyped as passive, unintelligent, and sexually promiscuous girls. Yet, in recent years, cheerleading has enjoyed a resurgence, perhaps because it resonates with postfeminist and third-wave feminist women like Amy (cited at the top of this chapter) who use the *girlie-girl* concept to define femininity. To Amy, female athletes still must adhere to emphasized femininity tenets of traditional beauty without an abundance of muscularity. In this way, cheerleading serves as the perfect feminine sport. Its current position as a bonafide sport synonymous with gymnastics has catapulted cheerleading to rank as perhaps the most feminine of high school girls' sports for its attention to sexual attractiveness—a paradox, since cheerleading also involves physical strength and toughness (Grindstaff & West, 2006).

Several women interviewed for this book had fond memories of their cheerleading career. Once a high school cheerleader and dancer, Lorraine, a thirty-eight-year old African-American/Black woman who participated in a focus group session for this book, concurred that participation in sports helps girls build confidence: "I was like super duper active. I was really, really toned. I recently saw a picture of me doing a handstand and I had all this muscle tone and I said, 'Oh my God!' I felt pretty

Figure 6.2.   Cheerleading long has been considered to be a sport that emphasizes and amplifies girls' femininity. Copyright: ViewApart. Source: Mirko Vitali/
Depositphotos.com.

confident." She is the aunt to one of the college women who participated in a different focus group discussion for this book and opined that despite the muscles she had as a cheerleader, it's the hair ribbons, colorful short skirts, matching socks and glittery pom-poms that make cheerleading more about expressing femininity than about showing off muscles. Findings among Adams' (2005) study of *girl power* suggested that cheerleading is a predominantly middle-class sport and resolved, "today's version of ideal girlhood that says it is desirable to assume some of the signifiers of masculinity as long as they remain feminine" (p. 110).

SPORTS, FEMININITY, AND
GENDER ROLE STRESS/CONFLICT

The gender role stress/conflict (GRS/C) paradigm (Pleck, 1995) introduced in chapter 3—when applied to female athletes' experiences—may be used to explain how and why they are stigmatized, conflicted, misplaced, or otherwise considered abnormal for acting outside of prescribed emphasized femininity norms. Effects of GRS/C which involve restrictions to one's achievement of her/his human potential, include poor body image, disordered eating, and low self-esteem. It is a psychological state brought about when socialized gender roles play out negatively, as when someone devalues, restricts, or violates another person who deviates from or conforms to gender norms. GRS/C may occur during gender role transitions (e.g., puberty), occur internally, and be experienced interpersonally (O'Neil, 2008). Sexualizing of female athletes' images increases dissonance and can cause women to limit degrees of athleticism they display (Roth & Basow, 2004). The context of girls and women playing sports typically considered masculine or in men's domain sets females up for experiencing GRS/C.

Since the *generic sporting woman* is a Caucasian/White, heterosexual prototype (Dewar, 1993), women of color may experience unique forms of GRS/C. Female athletes live among two cultures—a sport culture that is inherently masculine and a larger social culture where women are rewarded for displaying emphasized femininity. In college settings, this dynamic establishes higher status and privilege for female non-athletes and a marginalized position for female athletes. Failure to live up to ideals of femininity can produce psychological stress that may lead to negative health outcomes and coping behaviors. For example, researchers have found a relationship between femininity and eating disorders (e.g., anorexia, bulimia) in women (Readdy, Cardinal, & Watkins, 2013).

As part of interviews and focus groups conducted for the study reported in this book, women had very definite opinions about sports as it relates to their personal definition of *femininity*. For example, Mariana, 21,

Dominican, told her focus group peers about her struggle to negotiate femininity with athleticism in high school:

> I ran track. I was athletic, and none of the girls on my team sweat. . . . They're running around looking all cute and I'm like a dude, I'm sweating and I'm drenched and I smell. And I'm looking around and I'm like, "Really? I'm the only one that got that memo?" Thanks. But when I came out of that and I was in school it was like I looked nice. I looked cute.

What Mariana described was feelings about leading a dual life required when society deems girls who play sports to be *un*feminine. To avoid being ostracized by other students, athletes like Mariana are sure to dress up and emphasize their femininity in other realms of high school life. Other college women who participated in focus group discussions for this book told of their early resistance to sports in high school. It is as if they do battle with social stereotypes and redefine for themselves what it means to be an ideal girl or woman. Melanie, 20, Caucasian/White explained how she handled this stress:

> I didn't make the soccer team freshman year in high school. . . . I thought it was me and that girls maybe weren't supposed to play any-way. . . . My friend convinced me to join cross country. I cried the whole three miles through. I thought it was torture. And somehow I ended up doing winter track, spring track, cross country. Every day I hated it. I'd say "This is my last day. I'm never coming back." And ironically, I think it's the one thing I took from high school and now I still do it. Now I can say I actually enjoy it. . . . It's not the running I enjoy. It's finishing. It's something I'll always have because I like the way I feel afterwards.

Melanie endured internal conflict because she wanted to play sports. As she told her story, another young woman, Patricia, 19, Caucasian/White, agreed:

> I feel the same way. I stuck with sports, volleyball, all throughout high school . . . even though I was afraid of being considered a dyke. . . . [E]very single day I'd do the same thing—say I'm quitting and then I'd never quit. And now I feel like sports for women in high school and younger is so important—a routine—and then when you get back into playing sports, you remember how good you felt when you were play-ing sports. . . . I also learned to not really care so much about what other people thought.

Women need not be professional athletes to feel social pressures and restrictions placed on their body when it comes to working out, stressors that influence women's physical and mental health. Some contemporary definitions of *emphasized femininity* include greater degrees of muscularity than in previous decades. Women who seek the health, fitness, and aes-thetic benefits of going to the gym engage in conscious internal negotiation about limiting the size and strength of their body in order to achieve *appropriate femininity* without sacrificing social acceptability. Media representations of objectified, sexualized, hyperfeminine models, athletes, and other celebrities bear down on everyday women with not-so-subtle messages to be feminine and strong—but not *too* strong, physically. Many women share a common fear that weightlifting will increase their muscle size to the degree that they will bulk up, become masculine, and therefore, unattractive (Salvatore & Marecek, 2010). Ideologies associated with emphasized femininity have become the benchmark by which women may hold back on and limit their own success in physical fitness. Dworkin (2001) posited that weightlifting personifies a third-wave feminist strategy for physical self-empowerment, as well as self-defense in the event of attack, and healing after violence has been done to them.

Social expectations surrounding femininity and athleticism

Femininity and athleticism tend to be polarized concepts. Since large, bulky muscles deviate from traditional beauty ideals, female athletes may be considered ugly and *un*feminine. Describing an array of femininities ranging from *hyper-feminine* to *neuter*, Person (1999) examined cross-gender identifications used by women experiencing conflict between masculinities they value and femininities they eschew. GRS/C among female athletes may result when they attempt to embody and enact both feminine and masculine gender qualities; considered to be opposite and conflicting identities (Bem, 1993). Also, women athletes are at risk for homophobic harassment due to widely held social beliefs that women who play "men's sports" are "sexually suspect" (Lenskyi, 1999, p. 172). In Brazil, women are forbidden from playing sports deemed "against feminine nature" (Knijnik, 2015, p. 67) and many have urged for gender equity laws to make *futebol feminine* legal. Several college women whom I interviewed for this book talked about rewards they reap in intramural sports and gym activities. For example, Zumba was reported as a favorite. Ally, 20, Caucasian/White, explained how feminine Zumba makes her feel because it eliminates any sense of stress/conflict she might otherwise feel by participating in other sports activities:

> Everyone loves it. [T]here's all these success stories about how you lose weight. . . . The instructor, she motivates you, and you do new sexy, fun movements. I really think that women just love it because, even if they don't feel sexy on the street, they'll feel sexy through that class. And, I think that feeling sexy is a huge thing for women, like, no matter what their weight is, no matter how their hair is, you know, I think that's a confidence issue. They're confident in their own bodies.

Research findings suggest that some female athletes negotiate and reconcile the social expectations surrounding femininity with athleticism and exert considerable effort to ensure that they are perceived as heterosexual and feminine to attract sponsors and male attention. Frameworks of *doing girl, being girl, resisting girl,* and *subverting girl* explain how femininity plays out in the lives of female athletes (Ussher, 1997). To minimize mannish or lesbian stereotyping, female athletes construct their own brand of emphasized femininity (Feder-Kane, 2000) by exchanging traditional femininity for a *game face* or *competitive spirit* while doing sports, but then reactivating normative emphasized femininity by attending to their hair, makeup and dress after the game (Krane, Choi, Baird, Aimar, & Kauere, 2004), moves that lessen peer pressure about heteronormativity (Shakib, 2003). Describing Russian tennis star Anna Kournikova, Trolan (2013) explained that *femininity* sometimes serves as code for *heterosexuality.* Yet, pre-empting stereotypes by overemphasizing feminine appearance or being seen in public with men as if apologizing for masculine behavior (Kaskan & Ho, 2014, p. 5) qualifies as a reaction to others' *microaggression* and disrespect of women's athleticism.

Female athletes may react similarly to these pressures, but type of sport is a key variable in gauging degrees to which they comply to social pressures. The controversial issue of uniforms for professional female athletes, first raised in the mid-twentieth century when the AAGSBL/AAGPBL teams were founded during World War II to entertain baseball fans at home, resurfaces periodically. In 2004, the president of the International Federation of Association Football (FIFA) recommended that female footballers should wear "tighter shorts" to enhance the game's popularity with viewers (Olympic boxing, 2011). Most recently, the International Amateur Boxing Association (AIBA) debated whether female boxers should wear trunks like male boxers, or skirts. An AIBA representative argued that wearing skirts would enable female boxers to "stand out from the men's competitions" (Olympic boxing, 2011). Some female cricketers have resisted managements' uniform change plans from trousers to skirt (Russell, 2002). Both heterosexual and bisexual women rugby players may feel compelled to appear feminine and heterosexual, so are sure to bathe before after-game parties, wear ribbons in their hair during competition, and put on makeup, jewelry, and feminine clothing (Baird, 2001; Fallon & Jome, 2007). Some women's volleyball coaches require players to grow their hair long and tie it back in a ponytail with ribbons to sell their femininity *and* the sport (Lenskyj, 1999). Female softball players are more likely than basketball or soccer players to exhibit apologetic attitudes with strategic femininity displays (Davis-Delano, Pollock, & Vose, 2009). Female tennis players seem to succumb to these pressures by attending to a hyper-feminine appearance more so than female rugby and hockey players (Krane, Choi, Baird, Aimar, & Kauer, 2004). Women rugby players reported balancing their desire to play well with wanting to still look feminine and responding to warnings that women are too fragile for a physical team sport like rugby (Fallon & Jome, 2007).

Individual, non-team sport contexts offer another view on women, athleticism, and femininity. Bodysculpting, a women-only sport in Australia and the United States, reveals stress and conflict undergirding the *femininity* concept itself. Bodysculpting is a body figure competition—not quite like bodybuilding which rewards muscle mass and not quite like traditional beauty pageants. The bodysculpting sport requires competitors to emphasize femininity, symmetry, proportion, tone, definition and grace rather than physique and muscularity (Rosdahl, 2014). Guidelines for bodysculpting can be contradictory and ambiguous (Boyle, 2005) and the sport has been critiqued as amplifying only youthful, athletic, slim, graceful, and pretty qualities (Bolin, 1998). Meanwhile, the *muscular woman* ideal suggests that femininity "denaturalizes" the female body, demands time-consuming work to emphasize compulsory heterosexuality, and sets up a paradoxical relationship between femininity and muscularity. Rosdahl (2014) argued that "discouraging women from creating their full physical potential in the name of femininity" is "unnatural" (p. 41).

Despite physical fitness trends for women which have promoted health and eroticized *moderate* muscularity in recent decades, most women whom I interviewed for the study reported in this book expressed lukewarm opinions about women in sport when it comes to defining femininity. They were acutely aware of social expectations surrounding femininity and athleticism as they attend to beauty, health, lifestyle, and entertainment industries' convergence in rewarding fashionable, feminine bodies in sport. Yet, perceptions that sport and certain hobbies are *un*feminine persist. Among the magazine images used to stimulate discussion during interviews and focus group conversations about femininity for this book, an image of a young woman astride a motorcycle from *Ladies Home Journal*, 1990s, and another of an older fisherwoman from *Redbook*, 1945, were dismissed as *least feminine* across age cohorts of research participants. Explained Luciana, 20, a Latina: "I love motorcycles, but her posture . . . slouched over as if she's about to grab her pants, just kind of manly-ish . . . not really groomed. She doesn't look too ladylike. If she had a helmet on and was riding her motorcycle, I don't think many people would think that's a chick under that helmet." About the image of an older woman who posed with a row of four large vertical tuna and a fishing rod, Carolina, 19, Latina, said: "She looks like a cute little old *grandpa.* . . . She's got the hat on, her pants all the way up to here." On the other hand, Caitlin, 22, who identified as Bhutanese-Jewish-American, admired the image of an older woman displaying athletic achievement: "Did she really reel those in? That one just stood out. I was impressed by her. I'm vegetarian, but I was impressed." Across age cohorts, college women were particularly harsh critics of women's involvement in athletic activities as being *un*feminine, as many of the words and phrases they used to define femininity largely were associated with appearance. As explained in Table 2.1, women aged eighteen to twenty-nine who participated in focus groups most frequently defined femininity using words like *delicate, docile, gentle, graceful, ladylike,* and *submissive.* While I also heard definitions of femininity that included words of *powerful* and *strong,* these women were not referring to contexts of athletics or muscularity. Rather, they defined femininity in terms of women being independent and free to choose their lifestyle.

Female athletes' coping behaviors

Girls and women who play sports resiliently develop coping mechanisms for dealing with GRS/C and expectancy violations with regard to popular definitions of *femininity.* They maximize new media technologies and social networking spaces for self-representation that challenge mainstream sports media discourse and enable girls and women to find support for their marginalized experiences. Also, some female professional athletes are fighting for pay equity on par with male athlete counterparts, as expressed by tennis superstar Serena Williams: "I really hope that I can be helpful in that journey, because I do believe that women deserve the same pay. We work just as hard as men do. I've been working, playing tennis, since I was three years old. And to be paid less just because of my sex—it doesn't seem fair" (Tsuji, 2016). See Figure 6.3. The Women's Sports Foundation reports unequal funding for women in both college and professional sports, an outcome that may discourage women from pursuing sports and offers female athletes less incentive to push further (Pay inequity, 2016). Female athletes define *femininity* more as characterizing interpersonal qualities of good listening skills, and being nurturing, tender, and compassionate—than looking a certain way (Fallon & Jome, 2007).

Some female high school and college athletes who play team sports such as soccer resist the emphasized femininity archetype by consuming massive amounts of food, belching loudly, and eating in ways generally considered to be *unladylike.* They seem to do so without worry of weight gain due to high levels of calorie-burning physical exercise associated with training and play. Finding humor in a femininity paradox of conflicting demands of emphasized femininity and athleticism through *Soccer Girl Problems,* female soccer players celebrate control over their athletic bodies and satirize anxieties associated with it while "subvert[ing] ideologies of femininity via carnivalesque celebrations" of their unruly body and behavior (Heinecken, 2015, p. 1036). Their YouTube videos garner thousands of views (www.youtube.com/watch?v=n7r5lA3h-3M) and @SoccerGrlProbs Twitter account opens a community space for female soccer players to unite and share experiences—such as being unable to fit into skinny jeans due to well-developed, muscular calves and thighs. Similarly, female skateboarders resist conventional femininity discourses through gender-neutral online self-representations (MacKay &

Figure 6.3.   Multiple-award-winning tennis champion, Serena Williams, has endured sexist commentary about her powerful physique. She is waging a campaign for gender equity in pay for athletes. Copyright: zhukovsky. Source: Leonard Zhukovsky/ Depositphotos.com.

Dallaire, 2013). Similarly, female athletes' blog texts often oppose male-dominated sports models which emphasize competitive domination (Antunovic & Hardin, 2013). Because traditional female gender norms suggest girls and women are supposed to be emotional, nurturing, friendly, and approachable, women rugby players' appearance and behavior tends to violate others' expectations so coaches warn them to avoid being "rude, crude, and lewd," such as when singing traditional rugby songs with sexually explicit lyrics, paradoxically behaviors for which male athletes are celebrated (Fallon & Jome, 2007, p. 316). Female college athletes who play soccer, volleyball, gymnastics, track, swimming, basketball, softball, and tennis, rugby, and ice hockey deal with GRS/C by exhibiting pride in their strong bodies, feeling empowered, and advancing confidence from their sports environment (Krane, 2012; Krane, Choi, Baird, Aimar, & Kauer, 2004). Athleticism and femininity need not be contradictory, mutually exclusive arenas.

Sports, science, and women's feminine bodies

During the last decade, Olympic Games have witnessed a new wrinkle in social identity stress and conflict as it relates to femininity: sex verification testing of female athletes to ensure that they are, indeed, biologically women. The concept of *gendered physiological discrimination* has emerged to explain how sex-testing enables scrutiny of internal bodily processes (e.g., hormones, chromosomes) which promotes discrimination at intersections of imperialism, patriarchy, racism, and sexism, since the competitors most often suspected of not meeting sex standards are non-White athletes. The practice draws intense international news media attention and is considered "a new field of power that primarily discriminates against non-normative bodily processes" (Blithe & Hanchey, 2015, p. 486) which sustains a penchant for questioning the femininity of female athletes considered to be too strong or fast to be women (Buzuvis, 2012). Consistent with Western Eurocentric anxieties, the most recent Olympic Games sex-testing episodes involved female athletes who represent nations from the Global South (e.g., South Africa), women whose musculoskeletal features do not conform to typical Western femininity ideals (Ray, 2009). As science increasingly is applied to sport, physiological discriminations persist and limited definitions of *femininity* are invoked. No doubt, questioning of female athletes' femininity shall endure.

SPORTS INDUSTRY AND MEDIA
REPRESENTATIONS OF FEMALE ATHLETES

The role media play in representing female athletes and ultimately transmitting femininity ideals through visual images and words is undeniable. Female athletes' activities and accomplishments are filtered through a male gaze (regardless of a reporter's gender) and negotiated through conflicting discourses about sport and femininity. A popular explanation for women's exclusion from most organized professional sports underwritten by commercial enterprises is that it takes time to build franchises and audiences. The critical view is that female athletes (both girls and women) are underrepresented, trivialized, and sexualized. Their sexuality is considered more important than their athletic talents, an explanation for why much of sports journalism is sexist, racist, homophobic, and fueled by fears of men struggling to hold on to their privilege and male dominance of sport. Even the names of Olympic Games' women's sports

overemphasize femininity, systemically, with a *ladies* label, as with Ladies' Figure Skating and Ladies' Ski Jumping, for example.

Dominant representations of sport saturated with masculine gender
ideology persist and have proved highly resistant to change. Examples of
female athletes' supposed inferior status are plentiful from 2012 Olympic
Games coverage. When Team USA's Brittney Reese and Janay DeLoach
won long jump medals, post-competition news coverage included NBC's
Lewis Johnson asking, "Okay, ladies, where's that Olympic smile?" Regarding the athletes as *ladies* and demanding they smile so as to project a
pleasing appearance was to focus on stereotypical emphasized femininity
and preeminence of the male gaze rather than the athletes' significant
achievements. It was an epic double diss. For in-depth discussion about
women, femininity, and being urged to smile as microaggression, see
chapter 8. Other evidence of sexism and racism during the 2012 Olympic
Games included media's prolonged and ill-placed attention on gymnast
Gabby Douglas's hair, volleyball player Missy May Treanor's skimpy
uniform, weightlifter Holly Mangold's weight, and a water polo player's
exposed breast due to a wardrobe malfunction, all of which diminished
the athletes' talents and accomplishments (Taylor, 2012).

As I edit this page, twenty-year-old Simone Manuel just has become
the first African-American woman to ever win the individual 100-meter
freestyle in women's swimming and has dedicated her 2016 Rio Olympic
Games Gold Medal win to fighting against police brutality. Her achievement has proven highly emotional on Twitter, given a racist history in the
United States when segregation was law and African-American/Black
people were denied access to public swimming pools. As discussed
above, *sport typing* practices suggest that women who participate in a
feminine sport like swimming are judged for their beauty (more so than
their talent). In the months to come, I wonder how Simone Manuel's
femininity as a young woman of color will be represented and scrutinized amidst news media coverage?

Female athletes' successes during the 1996 Olympic Games inspired
founding of women's sports magazines in the United States. Unfortunately, coverage maintains a status quo of stereotypical heteronormative,
hyper-feminine representations that resonate with advertisers and readers (Fink & Kensicki, 2002). Sports journalists such as those at *Sports
Illustrated for Women* may acknowledge social changes with regard to
acceptance of female athletes (Kane & Greendorfer, 1994), but resist by
perpetuating hyper-feminine stereotypes when writing about female athletes' personal caregiving roles and by perpetuating homophobia when
focusing on female athletes' male partners (Griffin, 1998). Seemingly, female athletes go along with these sports journalism trends of amplifying
an emphasized feminine image so as not to lose or discourage sponsors
which offer financial advantage in the form of product endorsement/
advertising deals and modeling contracts. Feminist scholars offer mixed

reactions, with some arguing that this dynamic reinforces patriarchy (e.g., Markula, 2009), while others posit that female athletes engage in agentic behaviors and assert their "female presence," even though female athletes rarely control images produced by the mainstream news media (Heywood & Dworkin, 2003, p. 83). Research findings suggest that team and individual event female athletes would prefer to be represented for their competence and not necessarily how they look (Fink, Kane, & LaVoi, 2014). During our interview for this book, Cathy, 53, Caucasian/White, critiqued popular culture's celebration of the *Sports Illustrated* swimsuit issue for contributing to stress her daughter feels about body image:

> I think that the pressure has been put on those born in the eighties and the nineties—the pressure has been put on them to maintain a certain body image for life. Otherwise, they're going to lose out—they're not going to be able to hold on to their husbands, they're not going to be able to be successful in the business world. That's a shame . . . with the launch of the *Sports Illustrated* swimsuit issue and everybody's got to look like them . . . there's been a lot of pressure put on the young women who are in their twenties now to maintain that body image for life. Otherwise they're not going to be successful.

Sports Illustrated began publicizing photographs of female athletes as swimsuit models in 1997 and the first female athletes to appear were bikini-clad members of the U.S. beach volleyball team. A comparison of athletes versus fashion models in *Sports Illustrated* swimsuit issues revealed few differences between groups since all women were positioned in ways that emphasized femininity rather than athleticism, and sexually objectified women, collectively perpetuating female gender stereotypes (Kim & Sagas, 2014). In fact, sexualized images of female models in the sports industry have increased in popularity over time (Daniels & Wartena, 2011), and *Sports Illustrated* also features NFL cheerleaders, NBA dancers, and wives or girlfriends of male athletes as swimsuit models.

Undeniably, women are treated differently in the world of sports media; sexualized as objects and marginalized in the newsroom and as news audiences. Sports journalists have developed a hierarchy of most- and least- feminine sports for women, or gender marking, which paradoxically facilitates sexploitation and infantilization of female athletes as nonthreatening *girls*. Print and television sports journalists do not consider women who play sports as *real* athletes (Trolan, 2013, italics added). Instead, journalists engage with *sport typing* so that individual, non-contact sports like figure skating, gymnastics, and tennis effactually maintain normative emphasized femininity standards and receive greater media coverage than team sport events perceived as masculine (Hardin & Greer, 2009) which may have "less glamorous" female athletes (Trolan, 2013, p. 219). Media consistently emphasize female athletes' femininity, heterosexuality, and heterosexual appeal over their athletic performance (Kane & Maxwell, 2011). Furthermore, lesser coverage of women's sports as compared to men's sports continues and television coverage is lower than ever with just 1.6 percent of sports airtime devoted to women's sports (Cooky, Messner, & Hextrum, 2013). Effects of these negative trends suggest lowered expectations for and perceptions of women's athletic ability, and negative body image among girls (Daniels, 2009). Findings of a study of global newspaper coverage of the Olympic Games suggested that sexualization may be contextual, with New Zealand, Japan, South Korea, and Turkey reporting that it is primarily athletes from outside the home nation who are sexualized (Bruce, Hovden, & Markula, 2010).

Female sports journalists experience their own fragmented professional identity and gender role stress/conflict when it comes to femininity. Men "own sports journalism because they own sports" (Hardin & Shain, 2006, pp. 335–36). On the one hand, female journalists are expected to conform to a social definition of *femininity*, while also adapting to professionalism standards developed by men. Feminine values of nurturing, kindness, and compassion conflict with the detached, tough journalist's manner (van Zoonen, 1994) and set female journalists up to fall into a "friendliness trap" when their open-communication skills may get them in the door, but then work against them when they seek career growth opportunities (Frohlich, 2004, p. 67). On the whole, female sports journalists can reconcile the contradictions but never may be wholly accepted as equals with men in sports newsrooms (Hardin & Shain, 2006).

THE MAKING OF TOMBOYS
AND FEMALE CELEBRITY ATHLETES

Changes in media platforms and proliferation of messages over the past few decades have shifted the making of media celebrities out of women who excel in sports into commercial overdrive. The abundance of female athletes' images and narratives about their backgrounds has magnified sexploitation of their bodies and further underscored ways media shape women's emphasized femininities and their social identities according to ethnicity and sexual orientation. Emphasized femininity and heteronormativity among media representations of female athletes means sportswomen may be either completely sexualized, ridiculed as complex and troubling figures, or overlooked entirely by reporters who recoil at women who do not fit the traditional emphasized femininity norm. Sports journalism's coverage of a 1994 competition that turned violent in the women's figure skating rink between the athletic, masculine, married Tonya Harding and the artistic, feminine, single Nancy Kerrigan broke ratings records for television news programs. The feminine ideal for television sports news coverage, according to Fabos (2001), is female athletes who "look the part, but . . . exhibit sexual availability and uprightness" (p. 197). In this feud, Kerrigan was infantilized as the feminine victim and made into a media darling.

Beyond figure skating and sometimes tennis, professional female athletes experience significant challenges from sports organizations and reporters who do not know how to handle the fact that female athletes have athletic bodies, including well-developed muscles. Athletic women who embrace their power fall victim to a society only too willing to shame them for *not being feminine enough*. In recent years the multiple Grand Slam and Olympic Game–winning tennis star sisters, Venus Williams and Serena Williams have endured inflammatory racial discrimination by sports media who refer to their powerful thighs, chiseled arms, and abs as masculine. When head of the Russian Tennis Federation referred to the women as the "Williams brothers" in 2014, he was fined $25,000 for making the comments on Russian television while Serena Williams called him out for "extremely sexist, racist and bullying" remarks (Serena Williams, 2014). African-American/Black female athletes also have been criticized in mainstream media and social media for wearing braids, considered "ghetto," and for having "big butts" and dark skin (Wellington, 2015). Through strategic marketing, the WNBA has sought to engage with a representational double bind—promoting its players as both skilled and feminine while staving off the "sports dyke" stereotype with soft feature media placements and website stories about the athletes' family involvement, including interviews with their mothers and children, as well as beauty tips columns (McPherson, 2000, p. 188). Some WNBA stars who fit "femme-y femininity" norms as "slim and well coiffed" women, while others possess a "more muscular, physical" femininity (McPherson, 2000, p. 188)—have found commercial success with modeling contracts, product endorsement contracts, and spokesperson duties for breast cancer awareness nonprofits. Framing African-American/Black female athletes as role models succeeds primarily when their athletic abilities can be blended with "acceptable images of blackness and femininity" (Tasker & Negra, 2007, p. 8). As compared to male athletes, female athletes receive significantly fewer endorsement campaign deals—and when they do, women are expected to represent their bodies in sexually provocative poses rather to display their athletic skill.

Some sports journalists interrogate WNBA athletes' personal lives by invoking the *superwoman myth*, claiming they *can do it all*. This rhetorical device, popularized in the 1980s, is used to describe working women who have a career outside the home to make money, but also prepare food, clean, manage the house, bear and raise children, and sexually please their husband (Rakow, 1989), praising women for balancing paid and unpaid work. By romanticizing the *superwoman myth*, media reportage serves a discrediting function, dilutes broader issues, and further entrenches socialized norms and traditional female gender roles. Similarly, the *invincible Black woman syndrome* defines African-American/Black women who place unrealistic demands on themselves, women who consequently suffer internal stress and conflict (Childs & Palmer, 1999).

During the twentieth century, a handful of female athletes captured public attention through media which bestowed celebrity status upon them. Heteronormative standards of the day mandated that post-war news media address any ambiguity about the woman athlete's sexuality and clarify it in the form of emphasized femininity frames for girls and women. Olympic track star and LPGA Hall of Famer Babe Didrickson-Zaharias performed her gender with a combination of femininity and masculinity which did not fit comfortably with a binary dualistic framework wherein a girl or woman must be one or the other—but not both feminine and masculine. Strong links between sports and lesbianism emerged in conjunction with African-American/Black athletes' achievements during the 1950s (Cahn, 2010). The *tomboy* moniker liberally was used to describe female athletes who failed to measure up to emphasized femininity norms and it was applied to Althea Gibson, the first African-American/Black woman to win Wimbledon (*Baltimore Afro-American*, 1957). An *Ebony* magazine article inferred that she was a lesbian with a "psychological illness" since "entirely feminine" African-American/Black female sports stars "like boys, dances, club affairs" (Fastest woman, 1955, p. 28, p. 32). During our interview for this book, Finn, 62, Caucasian/White who identifies as heterosexual, fondly referred to herself as a *tomboy* as she shared her stories about negotiating stress/conflict as a feminine girl and then woman:

> Even though I'd always wanted to model, I've always been a tomboy. My programs that I loved growing up were *My Friend Flicka, Lassie*, you know, being outdoors on a farm. *Sky King*. Another, a vet who flew in and took care of the animals. *Sea Hunt*, too. No woman on those programs cared about her fingernails or makeup. They were living their lives in real terms in nature.

Finn also explained how she became more aware of flexible and deep meanings about femininity as she raised her own children and now cares for her grandchildren. Among college women who participated in focus groups, Meagan, 20, Caucasian/White, said transitioning from a *tomboy* is a process:

> I was raised by boys. I played in the dirt. *I* was a boy and wore boys clothes until I was in tenth grade. I had two older brothers and just wore their hand-me-downs until I realized, "Oh, wait. I don't want to look different from everybody else." I was less feminine than I am now. . . . I'm not gonna lie and say I don't care about what guys think, because obviously I definitely do. It's important.

Meagan's story underscores the salience of social norms and peer pressure that high school and college women experience with regard to their sense of femininity.

The *tomboy* label may be falling from common parlance as LGBTQ identities gain acceptance in the United States. Yet, tomboyism is seen as synonymous with homosexuality for many women, regardless of how they self-identify, and this could be a contributor to why stigma still is attached to the label. Failure to discover consistent usages of the *tomboy* label across diverse sexual orientation groups led Carr (2007) to resolve that women who identified as a tomboy in childhood or adolescence equated it with multiple factors, including lesbianism, immaturity, athleticism, and masculinity. Tomboys in adolescence may be considered sexually suspect (Shakib, 2003), but other researchers' findings have suggested that tomboyism is a transitory stage in girls' development (Martin, 1995), one that fades with maturation (Halberstam, 1998) as young women succumb to social pressures to conform to dominant heteronormative femininity ideals (Currie, 1997). Finally, a dearth of positive language for androgynous, athletic, strong, muscular, independent women may account for some girls' and women's dropping of the tomboy label from a list of self-identifiers (Carr, 2007). In the 1960s, the news narrative about professional female athletes pondered how/if they would "regain their womanhood through sexual surrender to men" (Cahn, 2010, p. 293). Such a framework suggests that athleticism and sports play represent phases in girls' and women's lives—rather than important lifestyle choices that set the pace for healthy lives.

DISCUSSION

This chapter has examined the world of athletics for girls and women—and sports' role in shaping social and individual definitions of femininity. Intertwined throughout are pressures, stresses, and conflicts associated with being muscular enough to perform well in sports while also conforming to contemporary ideas about how girls and women should look without going too far and looking too masculine. The line is a fine one, and not easy to find. The role of legislation in the United States known as Title IX was passed in the last century to provide equal sport opportunities for girls and young women that traditionally had been available to boys and young men. While many positive changes have been attributed to Title IX, critics suggest that hegemonic patriarchal norms persist which prohibit females from achieving their maximum potential. Fluctuating economic conditions also threaten budget cuts to school athletic programs and fears arise that girls' athletics programs will be the first axed since they are less respected than boys' athletics programs. The professional sports industry, including the Olympic Games, also perpetuate systemic discriminatory practices which diminish female athletes' achievements and present them as second-tier in comparison to male athletes' achievements. Professional female athletes face a double bind every day they train and play—maintaining (and emphasizing) traditional femininity standards while pushing their bodies to their limits to meet the demands of their sport. While journalism supports the sports world, women who work in the newsroom and appear in sports news products are treated in sexist ways. Even female athletes who have achieved the utmost in human capacity and are in a position to reap the rewards of celebrity are discriminated against, sexualized, and held to normative emphasized femininity standards that may not resonate for their powerful bodies or personal desires. Despite ongoing proof of their astonishing physical talents, female athletes are expected to remain conventionally feminine, attractive, and demure.

What remains unknown is how many girls and women hold back from pursuing any manner of physical challenge for fear that they either cannot do it because they're *only girls/women,* or for fear that they will become *un*feminine. Being held to some one-size-fits all notion of femininity and piling on loads of guilt, anxiety, stress and ambiguity sets girls and women up for a lifetime of unhappiness. Ideal femininity representations shared with little girls offer myopic views of what they can do and could become. In general, all girls and women deserve to feel positively about their inner *and* outer qualities that make them uniquely feminine.

SEVEN

Femininity as Shaped by Intersectionalities of Social Identity Dimensions

> I was never a big feminist, like girl power, because I never thought I *missed out* as a girl. Do you girls ever feel like you missed out on opportunities because you were a girl and have a vagina?
> —Research participant, Nicole, 18, Black-Japanese, heterosexual

There are as many forms of femininity and definitions of it as there are people inhabiting social identities featuring intersecting dimensions of age, ethnicity, faith/religion, gender, sexual orientation, and more. Even though a woman is aware of traditional, emphasized femininity standards, these may not be reflected in her own personal definition of femininity and she will develop her own, perhaps adjusting it over time as desired. Connell's (1995) path-breaking and inspired notion of multiple masculinities to explain hegemonic masculinity provides inspiration for codifying ways we think about femininity in the plural, too. So long as patriarchy persists, femininity itself may not be hegemonic—even though there exists a *hierarchy of femininities* wherein some are valued more than others. Some configurations of femininity are held up as ideal, normal, or serve as a benchmark by which other configurations of femininity are deemed abnormal, inferior, deviant, or wrong. Traditional, emphasized femininity norms offer a paradoxical privilege to a select few—by offering limited rewards for subordinating girls and women who do not measure up and for further strengthening patriarchy across social structures. While attention to specific social identity dimensions and their intersections is afforded to rhetorical explorations of femininity-in-context throughout this book, this chapter offers a deeper exploration of the intersectionality concept and a more textured application beyond simple piled-on-layers of demographics.

Examining intersectionalities of social identity dimensions offers an important point of entry for examining female gender role stress/conflict (GRS/C) in a femininity context. Discrimination along social identity dimensions operates in a given milieu with oppressions working in conjunction with one another, interlocking with complex effects. Collins (1991) wrote about triple jeopardy (e.g., ethnicity-gender-lower social class) of interlaced oppressions, warning that each cannot be considered as either separate or piled on, and concluded that the potential for discrimination is greatly increased for people who possess multiple undervalued social identity dimensions. Furthermore, because *avowed* and *ascribed* social identity dimensions surface through a historically- and socially-constructed and organized "matrix of domination" (p. 18), intersecting oppressions tend to occupy ranked positions in people's minds. Just as possessing two or more low-status qualities can result in "multiple jeopardy," conversely, display of two or more high-status dimensions can result in "multiple privilege" (Bowleg, 2008, p. 313).

Thinking about femininity in the United States and other parts of the world that are exposed to U.S.-based fashion-beauty complex global advertising and popular culture more than likely means evoking the image of an attractive young, thin, Caucasian/White, heterosexual woman. She is the benchmark by which many women, unfairly, are gauged. For some girls and women of intersecting social identity dimensions such as non-heterosexuals, women of color, and women who are not thin, this foundation serves as a source of GRS/C if they suffer in striving to achieve that ideal. Such a specific and limited femininity ideal may be inconsistent with the religion/spiritual faith structure of some women, and may not be achievable easily by others of lower socio-economic class.

While searching for images of women in magazines over the past 100 years to use as stimulus materials for interview and focus group discussions about *What is femininity?* as I collected narratives for this book, it is relevant to note that finding images to represent multiple social identity dimensions and their intersections was a challenge. To begin, the search was limited by only visible markers of difference. Visible characteristics apparent in a printed image may include *degrees of* age, culture, ethnicity, faith/spirituality, gender, hair texture, body size/shape, physical appearance, skin tone, and social class (to name a few)—while nonvisible characteristics tend to be less apparent, such as education, health/illness, national origin, occupation, regional affiliation, sexual orientation, and worldview. Unfortunately, dynamics of nonvisible social identities generally have received significantly less attention among social identity researchers, in general (Clair, Beatty, & Maclean, 2005). Even though they were in the minority, women's magazine images of women of color, of older women, and of women with physical disabilities were discovered because these social identity dimensions fall into a visibility range. Yet, external displays of religion/spirituality or sexual orientation were exceptionally difficult and I became painfully aware of the power of stereotypes used to represent women's social identity and to shape my own perceptions. As I have explained in this book's Introduction and Acknowledgements section, I carefully considered the pitfalls of using women's magazine images to generalize about social identity. In the end, I uncovered forty-five images among women's magazines published over the course of 100 years to stimulate conversations about how femininity is defined, images that depicted a wide variety of visible social identity dimensions. Despite challenges inherent in representing social identity diversity and intersectionalities, I know that using the images enriched women's discussions as a starting point for defining *femininity* and for critiquing this complex concept.

So, femininity as shaped by intersectionalities of social identity dimensions is addressed in greater detail throughout this chapter via these sub-topics: 1) Femininity and body shape/size, 2) Non-heteronormative, pariah, and oppositional femininities, 3) Non-cisgendered people and femininity, 4) Religion/spirituality and women's femininity, 5) Women of color and femininity, 6) Femininity and physical disability, 7) Femininity and socio-economic class, 8) Adding feminism to the social identity intersectionalities mix, and 9) Discussion.

FEMININITY AND BODY SHAPE/SIZE

One's *body* serves as visible evidence of where one fits amidst a hierarchy of overlapping and intersecting social identity dimensions which are interpreted as defining degrees by which a girl or woman is considered feminine (or not). Fatness may be the most unforgiving of dimensions in societies that prize a thin body shape/size. Today, omnipresent global media perpetuate images of the perfect feminine body as thin so that girls and young women of Western cultures associate emphasized femininity with thinness, compare their body to this ideal, and may conclude that their body does not measure up, an outcome which may lead to eating disorders and other unhealthful body practices associated with fat stigma. A thin ideal persists in Western cultures as closely linked with perceptions of femininity and self acceptance (Tiggemann, 2004). Upon viewing thin-ideal stereotypical images, adolescent women report experiencing more body dissatisfaction than older women (Groesz, Levine, & Murnen, 2002) and other study findings concur that the drive for thinness abates somewhat with age (McKinley, 2006).

The intersecting social identity dimensions of female gender, body size/shape, and ethnicity have provided fodder for media producers to mock femininity (or lack of it) as a source for entertainment. In early twentieth-century political cartoons, fat represented greed and uncontrolled impulses. The fat female body of single women served as a target for anti-women's rights advocates who simply wrote off suffragists as bitter spinsters unable to find or keep a man—or as *un*feminine, masculine, and/or lesbian. Sometimes Caucasian/White suffragists were depicted as being African-American/Black in order to suggest "that the suffrage movement was pulling white women down to the lowest strata" since ethnic minorities were considered as having a "primitive body" which was "not yet civilized" on the evolutionary scale (Farrell, 2011, p. 91, p. 83). So, overlap of fatness, Africanness, and queer femininity provided ample material for satirists. During first-wave feminism, suffragists were lampooned in propaganda used to delegitimize the movement, women thought to be shirking their female role responsibilities in the private domestic sphere, and ruptures in a heterosexual status quo. In reaction, some suffragists were sure to dress stylishly to promote their own concept of femininity shaped by charm and virtue. They sold *votes for women* messages by illustrating how likable and contemporary they were (Finnegan, 1999). Second-wave feminists during the 1960s, similarly, were chastised as lesbians for nonconformity to traditional emphasized femininity norms (Hesford, 2013). In fact, women's rights advocates were said to "threaten to unsex women" and to disrupt some "natural order of higher civilizations" by challenging male privilege (Farrell, 2011, p. 86). Degrees of mockery unleashed on certain varieties of femininity persist—as addressed in chapter 6, when a large body among some female Olympic Games athletes such as bodybuilders often is ridiculed across popular media. This issue also is picked up with regard to attention to femininities and politics in chapter 10.

NON-HETERONORMATIVE, PARIAH
AND OPPOSITIONAL FEMININITIES

Socialized beliefs about femininity are undergirded by heteronormativity and ultimately, homophobia persists. Acceptance of women's sexual and romantic relationships with other women has fluctuated over the years in the United States. In the eighteenth and nineteenth centuries, women were expected to have *emotional romantic* attachments with other women, but not *physical* ones (Weitz, 2010). Victorian ideas about middle-class Caucasian/White women's sexuality reinforced a sexual double standard—with girls and women positioned as objects of male desire while females' own desires were ignored. Girls and women perceived to lack a healthy interest in boys and men were negatively labeled as *lesbian* by both men and women. Women who had physical relationships with women tended to be married to men. However, by the early twentieth century more women pursued higher education and joined the labor force and could support themselves financially without having to marry a man. So, lesbianism became more visible. Following two World Wars and an economic depression in the United States, anxieties ran high during the mid-twentieth century that women had become masculinized out of necessity. Lesbians were on the receiving end of a "panic over the homosexual menace" (Cahn, 2010, p. 292) for contributing to a collapse of gender distinctions that, ultimately, could disrupt family relations (Penn, 1991). For a significant portion of the twentieth century, the medical establishment supported/contributed to social stigma of lesbianism and female bisexuality, labeling these behaviors as deviant (Friedman & D'Emilio, 1988). In particular, any muscular woman roused suspicion, an outcome which complicated femininity as expressed by women who played sports who were considered "literally un-becoming women" (Cahn, 2010, p. 291). Hence, femininity long has been defined as the object of masculine desire, a heterosexual matrix that reinforces power dynamics of dominance and submission.

Some girls and women seem to make it their duty to police for femininity among their peers. *Pariah femininity* is a category describing women whose biological sex category is considered inconsistent with their lived sexual experiences and who may enact aspects of masculinity, challenging women who become stigmatized as gender deviant (Schippers, 2007). Pejorative terms used to sanction these girls and women signal their threat to a social order, including *bitch, dyke,* and *slut.* Also, the term *oppositional femininity* is used to characterize women who challenge patriarchal gender relations and resist labels (Messerschmidt, 2011), categories that may include nuns, celibate women, and single women who opt out of emphasized femininity norms. In the workplace, some lesbians challenge heteronormativity and female gender expectations and conventions, such as by wearing a dress but refusing to shave their armpits or by wearing traditional men's clothing in meetings when they are the sole woman present (Trethewey, 2000). Categorizing various forms of femininities as they play out within unequal gender dynamics recalls Foucault's (1990) introduction of queer theory and the premise that gendered identity is a *performance* rather than some inherent, biological (aka *natural*) form. Charlebois (2011) poignantly argued that lesbians disrupt hegemonic masculinity norms and heteronormativity by occupying spaces as "both subjects and objects of sexual desire" (p. 34), a position which sometimes proves empowering to girls and women.

Some lesbians define *femininity* independently of their sexual orientation, feeling confident as females for a wide variety of reasons. As such, MacKinnon (2003) reminded us that gender markers such as femininity-masculinity are flexible, subject to change, and therefore unstable. I concur, re-emphasizing the need for scholars to think of femininity in its *plural form*—femininities—and to persist in producing research findings that chip away at the feminine/masculine binary dualism which ultimately benchmarks some groups as representing a desirable norm—while marginalizing others.

NON-CISGENDERED PEOPLE AND FEMININITY

Gender identity and degrees of femininity possessed or expressed play out along an axis of (in)equality, with some social identity intersections and performances of them holding greater social value than others. *Cisgendered* (sometimes shorted to *cis*) people are those who perform a gender identity that conforms to dominant social norms considered appropriate for one's biological sex, often simply referred to as heteronormative. Because just *What is feminine?* may have once seemed obvious or simple, answers today are more complex and complicated—reminding us to acknowledge social constructionism, as discussed in chapter 1.

Transsexual, transgendered, and other non-cisgendered people still encounter stigma and the very idea that one may become a gender (socially constructed) or sex other than what one biologically is born with still ranks among taboo topics in many parts of the world, including the United States. Outward appearances and other conscious expressions of emphasized femininity serve as a key marker for biologically born males who may wish to perform a female gender socially. It is reported that .3 percent of the U.S. adult population identifies as transgender (Gates, 2011), and *Time* magazine declared in 2014 that a transgender tipping point had been reached following the transition of former Olympic athlete Bruce Jenner to Caitlyn, and the success of Emmy Award–celebrated transgender actress Laverne Cox of television's *Orange is the New Black*— collectively establishing gender identity as the next civil rights frontier (Steinmetz, 2014). Sociologists and other researchers are urged to avoid using *transgender* to mean *different* (subordinate, marginal, extraordinary) and *cisgender* to mean *normal* (default setting) (Johnson, 2015). Setting up a cissexist false binary dualism marks certain genders and sexual traits as natural/unnatural or good/bad and threatens marginalization in social research (Serano, 2013), policymaking, and daily living. Indeed, words matter. How we use these and other terms which bring to bear on how *femininity* is defined must be done with care and respect.

During focus group discussions, college women shared mixed perceptions about femininity as something that is *performed* versus femininity as something that is an innate quality. In particular, this aspect of the femininity concept is central to gender transitions of people born as men who wish to become women. Wanda, 20, who identified as biracial, African-American and Caucasian/White explained: "I know that Caitlyn acts a lot more feminine than she used to. You know, with flipping the hair, growing the nails, and walking. That can't be easy to learn when you've been a man all your life. But, hey, if that's what she wants, then that's feminine enough for me." Wanda's acceptance of a broader definition for *feminin-ity* to include people who were not born women was not universally shared among some women who participated in focus group discussions and interviews, however.

In particular, older women among the age cohorts who participated in the focus group and interview discussions found transgenderism some-what perplexing and said they continue to think of femininity only in a context of girls and women. Shirley, 65, Caucasian/White, explained: "I don't know. I don't really understand it. I get that some men love other men, but how can men actually want to become *feminine* women?" In the same focus group discussion, Valeria, 58, Cuban-American, concurred with Shirley, but switched the conversation to talk about children who seem to identify with an alternate gender group: "What I don't under-stand is when celebrities have girls and then raise them like boys on purpose, like Angelina Jolie and her daughter Shiloh. That's a real shame." Valeria said she worried that such girls could grow up being very confused about femininity. She also referred to her Catholic up-bringing and lamented that she found the idea of femininity among for-mer men highly disconcerting.

RELIGION/SPIRITUALITY AND WOMEN'S FEMININITY

Common threads connecting many organized religions and faith struc-tures with other social identity dimensions which shape ways *femininity* is defined include a protectionist worldview of femaleness as constituting *the weaker sex* and preservation of a default female gender caretaker role. Among several Christian religions, the figure of the Virgin Mary pro-vides a "supreme exemplar of this feminine whiteness" and an ideal image of virtue and motherhood (Dyer, 1997, p. 74). Undeniably, in many circles, the ability to have a biological child is "reified as the gold stan-dard of motherhood" (Martin, 2010, p. 540) and is synonymous with traditional femininity as communicated across the ages in religious teach-ings.

Camila, a nineteen-year-old Latina, selected an image from a 2000s issue of *Ladies Home Journal* that featured a young woman who may be Muslim and wearing a hijab as *most feminine* from among the magazine images displayed for women during focus group discussions about *What is femininity?* Then Camila shared this story:

> One time I was in a restroom at like a Wendy's or something and this woman comes out of the stall and she's *beautiful*. She had this gorgeous curly hair, and she was *so* pretty. I was really taken back. . . . And then she looked in the mirror and started putting on her headdress. And I was like wow, you know? I know it's your religion, and I respect that.

But damn, these men hide their women good because she was breath-takingly beautiful.

Also classifying this magazine image of a woman wearing a hijab as *most feminine*, Kathleen, 54, Caucasian/White said, "You only see the eyes, but you could never mistake her as being masculine. Her eyes are made up, too. It's like she's saying 'Even if men want me to hide my body against temptation, they can't hide my feminine spirit.'" Sally, 60, Caucasian/ White, concurred: "There's something about this woman's eyes. You can totally cover her but her eyes tell a million stories. She is a person and a woman. She is feminine and this resonates even though we only see two inches of her." So, Camila, Kathleen, and Sally concurred that a woman's eyes can communicate so much about her internal qualities. With regard to this magazine image, these three women said it was femininity being communicated in the image of the hijab-wearing woman. See Figure 7.1 for a close facsimile of the magazine image women considered.

Conflicts may arise from reconciling organized religions' rules about femininity with lived experiences, however, as women experience intense pressures to live within the margins of a limited female gender role. Findings of a study about gender-role conflict and suicide rates among adolescent girls across ethnicities and religious backgrounds suggested

Figure 7.1.   Research participants considered a women's magazine image of a woman wearing a hijab like this to be among the most feminine images they examined as part of the discussions for this study. Copyright: patronestaff. Source: Luca Patrone/ Depositphotos.com.

that norms imposed upon young unmarried women, such as telling them what is and is not feminine or appropriate for them, are limiting and restrictive (Pinhas, Weaver, Bryden, Ghabbour, & Toner, 2002). Older women—mothers, grandmothers, aunts, and other female relatives—are expected to serve as a bridge connecting church and home and are charged to educate youth about all aspects of religious life, including instructing girls on how to be properly feminine (Taylor & Chatters, 1991). During interviews conducted for this book, Paloma, 46, Dominican, explained that church is an arena where older women emphasize their femininity: "Old ladies in Church still take care of themselves. Maybe they don't have the same body that they once had, but they dress well, put on makeup, and make themselves presentable." Paloma's description of older women of faith and emphasized femininity resonates with Luciana's narrative about ways culture influences emphasized femininity in her family—with her age 60+ grandmother maintaining her own appearance and then chastising granddaughter Luciana for failure to do the same. (See chapter 2). Indeed, culture, religion, gender, and ethnicity intersect uniquely in families and bear on ways *femininity* is defined.

Compulsory heterosexuality espoused by some organized religions generates stress and conflict for women who identify with other sexual orientations. Historically, some lesbian-, bisexual-, and queer-identifying women have been conflicted in their social identity intersections of female gender, sexuality, and religion/faith due to conservative religions' hierarchical and patriarchal values which demand that they conform to traditional female stereotyped roles of serving as homemaker, mother, and being subservient to men (Hagen, Arczynski, Morrow, & Hawxhurst, 2012). Frye (1983) attributed covert "pressures of compulsory motherhood" to religious views about femininity which frown upon lesbians, feminists, and childless women (p. 123). Overall, Ward (2005) posited that "religion-driven homophobia" negatively impacts femininity.

Indeed, stress regarding one's sense of femininity can be significant for women who try to adapt to religious teachings. Evangelical wives and mothers employed outside the home, for example, experience stress associated with simultaneously maintaining their role inside the home as homemaker which is dictated by a dominant ideology of femininity in evangelicalism (Bartkowski, 1999, pp. 58–59). Czarnecki (2015) found that devout Catholic women struggle to "achieve a *moral femininity*" (p. 716, italics added) when those unable to procreate experience cognitive dissonance about using assisted reproductive technologies and reflect on their infertility "as a journey toward salvation" (p. 733). Feeling degrees of shame (partly fueled by Church silence regarding infertility issues), such women may find other means to express normative emphasized femininity when childless (Throsby, 2002) even though "fertility and femininity remain conflated" (Czarnecki, 2015, p. 738). On the other hand, some Protestant women report finding ways to celebrate femininity in their faith by developing female images of God and by advancing female sexuality expressed in worship (Mason, 2007). Some Jewish women have found solace by identifying only with aspects of Judaism and feminism which satisfy their feminine *and* spiritual needs—by using gender neutral and feminine God-language consistent with their own lived experiences (Dufour, 2000).

WOMEN OF COLOR AND FEMININITY

Understanding GRS/C as it plays out among Asian-American, Latina, and African-American/Black girls and women who do not identify as Caucasian/White, but live in a world where emphasized femininity is defined by that standard—is of utmost importance. Ideological difference impacts one's definition of *femininity* and in a culture where ideal femininity is benchmarked as predominantly thin, young, and Caucasian/White across mass media and popular culture, girls and women who identify with other ethnic groups may feel higher degrees of GRS/C if they try to fit in—or perhaps resist and develop their own standards and norms.

Historically, representations of femininity among women of color have proven inaccurate but revealing about wider cultural influences. Femininity and its representations provide a window to observe dominant ideologies in action. For example, representations of the legendary beauty and sexual allure of Cleopatra's femininity in European culture saw pre-nineteenth-century artists change Egypt's Queen of the Nile to a Caucasian/White woman so that her skin color would match Europeans' ideals (Hughes-Hallett, 1990). Feminist writers have underscored interdependent economic, political, and ideological dimensions as means for highlighting differences in femininities among girls and women across cultures. As Collins (1991) has warned, social identity dimensions intersect. They should not be thought of as adjuncts or piled on. Over time, Caucasian/Whiteness had become a *raceless* norm in social scientific research (Zuberi & Bonilla-Silva, 2008)—meaning that researchers may draw conclusions about people when really they are describing a Caucasian/White group as a generic stand-in for *all* people. This practice is inaccurate, irresponsible, and unfair. Doing so when studying an important concept like *femininity* would be a critical error since trying to understand how a wide variety of women define femininity means asking them and collecting diverse narratives as I have done for this book. As discussed in Chapter 4, the fashion-beauty complex's promotion of Caucasian/Whiteness and subsuming of difference into Western glamour reflects a limited range of cultural ideas about *femininity*, an effect that Shome (2014) described as a "kind of borderlessness of white femininity that marks our times" across geographies (p. 178) and across the bodies of girls and women. Accepting any variety of femininity norms as *universal* has serious implications for women of color.

Asian/Asian-American femininity

The term *multiculturalism*, so popular during the 1980s and 1990s, has nearly dropped out of common parlance—perhaps because attempts to create an East-meets-West world culture where ethnicities all are embraced and respected has failed. Emphasized femininity is "unapologetically and invariably white," so exclusion of "non-white femininities" and persistent "racial divisions" has undone any promise of multiculturalism (McRobbie, 2009, p. 70). In the private domestic sphere where emphasized femininity norms are localized and enforced, second-generation female South Asian teens in the United States have reported a gender double standard associated with intersections of female gender, culture, and ethnicity. Brothers and male cousins are given much more personal freedom, such as being allowed to stay out later and learning how to drive a car earlier than females (Best, 2006). Asian cultures steeped in Confucian philosophy tend to be particularly oppressive toward women who are expected to be submissive (Pyke & Johnson, 2003) and are conflictingly stereotyped as either sexual (young women) or as androgynous (older women) (Bradshaw, 1994). Poet Michelle Myers performs as part of *Yellow Rage* on college campuses to critique representations of Asian-American women and their femininities, as well as the appropriation of Asian cultures in the United States. See Figure 7.2. An excerpt of her poem, *I'm a Woman, Not a Flava* underscores the disrespect that Asian-American women experience and anger she feels about how femininities of women of color are sexualized and commodified:

> Wet dream fantasies of easy coochie delight
> against such stereotypes must we constantly fight.
> and it don't help that other women
> compromise our integrity through titillating Asian cultural fantasy.
> Some will be your Chyna Doll, your mami with the slanted eyes,
> body tattooed with Asian calligraphy.
> Others ho their own Asian fashion exotica, from India to China,
> making millions off of images of Asian female erotica.
> They say imitation is the sincerest form of flattery
> so should we take as compliment this appropriated cultural chicanery
> that beats off on our sexuality?
> Well, personally, I feel this way—
> Let's untie our tongues and say:
> Fuck you, fuck you, and fuck you, too!
> 'Cause I'm a woman not a flava
> I'm a woman not a flava not the flava of a woman
> I'll knock the taste out your muthafuckin mouth
> If I don't like your behavior

Figure 7.2.   Poet Michelle Myers of Yellow Rage performing her poem, "I'm a Woman, Not a Flava," 2015, at Temple University in Philadelphia, PA, in protest of ways Asian cultures are appropriated and to critique representations of Asian-American women. Source: Photo by Elizabeth Maver.

I'm not a flava I'm a woman

There has been a dearth of representation of Asian or Asian-American women and their femininities across popular culture and mass media, beyond token models or actresses emphasizing femininity for their exotic sexuality. Consistent with Michelle Myers's anger about ways Asian women are stereotyped, Caitlin, 22, self-identified as Bhutanese-Jewish-American, and explained during a focus group discussion conducted for this book, how she rebels against standard, emphasized femininity steeped in a Caucasian/White identity:

> I just can't stand it. It's been a battle for me, too. I basically reject society's standards in terms of the media. . . . Super skinny, blonde and White. I'm not saying that those women aren't beautiful, because I think all women are beautiful. I am saying that I think that it's harmful to think that you have to mold into that image. That seems to be the message that we've been getting for a long time now. . . . Even in the commercials where there are women of ethnicity, they're usually quite light in their complexion—very, very pristine, clean looking, skinny, tall—so I feel that's a really harmful message. I very rarely ever see very dark or voluptuous women for a lotion or something like that. Asian, as well. I'm half Asian, so I think about that, of course. I don't

really see any Nepali or Indian women in commercials . That's something I think about, too.

About a 1980s *Good Housekeeping* image of an Asian woman wearing a red tunic jumper dress with black turtleneck underneath and black stockings, heels, and gloves, Caitlin criticized a common stereotype about Asian women and skin color: "[A] lot of people would think she's pretty—is that an air hostess thing she's modeling? [S]he is a really pale Asian, which goes back to what I was saying before. Those are the only Asians that we really see."

For college student Nicole, 18, Japanese-Black, who participated in a different focus group discussion for this book, the femininity concept is highly confusing. She regularly travels between the United States and Japan, and often encounters cultural dilemmas when it comes to emphasizing her femininity (or not):

> Back in Japan when I had to wear a traditional kimono. I had to go through, well, trying to get these boobs to go down, so I didn't look like a prostitute. That's an exaggeration, but it was definitely an issue where I had to definitely alter my way of wearing the kimono to look like what was considered a modest, well-dressed Japanese girl and there are not many curvy women in Japan. I mean I go over there and people ask me if they [my breasts] are *real*.

While display of a woman's breasts may be considered quite feminine in the United States (as I discuss at length in chapter 2), Nicole does not find this to be the case in Japan. So, she struggles with her own body in terms of binding her breasts so that she will be accepted when visiting Japan.

Meanwhile, Asian-American women who seek to emphasize their femininity in the West are expected to adapt to the fashion-beauty complex's Caucasian/White-coded products that promote mimicry and accommodation while precluding expression of cultural diversity or ethnic difference (Dyer, 1997). Among magazine images shared with women to stimulate discussions about femininity was a *Redbook* 1990s photograph of a short-haired Asian woman wearing a black suit with short skirt. Luciana, 20, a Latina, selected this image as being what she considered *most feminine*:

> [S]he looks really professional but at the same time, she's got it going on! She has the all-black everything. She has stockings and that's a big thing I think about being feminine. If you don't want to show too much, you have stockings on. She has shoulder pads which was a big thing back in the day. Her hair is groomed. She has on bright red lipstick.

Among second-generation young Asian-American women, daughters of Korean and Vietnamese immigrants living in the United States, the concept of *femininity* involves complicated challenges. Women of Asian descent internalize oppression, engage in subordinated femininity marked by submissiveness, and acquiescence to caricatured Asian femininity in mainstream settings (Pyke & Johnson, 2003). Consequently, second-generation Asian-American women in the United States experience conflicted femininity in conjunction with assimilation into a Caucasian/White world (Pyke & Dang, 2003). In Vietnam, young, unmarried, educated women struggle to negotiate expectations for their feminine identity, too. They receive confusing messages about ideal femininity and experience dissonance as they define femininity in relation to their perceptions of masculinity, their own sexual inexperience, obedience, and passiveness—a dynamic Quach (2008) characterized as "fluid femininity" (p. S158). Earlier, George (2002) described a similar dynamic among Indian women who embody femininity through discipline of their sexual bodies in conformance with social norms, internalizing patriarchal effects but defining them as constructed by their own choices.

Latina femininity

Marianismo, a term developed to describe traditional femininity ideology in the Latin world, suggests that women must be committed to men's authority, sacrifice their individual needs to their family, and maintain a good reputation (Levant, Richmond, Cook, House, & Aupont, 2007). *Marianismo* represents *machismo*'s opposite (Torres, 1998). Latinas living in the United States struggle with negotiating between being *una muchacha de la casa* (good girl, a girl of the house) and *una muchacha de la calle* (bad girl, a girl of the street) (Denner & Dunbar, 2004). Some immigrant parents are highly concerned about relaxed restrictions on girls in the United States that could make Latinas unmarriageable (Espin, 1997). Even girls in Cuba express their femininity through consumption and commitment to marianismo values while displaying a desirably feminine sexuality (Patierra, 2015). Other researchers have found that working-class and poor Latinas (e.g., Mexican-American) develop introverted styles to avoid family conflict should they speak openly and honestly (Taylor, Gilligan, & Sullivan, 1995), with effects that impact their conceptions of femininity associated with resistance to traditional expectations about how girls should be (Denner & Dunbar, 2004)—through self-expression and locating beauty internally (Parker, Nichter, Nichter, Vuckovic, Sims, & Ritenbaugh, 1995).

As addressed in chapter 4, the high school prom and Quinceañera 15th birthday represent an intersection of female gender, culture, ethnicity, and religion social identity dimensions. The extravagant costs associated with rituals celebrating femininity and marriage (and marking transition from childhood to young adulthood) may be cost prohibitive for families of lower socio-economic status, but they make them happen anyway (Colloff, 2009; Pompper & Crandall, 2014).

African-American/Black femininity

For African-American/Black girls and women, intersections of female gender, ethnicity, and socio-economic status dimensions of social identity—against a historical backdrop of racism—complicates any definition of femininity. In the United States before and after the Civil War, African-American/Black women endured rape and other inhumanities which have fueled an ideology defining their bodies as "hard/bad" (Weekes, 2002, p. 256) and "animalistically hypersexual" (Weitz, 2010), certainly not a legacy for considering African-American/Black womanhood out of historical context. Foreman (1990) has posited that given these contexts, "Black femininity, then, must be forcefully asserted" (p. 651) and Janiewski (1983) posited that after generations of performing heavy manual labor, African-American/Black women had to learn how to view themselves as "lady-like" (p. 33). Importantly, African-American/Black women and girls rely upon signifiers, such as clothing and hairstyles, to emphasize their femininity. Young African-American/Black women seek to move away from stereotypical links between Black womanhood and hypersexuality by incorporating some facets of emphasized femininity norms (e.g., purity, respectability), but do not go so far as to desire "Whiteness" (Weekes, 2002, p. 260). Yet, at least one college student, Nicole, 18, Black-Japanese, talked about how confused she has been about social identity intersectionalities and ways these play out in her own social identity:

> [E]ven as a little kid, I recently remembered going through this little identity revelation. One of my best friends was White, blonde, beautiful, with a beautiful White family and I used to go everywhere with them when I was young. One day when we had matching outfits, I realized that I didn't look like them. It was devastating for me. I wanted to be White so bad. I saw this Lip Smackers Chap Stick commercial with all these blonde-haired, freckled White girls putting on Chap Stick and in my head, I thought that if I put on this Chap Stick, I'll be White. So I bought the Chap Stick, put it on, and when I looked in the mirror and saw the same brown girl, I cried. I was convinced that I would be White. You don't think that affects you as you get older but as a kid, when you only see White kids, you only see skinny girls in commercials and you can't relate to that, it's devastating. It really is. . . . I'm very happy with myself and my ethnicity now. But there was a point when I wasn't.

Hair texture and skin tone are central to African-American/Black girls' and women's feminine identity and served as a symbol of resistance to Eurocentric notions of beauty and for celebration of black power in the United States during the 1960s and 1970s. Indeed, wearing of afro and cornrow hairstyles, and African styles of dress (dashikis) proved powerful images promoted by news media (Cranny-Francis, Waring, Stavropoulos, & Kirkby, 2003). Today, display of *bad hair* or *good hair* persists as an omnipresent social identity dimension (Banks, 2000) and a "badge of beauty for women" (Collins, 2005, p. 195). Over time, religious and scientific establishments have used body size, skin color, and hair texture as part of "anthropological and sociological justifications for racial and class hierarchies" (Farrell, 2011, p. 82). hooks (2015) noted that "the fair-skinned black woman" always has been perceived as a "lady" and rewarded with higher status as compared to darker-skinned African-American/Black women who were "seen as bitches and whores" (p. 110). The former sometimes "passed" as Caucasian/White women and experienced "limited social privileges" (Ligon, 2015, p. 57).

Variations in ethnic cultural practices associated with hair translate to "economic survival skills" for African-American/Black women. This is especially relevant for women who seek to work in corporate management shaped by institutionalized power inequities that play out in covert racism and classism (Houston, 1992). Without doubt, female popular culture celebrities who identify as African-American/Black know that "light skin, long hair, and small features" are important physical attributes for defining beauty (Durham, 2007, p. 241), based on emphasized femininity norms which use Caucasian/White body attributes as reflected across popular culture as invitations for African-American/Black young women to emulate. However, striving for those *proper femininity* ideals can take its toll on African-American/Black females' self-esteem (Leadbeater & Way, 1996). In a focus group discussion conducted for this book, twenty-year-old Karen, African-American, pointed out a 1970s magazine image of a thin African-American woman wearing a bright yellow short set whom she categorized as *least feminine*: "I think she looks ill, fragile. I would feel so helpless if I was like that. Where are her boobs? Her butt? Her skin is light and I know the natural look was in a long time ago, but she just doesn't look feminine to me." Karen expressed joy that social media vehicles, in particular, support display of emphasized femininity among African-American/Black women—who do so with pride.

Yet, the fashion industry's acceptance of non-Caucasian/White beauty has vacillated. As an extension of the 1960s' *Black is Beautiful* movement in the United States, ten African-American/Black fashion models walked across a Versailles gala charity event stage on Wednesday, November 28, 1973, in France, and enabled American designers to begin thinking beyond the Caucasian/White female form as a standard for emphasized femininity. These African-American/Black women with "their high cheekbones, brown skin, and slim hips" (Givhan, 2015, p. 258) performed at what has come to be known as *The Battle of Versailles Fashion Show*. The fashion world's acceptance of African-American/Black women as models began to wane in the mid-1990s, however (Givhan, 2015).

More recently, findings about body image norms among female African-American/Black media users today suggest a higher tolerance for the larger body as a standard for attractiveness and femininity. Duke (2000) found that African-American/Black girls reported higher self-esteem levels and more positive body images than Caucasian/White girls and that they use teen magazines as a lens through which to critique *White beauty culture* rather than as benchmarks for achieving some ideal feminine physique for themselves. In fact, Duke (2000) found that African-American/Black girls expressed sympathy for Caucasian/White girls, whom they saw as "unwitting victims" of unrealistic images of emphasized femininity, ones they do not fall for since elder female family members recommend a heavier physique for good health and for sexual appeal among African-American/Black men who "prize 'thick' or amply filled out girls" (pp. 384–85). Most of the African-American/Black women who participated in research for this book mentioned that unique to their culture is admiration for having a "large butt." College student Angela, 20, African-American/Black, explained: "I remember walking home from school and I would look at the reflection of myself in the car mirror and my butt would look so big and I loved it, but it really wasn't *that* big." A member of the same focus group discussion, Nicole, 18, Black-Japanese, agreed: "All my Black cousins had ass and I'm that Asian cousin without the ass . . . . I'd like a little more donk." In the United Kingdom, African-Caribbean young Black women use mediated portrayals of Caucasian/White females' overt sexual behavior as a benchmark for what they *do not* want to do. By engaging in decision making shaped by denigrating sexual activity of peers, young Black women represent themselves as properly feminine and sexually respectable by declining to participate in behaviors attributed to "White femininity" (Weekes, 2002, p. 255).

The concept of femininity, simply, has seemed inconsistent with controlling images of the hypersexualized *hot momma, Jezebel, Sapphire, asexual mammy, mule, matriarch, welfare recipient* and *baby-momma* which have subordinated African-American/Black women and threatened to negatively impact others' and their own self-perceptions. Collins (2010) persuasively has argued that these stereotypes persist as forms of *new racism* that play out via mass media, simultaneously as empowerment images for girls and women to assert control over their bodies and lives—and new forms of discrimination. Rather than seeing "racist, classist, and sexist prejudice and discrimination," some Caucasian/White audiences see African-American women of lower socio-economic status as suffering from "moral failings" (Collins, 2010, p. 9), and as "Black bitches and bad mothers" who are "defeminize[d]" (Collins, 2005, p. 148, p. 198). In addition to providing their daughters with race socialization messages for dealing with discrimination, African-American/Black mothers teach them about femininity and racial pride (Thornton, Alwin, & Camburn, 1983).

FEMININITY AND PHYSICAL DISABILITY

Femininity shaped at the intersection of female gender and physical disability sometimes involves negotiating *an almost passing body* in order to engage with emphasized femininity. Lived experiences of girls and women with disabilities are further complicated by an expectation that girls and women should be and look feminine, what some feminist disabilities scholars characterize as navigating the "politics of appearance" (Garland-Thomson, 2005, p. 1559). This dynamic highlights the degree to which emphasized femininity ideals and female gender norms co-mingle. Disabled bodies often are construed as sexless and infantilized, stripped of the ability to pleasure or to be pleasured—so that women with disabilities are denied an identity as sexual beings (Colligan, 2004). So, girls and women may strategically downplay or mask a physical disability to feel more feminine and/or to be perceived that way by others.

The drive for perfection, when co-mingled with the concept of femininity, presents complications for girls and women whose bodies are visibly disabled. Some women with disabilities may be able to enjoy greatest degrees of social acceptance and value, so long as their bodies do not disrupt cultural expectations of able-bodiedness enveloped in femininity and perfection. The *disabled* label can be applied to almost anyone with "impairments whether physical, sensory or intellectual" (Barnes, 2003, p. 7). The acronym, *TAB* (temporarily able-bodied) serves as a reminder that most people experience a disability at some point in the life cycle (Edison & Notkin, 2010). Disability activists diligently have fought to have negative labels removed from the everyday lexicon, including *cripple, deformed, gimp, retard,* and *vegetable* (Linton, 1998), as well as pejorative terms like *wheelchair-bound* and *victim of paralysis* (Lunsford, 2005). Girls' and women's femininity while inhabiting a body considered disabled is subject to additional sets of stereotypes and other biases by able-bodied biased cultures that value autonomy and physical agility *as a given* for femininity and perfection. Overall, a medical model suggests that people with a disability are sick or in need of rehabilitation, often represented as poor, helpless victims, and villains earmarked by secrecy and shame (Kessler, 1998). Thus, mass media characterizations of people with disabilities as "sickly and helpless victims" prove stigmatizing and can foster low self-esteem among people with disabilities (Zhang & Haller, 2013, p. 330).

During focus group discussions and interviews, a 1965 *Ladies Home Journal* black and white image of a young woman wearing ponytails, slippers, and a puffy quilted bathrobe while using a walker was ignored by women as they listed the magazine images as either *most feminine* or *least feminine*. When I inquired as to why this particular image seemed to evoke no reaction at all, women shrugged their shoulders and shared feedback such as, "I didn't really think about that one at all," or "She's cute and all, but I didn't see her as feminine in any way." So I resolved that even in a discussion about a concept so common and pervasive as *femininity*, the one image of a girl with a disability remained invisible.

Findings of a study about representations on the U.S.–based reality television show, *Push Girls*, revealed that the four hyper-feminine women who used wheelchairs perpetuated the *sex object* stereotype by emphasizing their feminine identity with sexy and revealing clothing, makeup, and fashionably styled hair in order to make their bodies acceptably feminine and to demonstrate how their bodies can appear desirable (Lenhard & Pompper, 2015). The physical accommodations and equipment required (e.g., wheelchair) and extent to which these are perceived as disruptive to women's ability to perform cultural roles deemed traditionally feminine also play a significant role in women's feminine body and an ability to "pass" (Scott, 2015). Consequently, being a woman with a disability involves a double discrimination or double jeopardy (Traustadottir, 1990).

FEMININITY AND SOCIO-ECONOMIC CLASS

Rhetorically, people of lower socio-economic status frequently are blamed for their lot in life and are presumed to be unwilling to *improve* themselves. For girls and women, emphasizing femininity is easier to do with a robust income, but consumerism and mass media regularly bombard women with messages about ways to enhance their feminine selves whether they can afford it or not—with subject positions of upper-class Caucasian/White women (and some wealthy women of color) setting the fashion trends and serving as model citizens. Women of color, women of the global South, and working-class women are exposed to "glamorous images of white female celebrities and their beautiful bodies" who embody cultural and economic privilege (Shome, 2014, p. 206), images used as templates for defining femininity that some girls and women of lower socio-economic status struggle with and are anxious about emulating for themselves.

At the outset of the twentieth century, working women developed their own definition of femininity, one that challenged middle-class perceptions of labor as degrading to femininity. There is little to suggest that working-class women were any less attracted to emphasizing femininity than the more privileged women who did not work outside the home for wages (Bartky, 2010) and still subscribed to Victorian ideas about women appearing pretty, but frail and helpless—as both groups of women immersed themselves in consumerism. Enstad (1999) explained how connections among hard work, fashion, and consumption formed a new definition of femininity for working-class women which included pride in their work in the public sphere.

When considering a black and white image from a 1945 issue of *Red-book*, a woman wearing a blouse and slacks seated at a table with chairs next to a small wood-burning stove in a room with sparse decorations, women I interviewed for this book project were horrified. They made faces and scoffed. This image made the *least feminine* pile every time. As I followed up to learn more, women told me that the image was the "exact opposite" of how they defined femininity.

As I collected narratives for the study reported in this book, I listened to ways women spoke about socio-economic status and how this inter-plays with femininity. To emphasize femininity with beauty and fashion accoutrements can prove highly expensive—even for girls and women who can afford it. But what does this dynamic mean for those who can-not? I heard Amanda, 61, African-American/Black, as she spoke during a focus group about ways social class status factors into a definition of *femininity*. She lovingly recalled family stories about how socio-economic conditions were an important consideration undergirding her parents' union:

> [W]hen I go back and think about some of those women, the men chose them for completely different reasons—it was more like their sturdi-ness and money. A lot of them were stocky. My dad's mother had ten children, my mother's mother had four. . . . My mom was a stunner. My dad's older brother convinced them that they should leave Mobile [AL] to go to New Orleans, because that's where they had the prettiest women and whose families had money. . . . So, the older one married a really sweet, petite and pretty lady whose dad owned a drug store. Then the other one was my mother who worked in her family's busi-ness. They'd had a business in New Orleans for a couple generations.

Amanda laughed with other women in her focus group as she talked about how it all could have ended very differently if her parents lived in other areas and under different conditions. She spoke of how "strategy" and "true love" seem like contradictory concepts, but resolved that the expression "true love knows no bounds" is simply fantasy. Instead, Amanda stressed that femininity, beauty, and money can "help to make *real* love last."

In a different focus group discussion, Alonda, British exchange stu-dent born in Nigeria, 20, told other college women about how display of emphasized femininity is affected by social class, health, and body image beyond U.S. shores, too:

> My parents are both Nigerian. I'm English. They're not as obsessed with skinniness as something to strive for, necessarily. It's more about getting enough to eat and actually having money, that you can afford to eat. The fact that you're skinny probably means that your family is poor and you can't afford to eat.

Alonda explained that "girls with some meat on their bones" are considered more feminine and healthy in Nigerian culture—and that *this* makes them more marriageable: "Healthy women make the best mothers," she added. So, considered together, these narratives of two women separated by forty-one years shared many similarities. Amanda and Alonda suggested additional dimensions shaping the concept of *femininity*, a complex term that is defined by more than surface value of how a girl or woman appears or behaves. Socio-economics play a significant role in determining what's valued as feminine—and the long-term implications of people's perceptions of feminine. In the end, both narratives underscore the ways girls and women are objectified by men as marriage partners and future mothers—and the role the concept of femininity interplays with those processes.

Working classes of all social identity dimensions struggle and feel marginalized from traditional emphasized femininity norms adhered to by middle-class girls and women—with effects compounded by age and ethnicity. During girlhood life stages, social identity shaped by a lower socio-economic status significantly impacts girls' representations of and behaviors associated with femininity. They rely on mass-mediated images of predominantly Caucasian/White middle- to upper-class girlhood as perfection benchmarks to transcend social class boundaries and end up feeling marginalized as a consequence (Thiel-Stern, 2014). McRobbie (1978) found at the outset of her girlhood studies that U.K. working-class girls expressed a social identity that conformed to traditional femininity—in terms of future marriage with children. The girls then developed coping mechanisms for dealing with mediated images that put representations of fantasy-emphasized femininities within their view. *Working-classness* binds girls to one another in their consumption of the messages about what femininity *could be*. This dynamic persists on the United States side of the Atlantic with a key additional ingredient today: social media. Using self-produced "Am I pretty or ugly?" YouTube videos, working-class girls of color seek public validation for enhanced self-esteem by offering up their bodies for public scrutiny. Yet, they risk being disciplined through posted feedback shaped by heteronormative femininity ideals presented in often racist, violent, and sexualized language for how to become more beautiful and how to be a better person (Rossie, 2015). While these girls are actively engaged with social media (rather than mere passive observers of teen magazines), the cultural currency of feminine visibility involves risk of exposure to damaging words and online experiences that may scar for a lifetime. Media embody the potential to empower girls to explore female gender roles and interpretations of femininity in terms of marriage, motherhood, full economic participation, and any other goal they may choose for themselves. It is regrettable that dynamics associated with the femininity concept too often involve high levels of stress and conflict for girls and women.

ADDING FEMINISM TO THE SOCIAL
IDENTITY INTERSECTIONALITIES MIX

Ways femininity is qualified and defined in the United States has become intertwined with feminism and its various waves and interpretations for more than 100 years. In the United States, first-wave feminism began in 1848 at the Seneca Falls Conference to secure the vote for women and culminated in the ratification of the Nineteenth Amendment in 1920. Yet, Elizabeth Cady Stanton and other middle-class suffragists virtually ignored African-American/Black women (Davis, 2010). Second-wave feminists' goal to achieve equal rights for women emerged amongst the civil rights, peace, and free-speech movements. Meanwhile, Betty Friedan's (1963) *The Feminine Mystique* overlooked working-class women and African-American/Black women (Smith, 2015). Both first- and second-wave women's movements have been criticized for inadequately considering ways that female gender intersects with other social identity dimensions, including ethnicity, physical and mental disability, social class, and sexual orientation.

Luciana, 20, who self-identifies as Latina from a lower-class upbringing, explained during a focus group discussion conducted for this book why she considers herself a feminist: "[M]y definition of feminism is the fact that I embrace my womanhood and I put that first above anything. It's not to bash men. It's just that I'm proud to be a woman. . . . I love the way I am. . . . I feel like every woman wants to feel—feminine. That's part of being a woman." Luciana's words prompted many women sitting around the focus group discussion table to nod their head in agreement and some even clapped their hands.

Yet, many young women today have negative perceptions of feminism and completely separate the movement from ways they define femininity. Some women simply see no connections between feminism as a movement and ways femininity is defined. For example, Nicole's epigram at the top of this chapter suggests that she considers feminism irrelevant to her own lived experiences because she does not feel as though she has "missed out" on any opportunities. As discussed in chapter 4, the Twitter hashtag campaign, #WomenAgainstFeminism, inspired several young women to explain why feminism is not for them. They, too, expressed opinions that suggest feminism, as a political movement, is irrelevant in their lives—while some seemed to inaccurately equate feminism with manhating. During one of the focus groups I conducted with college women when collecting narratives for this book, Caitlin, 22, Bhutanese-Jewish-American, shared her own definition of feminism: "It is about equality for all, not hating men—which I just think is ridiculous." Rebecca Walker (1992), daughter of second-wave activist Alice Walker, wrote *Becoming a Third Wave* for *Ms.* magazine to say, "We're different, but we're part of this history" in response to sentiments on college campuses that feminism was irrelevant and dead (Anderson, 2013). In the documentary film, *The Punk Singer* (2013), Jennifer Baumgardner explained third-wave feminism: "The third wave cliché is like a hot but angry bisexual girl who is wearing a mini dress with combat boots. I mean, there's like, a lot of I think attempting to reconcile a lot of extremes that are in all of us" (Anderson, 2013). Yet, today's third-wave movement is critiqued for equating female sexuality with freedom to consume for a *postfeminist masquerade*, for *undoing* feminism's gains with acceptance of class positions in the United Kingdom (McRobbie, 2009).

In bell hooks's (2015) *Feminism Is for Everybody*, she argued that post-feminism operates inconsistently with goals for moving toward an open society wherein all people are valued for their distinct social identity. Moreover, hooks and other feminists have argued that ideological assumptions at work in postfeminism limit inclusion by "certain women within privileged educational, professional, and other work contexts" and also are linked to consumer-led capitalism (Tasker & Negra, 2007, p. 2). The *whiteness, heteronormativity,* and *middle-classness* of women's liberation had been part of the second-wave feminist movement's rhetorical strategy and also attributable to news media framing of it (Hesford, 2013). In sum, the women's liberation movement was and is primarily Caucasian/White and middle class—which helps to explain why emphasized femininity reproduces a heteronormative Caucasian/White and middle-class ideal or standard.

The Equal Rights Amendment was reintroduced in 1972 but failed to pass, so that today there is still no Equal Rights Amendment in the United States, and feminism has fragmented. Globally, feminist theorists tend to agree on the importance of protecting girls' and women's bodies, supporting their rights, contesting backlash, and debating about how femininity is made to mean. Challenging accepted ideas about girls' and women's social position is a battle worth waging. Self-reflexivity involves bringing together multiple, intersecting social identity dimensions and contexts overlooked by anti-feminists without ignoring discrimination's patriarchal, racist, and classist roots. Holmlund (2010) argued that post-feminism represents "a white chick backlash that denies class, avoids race, ignores (older) age, and 'straight'-jackets sexuality" (p. 117). Meanwhile, social pressures for women to maintain a certain appearance, to take full responsibility for private sphere responsibilities, and to perpetuate female gender roles in the domestic sphere produces internal conflicts with physiological effects for women who struggle to negotiate time spent on work outside the home for pay with non-paid work at home. Backlash against feminism grows proportionally to the forces girls and women endure to control the shape of their bodies, their age through surgical procedures, amount of makeup they wear, and fashion trends they keep up with—often with limited regard for the size of their budget.

DISCUSSION

Without doubt, social identity intersectionalities impact one's definition of femininity. This chapter has examined femininity as a concept shaped by social identity dimension intersectionalities, including class, ethnicity, faith/spirituality, gender, physical ability, and sexual orientation, with additional attention to the social importance of body shape/size and the role of feminist social movements. Indeed, as amplified among voices of women who participated in study findings shared throughout this book, femininity is a subjective concept, fluid and flexible enough to accommodate multiple social identity intersectionalities. Femininity, as a concept, must continually be problematized as a set of culturally inscribed social practices and include debates/discussions to exorcise the concept of its privileged, middle-class, "heterorespectability" (Hesford, 2013, p. 70). Doing so should make the concept of femininity available for interrogation among women of color so that they need not relinquish signifiers of racial difference en route to developing their own definition of femininity (McRobbie, 2009, p. 70).

One's sense of personal femininity, emphasized femininity, performances of femininity, and others' perceptions of femininity operate under structures of domination which contribute to girls' and women's subordinate position in society. Hence, girls and women shall continue to actively engage in their own contextual definitions of what femininity means by combatting forces which threaten to make them obscure, deviant, ignored, or marginalized. Such acts of resistance to idealized, standard, normalized versions of emphasized femininity and any ideas about perfection eventually should chip away at the feminine/masculine binary dualism borne out of axes of power relations which persist in a failure to view girls and women as multiple groups of individuals possessing unique gender identities shaped by their intersecting social identity dimensions.

EIGHT

Sexuality, Masculine Femininity, and Feminine Masculinity

Part of femininity is loving your body and having the strength, you know, to love your body.

—Research participant, Carol, 19, Caucasian/White, lesbian

Worldwide, there are nearly as many signifiers of femininity and masculinity as there are people. This may make unambiguous identification of people challenging, but what opportunities exist for individuals to express themselves by emphasizing how feminine or masculine they want to be in any given context! Signifiers of femininity and masculinity go far beyond one's physical body to include presence or absence of certain elements, including dress style, makeup, language/speech, work/occupation, gestures/body language, occupation, recreation, and so much more. Mutually exclusive binary labeling for women who *must* be masculine if they use assertive speech and men who *must* be feminine if they use passive speech slowly is becoming outdated as it becomes more socially acceptable for any one person to exhibit a full range of characteristics. For those who still believe one's bodily performance must be congruent with biological sex, stereotyping and negative consequences endure for the masculine female considered a *bitch* or *butch* who needs to be put in her place—and for the feminine male considered a *fag* or a *pussy* who needs to be toughened up. Polarizing binary labels serve as blinders for a range of diversity across social contexts and cultures. In the United States, femininities and masculinities are becoming much more fluid concepts as applicable for any gender group, even though transgendered people may experience conflict in choosing combinations to fully characterize their identity.

There is no *single* definition for femininity, as each individual woman may change her ideas about it multiple times across her life course. Women interviewed for this book affirmed that. Dynamics are rife for stressful and conflicting experiences among women as expressions of socially defined female gender roles and identity vary. Also, traditions associated with femininity and expectations of attractiveness and female roles of caretaking of others persist. Women who are ambitious in their career are just as likely to be considered approvingly by some and disapprovingly by others. Women who raise their children full-time at home are just as likely to be respected by some and disrespected by others. Bearing in mind that femininity is not the same as a girl or woman's biologically sexed body, and because so much diversity exists within both femininity's and masculinity's manifestations and representations, considering femininities and masculinities in their plural forms is more accurate than considering them as singular, oppositional, or complementary. The postmodern cultural studies concept of *bricolage*, a combination of mixed media and eras so that *anything goes* (Hebdige, 1988), metaphorically supports the idea that individuals experience multiple femininities and masculinities regardless of biological sex. MacInnes (1998) argued that gender, femininity, and masculinity represent "an ideology people use in modern societies to imagine the existence of difference between men and women on the basis of their sex where, in fact, there is none" (p. 1). For these reasons, femininity and masculinity have become "more amorphous and difficult to define in our society than even in the recent past" (Beynon, 2002, p. 3).

Addressed in greater detail throughout this chapter are these sections: 1) Theorizing about femininity and masculinity in a context of sexuality, 2) Femininity-inspired microaggressions, 3) Heteronormativity as social control on femininity, 4) Drag queen and king culture for emphasized femininity and masculinity, 5) Women in the military, and 6) Discussion.

THEORIZING ABOUT FEMININITY AND MASCULINITY IN A CONTEXT OF SEXUALITY

All known societies distinguish between female and male and offer up models of behavior for each group. *Femaleness* and *maleness* suggest something about an individual's essence, while *gender identity* refers to one's subjective feelings about that femaleness or maleness (Hoffman, Borders & Hattie, 2000). The concepts of *femininity* and *masculinity* do more than shape gender identity, for each is a "critical element in our informal social ontology" (Bartky, 2010, p. 91). Feminist, girls', and men's studies scholars long have considered theoretical issues associated with gender identity, a woman's sense of her own identity and desirability—and a man's, too. For a long time, the biological sex-role socialization model has posited two fixed, bipolar, and mutually exclusive categories of woman and man (Kimmel, 1987), effectively reinforcing for centuries *opposite sex* roles shaped by either femininity or masculinity. Yet, in addition to lack of parsimony making for theoretical inadequacies, the biological sex-role socialization model no longer holds fast (if it ever did). Perfection of surgical procedures are used to change a person's biological sex orientation, and expanded research on the social construction of gender attributes tells very little about one's gender according to biology. Exceptions include linking masculine aggression to testosterone, the primary male sex hormone (MacKinnon, 2003, p. 3).

As I conducted one-on-one interviews and focus groups with women for the study reported in this book, Denise, 52, Caucasian/White, intently pondered ways to express her definition of *femininity* when sorting through the magazine images used as stimulus materials and separating them into lists of *most feminine* and *least feminine*. Here is how she referred to a 1980s *Good Housekeeping* image of a woman cradling a baby: "Well, it's the essence of what differentiates *masculine* from *feminine*. . . . [T]hings that men cannot do, like giving birth . . . things that are own-able by women that are not own-able by men." In the end, Denise (and several other women, too) used biological markers to define femininity. In a different interview, Caitlin, 22, Bhutanese-Jewish-American, used this same image of a woman cradling a baby to share a similar opinion about defining *femininity*: "Probably one thing that most people could agree on is that you're in your most feminine stage if you're pregnant—or at least you're in your most woman state . . . because it's the one thing we can do that they [men] can't."

Patriarchy, a theoretical concept that long has captivated feminist scholars, structures social life in such a way that men and masculinity are positioned as superior and dominant over women and femininity. Throughout interviews and focus group meetings, women raised many issues, concerns, and questions about *femininity* as it overlaps with multiple aspects of being a girl or woman. For example, several college women told stories about how the concept of *femininity* complicates relationships and fuels misperceptions and insecurities for themselves and for their partners. Angela, 20, African-American/Black, explained:

> I think both boyfriends I've had didn't think of me as feminine—not because of my appearance, but in my personality. Like, I'm very argumentative. I'm very dominating. One guy said I should wear a night gown instead of shorts and t-shirt. I think the big problem was that it made him feel like less of a man and that was a big issue. Now lucky for me I could realize that's not *my* problem, it's *his* own insecurities. . . . I am comfortable enough with myself as far as my personality goes that I don't care that much. . . . [S]ometimes I find myself trying to not be feminine because I want to appeal to someone as not being a girlie-girl, but I want to appeal to them because I love video games, I

like boxing, and I wear baggy jeans. I don't want to be liked because
I'm submissive, passive, or not confrontational. . . . I'm proud and want
guys to respect me. I think that reflects their confidence as an individual in which case I can rely on *them* to be OK with *themselves*. I don't
have to make them feel better about themselves. That's not my job.

As Angela shared her story, many other college women in the room
nodded their heads in agreement. Some applauded Angela for standing
her ground and not succumbing to pressures to conform to her boyfriend's demands or his perceptions of how a girlfriend *should* emphasize
her femininity. Other women concurred that they, too, have felt the need
to suppress or augment aspects of their feminine identity in order to stay
in a relationship. Overall, patriarchy demands that females be exploited
and sexualized to satisfy male desires. Males are socialized into patriarchy and find themselves marginalized if they refuse to either comply
with it or easily fit into traditional masculinity patterns (Craig, 1992).
Also, it is possible for certain forms of femininity to be emphasized, more
celebrated, or promoted as ideal—especially when based on a young,
thin, Caucasian/White ideal. Certain types of femininity also may be perceived as *better* or *more powerful* than some other forms of femininity.
Despite culture-specific contexts, MacKinnon (2003) posited that, generally, social science scholars across multiple fields concur that the standard
conceptions of femininity and masculinity are universal due to patriarchy's endurance as an organizing framework.

This chapter's focus on sexuality, masculine femininities, and feminine masculinities is rooted in an understanding of ways femininity and
masculinity are intertwined with gender, power, and sexuality. Carol's
plea cited at the top of this chapter may seem to be a simplistic statement,
but her urging that women embrace their femininity and love their body
is rooted in Carol's understanding that so much of what girls and women
are told by popular culture, the fashion-beauty complex, mass media,
and even family members is that *they are not perfect* and that they need to
make improvements so that they will be loved. Just how these notions are
communicated to girls and women constitutes and relies upon *discourse*—ways we use language to construct issues, talk about them, and
communicate about them. Discourse impacts social practices and establishes norms (Foucault, 1980, 1990). Freud (1933) closed his (in)famous
Femininity lecture by alluding to *puberty* as the turning point wherein
girls push aside masculine qualities to accommodate a developing femininity. In the end, what Freud endorsed was a prescription of *emphasized
femininity* as the benchmark for girls and women. *Emphasized femininity*
legitimates unequal gender relations between women and men because it
takes on meaning only in a context of complementing *hegemonic masculinity* (Messerschmidt, 2011). Sharol, 42, African-American/Black woman

interviewed for this book, associated seeming contradictory terms of *soft-ness* and *strength* when defining femininity:

> [T]here is a *softness* to women, but I also think that there's a *strength* that we possess even though it doesn't always show. Some women are very strong on the outside and that's their bravado. What makes wom-en women is that we possess a strength that is an inner strength—that emerges when it's necessary. I do think that we also have a softness to us—even the hardest woman. . . . I believe that every woman has that softness to her. . . . I think that women are able to use their femininity in a way that gives them confidence—to use their femininity to advance whatever they're trying to advance. . . . There's an interplay between men and women—even in a business setting—women have an ability to use their femininity in a way to get what they want. I don't mean it in a slutty way. It's very interesting in terms of men feeding off of that.

Sharol's definition of *femininity* as a continuum with softness at one pole and strength at the other complements thinking about femininity in its plural sense—femininities, a flexible concept that may be used by girls and women of multiple intersecting social identity dimensions and con-texts. I shall return to this discussion in chapter 11. In a separate one-on-one interview, Jenni, 42, Korean-American, seemed to agree with Sharol by equating femininity with *softness*:

> Femininity is being tidy and neat, ladylike. . . . [Y]ou can be tough and do all the things you want to—but what makes a woman unique is that you can approach it in a way that's more feminine, more ladylike, and still be able to accomplish the same thing. You don't have to be so rough and bullish to get what you want. There's a unique approach that a woman can get away with. . . . I don't think you need to be bullish about it. Even a man can use some feminine qualities—a little sensitivity.

That both Sharol and Jenni talked about *utility* of femininity as a *strategy* for acquiring what a woman wants suggests an outcome of women learn-ing to navigate their second-class status under patriarchy.

Male identity steeped in masculinity generally requires distance from female identity and femininity. Otherwise, men who display feminine qualities are considered the *opposite* of masculine and become subject to violence and marginalization because they are considered homosexual (Pompper, 2010). Hence, anti-femininity rests at the center of historical and contemporary ideas about manhood such that masculinity is "de-fined more by what one is not rather than who one is" (Kimmel, 2004, p. 185). When we spoke one-on-one as part of an interview for this book, Sally, 60, Caucasian/White, talked about men who display feminine qual-ities: "I have two bosses for fifteen years. Fantastic! They are the most gentle, pro-women, feminine men and yet they are straight guys." Sally's commentary suggested her surprise at a seeming disconnect between these bosses' gender and sexual orientation. She offered that non-heterosexual men have something to teach heterosexual men about understanding femininity, managing employees, and working well with women of all stripes. Nineteen-year-old college student, Mimi, Asian-American, reflected on a *Ladies Home Journal,* 1955, image of a nurse and pondered gender stereotypes that reflect on ways she interrogates the concept of *femininity.* Mimi shared a poignant example of how men are stereotyped if they pursue careers deemed feminized:

> I know a guy from church who said he was studying to be a nurse. We feel bad for him, and we were all like, "Boy, are you crazy? Are you going to walk around wearing skirts, too, and stuff?" I mean, I know that's not what they wear. That's what it's like to have a typical stereotype that women are more nursing and nurturing types than men are.

Undeniably, an assumption of heteronormativity determines ways many people constitute femininity and masculinity. Mimi expressed a bit of shame for the way she and friends teased the man at her church and offered this follow-up: "I know. It was wrong. But, come on, that's how it is. People associate femininity in guys with being gay."

Narratives that women shared clearly underscore the salience of unequal social power relations attached to ways we define femininity. Because girls and women embody degrees and varieties of femininity as they feel appropriate and across their life course, femininities in the plural form is more accurate and flexible so as to accommodate multiple contexts of girls' and women's lived experiences. Based on the patriarchy framework discussed above, we know that *femininity* never can be hegemonic in ways that masculinity is hegemonic. As noted throughout this book, the traditional form of *emphasized femininity* expressed by girls and women involves body displays of dresses, jewelry, makeup, shoes, and stylish hair. *Subordinate femininities* are those defined in terms of resistance or noncompliance to emphasized femininity traditions. As noted in chapter 7's attention to femininity when female gender and attention to sex intersect, there exists a *hierarchy of femininities* in terms of non-heteronormative, pariah, and oppositional femininities. Navigating what girls and women *are supposed to look like and behave* in order to be considered feminine may conflict with their own sense of *how they are.* For example, some lesbians and women who are bodybuilders are considered more masculine than feminine and may experience difficulty fitting in with everyday situations (Bartky, 2010). Moreover, not only are girls and women criticized by men for being *un*feminine, but girls and women expressing emphasized femininity also may engage in bullying with verbal and physical abuse of those considered to possess oppositional/subordinate femininities. In short, girls and women suspected of nonconformity with regard to emphasized femininity—as in school settings—may find themselves physically attacked by other girls or women (Adams, 2005; Messerschmidt, 2004, 2011).

For girls/women and boys/men considered to be nonconforming to traditional femininity and masculinity ideals, levels of gender-role anxiety, stress, and conflict may be more escalated than for those who appear to be conventionally feminine or masculine. In general, people report higher levels of well-being and enjoy their jobs more when their femininity or masculinity levels resonate with workplace norms (Wolfram, Mohr, & Borchert, 2009). In other words, women who scored low on femininity reported greater satisfaction with jobs in gender-atypical, male-dominated occupations than those considered gender-typical (Long, 1989).

FEMININITY-INSPIRED MICROAGGRESSIONS

Emphasized femininity, as discussed above, complements *hegemonic masculinity*, an outcome of patriarchy's roots in many societies. For girls and women, dressing and behaving in feminine ways consistent with expectancies for girls and women may have its rewards in love and acceptance. Yet, women who follow emphasized femininity's demands may not always come out on top—as when they are exposed to microaggressions by males who believe femininity means females are continuously available to them as desirable sexual partners. Demanding that girls and women smile and insulting them with catcalls and street harassment is a form of verbal violence often expressed in conjunction with physical violence. Microaggressions such as these are rooted in social power relations and are operationalized as "brief and commonplace daily verbal, behavioral and environmental indignities, whether intentional or unintentional, that communicate hostile, derogatory, or negative . . . insults to the target person or group" (Sue, Capodilupo, Torino, Bucceri, Holder, & Nadal, 2007, p. 273). Consequences for those offended manifest in a hostile and invalidating climate (Solórzano, Ceja, & Yosso, 2000) and mental health issues (Sue, Capodilupo, & Holder, 2008). Critical race theorists have posited that covert microaggressions are a symptom of an unconscious exclusionary worldview toward others (Sue, Bucceri, Lin, Nadal, & Torino, 2007). Furthermore, microaggressions perpetuate stereotypes which oversimplify or reduce someone to certain qualities or exaggerate group differences (Watzlawik, 2009).

Recent Internet-transmitted video satires have crystallized a micro-agression against girls and women—and inspired public discussion about gender disparities in perceptions about facial expressions. The ancient Greeks believed that our character is visible on our face and it takes only one-tenth of a second to judge the character of an unfamiliar face (Willis & Todorov, 2007). In 2013, a parody public service announcement released on *Slate V*, an online video magazine, showed differences between women's and men's smiling face and their at-rest face, linguistically labeling the latter a *Bitchy Resting Face. BRF* is when an expressionless face is at ease or deep in thought. A *BRF* may be perceived as angry or irritated. A mock public service announcement video on the comedy website *Funny or Die* (Broken People, 2013), re-labeled the phenomenon, *Resting Bitch Face, RBF.* These satire phenomena became linked to girls and women as an Internet meme across YouTube, Facebook, and other social media through images of celebrities such as Vivien Leigh (as Scarlet O'Hara), Kristen Stewart, and Victoria Beckham without smiles as they were *urged to be feminine and to smile.* In a first-person *New York Times* piece, Bennet (2015) wrote about the "tyranny" of *RBF* as inspiring women to consult plastic surgeons to surgically correct their permafrowns. In a New Jersey business journal, *NJBIZ,* Fry (2015) reported on physicians who explained how women's faces sag as they age and women speculated about how a perceived scowl could be holding them back at work. She called femininity a "double-edged sword" since women who are *too serious* may be deemed "bitchy" while those who smile and laugh too much may not be taken seriously (Fry, 2015).

Framing of these natural phenomena so negatively constitutes microaggressions. The arrangement of facial features and expressions is gendered, with girls and women policed in attempts to control them. Simply, humans make judgments based on facial cues and verdicts for women are much more critical and harsh. Somewhere along the evolutionary chain, smiling has become an unspoken given for girls and women since they tend to smile more and happy displays have been associated with femininity (LaFrance, Hecht, & Paluck, 2003). Ironically, girls and women suffer higher rates of depression than boys and men (Mayo Clinic Staff, 2016). Smiling babies are more likely to be labeled female and good-looking people get the most valentines (Highfield, Wiseman, & Jenkins, 2016). Happiness is the most attractive female emotion expressed, and men consider *serious* women less sexually appealing (Tracy & Beall, 2011). By contrast, smiling men appear "too feminine or more desperate for sex" (Dowd, 2011).

Feminists and others associated with the movement against street harassment use a "Stop telling women to smile" campaign theme. "Show me a smile" is common in street harassment and when girls and women do not comply, they are mocked (Waldman, 2013). In Atlanta, GA, a painter-illustrator and her helpers plastered posters on vacant buildings with the headlines, "Stop Telling Women to Smile," "My Outfit Is Not an Invitation," and "Women Do Not Owe You Their Time or Conversation" (Lee, 2014). Across the United States, women are campaigning through their writing, public meetings, and anti-harassment groups like "Hollaback!" and "Stop Street Harassment" to end objectification and demoralizing slurs, microaggressions against women simply for expressing their feminine identity (or not).

HETERONORMATIVITY AS
SOCIAL CONTROL ON FEMININITY

Research findings suggest significant backlash associated with being unable (or unwilling) to fulfill social expectations about one's gender-sexual role as expressed through femininity or masculinity. When a man is *un*-masculine or woman is *un*feminine, each is believed to be acting not only contrary to their biological sex, but contrary to a heteronormative ideal. Heterosexism is a potent ideological system in the West that emphasizes the primacy of heterosexuality and perpetuates heterosexuals' privilege and social power (Hegarty, Pratto, & Lemieux, 2004). Femininity and masculinity are manifested in appearance and behavior—or, as Watzlawik (2009) posited, "they capture how men and women are believed to be like (or more likely to be like)" (p. 134). Masculine women often are considered lesbian and feminine men often are considered gay. As part of my research for this study, Camila, 27, bisexual, Dominican, participated in a focus group and used a 2000s *Ladies Home Journal* image of stand-up comedian Ellen DeGeneres to explain how the concepts of femininity and masculinity complicate life experiences for non-heterosexuals who simply want to *be*:

> I feel that's a big problem with lesbians and women that want to appear to be strong and independent. They always feel like they must be manly. I think that in the long run, that's horrible because you don't want to teach the younger generation that in order to get respect, and in order to surpass everyone else, you have to be like a man. I think that's what Ellen [DeGeneres] does. I love what she represents—that she's open about her sexuality and she has all this opportunity to reach out and share her thoughts with the world. . . . I don't think femininity and masculinity have to be connected. I think that there's always some sort of—a firm balance. Among my friends who are lesbians, there's always one woman who has to portray a man in the relationship and they always bothered me. Why can't there just be two women who embrace the fact that they're women? Why is there some sort of male perspective mixed in there? Why do they have to be connected? When there's a discussion on men, it's always woman is a part of man and that's frustrating because I feel like they're two separate entities that shouldn't be compared or connected. Why can't there just be women and men, you know?

Camila experienced some difficulty with the *most feminine* and *least feminine* magazine image exercise conducted for this book as I sought to discover how women defined femininity. As a woman who identifies as bisexual, Camila encouraged dissolution of the feminine-masculine binary dualism, explaining how it complicates human relationships and contributes to individuals' internal confusion and stress.

Overall, gender role stress/conflict (GRS/C) among men is a consequence of heteronormativity and traditional ideas about masculinity which end up inhibiting men's relationships with other men and intimacy with children and women. As compared to heterosexual women, heterosexual men worry more about not appearing to be feminine or homosexual (Bosson, Prewitt-Freilino, & Taylor, 2005). This outcome constitutes a social control on men—wherein they are expected to be straight and to be masculine. Slurs such as *fag* and *queer* are considered to be more hurtful to men than equivalent verbal insults are to women (Burn, 2000). Two generations of men across four ethnic groups reported anxiety, confusion, and frustration with regard to the *metrosexual* concept (men who attend to fashion and personal grooming) and perceptions of inadequacy when considering how they measure up to media-promoted male body images (Pompper, 2010). African-American/Black men are told to enact a particular performance of Black masculinity and the Black church rhetorically rejects homosexuality through code words of *punk* and *sissy* expressed from the pulpit to warn against weakness and femininity (Pitt, 2010). In these ways, men are controlled to conform to traditional male gender role norms associated with masculinity.

Heteronormativity as a social control plays out uniquely for girls and women. In the wake of *girl-power, riot grrrl,* and *punk girl* trends are concerns that young women, in particular, may use emphasized femininity to take *wild girl, saucy flirtatious, pleasure-loving,* and *sexy girl* stereotypes to extremes for unrestrained sexual experiences. Social norms dictate that the pleasure-loving young woman will settle down over time to become the selfless devoted mother (Glover & Kaplan, 2009). The *laddish girl* stereotype of young women who dress in traditional male clothing and experiment with sexual lifestyles other than those sanctioned by heteronormativity serves to "counterbalance" the hyperfeminine forms which are critiqued as "excessive" or "transgressive" (Dobson, 2014b, pp. 264–65). Such critiques serve to point out moral transgressions and to restrain girls and young women along the more traditional lines of bygone days. Rather than thinking in either/or terms (feminine *or* masculine), I consider all of the above phenomena as residing along a femininities continuum within an individualized context of a girl's or woman's complete social identity dimension of gender as it intersects with age, culture, ethnicity, and more—in addition to sexual orientation. Framing girls and women as masculine not only stimulates social critique about their non-heterosexuality and disruption of a long-standing gender order, but also may serve to suppress further feminist intervention if women are considered free to act like men (McRobbie, 2009).

Research findings suggest that people still rely on visual and gender-role stereotypes when defining femininity and masculinity—those driven by heteronormativity. As discussed in chapter 2, women across three age cohorts who participated in the study reported in this book defined femininity referring to appearance—especially among women ages eighteen to twenty-nine—with words such as *beautiful, curvy, elegant, medium height, muscular, poised, pretty, thin,* and *toned.* In earlier studies, when research participants were asked to illustrate their open-ended descriptions of what femininity looks like and what masculinity looks like, they came up with female types of *housewife, whore, career woman,* and *feminist* and male types of *business executive, ladies' man, homosexual,* and *nerd* (Green & Ashmore, 1998)—and attributes concerning their physical appearance, occupation, social roles, and sexual behavior (Six & Eckes, 1991). From childhood through adulthood, people are socialized to their cultures' gender-related stereotypes and role expectations. The stereotypes lead ideas about femininity and masculinity associated with gender identity rather than the other way around (Spence & Buckner, 2000). According to an earlier study, changes in culture and environmental context inspired college-aged women to endorse more masculine-stereotyped traits for themselves while college-aged men continued their non-endorsement of feminine-stereotyped traits for themselves (Twenge, 1997). Boys playing rugged sports such as football and girls dancing with pink tutus shape young people's behaviors in socially acceptable ways (Lenskyj, 2012) and further entrench hegemonic masculinity with femininity as subservient. Effects of visual stereotypes emerged among findings of a longitudinal study, 1983–2003, with mothers displaying increased femininity levels with more marital support in the private, domestic sphere—but decreased femininity levels when unmarried, with more children at home, and while working full or part time (Kasen, Chen, Sneed, Crawford, & Cohen, 2006). Those findings paint the picture of a woman who wishes to emphasize her femininity as someone who is married, works only at home, has children (but not too many), and has a husband who helps with the housework. Heteronormativity, reinforced by visual stereotypes across popular culture and media representations serves as a powerful social control on the type of femininities women and men embrace.

DRAG QUEEN AND KING CULTURE FOR
EMPHASIZED FEMININITY AND MASCULINITY

For hundreds of years (if not more), drag queen and drag king performers have been breaking social rules/roles that female gender characteristics can be performed only by women and that masculine gender characteristics can be performed only by men. Audiences are afforded the opportunity to see both femininity and masculinity *over*produced as part of a parodic gender performativity which dissociates biological sex from socially constructed gender (Butler, 1990). Drag queens and kings allow a rupture in gender guidelines while also reinforcing the social image of what it means to exaggerate femininity or masculinity when a man wants to look like a woman (e.g., Cher, Dolly Parton, Reba McEntire) with large wigs, pancake makeup, sequined gowns, big jewelry—or a woman wants to look like a man (e.g., Issac Hayes, Elvis Presley, Michael Jackson, Tim McGraw) with cigars, neckties, business suits, beard/moustache. *Doing gender* involves a complex of socially sanctioned behaviors and attitudes which cast particular pursuits as expressions of feminine and masculine "natures" (West & Zimmerman, 1987, p. 126). Yet, Greaf (2015) persuasively argued that drag queens' femininity performances ultimately reproduce traditional femininity and male privilege, reinforcing heteronormative ideas about emphasized femininity defined as a certain style of hair, clothing, makeup and body language. Drag queens "bear the stigma of gay male femininity," and make visible gay and transgender social identity intersectionalities with jokes about sex in their performances which suggest that sexual acts are the same regardless of sexual actor (Taylor & Rupp, 2005, p. 2133).

Study of drag king culture offers a particularly fascinating opportunity to interrogate how femininities are performed when women dress and act as men. If men are presumed to look "unprepared and natural," while women are complimented for looking "well put together" (Brown, 2000, p. 44), how is this dynamic complicated in drag king performances? The director of *Venus Boyz*, a documentary about drag king culture, does not equate the art form with any political movement, but she argued that it raises awareness about women performing femininity in new ways. Baur (2002) explained:

> Drag king is not . . . in this way a political movement, but I think it does a lot of new ways of perception—how we can look at man and woman. And it's opening up for a lot of women the possibility to discover in themselves certain things which they were not allowed, perhaps, to live out.

Drag king performing is quite empowering for women, perhaps an opportunity to explore the gender privilege men have enjoyed for so long. Baur (2002) explained:

> Like Mo [Fischer] always says, "I don't do drag kinging to become a strong woman. . . . I'm *already* a strong woman. I don't need that." We are strong as women. But, to perceive—to see through certain power strategies. If you *know* them, you have the option to *use* them when you need them.

Drag king performer Mo Fischer has been described by the *Venus Boyz* director as using and embodying femininities on a continuum. What she does may be considered to be a form of *subversive femininity*—women who challenge patriarchal gender relations and resist labels—as described earlier in this chapter. But to Mo Fischer, drag kinging enables her to perform what she feels and is.

Challenging drag queen performers on the quality and authenticity of their femininity exhibition has been a staple of live performances, as well as fodder for the U.S. reality television show, *RuPaul's Drag Race*. In stage performances, perhaps some women feel threatened by drag queens' performance of femininity (Schacht, 2004), or it could be feelings of "anomie . . . when confronted with the subversion of the drag performers" (Egner & Maloney, 2015, p. 15). On the award-winning reality television program, intersectionalities of gender, sexual orientation, and ethnicity are depoliticized and gender boundaries are breached, moves that advance the public discourse of what is *feminine* (Strings & Bui, 2013). Gender identities communicated via drag, camp, and parody through performances of femininity and masculinity also advance deconstruction of heteronormative gender standards.

Both female and male drag performers strategically seek to be subversive while appearing sexually fluid, displaying both feminine and masculine qualities—sometimes within the same time span of an act. Overall, the concept of gender identity can be a "malleable site of subversive resignifications" (Escudero-Alías, 2010, p. 167). Often, audiences represent a diverse group of LGBTQ members and performers themselves identified according to diverse sexual orientation labels. Drag performers undermine the power of heteronormative gender roles as they expose a restrained masculine side—or a restrained feminine side—of one's gender identity. While the drag queen phenomenon has attracted significant scholarly attention, the drag king phenomenon has received significantly less attention. For the current discussion, examining drag culture provides an opportunity to examine masculine femininities, feminine masculinities, and ways we need a more flexible and expanded definition of *femininity*.

WOMEN IN THE MILITARY

In a world of the heterosexual status quo wherein women are urged to display only emphasized femininity, norms spectacularly are turned upside down in a context of war, which is gendered as male and masculine. Femininity "sits uncomfortably with wars and conflicts" (Afshar, 2003, p. 180) and although much is made of male muscularity, Still (2003) remarked that "the image of the (ideal) male physique is a product of ideology and fantasy just as the images of perfect womanhood have been shown to be" (p. 6). Consequently, nearly 100 years ago it was declared that male virtues are called into service during wartime but that women "cannot go over the top" (Hall, 1920, p. 102). Since that time, military regimes in the United States and United Kingdom have cracked open the doors for women to play predominantly non-combat roles in addition to nursing, caregiving, and other traditionally female gender roles women have played in U.S. wars since the Civil War.

Resisting or challenging hierarchical, gendered military establishments to be accepting of a full range of femininities is an ongoing process. Earlier, during World War I, many U.S. women wore man-tailored clothes to work outside the home while men did battle abroad, but were expected to return to feminine clothing once the war ended. Critiquing a 1919 *Vanity Fair* cartoon, Behling (2001) opined: "[A] woman's world outside the home is more constrained than her world inside the home; in public, her services unwelcome" (p. 160). More recently, while Reserve Officers' Training Corps (ROTC) women defy social norms proving women are more than sexual, passive beings—through building muscles, displaying leadership, and developing weaponry skill—they end up reproducing traditional femininity and male privilege. ROTC women modify their internal definition of femininity as one accommodating motherhood *and* soldiering, rather than actively transforming the military's long-held belief that a woman's place in war (if involved at all) is associated only with caretaking (Silva, 2008).

Women wearing military uniforms seem to offer a disconnect for women considering a definition of *femininity*. A *Redbook* magazine image from 1945 which showed a blonde woman wearing a U.S. Cadet Nurse Corps light gray military uniform elicited limited reaction from women who participated in focus groups and interviews for the current book project. They could not seem to envision the image as being at all related to their definition of femininity—as either *most feminine* or *least feminine*. See Figure 8.1. For women who volunteered to support U.S. military efforts, wearing a uniform meant unity and authority. In 1941, Eleanor Roosevelt explained that as volunteers, women needed a uniform: "It saves time, explanation and the trouble of identification. . . . It is a passport and a protection" (No Sam Brown, 1941, p. 6). As part of a focus group meeting of college women for this book, Andrea, 19, Caucasian/White perceived a conflict experienced by women involved in the military:

> I, honestly, have yet to meet a female that doesn't want to be viewed as feminine. And, I have friends that are in the Army; they're in the ROTC program. Based on appearance alone, they're very masculine looking. And, still they want to be viewed, you know, with her partner or whatever—she wants to be seen as feminine. So, I think it is a big thing if you're *not* seen as feminine.

Participating in a different focus group hosted with women to define *femininity*, Lisa, 21, Caucasian/White, agreed that military and femininity do not seem to go together:

> I got into the whole military thing when I was younger and I don't think it's a very feminine thing. Not that I find it unattractive, per se. I have respect for it, but as far as my personal femininity, I don't recognize or identify with it. . . . I can't help it. I'm just being really honest. Like, in my head, when I see a woman with an apron on, she's more feminine to me versus a bulletproof vest. Domesticated things, like, watching someone at home doing laundry, like that just seems like something that's feminine.

News media play a crucial role in shaping images and providing information about women soldiers who die on battlefields and those who are affected by war at home. U.S. news media seem only too satisfied to frame women's involvement in military operations using traditional femininity ideals as benchmarks for rhetoric about militarized femininity (Enloe, 1993). During the Tunisian Revolution of 2010–2011, print and wire media consistently clung to traditional female gender stereotypes, representing women as emotional, communal, and nurturing mothers and wives, whereas blog content produced by non-mainstream news reporters represented women as fully engaged agentic leaders and citizens (Pompper, 2014b). Media discourse of the Iraqi war and military protocol converged in coverage of deaths of four British service women when their identity as soldiers and their accomplishments were minimized, effectively reinforcing marginalization of women in war narratives (Ette, 2013). Moreover, Ette (2013) found a gender dichotomy, with the servicewomen's femininity emphasized in media coverage as they were "stripped . . . of the tough soldier identity" and described in relation to others, such as "daughter, wife, sister . . . best friend . . . beautiful, bubbly, caring" (p. 255). Hence, news media consistently downplay femininity in war narratives and rely on hackneyed female gender stereotypes and gendered news frames to represent women engaged in active combat.

DISCUSSION

For any who believe the feminism political movement in the United States has succeeded in affecting gender equality and therefore, there is no need to persist, this chapter's argument about how women and men each possess both feminine and masculine qualities which are not only under-appreciated, but are used to discriminate and marginalize, provides an alternate view on perceptions of gender equality. When men are denigrated for possessing feminine qualities and women are harassed for not being feminine enough or for being too masculine, clearly, gender equality has not been achieved. Post–1960s social movements, women have begun to emphasize more masculine characteristics (Spence & Buckner, 2000). MacInnes (1998) posited that at some point, there shall be no difference between women and men beyond anatomical arrange-

Figure 8.1.   U.S. Cadet Nurse Corps uniform worn by women 1943–1948 during World War II. Source: Image copyright © The Metropolitan Museum of Art. Image source: Art Resource, NY.

ments, a future moment when binary dualisms such as feminine/masculine could disappear completely or it shall become commonplace knowledge that both concepts describe qualities possessed within each biological sex. Beynon (2002) qualified masculinity for men in terms of a "hybridized masculinity . . . experienced and displayed differently at different times in different situations" (p. 6). Yet I prefer the simplicity of a continuum metaphor representing a universal measure for plural versions of femininity and masculinity as applied to women and men. See Figure 8.2.

Femininities   **Masculinities**

Figure 8.2.   Femininities and Masculinities Continuum. Source: Created by Donnalyn Pompper.

For now, we have much work to do before widespread social acceptance of individual women and men performing both masculinities and femininities is realized. Moreover, the concept of femininity must gain new respect and not be used to chastise men or to sexualize women to the degree they are victimized by microaggressions or full-on violence. Gender identity and its feminine and masculine qualities have much less to do with biology than with cultural, economic, and social conditions—as social construction theorists have posited.

This chapter addresses ways a sexuality lens proves helpful for building upon and advancing application of theory about femininities and masculinities and examining instances wherein femininity is used to threaten girls and women in the form of microaggressions. Also covered are contexts wherein women and men of multiple sexual orientations emphasize their femininity and masculinity through accentuated drag performances, sometimes to make radical political statements through entertainment. Offered is a deadly serious context for looking at ways women seek to express their femininities both internally and in ways regarded as acceptable in a military setting. Clearly global news media still struggle with reportage about women and war due to entrenched news frames rooted in old stereotypes. Enabling biology to trump lived experiences among women and men shortchanges the social constructions of femininities and masculinities—and continues to hold back women and men from achieving their maximum potential.

NINE

Age, Health, and Femininity

Of course, there are clothes and fashions and styles that I wish I could wear, but are more suitable for younger people. As you get older, you have to realize there are certain boundaries and you need to not cross certain lines. When I go shopping with my younger daughter, 17, I see some really trendy clothes out there that I think are so neat. I'd love to wear something like that and she says to me, "Mom, you've got to act your age." And I say, "That's really unfair," and she says, "Well, it's true. It'd be so weird to see you wearing something like that."
—Research participant, Yifang, 52, Chinese-American

Age may be only a number, but tell that to women who have been socialized to fear aging. Age is a social, political and economic issue rooted in anxieties about the ever-advancing life course. Emphasizing femininity post–age forty is particularly difficult for some women, especially those who are ill and have lost their hair while battling cancer or cannot afford expensive clothes, plastic surgery, spa treatments, or stylish retirement communities that promote active lifestyles. Contemporary age relations mean that growing older, as a woman, involves stress and conflict associated with the (in)ability to continue embodying the youthful standards of idealized femininity. Older women interviewed for this book openly discussed body shame and young women talked about unhealthful behaviors, all to achieve social acceptance as feminine women. Women who participated in interviews and focus groups expressed hope that Photoshopping critique advanced by singer-songwriter Meghan Trainor (and others) affects positive change in ways images of girls and women are manufactured for magazines. In a focus group discussion, college student Nicole, 18, Black-Japanese, expressed her dislike of manipulating photos in the service of persuasion for selling products and services:

It's really disturbing. Just look up Photoshop on YouTube, and I saw a clip of an artist fixing a picture of Penelope Cruz on a magazine cover and they even shrunk the width of her rib cage so she would have a thinner waist! . . . Penelope Cruz apparently has too wide of a rib cage to be on the cover of *Cosmo*. It's a little ridiculous.

Women aged 30–49 and 50+ who were interviewed for this book shared optimism that groundbreaking super models such as Beverly Johnson, Christie Brinkley, Jerry Hall, and others can help to change negative stereotypes about older women considered to be *un*feminine simply because they are older.

Among patriarchal cultures that increasingly glorify youthfulness, older women experience much fear, anxiety, stress, and inner conflict when they perceive an inability to measure up to a feminine ideal based on youth. Fear of aging can be debilitating for women who invested the first half of their life emphasizing their femininity. Ray (2006) characterized a "lonely terror at 40" for women whose sense of femininity is negatively impacted by menopause, empty nest syndrome, and "a culture that renders older women sexually invisible" (p. 26). The price for *under-emphasized femininity* is high at any age, but because femininity is considered to be intrinsically connected to a woman's core sexual identity in a finite quantity that lessens with age, emphasizing femininity later in life presents challenges when a woman's body seems to turn against her. Sally, 60, Caucasian/White, spoke of negative aging during an interview for this book:

Parts of old age really suck. I'm now a NY Jew, but I grew up a New England Protestant. Simple was good. I was never a person who dyed their hair or was into fashion or wore makeup—but there are certain things as I get older. *Depression* is an overused word. As I get older, the pot belly or the age marks, I think get me down a little bit. . . . Our self-image is based upon a zillion different things. It's different if it's with a mate, in a group. In one way I pride myself. I'm sixty, I'm raising two girls, I'm frugal, not wasteful. In another way, you look in the mirror and wonder if that's an excuse for being schlumpy? . . . My friend at work who I think looks much better when she walks out the door than I do. She says, "Oh, I'm so superficial when I stand next to you." And I'm like, "Oh my God, I wish I could take the effort to do certain things." My self-image also is a little bit about getting old alone.

What Sally meant by "being schlumpy" could be interpreted as simply a woman chosing not to emphasize her femininity. This raises questions of *Why does a woman have to emphasize her femininity? Is this something she must do for a lifetime? When will others be satisfied with a woman however she chooses to be or to present herself? Must a woman always be chained to others' perceptions or social mores?* Some men consider older women who appear to insufficiently care about themselves to be "mannish or neutered or simply unattractive," which means older women cannot be considered feminine at all by such men (Brownmiller, 1984, p. 150). By contrast, fifty-two-year old Yifang was quoted at the top of this chapter about a desire to be fasionable, but her daughter chided her for *trying to* emphasize her femininity. In Sweden, Wärn (2012) explained that fashion that is functional and practical signifies a "more equal society" (p. 177) with regard to gender, one that may be more accommodating of women who possess degrees of masculinity and males who possess degrees of femininity. Femininity, among older women, seems a double-edged sword.

Throughout the life course, heterosexual women unwittingly make themselves "object and prey" for men (de Beauvoir, 1968, p. 642) as they remain perpetually surveilled and judged. Such imposed limitations play out in public sphere workplaces where preferences for the "pretty young woman" may emerge and in the private-domestic sphere where a "well-preserved older woman" must not "let herself go" for risk of losing her husband (Bartky, 2010, p. 86). From an early age, we are socialized to think of older women in the United States in limited communal and caregiving roles. Girls and women are oriented to internalize qualities associated with the female gender role such as homemaking (Friedan, 1963), and a "biological imperative to procreate" (Ray, 2006, p. 26) undergirds many a definition of femininity. Thus, after middle age, women may encounter difficulty transitioning to a post-reproductive female identity and new ways to think about femininity as they ponder how to live the rest of their life.

Women's social identity dimensions intersect in ways that can further complicate a female gender old age social identity. Because the body is a critical marker of age, it serves as a visible reminder of ways ageism manifests, both internally and externally. Older lesbians' social identity can uniquely inspire resistance to heteronormative standards (Copper, 1988), as their lived experiences include dealing with homophobia, sexism, *and* ageism (Slevin, 2006). Some women who identify with radical lesbian communities may reject hegemonic emphasized femininity images and opt instead to replace an oppressive drive for female beauty through youth with a new female aesthetic valuing physical strength, health, "character lines," and gray hair that complement and enhance a woman's attractiveness (Bartky, 2010, p. 96).

Of limited support for older women struggling with how to feel good about their feminine identity in old age is second- and third-wave feminist ideology, which are both critiqued as intensely ageist. Friedan's (1963) manifesta written from her early forties, Caucasian/White middle-class standpoint, primarily targeted women in their twenties and thirties. This is ironic since Friedan criticized the *feminine mystique* as leaving women with "a terrifying blank which [made] them unable to see themselves after 21" (Friedan, 1963, p. 64). As a political location, old age largely has been ignored and feminist researchers have seemed unwilling to talk to older women to explore their lived experiences (Calasanti & Slevin, 2006). Feminist psychoanalytic criticism in the United States categorically defines women as "mother to young children" and no older than early middle-age (Woodward, 1995, p. 88). A body of research that investigates mothers' relationships with their adult daughters further entrenches women in the *eternal mother* role consistent with a liberal feminist perspective which suggests gender equality shall emerge eventually. MacDonald (1983) argued that "youth is bonded with patriarchy in the enslavement of the older woman" as female generations compete for power to the degree that youth culture depends on "the powerless old woman" (p. 39) to benchmark its salience. Copper (1988) concluded that while women typically spend their lives caring for others, lack of reciprocity once they get older fuels ageism trends, too. Workplace experiences of older women largely have been less explored in favor of younger women's workplace experiences (McMullin & Berger, 2006). The exclusion of older women from feminist writing reflects the wider culture's *gerontophobia* (Arber & Ginn, 1991), fear of growing old or fear or hatred of old people. For some reason, issues about and surrounding women's aging seem to garner little interest as part of larger feminist agendas.

This chapter addresses issues associated with femininity in the context of female age and health: 1) On becoming socialized to emphasized femininity as girls and young women, 2) Older women, femininity, and power, 3) Beauty-fashion-media shaming of older women, and 4) Discussion.

ON BECOMING SOCIALIZED TO EMPHASIZED FEMININITY AS GIRLS AND YOUNG WOMEN

By the time women reach middle and old age, they have been fully socialized to emphasize femininity through years of surveillance, restrictions, and training in *female gender knowledge*. Twenty-year-old Luciana, a Latina, explained in a focus group discussion organized for this book how she learned about femininity:

> [B]asically it's been instilled in me since I was born. Like, as a little girl, I couldn't be playing around or even sitting without my legs being crossed. My legs were open, I would get yelled at—"You're a lady, close your legs." [W]hat it is to be a lady is pretty important in my family, and as you get older it's kind of like you already know what it is.

Luciana's story evoked significant agreement during the focus group discussion, with several college women wondering aloud, "Yeah, why *is* that?" College women further probed this larger question, sharing stories about how *female gender knowledge* is transferred as girls are taught to "sit still" and to "fold your hands" at church and elementary school—and to "say please and thank you"—but that these lessons are not imposed as regularly upon boys. Understanding how/why girls, historically, have been controlled more than boys reveals much about how femininity is socially constructed.

Girls seem to encounter all manner of restrictions as they are being socialized to be feminine. Girls are encouraged to "work, play sports, be tough, but don't do it while wearing nail polish, pink uniforms, or crying" (Baumgardner & Richards, 2004, p. 60). It seems that four, five, and seven-year-old girls have more *female gender knowledge* than boys have male gender knowledge because they have been taught what belongs to girls and what *does not* (Tenenbaum, Hill, Joseph, & Roche, 2010). The founder of adolescent development theory argued that girls' *feminine nature* makes them sexually and morally weak (Hall, 1931, italics added), ideas that may seem arcane today, but persist nonetheless through socialization. In response to ideas that femininity makes girls vulnerable, parents may seek to protect them with extra rules and earlier curfews which end up limiting girls' agency and individuality. See chapter 3 for a more detailed description of Best's (2006) fieldwork study. Perceptions that femininity equals weakness also play out in terms of spaces that children are permitted to occupy. Girls' private space is their bedroom, where girls of economic means practice emphasized femininity through decorations, makeup, and clothes (Griffin, 2001). For boys, their space is the street, playgrounds, or other out-of-doors areas where they are more free to exercise, explore, and develop critical thinking and social network building skills.

On the other hand, some girls and young women actively challenge gender boundaries and negotiate ideal, emphasized femininity in mixed and single-sex physical education classes, as well as during leisure time off school grounds. Hill (2015) found that girls who consider themselves physically active carefully manage activities they participate in, especially when choosing to deviate from "the fit, slender, girlie-girl" norm (p. 666). See chapter 1 for detailed explanation of *girlie-girl femininity*. Undergirding *girlie-girl femininity* are consumer messages which target girls from an early age. Consumer culture has become the crowning feature of contemporary modes of feminine membership—with postfeminist teachings about associating sexual freedom with equal rights. By the time girls reach high school, they have learned to equate purchase behavior with femininity, for beauty and fashion advertising has socialized them well—as detailed in chapter 4. As girls grow up and advance in their education to middle school and high school, they practice emphasizing their femininity on classmates. In fact, girls and young women are encouraged to use school as a personal training ground for performing emphasized femininity while under the watchful eye of adults (McRobbie, 2000).

In the current twenty-first century, college women relish modified mores acknowledging that age twenty-five no longer represents some arbitrary deadline for marriage and motherhood, the *proper enactment of femininity*, according to *tradition* in the United States. For young women who consider themselves to be postfeminist or third-wave feminists, there are traces of questioning and moving away from hegemonic representations of emphasized femininity and toward qualities such as strong/ determined, self-awareness, and self-confidence. These qualities, paradoxically, also may contribute to higher levels of gender role strain (Robertson, Johnson, Benton, Janey, & Cabral, 2002), given workplace and other contexts where effects of patriarchy endure and keep young women at second-class status in spite of their talent, strength, determination, and confidence. If anything has been learned from the teen girl punk movement of the late twentieth century, it is that girls don't want to stay home and can be comfortable with *un*feminine behaviors in public—such as when slam dancing, displaying shaved heads and unshaved armpits or legs, and featuring multi-colored hair. College "girls" may be considered as living an "extended version of their teenage years" while living away from home to receive their education (Thiel-Stern, 2014, p. 163), yet some do cling to traditional traits associated with "prototypical femininity" (Robertson, Johnson, Benton, Janey, & Cabral, 2002, p. 19). Discussions throughout this book about college women aged eighteen to twenty-nine defining femininity in terms of appearance and visualizing femininity in terms of long gowns, pink, pearls, lace, and motherhood bear out these earlier findings, too. As addressed in chapter 2, members of this age cohort also associated femininity with words/phrases about behaviors such as *ability to bear children, can cook, non-competitive, obedient, passive, polite,* and *restrained*—as well as internal qualities/virtues such as *caring, comfortable, compassionate, docile, supportive,* and *sweet.* Decisions young women make about whether or not to act upon emphasized femininity norms steeped in assumptions that they are headed for marriage, motherhood, and limited economic participation—in conjunction with decisions about their education and employment—all impact a lifetime of possibilities. A variety of outcomes depend upon social identity dimensions and intersectionalities of female gender along with ethnicity, social class, and sexual orientation, for example.

Older women who spoke with me for the study reported in this book were comfortable reflecting on ways their ideas about femininity have changed over the years. During our interview, Finn, 62, Caucasian/White, spoke of femininity in terms of displaying her body as a model and then in terms of keeping her body healthy and fit:

> When I was young I was very, very shy. . . . I wanted to have people acknowledge me. I thought I'm going to model and that's what I did— locally. Then the Ford Agency in NY wanted to hire me. But my father put his foot down and didn't want me to do any of that. . . . Now, I'm married to this person who's just a wonderful individual and he makes me feel good about who it is that I am. . . . We were sixties people. I never felt like I had to be anything other than who I was. . . . Over the

years I think I've relaxed a lot. I've chosen not to wear makeup anymore. Not that I wore a lot before, just blush and mascara. I've gotten
away from that. As far as my body image, just as long as I'm healthy
and fit. I'm gravitating more into . . . neighbors involved in bowling,
rollerblading or bicycling. . . . I don't go out on the bike trails by myself
because people have gotten into trouble doing that. . . . It's more just to
make sure I keep my body moving. It doesn't have anything to do with
physical appearance—although those are the side benefits.

Women like Finn, who have made peace with social norms attached to
emphasized femininity, seemed more comfortable and relaxed than
women who shared stories of exhaustion associated with coloring their
hair every month, going for manicures every week, and shortness of
breath due to overweight. While older women who subscribe to emphasized femininity standards and a drive for perfection said that doing
body work makes them happy, many couched their praises with grum-
bling about how much time it takes and how much money it costs. Some
older women who participated in interviews and focus groups complained that living on social security cannot accommodate anything extra
like a "frivolous" pedicure.

OLDER WOMEN, FEMININITY, AND POWER

Age serves as a social organizing principle, with various age groups'
identity and power shaped in relation to one another. In this way, age
serves as a *master status* characteristic with power relations intersecting
with other social identity dimensions, such as gender, ethnicity, social
class (Laz, 1998). Age represents a fluid social identity dimension. People,
as individuals and as groups, experience varying degrees of privilege
and disadvantage as they move through the life course. Old age inten-
sifies other inequalities and represents a social location in itself, one
marked by a loss of power, authority, and status (Calasanti & Slavin,
2006). People create meaning about age, making it a social construction.
However, Gullette (2004) posited that aging has been "overnaturalized"
(p. 102), as many people tend to focus on biological manifestations rather
than assessing ways society and individuals shape its relevance.

The HBO documentary, *About Face: The Supermodels Then and Now*
(Greenfield-Sanders, 2012), explored relationships among femininity, the
beauty business, and women's physical appearance. The documentary
was an official selection of the 2012 Sundance Film Festival and featured
interviews with supermodels Christie Brinkley, Carmen Dell'Orefice, Jerry Hall, Beverly Johnson, China Machado, Paulina Porizkova, Isabella
Rossellini, and other age 50+ women who shared their views on roles
they played in defining beauty and emphasized femininity norms. Supermodel and actress Jerry Hall explained: "Of course it's no fun getting old

and sick and dying. We all know that's coming and it's a bore. . . . Why shouldn't we be allowed to age? When I turned fifty, I felt a sense of achievement" (Greenfield-Sanders, 2012). This documentary featured interviews with several women who coined the term, "supermodel." Hall is a global phenomenon, featured on numerous fashion and beauty magazine covers over the course of her long modeling career, married to rock legend Mick Jagger, and currently married to media mogul Rupert Murdoch. Her voice in the documentary was one of associating femininity with positive aging.

During our interview for the study reported in this book, fifty-one-year old Connie, identified as "mixed ethnicity" (African-American/Black and Caucasian/White), shared a story about ways she observed age-female gender intersectionalities grouped with femininity and body image at a Delta Sigma Theta sorority luncheon she recently had attended:

> I think women are very conscious of femininity and body image. It is one of the things that women have been faced with all of our lives. I know women that are older than me—where body image is *everything*. And I'm not just talking about the figure now. I'm talking about how she looks. I love to go to church. I watch the old women there. I just crack up laughing because sometimes they are so cute. They have not lost their girlish charm. As a matter of fact, I was at a luncheon this weekend and it was a Delta big hat luncheon. . . . They had to pick a woman from each table that they thought could win for the table, because I think the whole table got prizes. Anyway, I was chosen from my table to be in the parade along with the other thirty or forty people that were up there. There was one little old lady. . . . She was a gorgeous seventy-year-old woman that had her blue leather gloves with the blue suit and the fur around a big old beautiful blue hat. This woman, she literally strutted her stuff. She danced. I was even applauding for her. I said "Oh, Lord, if I can even look half that good when I'm her age, I'm going to be all right." It just touched my heart and really made me smile and say, "You know, that's how I want to be." Enjoy being a woman, enjoy being who they are.

Connie's narrative underscored the joy she and her friends feel about emphasized femininity as an older woman. Ways women like Connie consider femininity later in life stand in stark contrast to messages of the fashion-beauty complex about older women being ugly, broken—or invisible.

Female gender and age intersect in systems of social inequality which intensify after middle age, further complicating circumstances for older women in the workplace and at home. Meanings associated with age and aging are fundamentally gendered with women and men experiencing aging processes differently. There are contrasting degrees of privilege and status loss projected upon gender groups (Stoller & Gibson, 2000). Men, as the standard in social hierarchical power structures, tend to move through life with little regard paid to their gender or age (until extreme old age). Wives' tendency to outlive husbands has been qualified as a "dubious privilege" (Lewis & Butler, 1984, p. 203), for women often persist under a cloud of oppression (King, 2006). An old body is interpreted amidst contexts of multiple power relationships (Furman, 1999) — and the older woman generally lacks power in all of them.

Negative outcomes of aging spill over into the workplace, too, where older women are devalued—both in relation to younger women and in relation to men. For women who work outside the home, midlife is the point during which private and public spheres collide as women seek to balance needs of children and aging parents with their own career (Carr, 2002). Peak earning for women is age forty-five while men continue to out-earn women far beyond. People in the United States now entering old age are experiencing the highest gendered wage inequality of any recent generation (Gullette, 2011). Women are stereotyped at a younger age than men are—and older women face more severe ageist stereotypes about femininity loss (Hummert, Garstka, & Shaner, 1997). Unattractive people are paid less (Hamermesh, 2011) and older women feel the brunt of this discrimination (Phillips & Dipboye, 1989). Older women of color encounter unique stereotypes consistent with gender-ethnicity, social identity, dimension overlap. Those who are lower on the socio-economic scale perceive even greater incidences of discrimination (Kessler, Mickelson, & Williams, 1999; Thornton, 2002). This could explain why midlife-aged African-American/Black women and midlife-aged Latinas seek support from one another about their changing bodies and social circumstances through informal social networks (Pompper, 2011). Resumes are gendered documents and interview settings provide employers the opportunity to observe older employees' bodies. Linking of age with experience reflects a positive bias toward men who rarely leave the paid workforce to raise children, while women are perceived negatively when they take "on ramps" and "off ramps" as primary caregivers to children (Hewlett, 2007). An aged body is considered an obstacle to finding employment, so women color their hair to present a younger appearance to potential employers (McMullin & Berger, 2006).

After a lifetime of being told their value rests in *emphasized femininity*, older women can fall victim to constant media messaging from the fashion-beauty complex. Social construction of what it means to be an old woman teaches us to read the older female body negatively. Indeed, older women may internalize negative critique and may be *less satisfied* with their body image than their younger cohort. Perceptions of a person's physical attractiveness diminish with age—especially for women (Cruikshank, 2003), with those who are chronically ill or impaired considered to be "problem old people" (Holstein & Minkler, 2003). During our one-on-one interview for this book, Sharol, 42, African-American/ Black, offered critical commentary about girls and young women who are influenced by mediated images and succumb to plastic surgery—but then admitted she recently had undergone breast reduction surgery herself:

> [T]hese young women, they're growing up where plastic surgery is the norm now—not just for the elite—where anybody that, if your body doesn't fall within that certain standard, then you can have it corrected. . . . For this generation, I think they're inundated with that same sort of mantra of *You have to look a certain way or there's something wrong with you.* . . . I had a breast reduction last year with a breast lift. I will say that I appreciate the fact that my breasts are a little bit higher than they were last year. Gravity had already taken hold. . . . As I got older, my breasts became so enlarged—felt like I was out of balance, the top part was so heavy and the bottom part was so little that I'd just topple over. The breast reduction enabled me to kind of even it out a little bit. I still don't have hips or the butt. In fact, my husband jokingly says I have an *assitol*—no ass at all.

Sharol's story framed plastic surgery for older women in terms of health with fringe benefits affecting her body image for emphasized femininity. In her view, this action is quite different from having breast enlargement in order to feel more socially accepted.

Negative effects of aging according to emphasized femininity standards are felt by young women, too. During a focus group discussion of college women, the subject of anti-aging cream being used among peers emerged. Andrea, 19, Caucasian/White, questioned the beauty industry's decision to use Kim Kardashian as a spokesmodel:

> It's so crazy, but it keeps going back to the Kardashians. Kim Kardashian is now the spokesperson for Illumifill, which is like a wrinkle reducing make-up and skincare line, and she's still young! What? You're going to tell the whole world "Oh, look at my face. It's so flawless and wonderful," to, like, a fifty-year-old? You're not going to look like that. It's not up to you. Even if you get a face-lift, you still will not look like that.

Andrea's commentary about ways of putting down old age in order to sell youth-promising products and services illustrates just one of the many ways old age and maturity is disrespected and disregarded in the United States. Degrees of deception used by the fashion-beauty complex also were stridently criticized by college women throughout focus group discussions about defining femininity. As explained in chapter 4, women aged eighteen to twenty-nine critiqued how Photoshop and other editing tools are used to make women appear more perfect in images in order to sell to them. Krystol, 20, an African-American/Black college student who participated in focus group discussions for this book, said she and her mother constantly debate about fashion magazine images' authenticity: "It's just hard. You can't take it to heart because a lot of people know that it's airbrushed. It still plays with your mind a little bit." Like Andrea, Kierra, 23, African-American/Black, had a story to share about aging cream and one of her friends in a different focus group discussion:

> This is ridiculous, but, I mean, I love the girl to death. She's my best friend growing up. And we both went somewhere together, and we were in a hotel room. And, I go into the bathroom to brush my teeth, and there on the sink was like this fifty-year-old person's anti-wrinkle face wash. And, I'm like, "What? Did grandma come in when I was, like sleeping? What is this?" And, she's like, "I just think it's a good idea to start early." I said, "You're twenty!" There's so many women. . . . I worked at Sephora, and I would see so many young girls buying these $95 anti-wrinkle creams. And I'm like, "I'm supposed to sell you stuff, but come on. Like, you do not need."

Kierra's anecdote elicited bouts of laughter among other college women who participated in the focus group discussion, but they were deadly serious about the negative effects that women suffer. This and other focus group discussions exposed the age eighteen to twenty-nine cohort's anger about the cosmetics industry's success in making girls and women feel stress and conflict about their bodies and ways it uses their attention to emphasized femininity as a means to turn a profit. Age scholar Margaret Gullette (1997) once posited that women begin to experience effects of social pressures to avoid decline in their thirties, but more recently has suggested it begins even earlier in life when describing "new ageism in America"—where *all that old women are* is in contrast to what societies value most highly (Gullette, 2011). Kierra's anecdote above personifies Gullette's attention to new ageism trends.

Research findings are mixed as to the specific age women report feeling the highest and lowest degrees of femininity—which suggests that women may not think of themselves as any more or less feminine as they age, even though others' definitions of femininity tend to associate the concept with younger women. Doris, 53, Caucasian/White, compared/contrasted her views on femininity with those of her co-workers:

> I don't think aging will be an issue for me. Well, hair will. And wrinkles are important. I remember years ago, a woman at work had a facelift in her early fifties. She was ten to fifteen years older [than me] at the time. I would never have a facelift. I know people in their forties that do it, in their thirties . . . Botox. I'm so nervous about putting anything into my face.

Doris explained that she's always felt feminine and anticipates no change as she ages. However, it is the representation or emphasis in terms of appearance that complicates perceptions and foments stress and conflict for women.

Other research findings suggest women's preoccupation with body shape and size persists over the life course and even may become more pronounced over time (Fey-Yensin, McCormick, & English, 2002). Older women feel stigmatized by their changed physical appearance (e.g., over-weight, deep facial wrinkles sagging breasts) and others' negative judg-ments (Meadows & Davidson, 2006). These physical manifestations are celebrated in some cultures as signs of wisdom and achievements (Young, 2010). In the United States and many other Western nations, *aging well* presumes a feminine elderly woman who is healthy, slim, and sexy (Ruddick, 1999). In my research for this book, Kathleen, 54, Cauca-sian/White, told women in her focus group discussion how she differen-tiates *feminine* from *sexy*: "To me, *feminine* is an attitude and *sexy* is what you look like on the surface—so it's a mixture. How you present it." Kathleen's collapsing of *feminine* with *sexy* is typical when considering an emphasized- femininity-as-norm framework, underscoring the complex-ity with which I have considered in this book the many ways femininity is defined. Indeed, the aging female experiences intense conflict with social representations of ideal, perfect, or emphasized femininity.

In addition to the beauty-fashion complex's contribution to stress/conflict girls and women feel about their feminine body, the pharmaceu-tical industry has formed an uneasy liaison with one of women's biologi-cal maturation phases. Menopause has been positioned as a femininity-stripping deficiency disease. Through the nineteenth and early twentieth centuries, women who moved beyond stages of "younger female sexual-ity" and ceased to possess "functionally reproductive bodies" were thought to be diseased, in decline, and henceforth dependent on others (Marshall & Katz, 2006, p. 76). Since the 1960s, hormone replacement therapy (HRT) capitalized on—and mass media heavily promoted—what was qualified as "defeminizing risks of physical decline" *by promising to restore women's essential femininity* through replenishing estrogen (Mar-shall & Katz, 2006, p. 81, italics added; Wilson, 1966). The movement reinforced patriarchal norms of traditional marriage, reinvigorated stereotypical female beauty norms essential for the male gaze, and ulti-mately, contradicted feminist movements' demands for gender equality. Profit motives of the biomedicalization of natural aging processes for women have met serious criticism of health risks associated with an HRT *cure* (Joyce & Mamo, 2006). At a focus group discussion conducted for this book, college student Chloe, 22, Caucasian/White, shared an anec-dote about her grandmother's health issue as it relates to her sense of femininity:

> [O]ne of my grandmas did that [took HRT] and years after they found out it gives you terrible osteoporosis. Like, my one grandma now has really bad osteoporosis because she did this thing to avoid meno-pause. . . . When I told my grandmother once that I wanted a breast reduction, she said, "Absolutely not. What are you—crazy?"

Embedded in Chloe's narrative (and those of many other women) are fears about the pharmaceutical and medical industries, institutions which are supposed to help people live quality lives. When women distrust authorities to help them, the stress and conflict they experience about their body is compounded. No doubt, establishing menopause as a pathology, combined with anti-aging rhetoric urging women to avoid displaying bodily changes associated with aging, has contributed to older women's high levels of inner conflict.

BEAUTY-FASHION-MEDIA SHAMING OF OLDER WOMEN

The beauty industry, fashion industry, and mass media endorsement and promotion of *emphasized femininity* accoutrements which give girls and young women (who can afford it) so much joy in their youth tend to turn in upon older women by shaming their failed femininity. Like Lövgren (2015), I appreciate the concept of *doing age* for its nod to power overlays impacting internal perception formation, as well as shaping of external social values. When women's magazines and bloggers share tips about how to do age—*how to look fabulous over age forty*—readers are instructed to think of middle age as a femininity graveyard, a self-esteem-lowering make-or-break moment in a woman's life. Combined, these industries compound the strategy of making people feel bad about themselves in order to sell them products and services.

Focus group participant and college student Liz, 21, Caucasian/White, said she hopes to be like her grandmother one day: "My grandma, she's eighty, but is just so beautiful from the inside out. . . . She just carries herself and she's healthy." Yet, older women often are on the receiving end of the harshest critique by the beauty-fashion complex. Even younger women—college students—shared fears that they shall somehow "fall apart" with age, messages reinforced by the beauty complex. In a focus group discussion conducted for this book, Alejandra, 22, Dominican, explained: "When I'm older, I hope I still care and try to keep my shape. Even though I don't work out now, I still don't want to be one of those people that lets themself go when they get older." Whereas men are promised the chance to perform as if still young men—through products such as Viagra—women are promised that they could *look* young with the right diet or make-up (Gott & Hinchliff, 2003). See Figure 9.1.

With all of the negative messaging by pharmaceutical and beauty-fashion complex advertising about aging women's lost femininity, it seems counterintuitive that a handful of magazines targeting age 40+ women launched in the late twentieth century folded after only a few short years due to foundering advertising support. These magazines included *Lear's, Mirabella, More, My Generation,* and *New York Woman.* The magazine medium, historically, has attracted more female readers than

Figure 9.1.   Both women and men have discovered cosmetic surgery and injections as a means for combating negative stereotypes associated with aging so that they may continue to emphasize a youthful appearance. Copyright: lisafx. Source: Lisa F. Young/ Depositphotos.com.

male, and has established ideals and standards for femininity. It seems the magazines did not mind telling older women their femininity needed a boost, showing an ideal that was just as unrealistic for younger women (Kitch, 2003). Perhaps some advertisers simply chose not to associate their products with older women? Cultural historian Lois Banner (1992) opined that even Freud experienced difficulty in writing about aging women. Moreover, feminist critics have complained for decades that media fail to represent age 35+ women—and that representations of senior citizens set up unrealistic expectations about active lifestyles that reflect higher socio-economic audiences (Nussbaum, Pecchioni, Robinson, & Thompson, 2000). Lauren, 23, Caucasian/White, shared a story about her mother's stress associated with working to emphasize her femininity:

> My mom is divorced and dates. Now it's a huge thing thinking about the surgery—"I want a tummy tuck. I want this and I want that." . . . Stuff she sees in magazines. . . . I know it bothers her a lot and she's fifty. . . . Any other time she doesn't care, but when she's got a date, she's like competing with women my age—fit and tan. It bothers her. . . . My mother still loves shopping and the latest fashions and she likes to look good. The pressure is there.

Lauren explained that she and her mother share magazines and watch a lot of the same feature films and television programs. When I followed up to ask women in her focus group about any media influences on one's definition of femininity, Lauren was the first to raise her hand and say, "Oh yeah, social media is girls' own pictures, but magazines like *Self* and *Cosmo* set the trends."

Beyond women's magazines, representations of women in film, reality television programs, and other pervasive forms of popular culture are intensely age conscious. Arguably, postfeminist ideology suggests that we now live in an era of equal rights and opportunities across gender groups, that the work of second-wave feminism has been accomplished and there remains no more work to do. *Why then are women middle-aged and older shamed and victimized in media representations that contribute to stress and conflict about their sense of femininity?* Tasker and Negra (2007) posited that postfeminism itself has inflated the value of youth with advertising and mainstream pornography images projected back for us to compare ourselves with some ideal of perfection, a painful task for older women. "Chick flick" films such as *How Stella Got Her Groove Back* (1998), *Bridget Jones's Diary* (2001), and *13 Going On 30* (2004) mince no words about impending decline awaiting post–thirty women. Hollywood feature films like *The Hunger Games* franchise have been applauded for providing a female protagonist, but *how many Hollywood films feature older women as protagonists—unless their character represents comic relief or tragedy, as in Tyler Perry's Medea films?*

Clothes and fashion accessories serve as trimmings for emphasizing femininity, as well as to reflect subject position with regard to age. At a focus group meeting discussion for this book, Luciana, 20, Latina, raised questions about a double standard when it comes to aging women and fashion: "A lot of older women in my family in their thirties and forties they're acting like girls my age. Like a lot of my aunts are getting breast implants, like makeup all the time, their nails done." Yet, how many times have we seen social media items about clothes and styles older women *should not wear*, such as leather mini skirts? Luciana's rhetorical question set off a firestorm among one set of college women who defended an older woman's right to wear whatever she chooses and another set of peers who made faces and sounds indicating their disapproval of older women emphasizing their femininity.

The *authority* of media to set rules and conventions—and to define *femininity*—may be debated, but there is no doubt that it occurs. *The Daily Mail* set the cut-off age at forty in conjunction with photographs of age 35+ actresses and fashion models, including Victoria Beckham, Elle McPherson, and Gwyneth Paltrow (How old's, 2009). Lövgren (2015) interviewed twenty-one women ages sixty-two to ninety-four and discovered that most "struggle with being part of the age category of *old*" (p. 3, italics added). Older women do feel invisible with increasing years

(Lövgren, 2013a), but prefer to "fit in rather than stand out" as empha-sized femininity norms demand, as well as to feel comfortable and to accommodate stiff joints when choosing clothes—one reason why they have forsaken high heels, which means "letting go of an acquired ability to display femininity" (Lövgren, 2015, p. 13, p. 7). In our one-on-one interview, Cathy, 53, Caucasian/White, talked about femininity in a con-text of growing older:

> I think I'm a lot more comfortable with myself. As you get older, you find that you have to like yourself more and not worry about how everybody else perceives you. . . . [Y]ou don't have anything to prove to anybody any more. You have to live your life the way you want to live it because you are at the last quarter of your life—you want to make it count and you want to make it meaningful for you and your family rather than anybody else. You don't really care what everybody else thinks at that point.

In the HBO documentary, *About Face: The Supermodels Then and Now*, model and actress Isabella Rossellini concurred, "As you grow old, you don't count anymore. For sure my social status has diminished because I know I'm not invited to the A parties anymore. My daughter is" (Green-field-Sanders, 2012).

Discussions about femininity among women I interviewed for the study detailed in this book included examinations of the few magazine images featuring women with gray/white hair that I selected to stimulate discussions. A 1955 *Ladies Home Journal* color image of Vijaya Laskshmi Nehru Pandit, Indian diplomat and politician, first woman President of the United Nations General Assembly (1953), showed her standing in a colorful meadow of wildflowers wearing her gray hair, a purple sari, wristwatch, and lipcolor. Caitlin, 22, Bhutanese-Jewish-American, ex-plained how the image jumped off the page to her as *most feminine*:

> Oh my gosh. Really, really love that one. I just love the look, in gener-al—that contemplative look—that she's in a natural environment and she looks really comfortable there. She's totally curvy, lots of substance and juice. She looks wise—and aware. She looks conscious—like she has some experiences that I'd probably want to know more about.

Of the other women's magazine images covering the past 100 years, none of the older women images elicited much enthusiasm for being *most femi-nine*. A 1910s *McCall's* line drawing of a woman with gray hair wearing a floor-length coat was described by women across age cohorts as "old-fashioned" and "frumpy. A 1982 *Ladies Home Journal* black and white photo of a woman with graying hair and circles under her eyes was criticized in focus group discussions for looking "tired" and for wearing a "baggy" business suit with scarf that "looks like a tie." A 1971 *Good Housekeeping* image of a gray-haired woman wearing a seersucker rain-coat tied at the waist was described as "stylish, but not necessarily feminine." It would seem that defining *femininity* in terms of *style* has its limitations.

DISCUSSION

Institutionalized emphasized femininity norms hover over women into old age like a specter. Examining age explains just as much about socialization into femininity and ideal standards for perfection as it does about individual women conflicted about whether or not (and how) to measure up to those ideals. This chapter has examined issues associated with femininity in the context of female aging and health over the life course through old age, focusing on femininities and power, as well as the role of the beauty-fashion complex and media in shaming of older women. We were reminded several years ago that the feminine concept is steeped in youth and we are taught to believe that "femininity is *not* something that improves with age," such that women who rely on some "feminine strategy as their chief means of survival can do little to stop the roaring tide of maturity as they watch their advantage slip by" (Brownmiller, 1984, p. 236). Hence, the pharmaceutical and medical establishments, in league with the beauty-fashion complex, persuade girls and women that money can buy them options for extending a youthful appearance and acceptance through old age. Orenstein (2011) pondered the paradox of girls "getting older younger *and* staying younger older" with the help of Botox injections which cosmetically remove wrinkles by immobilizing facial muscles.

Overall, most Western cultures worship a postfeminine heroine who is youthful, playful, and vital, offering an impossibly steep challenge for middle-age and older women who still feel feminine and want to be regarded as such by others. Postfeminist rationales that gender equality has been achieved further antagonizes age differences among women and alienates age cohorts from one another. For, unless the beauty-fashion complex offers young women an *other* in the form of a middle-aged-and-older woman upon which to heap anxiety, stress and conflict while serving as a benchmark for comparison, the pervasive power and privilege of youth in an ageist milieu pales. Likewise, feminism itself is deemed old, outdated, and in decline. Considering that aging is framed as decline in conjunction with growth and omnipresence of the cosmetic surgery industry, actress and model Isabella Rossellini likened trends to the historic Chinese practice of foot binding for *lotus feet*, as a beauty aesthetic. She said: "Is this the new foot binding? Is this a new way to be misogynist? Is this a new way to tell women that 'you are ugly?'" (Greenfield-Sanders, 2012).

TEN

Femininity and Politics

Some women care more about being feminine than being feminist.
Some women care more about being feminist than being feminine. . . .
To be feminist means you're pro-women. . . . Being feminine can mean
many different things. I don't necessarily define feminine to mean
frilly, lacy. To me it's more about intelligence and confidence.
—Research participant, Amanda, 61, African-American/Black

Examining *femininity* in a political context, this chapter considers dynamics associated with women having/aspiring to a political career, girls and women achieving their maximum potential, as well as girls and women organizing around politicized issues fundamental to the femininity concept. Due to widely held understandings about femininity as being opposite of masculinity and inconsistent with what it takes to be a successful politician in a man's world, women actively involved with politics experience gender discrimination. Victoria Woodhull, a leader in the woman's suffrage movement, was the first female candidate for President of the United States in 1872. Margaret Chase Smith ran for the Republican nomination for the U.S. Presidency in 1964, Shirley Chisholm vied for the Democratic nomination for the U.S. Presidency in 1972, and Geraldine Ferraro was Gerald Ford's running mate in the Republican bid for U.S. President in 1984. Having one's femininity attacked was something Shirley Chisholm, the first major-party African-American candidate for U.S. president, knew something about. At the time of this writing, Hillary Rodham Clinton has made history by securing the Democratic nomination for U.S. President. Across multiple fields of study, research findings suggest that women leaders violate others' expectancies about femininity and consequently these women experience steep challenges in winning elections and advancing political movements.

207

Feminine stereotypes characterize women as warm, compassionate, nurturing, and sensitive, seemingly weak qualities unassociated with political leadership. More often than not, *leadership* is coded as male and masculine (Koenig, Eagly, Mitchell, & Ristikari, 2011). In fact, women politicians who avoid expressing emotions like anger and crying (Campus, 2013) then are accused of being too masculine (Hvenegård-Lassen 2013). When asked during her 2016 Democratic nomination run for the U.S. Presidency if "women's ambition is regarded as dangerous . . . [because of] . . . men's fears that ambitious women would take up space that used to belong exclusively to them," Hillary Rodham Clinton answered: "100 percent" (Traister, 2016b). Furthermore, women whose female gender intersects with their ethnicity, sexual orientation, and other social identity dimensions experience compounded bias effects, as expressed by abolitionist Sojourner Truth who spoke at a women's rights meeting in 1851 about the womanliness of her own body:

> That man over there says that women need to be helped into carriages, and lifted over ditches, and to have the best place everywhere. Nobody ever helps me into carriages, or over mud-puddles, or gives me any best place! And ain't I a woman? Look at me! Look at my arm! I have ploughed and planted, and gathered into barns, and no man could head me! And ain't I a woman? I could work as much and eat as much as a man—when I could get it—and bear the lash as well! And ain't I a woman? I have borne thirteen children, and seen most all sold off to slavery, and when I cried out with my mother's grief, none but Jesus heard me! And ain't I a woman? (Sojourner Truth's, 2016).

Soujourner Truth, an African-American abolitionist and women's rights activist, has been in the news in recent months when it was announced that her image may be printed on the back of the U.S. $10 bill (Reilly, 2016). The move to finally add women's images to money has spurned significant debate about the time gap in representing gender diversity on U.S. currency and recommendations that women be placed on the back, rather than the front, of paper money.

As greater numbers of women compete for political office at the local, state, and national levels, it is important to understand challenges women candidates encounter among voters—especially when stereotypes about femininity are communicated by media reports. While women have made some gains in U.S. politics, their underrepresentation across political life persists with exceptionally slow change for equality as compared with many other developed nations around the world. The global average of women serving in parliaments is only 23 percent, despite their proven abilities as leaders and change agents (Puri, 2016). Women who served as research participants for this book project concurred that the political arena proves especially harsh for women competing for political office due to ongoing stereotypes that leadership is more synonymous with maleness than it is with femaleness. Most women speculated that negative media coverage contributes to women being framed as less than capable—and reportage that demeans their potential by focusing on a woman's body image, hair, fashion, and family caregiving status, more so than their political acumen. During data collection for this book, research participants mentioned names of several female leaders who have received negative attention to their femininity in news reportage of politics, including Michelle Obama, Hillary Rodham Clinton, Sarah Palin, Sonia Sotomayor, and Michelle Bachman.

Enjoined throughout this chapter are discussions about distinguishing feminist politics from female political leaders who practice *equality femininities*, resisting emphasized femininity practices perceived to sometimes disempower women and counteract advancements for democratizing gender relations. For example, equality femininities are practiced when women who identify as lesbians disrupt heteronormativity (for example, U.S. Senator Tammy Baldwin), and women with disabilities disrupt ableism (for example, U.S. Congresswoman Tammy Duckworth). Also, feminist politics are addressed in a context of postfeminist popular culture and third-wave feminism. Worldwide political organizing by topless women protesters, FEMEN, and by political activists such as Pussy Riot both focus on concerns central to female identity and femininity, including sexism, sex tourism, homophobia, and policymakers' and religious institutions treatment toward girls and women.

This chapter addresses issues associated with femininity biases in the context of politics in these sections: 1) Stereotyping women and femininity biases in politics, 2) Generational differences among popular and third-wave feminism, 3) Girls' and women's activism and politicizing women's issues, 4) News media coverage of women in politics, and 5) Discussion.

STEREOTYPING WOMEN AND FEMININITY IN POLITICS

Enduring stereotypes prove particularly destructive for women in elective politics as audiences and critics have been socialized to expect women who perform their role in the public sphere to also discursively enact emphasized femininity. In the United States and many other parts of the world, we are expected to think of women as second—with men first. Moreover, we admire women who *think of themselves* as second, a move that "allows us to pretend we are not sexist" and reveals our hypocrisy when a female politician *actually does* put herself first (Caro, 2016). Media play a key role in determining what is symbolically important. Women who are perceived as too feminine are considered weak, incompetent, and inexperienced. Women who are perceived as too masculine are deemed deviant and scary. Backlash against women leaders around the world in recent years has made global news—with (at the time of this writing) Brazil's President Dilma Rousseff facing impeachment, former President of Argentina Cristina de Kirchner indicted in a finance scandal, popularity plunges of Michelle Bachelet in Chile and Aung San Suu Kyi in Burma—and even criticism of Angela Merkel for welcoming so many Syrian refugees to Germany. Potential for such backlash effects exists for all women who vie for and obtain political office, so image campaign communication is tricky as workers run the risk of challenging normative female gender identity standards and emphasized femininity norms when messaging about their candidate.

Current stereotypes about women in politics are rooted in experiences of suffragists of the early twentieth century first wave in the United States. These women grew accustomed to attacks on their femininity as a means to diminish the strength of their voice in demanding votes for women. Men of the day considered woman suffrage to be contrary to nature (qua heterosexual status quo), social conventions, and women's feminine essence (Smith-Rosenberg, 1985). In her study of the popular rhetoric used throughout the seventy-two-year campaign of women to secure the Nineteenth Amendment in 1920 permitting them to vote, Behling (2001) documented how the suffragist was caricatured as a "masculine woman, a character who is both female sexed and masculinely gendered" (p. 3) and discovered how anti-suffragists used science and the media to discredit and contradict women's demands for political agency. Clear patterns emerged revealing fear of lesbianism, what enfranchisement might do to advance economic independence for women, and what votes for women might do to destabilize male hegemony and the institution of marriage should suffragists eschew marrying men altogether. See Figure 10.1.

Today, voters who rely on stereotypes about femininity are less likely to vote for a female candidate. Baur (2015) found that individual characteristics leading to differences in feminine stereotype reliance when considering a female candidate included attention, knowledge, and partisanship. For example, higher degrees of partisan support may carry greater salience than a candidate's gender (Dolan 2014), yet voters who tend to pay low levels of attention to politics and those lacking strong partisan attachment may latch on to stereotypes and avoid voting for a female candidate because they consider women to rank high on scales of weak, lenient, soft, warm, and caring (Baur, 2015), qualities undergirding "the automatic concept-attribute associations that are thought to underlie implicit stereotypes" (Rudman, Greenwald, & McGhee, 2001, p. 1165). Other negative stereotypes for women applied in a political context are based on physical appearance in terms of age and weight; translating to the cultural stereotype of a *power-hungry* female (Charlebois, 2011). These stereotypes tap into ideas about *emphasized femininity*, about how a woman *should* look and appear.

Figure 10.1. Women's suffrage parade in New York City, 1913. Source: Manuscripts and Archives Division, The New York Public Library.

Perhaps the highest profile female U.S. politician who has encountered negative stereotyping on multiple social identity dimensions is Hillary Rodham Clinton, former U.S. Secretary of State, NY Senator, and U.S. First Lady. At the time of this writing, she has won the Democratic Party's nomination for President of the United States in the 2016 campaign. Over the course of her decades spent in public service, Clinton has been criticized for a failure to measure up to discursive markers through which women traditionally signal their femininity. Considered impersonal, Clinton generally is quiet about details relative to her domestic sphere, even though it is widely known she embodies female gender roles of wife, mother, grandmother, daughter, and sister. Rather, she amplifies her roles as politician, leader, advocate, expert, and lawyer.

Expectancies for a feminine rhetorical and leadership style from Hillary Rodham Clinton have been violated at many turns and critics consistently seem emboldened to attack her anew with advancement of her political career. In particular, Clinton was relatively slow to adapt to others' perceptions of mixed signals along a femininities-masculinities continuum and the intense and often mean-spirited attacks from political rivals, pundits, and media (Campbell, 1998). Clinton's rhetorical style is one of consummate professionalism indicative of her experience in the political realm and her years of formal education, arenas historically dominated in the United States by men displaying high degrees of male-gender-coded masculinity. As First Lady from 1993–2001, Clinton faced intense criticism for her hair styles, pantsuit outfits, and chunky jewelry. When Clinton lost to Barak Obama in Iowa during the 2008 Democratic Party nomination primary, she shed a tear and it captured media attention. Ironically, this framed her as emotional, subject to stress, and human. These were the same qualities that critics suggested she lacked when they called her an "ice queen" as she was framed in news media as emotionless (Curnalia & Mermer, 2014, p. 26). Clinton the candidate on the 2016 presidential campaign trail was hammered on social media as a *bitch, harpy, dumb,* and *ugly* (Leonard, 2016). Clinton's sexuality has been attacked multiple times over decades. She has been called frigid as a woman who could not satisfy her husband, with the *New York Times* actually tallying the total number of times she shared a bed with her husband, former U.S. President Bill Clinton (Traister, 2010). She has been called a lesbian and hermaphrodite (a slur, rather than label for sex or sexual orientation) (Traister, 2010) and lampooned on the cover of now-defunct satirical *Spy* magazine wearing conservative white male underwear featuring bulging male genitalia underneath and the headline, "Hillary's Big Secret." Margaret Thatcher, perhaps the most powerful British female politician in recent memory, also regularly was portrayed as not a real woman (Wajcman, 1998). Conservative political commentator Rush Limbaugh described Clinton's run for the White House in 2008: "Does our looks-obsessed culture want to stare at an aging woman?" Responding to a microagression upon Clinton's body when a reporter on the 2016 presidential primary trail asked her about calories in an ice cream sundae she was eating, she booed the reporter, saying "Oh, come on!" and a video clip went viral. Misogynist attacks and Clinton's endurance with grace has earned her the admiration and personal role-model status for many Americans. Hillary Rodham Clinton, through her public service, has invited U.S. citizens to reconsider ways they have been socialized to think about gender and power—and how they make meaning about femininity and masculinity.

Non-Caucasian/White women may be willing to erase nearly all signifiers of ethnic individuality in order to blend in as enthusiastic subscribers to dominant, normative Caucasian/White femininity. First Lady Michelle Obama, a five-foot-eleven African-American/Black woman, is popularly heralded for her personal style. She uses fashion to emphasize femininity, even though she holds an authoritative position and perhaps sought to deflect criticism for posing a threat to her husband's masculinity. In her last weeks as First Lady at the time of this writing, Michelle Obama also has brought her own embodiment and display of femininities to public service and introduced new ways of considering combinations of intellectual and physical strength on the campaign trail for Hillary Rodham Clinton. She, too, has confused pundits, media, and citizens socialized to expect women in the public sphere to discursively enact emphasized femininity based on some Caucasian/White ideal, and for herself possessing muscular arms which Traister (2010) opined had "become the subject of a national obsession" (p. 47). Michelle Obama's social identity was caricatured in terms of "popular apprehensions of Black femininity as angry, dominating and ultimately emasculating" that played out in media with sassy, nagging, Sapphire stereotypes (Traister, 2010, pp. 47–48). During an interview for this book, Sally, 60, Caucasian/White, spoke of her daughter's admiration for Michelle Obama:

> I have a twenty-five-year-old and she is athletic. She loves, loves, loves, both politically and just as a woman, Michelle Obama. I think a little bit of it is that she's built like Michelle Obama. She's polished, athletic, has broad shoulders that are well toned, she has long wild, curly hair and she's wide hipped.

Sally and many other women who participated in interviews and focus group discussions for this book expressed support for women in politics so long as they "don't forget they're women." As I probed this response, I learned that what women meant was *emphasized femininity*—wearing fashionable clothes and maintaining a perfect appearance with styled hair and manicure.

Traditionally, a feminine rhetorical style involves reaffirming woman-liness discursively. Both Hillary Rodham Clinton and Michelle Obama, in addition to many other women public figures in politics, tend to communicate their femininity in ways that run counter to female gender norms for governing and public advocacy. For example, when woman politicians engage in argumentation, clarify their position, respond to competing viewpoints, and offer compelling evidence—behaviors gender-coded as masculine (Campbell, 1998)—they tend to confuse audiences unaccustomed to women exhibiting what have come to be known as traditional masculine qualities. Rather, women are expected to embody emphasized femininity steeped in nurturance, domesticity, and intimacy (Tonn, 1996) while communicating experiential learning and drawing narratives from their domestic sphere—as compared to men's communication style shaped by use of tough talk and a confrontation style (Campbell, 1998). A certain brand of femininity has been made normative by patriarchal discourse and becomes visible when examining interactions during conversations. Whereas men speak and interrupt more, women use more hedges and backchannel more (Cranny-Francis, Waring, Stavropoulos, & Kirkby, 2003).

Multiple expectancy violations emerge when women political figures enact their femininity through communication. It is our beliefs about *women's place* and our expectancies that make their ability to compete so challenging (Caro, 2016). Whereas powerful men are deemed *successful*, powerful women are chastised for being *ambitious* and *aggressive* (Wajcman, 1998). Powerful women—a paradoxical phrase, given that the adjective is not necessary for qualifying men and since most people are not socialized to think about women this way—are held back since they are not considered viable candidates or because they are stereotyped as cold and barely human (Curnalia & Mermer, 2014). Here are five common female gender discriminations associated with the concept of femininity which negatively impact women in politics:

1. Femininity means incompetence—and competence is unfeminine.
2. Women are complimented more on their bodies (emphasized femininity) than on their intelligence or achievements.
3. Women have the choice to speak out and be shamed—or to be silent and invisible.
4. Women are subordinated; however, they must define themselves in comparison to men.
5. Aging women are perceived as irrelevant or invisible, while aging men are perceived as distinguished and honorable.

During the last thirty years, connections among politics with family and motherhood have provided common themes used in political campaigns—and both themes are deeply rooted in the femininity concept. Some researchers have qualified the trend as *politicized motherhood*, warning that while it may resonate among some women by inspiring them to political aspirations, it also resurrects traditional female gender stereotypes that undermine women's capacity to see themselves beyond "a restricted domestic and caregiving role," in effect, short-changing female candidates' potential (Deason, Greenlee, & Langner, 2014, p. 138).

Undeniably, women experience time pressures from family responsibilities more than men do—and this dynamic further complicates women's political careers (Fox & Lawless, 2011). See chapter 5 for an in-depth discussion of public-private sphere negotiation challenges for women. While *politicized motherhood* helped to present U.S. Vice Presidential candidate Sarah Palin as a wholesome, feminine woman during the 2008 campaign, critics questioned her ability to fulfill the duty while caring for a newborn son with Down's syndrome (Rubin, 2008). Palin also has endured a harsh media spotlight on issues related to her feminine identity—in terms of rumored marriage troubles and her daughter's marriage, divorce, and pregnancy. That these issues were made so public suggests news media expectancy violations—or, news sensationalism based on a very public woman politician with a wholesome feminine image.

GENERATIONAL DIFFERENCES AMONG
POPULAR AND THIRD-WAVE FEMINISM

The politics of being feminine also long has captured the attention of feminist activists, anti-feminism critics, and academics since second-wave feminism told us that the personal also can be viewed as political. Feminism has become cool, with the f-word appearing on catwalks, T-shirts, and billboards. Dubbed *popular feminism* in the United States and the United Kingdom for the playful ways assertion of women's rights is addressed by popular culture celebrities such as Beyoncé, Taylor Swift, Emma Watson, and Amy Schumer, this postfeminist approach moves as far away as possible from the Caucasian/White second-wave feminist movement. Therein lies the commodification and marketability of feminism, its decoupling from politics, wrote one of the three founders of the magazine, *Bitch: Response to Popular Culture*, who pondered what radical feminists might do to intervene and revive a potentially transformative political movement (Zeisler, 2016). A third-wave take on feminism in a postfeminist world is driven by energetic personal empowerment through consumerism and sexual enjoyment more so than fighting for women's gender rights. Such a shift entirely disconnects feminism from politics and social justice (McRobbie, 2000). Tasker and Negra (2007) concurred, characterizing *postfeminist culture* as an "erasure of feminist politics from the popular" (p. 5 italics in original) by silencing *feminist* concerns within postfeminist culture, rhetorically, through promotable slogans such as one borrowed from the African-American/Black idiom, "you go, girl!" (p. 2 italics in original). Goldman (1992) used the phrase *commodity feminism* to capture linkage of feminism and femininity in the service of capitalism—meaning that girls and young women "choose to be seen as sexual objects because it suits their liberated interests" (p. 133). Paradoxically, postfeminism requires girls and women to be silent in not offering critique of gender relations under patriarchy while they enjoy their personal freedoms as embodiments of femininity according to female stereotypes of sexual servility. Among the eighteen to twenty-nine age cohort of college women who participated in the study reported in this book, words often used to define *femininity* included *obedient, passive,* and *restrained*. When I asked why they also defined *femininity* by using words like *confident, powerful,* and *strong,* several explained the paradox in a context of heteronormativity: "I don't want to compete with my boyfriend or future husband," and "I want to work, but I also want to have kids—so, my husband probably will make more money than I do."

Another postfeminist manifestation, *girl power,* provides a lens through which to view changes in the feminist political agenda in recent decades. *Girl power,* as introduced in chapter 1, was promoted by the *Spice Girls* all-female band during the late 1990s. The *girl power* slogan has inspired girls' studies scholars to indict the hollow empowerment rally-

ing cry for failing to advance political aims of equality regardless of ethnicity, social class, or sexual orientation. For example, Adams (2005) examined experiences of high school cheerleaders and girls who fight in
school, resolving that emphasized femininity persists in a narrow version
of an ideal Caucasian/White girlhood as blended with "signifiers of masculinity as long as they remain feminine" (p. 109). The *girl power* mantra
both fails to consider social identity dimensions and life experience contexts, or to interrogate what is considered some idealized *high school girl*
concept. Similarly, third-wave feminism supports "girlieness as well as
power" as an appropriation of the word *girl* within a feminist context
(Baumgardner & Richards, 2004, p. 59), but some critics suggest that *girl
power* socializes young women to act as children in order to gain social
acceptance, while critics of third-wave feminism argue that it is entirely
divorced from its political roots anyway (McRobbie, 2009). During our
one-on-one interview for this book, Sally, 60, Caucasian/White, and
mother of a college woman also interviewed for this book, offered this
rationale to explain third-wave feminism and young women's mindset:

> I think maybe the younger girls in some ways are more comfortable
> with their bodies. They're used to being around men in ways that
> previous generations weren't—whether sharing apartments and bath-
> rooms, to sleeping, whatever. They'll put out if they want to put
> out. . . . I think a lot of girls follow the styles, trends. If right now the
> look is slutty, they don't worry about it—if it's short, little cleavage—
> but they have a certain confidence that they control their own bodies.
> There are women who totally feel that unless they put out, they don't
> have value. Unless they're pregnant, they don't have value. Unless
> they're desired by a man, they don't have value. I think some of the
> college girls are what we used to call promiscuous, or un-careful. They
> have a lot more liberty, opportunity, alcohol, drugs. I think a lot of
> them do feel very strong about themselves—even if we look at them
> and think "What the hell are you doing?"

The current rift between second- and third-wave feminist movements
bears more than a few similarities to age-line divides among first-wave
feminists of the 1920s. Back then, the older generation felt slighted by
new radical feminists criticizing elders who "wore flat heels and had very
little feminine charm" (Behling, 2001, p. 191). The younger generation
among first-wave feminists, instead, embraced fashion for their own political purposes after their rhetoric demanding equality was ignored. For
example, the younger set among first-wavers wore green, white and vio-
let jewelry (GWV) to symbolize and amplify their mantra, *Give Women
Votes* (Pham, 2012). Today, decrying the absence of political motive
among third-wave feminism, McRobbie (2009) critiqued it "as a kind of
shadow feminism, a substitute and palliative for the otherwise forced
abandonment of a new feminist political imagery" (p. 90). Unwilling to
entirely write off third-wave feminist perspectives, second-wave feminist

Bailey (2002) expressed hope that young feminists might embrace their femininity for its "subversive potential" (p. 145).

GIRLS' AND WOMEN'S ACTIVISM
AND POLITICIZING WOMEN'S ISSUES

Historically, political activism, movements, and rioting activities have been gendered as male-centered and masculine. Yet, there have been *gender differences* among roles and specific engagements across social identity intersectionalities of age, gender, ethnicity, and social class. Target concerns for women's activism during much of the eighteenth and nineteenth century involved what Thompson (2008) referred to as "consumption issues that tended to preserve the role of the family" (p. 24), basic issues relative to nurturing female gender traits. Women have been represented in fine oil paintings as peasants rioting for food, as victims, or as mythical, romantic inspiration for political action—such as Eugène Delacroix's 1830 bare-breasted heroine carrying the Tricolour in *La Liberté Guidant le Peuple* (Liberty Leading the People). By the end of the nineteenth century, however, North American women became inspired to extend their role by actively engaging in politics to gain access to a public sphere theretofore closed to them and were learning to be less fearful in emphasizing their femininity and in adopting more traditionally accepted masculine traits (Jackson, 1993). Throughout the twentieth century, women in the United States were especially active in campaigning for the right to vote and then later on for equal rights with men as part of social change movement campaigns throughout the 1960s and 1970s, with limited success, as addressed in various sections throughout this book.

Links between young activists and their parents have inspired researchers since student movements of the 1950s and 1960s to learn just how young people become civic minded and politically engaged. Pronounced across many of these movements are gender differences. Examined to a lesser extent: *Just how do girls and women learn about activism and possible use of rioting to affect change with regard to issues central to their feminine identity?* Gender shapes teenagers' sociopolitical development as engaged actors within their community due to parental constraints that generally are more restrictive for girls than boys (Gordon, 2008) due to safety concerns as girls move through communities (Best, 2006). Also, effects of gender inequality in the political arena for girls include fewer leadership roles with more behind-the-scenes work (Robnett, 1997) consistent with women's caretaker role, which can prove problematic when socializing girls to actively fight for their beliefs (Whittier, 1995). Westman (1991) coined the term *juvenile ageism* to qualify teen activists' need to navigate parental surveillance and mobility issues since they may not yet be legally permitted to drive. Socioeconomic and racio-ethnic contexts influencing gendered parenting may (dis)empower girls (Hill & Sprague, 1999), making them more dependent or passive (Fiese & Skillman, 2000). Social class also plays a role in parenting styles, with middle-class families practicing *concerted cultivation* that restricts children's activities to specific adult-supervised arenas (Lareau, 2003). The Internet and social media empower teens to get involved in political issues, but this may be no substitute for face-to-face participation (Bandy & Smith, 2005). Girls' engagement and activism play an important role in their ability to engage with politics and, possibly, ways they define *femininity.*

One area of the world where girls and young women are joining their older counterparts in political action is a global feminist protest movement sweeping local areas in Ukraine and Russia. The movement has spread globally via social media in advancing women's issues and expressions of femininity in new radical directions. Channell (2014) called it *sextremism.* In Ukraine and other parts of Eastern Europe, a group of female university student activists known as FEMEN, use the visual rhetoric of their topless bodies painted with slogans to support public image events and to publicize them across their internet network in efforts to raise awareness about femininity, sexism, sex tourism, women's reproductive rights, and other issues that impact women's lives. See Figure 10.2. FEMEN's protests from 2008 to 2013 played out in local activities, but these increasingly surpass transcultural levels (Thomas & Stehling, 2016). The women are young and emphasize their femininity by decorating their hair with colorful feathers and flowers, in protest of the sex trade in Ukraine, sexism in the Ukrainian government, and more. Post-Soviet countries such as Ukraine revere their cultural legacy. Here, the dominant model of femininity is attributed to the matriarchal Ukrainian goddess Berehynia, a hearth mother/protectress. Rubchak (2015) posited, however, that FEMEN prefers to advocate Western-style female gender discourses through provocative dress and actions in an effort to resist post-Communist norms and to break down male-hegemonic forces. Such tactics disrupt traditional emphasized femininity traditions and perforate boundaries established to contain women's "pseudo-purities" of religion, femininity, morals, and rights—generating online debates wherein the young women are labeled as *sluts* involved with *offensive* and *vulgar* activities (Betlemidze, 2015, p. 375). Despite mainstream media attempts to depoliticize FEMEN's protests by demeaning the women involved (Thumim, 2012), FEMEN has put gender hierarchies on the public's political agenda by inspiring debates about more fully changing society by fostering gender equality (Thomas & Stehling, 2016).

Somewhat like FEMEN, women of the punk rock band, *Pussy Riot,* also mobilize their political message (including imprisonment of three members) around emphasized femininity with provocative lyrics about sex. Both FEMEN and *Pussy Riot* label themselves as feminist, but the

Figure 10.2. FEMEN activists gathered in Kiev, Ukraine, to protest for women's rights, November 25, 2010. Source: Виталий Павленко/ Depositphotos.com

rationales differ since *Pussy Riot*'s songs are about more than feminist issues, often targeting protests against Vladimir Putin's presidency and government's clamp on dissent as these bear on women's ability to speak publicly about women's rights. Sextremism trends and these women activists are moving feminism into additional directions and vitalizing the political nature of feminism and femininity. I would argue that the activism of these groups is not necessarily new, even if the global protest movement components *are*. Indeed, they are important for solidarity in unifying women around the world on issues important to their femininities, health, well-being, and ability to achieve maximum human potential. Rather, what groups like FEMEN and *Pussy Riot* bring to the conversation is a broader continuum of femininities that include leadership, activism, and raw, brazen sexuality, values ordinarily attributed to men and masculinity.

NEWS MEDIA COVERAGE OF WOMEN IN POLITICS

Press *freedom* in the United States must not be confused with press *fairness*. The male-dominated scene of political journalism is notorious for constructing female gender in dismissive and stereotypical ways (Franks, 2013), as interrogated earlier in this chapter. Although some recent U.S. research findings suggest fewer gender differences in tone of media coverage of candidates (e.g., Hayes & Lawless, 2015), a study of twenty years' worth of newspaper coverage of the United Kingdom's women members of Parliament (MPs) offered mixed findings with degrees of gender parity. Some journalists have been calling one another out on sexist depictions, but women politicians still are infantilized and portrayed as weak and emotional, relegated more often than not to nonpolitical stories with greater emphasis on personal angles (O'Neill, Savigny, & Cann, 2016). Women with a political activist agenda have come to realize the importance of forming a symbiotic relationship with the news media, whether or not they respect the fourth estate's manufacture of political news. Over decades, women's rights have met resistance from mainstream media outlets, often resorting to attacking women's femininity when critiquing their political issues although it may not be considered newsworthy (rooted in media bias). First-wave feminists felt the brunt of negative newspaper and magazine coverage which demeaned their demand for the vote and represented suffragists as ugly, masculine women unfit for marriage and motherhood. Indeed, the masculine woman was marginalized in the popular press and across literature before, during, and after ratification of the Nineteenth Amendment to the U.S. Constitution which gave women the right to vote (Behling, 2001). By the time second-wave feminists took to the streets in the 1960s and 1970s demanding passage of the Equal Rights Amendment (ERA) in the United States, news media were equally prepared to ditch professional journalism standards for fairness and careful analysis of a political movement by ridiculing female protesters' demand for equal rights and reporting on "spectacle-ization of the women's liberation movement" (Hesford, 2013, p. 50).

Print and electronic reportage of the 1960s and 1970s clearly illustrated ambivalence toward the U.S. women's movement as an authentic political action and instead framed the proposed ERA as the product of Caucasian/White, middle-aged, middle-classed housewives with too much time on their hands rather than seriously considering their political demands. When the U.S. House of Representatives passed the ERA in 1970, a *New York Times* editorial, "The Henpecked House," severely criticized the outcome and "reduced the ERA fight to a spectacle of femininity" (The henpecked, 1970). Meanwhile, *Playboy* magazine framed women's liberation in terms of a threat to the heterosexual order and mocked the physical appearance of liberationists (Hunt, 1970). By the end of 1970, well-respected media such as *Time* magazine and the *New York Times* had resorted to attacking women's sexuality by introducing negative critique about lesbian lifestyles.

Persistent with U.S. news media's long-held tradition of attacking politically active women based on their physical appearance in contexts such as femininity, attractiveness, and respectability, reportage about women running for political office consistently objectifies female candidates and politicians in terms of emphasized femininity as expressed through fashion, hairstyle, and makeup. Women are constructed according to journalists' narrow understanding of what femininity is and female politicians often are constructed as *other* in comparison to male politician benchmarks (van Zoonen, 2006). Because media coverage plays no small part in U.S. political processes, when mediated representation of women's femininity marginalizes women (Ogle & Damhorst, 1999) or renders them invisible (O'Neill, Savigny, & Cann, (2016), discredits their credentials and capabilities (Siegel, 2009), or relies on stereotypes that demean female candidates (Baur, 2015), it is no wonder that so few women occupy the highest offices locally, statewide, and nationally. Among voters, a candidate's appearance can play a significant role in whether or not she is well received, useful information for campaign strategists in developing political brand images for the woman politician (Hoegg & Lewis, 2011). Fashion shapes perceptions of people and, in turn, impacts how those people are treated (Pham, 2012). So, when highly esteemed, authoritative news media criticize women politicians' feminine appearance, significant damage may be done to their reputation.

A backlash effect called the *gender double bind* means women in politics considered too feminine are chastised in the media for being incompetent and those considered not feminine enough are framed negatively as non-heterosexual and/or ugly. The gender double bind holds back women from fulfilling their leadership potential (Jamieson, 1995). Patterns in news coverage of appointments of women to high courts have emerged among Western nations of Australia, Canada, and the United States, including reliance on feminine stereotypes and highlighted deviances from such stereotypes in terms of ethnicity, religion, motherhood, or communication style (Escobar-Lemmon, Hoekstra, Kang, & Kittilson, 2016). For example, nearly every news article about the nomination of Sonia Sotomayor to the U.S. Supreme Court mentioned that she was "emotional and tough," commonly held stereotypes about Latinas, and Elena Kagan was labeled "inexperienced" (p. 265). For the Canada Supreme Court, Rosalie Silberman Abella was framed as the "first female Jewish judge" and Andromache Karakatsanis was accused of "jump[ing] the queue" ahead of more experienced justices (Escobar-Lemmon, Hoekstra, Kang, & Kittilson, 2016, p. 267). Women leaders in politics and elsewhere "must walk a razor's edge between looking powerful and still appearing appropriately feminine" (Pham, 2012), as they have to "work much harder to prove themselves as valuable leaders and stewards of the people . . . in the process they also need to look approachable, relatable, and feminine" (Sanghvi & Hodges, 2015, p. 1686). Berger (1972) characterized society's perception of gender in terms of "men act and women appear" (p. 45), crystallizing effects wherein women are judged by their looks rather than by their intellect, talents, or deeds. Such outcomes seem more pronounced in political journalism. As mentioned at the outset of this chapter, Shirley Chisholm was the first African-American/Black woman elected to the U.S. Congress, and first major-party African-American/ Black candidate for U.S. President. During her 1972 run for U.S. President on the Democratic ticket, Shirley Chisholm had her femininity attacked and she responded: "One distressing thing is the way men react to women who assert their equality: Their ultimate weapon is to call them unfeminine. They think she is anti-male; they even whisper that she's probably a lesbian" (Walston, 2012). Shirley Chisholm's legacy as educator, author, and politician, was commemorated on a U.S. postage stamp in 2014. See Figure 10.3.

News media coverage of the 2008 U.S. Presidential election showcased the gender double bind phenomenon when Republican Vice Presidential nominee Sarah Palin was depicted as *sexy* and *feminine*, but *incompetent*—and Democratic Presidential contender Hillary Rodham Clinton was depicted as *competent* but an *unfeminine iron maiden* (Curnalia & Mermer, 2014). Clinton had been no stranger to wardrobe critique—as when she was demeaned for wearing the power pantsuit, a "desexualized uniform" (Pham, 2012). Pantsuits strategically may hide or de-emphasize a woman's femininity, which can present a "serious liability" in certain circles (Euse, 2016). In an interview for this book, Sally, 60, Caucasian/ White, mother of a college woman also interviewed for this book, had this to say about Hillary Rodham Clinton:

> [S]he has made it her mission to use the media to push women's issues. And yet, many people looking at her would say—not that she's quote *un*attractive, but a little bit bottom heavy, wears the pantsuits, no spring chicken, had a philandering handsome husband. And yet, I think of her in some ways as being *very* feminine. When I think of Hillary Clinton, to use the vernacular, I don't think of a ballbuster, I think of someone who is feminine.

Ways Sally described a woman political leader suggests a broader definition of femininity that coincides with the Femininities and Masculinities Continuum that I presented in chapter 8. The Continuum suggests that every person (regardless of gender) embodies elements of each concept within and, flexibly, may enact any degree of femininity at will.

In the media scene, things heated up in 2007. News media coverage of Hillary Rodham Clinton's cleavage provided fodder for reporters attending to the political beat and beyond, elevating to the level of national public debate a discussion about a woman's femininity and ways it is communicated through clothes. The *Washington Post* fashion editor filed a 746-word article about Clinton's femininity and her cleavage, with the headline "Hillary Clinton's tentative dip into new neckline territory" (Givhan, 2007, p. C01):

> There was cleavage on display . . . Sen. Hillary Clinton . . . talking on the Senate floor . . . neckline sat low on her chest and had a subtle V-

Figure 10.3. The legacy of educator, author, and politician Shirley Chisholm (1924–2005) was commemorated on a U.S. postage stamp in 2014. Source: Olga Popova/ Depositphotos.com.

shape. The cleavage registered after only a quick glance. . . acknowl-
edgment of sexuality and femininity peeking out . . . it wasn't until the
early ninties that women were even allowed to wear pants on the Sen-
ate floor.

Politico, a political journalism news service, panned the media firestorm
about the kerfuffle: "We like her suit jacket—we thought it was a vision
in coral—but that is not why it was a stupid attack. Write this down,
guys: Attack her policies, attack her past votes, attack her personality if
you want to, but don't attack what she is wearing. It looks sexist and
cheap" (Simon, 2007). In sum, female politicians have an additional burden that male politicians do not—to meet society's expectations that they
appear authoritative, yet feminine. As de Beauvoir (1968) astutely
pointed out, women are required to attend to their appearance and dress
because their professional success depends upon it. *What would Simone de
Beauvoir have had to say about social media, I wonder?*

Yet, as political reporters explain, they simply are manufacturing
news within the constraints of certain journalistic routines and conventions. Workers at the Finnish *Suomen Kuvalehti* weekly news magazine
spent significant amounts of time planning for and producing cover
photography of the female Finnish Prime Minister and experienced conflict when trying to balance journalistic neutrality with feminine beauty
norms in a country with a reputation for high gender equality, but a
milieu where the public-private sphere overlap is deeply rooted in cultural practices (Huovinen & Weselius, 2015). Moreover, we live amidst an
unprecedented global celebrity culture which forces women to monitor
their femininity in terms of appearance and public image. The magazine's editorial and production team charted "slippery" new territory
when Prime Minister Mari Kiviniemi requested to use her own makeup
artist; the staff (in conjunction with the PM) pondered whether or not she
should smile and tilt her head—common articulations of femininity according to Goffman (1979). The magazine struck a balance between paral-
lel but competing scripts of journalistic neutrality and feminine beauty
(Huovinen & Weselius, 2015, p. 13) while pulling back the curtain on
ways news media construct gender in political coverage—for all readers
to see.

DISCUSSION

Valian's (1989) lamentation of *Why So Slow?* persists well into the new
millennium with many nations around the globe still offering a dispro-
portionate representation of women involved in and elected to political
leadership positions. As it turns out, research findings consistently and
persistently expose flawed systemic, patriarchal mindsets and traditions
that hold women's femininities against them. Expectancies based on gen-

der create problems for women in many professional fields, exponentially so in elective politics. As the level of office increases in power and importance, female candidates suffer from an ongoing feminist backlash and old-fashioned ideas about femininity as limitation in the political arena. Women's femininities are used against them, narrowing the possibilities for women's agency. People continue to be socialized to stereotypes of women as relegated to the private/domestic sphere simply because they are considered biologically inferior and incompetent to serve as stewards of the public will. *Who knows? Politicized motherhood could serve a purpose other than to self-aggrandize photogenic families.* Increased numbers of images of female politicians who seamlessly manage doing it all (Warner, 2010) in paid work *outside* the home and unpaid work *inside* the home could inspire more women to political activism. I worry, of course, about stress and conflict associated with negotiating between women's political leadership role and the mother role—especially among those lacking in support systems. I concur with Huovinen and Weselius (2015), as they urged for comprehensive analyses of the public-private division so that we finally may "understand why the old gender contract still persists even when women officially have equal rights to take part in politics" (p. 15).

Beyond addressing enduring stereotypes faced by women in politics, this chapter examined generational differences among popular and third-wave feminism as map makers for activism designed to affect social change—and posited that girls' involvement in politics is thwarted by other effects of ways femininity is regarded according to age, threatening to block a pipeline of potential for future female leadership. There is no room in today's global society for anything that stands in the way of girls and women considering political leadership as a viable option. Finally, this chapter offered an update on how far the news media have (not) come in representing gender equitably in the realm of politics and have used *femininity* as a means for attacking qualified women running for political office. This last point is particularly salient since journalism traditionally has fulfilled a public sphere function by providing information required by voters so that they may make informed voting choices. While women politicians, appointed leaders, and activists cannot rely on basic fairness from traditional media which make profits from perpetuating sexist images of girls and women and from sensationalizing women's issues, neither can they rely on a feminist movement that has lost its footing by exchanging political activism for real social change—for sexual independence and economic opportunity to fuel the capitalist machine and to blithely perpetuate a patriarchal system of economic power and domination. Popular self-disciplining practices linked to femininity serve to distract women young and old from femininities as an ingredient for political organizing. Instead of tending to their looks to satisfy the male gaze (or what they've become convinced is for themselves), girls and women have sociopolitical work to do by well-investing their time and energies in helping *all* people to improve their circumstances and ultimately to achieve their maximum potential. The growing possibilities for social media offer a beacon for global feminism fighting on multiple women's issue fronts, a means for women to circumnavigate corporatized media and unite globally—not unlike Eastern Europe's sextremism movements. These important discussions must grow and continue if feminism is to be relevant and vital. I anticipate the day when a female politician's partner is stereotyped as the adoring and supportive one, rather than our current reality in the United States where the compliant wife plainly stands behind her politician husband.

ELEVEN

Lessons and Moving Forward

Language is so difficult. How do you detach yourself from what has been instilled in what you think you should think *when it comes to femininity? As a woman, to be feminine is to be aware of the differences in language, of culture, and the media—and to just be aware of it so you don't fit into some sort of mold that has been laid out for you.*
—Research participant, Camila, 27, Dominican, bisexual

Women long have been attracted to the study of gender as a socially constructed phenomenon. Women scholars and policymakers were first to make masculinity visible as an analysis category (Kimmel, 2001) so that today, masculinity studies programs thrive in universities and colleges the world over. Meanwhile, even though the concept of femininity has attracted significant attention among feminist scholars, a formal study of femininity does not seem to have garnered the same degree of attention in universities and colleges in terms of discrete departments and programs of study. The purpose of this book is to pull together multiple disciplines' interrogation of the femininity concept and to add women's voices and lived experiences across generations to conversations about *What is femininity? What does it mean to you?* This phenomenon is intentionally wide-ranging and covers at least 100 years of history as I address it in this book, with attention to multiple media forms' representations, and a generalized description of stress/conflict women experience because of *femininity* definitions imposed by others. I used images from women's magazines that were representative (but not exhaustive) to stimulate discussion about femininity. Camila, as quoted above, seemed to capture well the confusion women generally feel about the term *femininity* once they move beyond what they have been told. What women resent is being universalized, taken for granted, and underestimated. Among the women I interviewed, *femininity* must be defined as a flexible concept which encompasses a range of possibilities.

New ways for thinking about femininities have been offered, which if used to supplant the traditional emphasized femininity most often amplified across media platforms, could change public discourses about femininity and supplant the limited social roles for girls and women. The focus group and interview research methods used for collecting data — and the hermeneutic phenomenological theme analysis technique used are consistent with a larger feminist methodology. I join many feminist researchers who use the term *feminism* to include the elimination of oppression among *all* people who are marginalized by a dominant culture, including but not limited to people of color, people with disabilities, people across ages and socioeconomic circumstances, and people across sexual orientations. Feminist values include respect, caring, reciprocity, self-determination, and interconnection. This book constitutes a research project driven by a desire to understand *femininity* without reproducing gender inequality and while embracing social identity intersectionalities as we work to create a society which no longer relegates girls and women to second-class status or celebrates male privilege as something *natural*. These qualitative research methods and rhetorical analysis promote the ability to *talk back to* the methodological assumptions of early scientific research inspired by Charles Darwin's 1872 ideas about middle-class women's frailty and how males steadily move toward perfection while females are outside of the same process of natural selection. Such attitudes remain entrenched as institutionalized social inequalities across gender and other social identity dimensions. This book is rooted in feminist communication theory which begins with an assumption that we are in need of *deep structural change*. Eradicating injustice, discrimination, and oppression must be our main objective advancing further into the twenty-first century.

The study of rhetoric continues to be relevant. The symbols and discourses that impose themselves upon our lives, transferring meanings, and sometimes limiting our ability to make brand new meaning permeate public and private spheres. Being conscious of how symbols and discourses function and being aware of their impact in socially constructing reality enables us to make independent and conscious choices about who we are, how we perceive others, and understanding the values that matter. Research participants' perceptions, stories, and recommendations which inspired this book project amplified most of the negative stereotypes about women and their femininities—but also offered nuances and optimism that change may be afoot. Women across age groups anticipate a future where stress associated with concern about how one looks becomes a thing of the past and that girls and women are assessed for how femininity shapes girls and women from the inside out—rather than the other way around. Associations between internalization of emphasized femininity norms/ideals and body image and self-esteem—and constant social comparisons—offer important intervention moments for exposing roots of female gender role stress/conflict. In general, women encourage ongoing and regular discussion about femininity and how it is made to mean, followed by social change for good.

Signifiers of femininity and masculinity emerged in our discussions about bodies, dress, patterns of consumption, work, as well as mediated representations of women in their gendered roles. Social researchers often focus on ways that media reproduce and sustain *natural, normal,* and *commonsensical* notions of masculinity and femininity as part of processes for meaning making about gender identity. Women who participated in this study did, too—to the degree that many, if not most, placed blame on media for articulating traditional versions of femininity as if they are facts. Paradoxically, however, when examining the images of women from the past 100 years of women's magazines, their eyes were transfixed on the fashions featuring skin, the colors pink and red, pearls, lace, satin, silk, corset, gowns, and jewelry—images of a bride and of women with babies as *most feminine.* I call this *paraphernalia of femininity*—items that women have been socialized to internalize as representing femininity, whether they personally wear or use these items or not. Meanwhile images selected by women to represent their own idea of *least feminine* were those of women wearing business suits, trousers, blue jeans, leather jacket, and engaging in activities like baseball, fishing, horse riding, gardening, motorcycling, and holding a handgun. Researchers have suggested that women attend to images of femininity and use them as guideposts for their own gender performances (Goffman, 1976), calling the images "seductive" (Bordo, 2000, p. 186) and omnipresent since they are available in advertising across television, billboards, newspapers, magazines, and the internet (Beynon, 2002). I intentionally chose not to use advertising images—only images from magazine editorial pages—to avoid images overtly designed to sell. I often wondered if women simply were so indoctrinated by certain images that they *instinctively* selected *what media tell us is most feminine.* Many women whom I interviewed said they want to be able to wear whatever they want and to define femininity much more broadly than in its emphasized form which is rooted in satisfying the male gaze. In particular, lesbian and bisexual women, as well as older women, advocated for a definition of femininity that included being able to wear clothing stereotypically associated with boys and men. See Figure 11.1.

This final chapter expands upon important points about lessons learned in order to advance femininities studies for better understanding of how *femininity* is defined: 1) Femininity in a world of female gender role stress/conflict, 2) Socialization and femininity expectancies holding back girls and women, 3) Femininities and masculinities on a continuum,

Figure 11.1.   Defining femininity according to a Femininities and Masculinities Continuum means that if a woman chooses to wear lace and silk, she can. If she wants to wear a top hat, tuxedo, and pearls, she can do that, too. Source: Scott Griessel/ Depositphotos.com.

4) Feminism now and later, and 5) On *not* defining femininity by exclusion and by alleviating unequal power relations.

FEMININITY IN A WORLD OF GENDER ROLE STRESS/CONFLICT

Among narratives collected, most disturbing were the stories shared about stress and heartache associated with feelings of not being feminine enough, having a bad body image, and worrying about how this all might play out as women age. These findings contribute to Female Gender Role Stress/Conflict theory building, which is an understudied area (as compared to Masculine Gender Role Stress/Conflict theory work) that requires greater attention to gauge and predict how women negotiate inner turmoil when considering the way they look in conjunction with roles they play in public and private spheres, and how they feel about themselves. O'Neil (1981) has urged for empirical research that would support counseling psychologists to "speak to the public more authoritatively on the dangers of restrictive sex-role socialization for men, women and children" (p. 76). In general, gender role stress/conflict is a complex, multidimensional paradigm describing an unconscious phenomenon produced when perceptions of gender roles deviate from, restrict, deval-ue, or violate norms. Research participants for the study reported in this book seemed acutely aware that women's bodies are objectified in mass media images, that women internalize female gender body image mes-sages, and that femininity is a product of historical processes.

Understanding how women across generations define *femininity* pro-vides empirical data, a broader and more robust set of operationaliza-tions when measuring GRS/C and when advancing dialog about promot-ing social justice for women, as well as for men. As posited by O'Neil (2008), the addition of research about GRS/C experienced by girls and women as their gender identity reflects social identity intersectionalities of ethnicity, sexual orientation, social class, and other dimensions—when combined with what is known about the phenomenon in the lives of diverse men and boys—provides an important baseline for eradicating and preventing GRS/C root causes as they develop and play out in schools, families, and interpersonal relationships. Each girl and woman experiences "unrelenting pressure to make the most of what she has" (Bartky, 2010, p. 87). The body is more than a passive surface upon which discourses are imposed, however. Girls and women possess the ability to resist discourses with which they disagree—and to write their own—living true to their own social identity as their female gender intersects with age, ethnicity, sexual orientation, social class, and more. As Foucault (1990) instructed, the body is a site of struggle.

Performing emphasized femininity can be fun, for a while. Presenting and performing a beautiful and sexy body oozing with femininity can mean attracting attention and even admiration. Yet for heterosexuals, as feminist critics point out, the male gaze rarely involves "real respect and rarely any social power" (Bartky, 2010, p. 87). Disciplining the female body to conform to limited ideas about emphasized femininity requires resources inequitably distributed in most cultures—and the payoff is short lived as women age. These processes can be unfulfilling since wom-en rarely rise above second-class status, anyway.

SOCIALIZATION AND FEMININITY EXPECTANCIES HOLDING BACK GIRLS AND WOMEN

Girls and women are expected to behave according to emphasized femi-ninity norms and these expectations ultimately either restrict girls and women who have aspirations beyond what is expected of them—or es-tablish barriers so that certain behaviors and career paths are not consid-ered options at all. In the extreme, girls and women who believe mes-sages suggesting that they are biologically, emotionally, or intellectually inferior to men will fulfill the weak role that defines sexism (Butler & Paisley, 1980). Disparagement of confidence and ambition in girls and women underscores ways success confirms masculinity but *dis*confirms femininity (Kimmel, 2008). Sexism's tentacles are long and enduring, with girls and women holding their second-class status to be a self-evident truth—given institutionalized sexism, years of socialization to think of femininity as synonymous with weak, and a norm of viewing women considered to have overstepped the boundaries of emphasized femininity as deserving of disparaging epithets. Gender socialization involves "a complex of socially guided perceptual, interactional, and micro-political activities that cast particular pursuits as expressions of masculine and feminine 'natures'" (West & Zimmerman, 1987, p. 126). Women who dare to put themselves first are harshly chastised for doing so, regarded as *aggressive, bitch, slut,* bad mothers, wives, co-workers, and leaders—*un*-feminine. As Caro (2016) explained, "[I]t isn't the women who seek power who are the problem. It is our expectations of them."

Girls and women are trained for a lifetime of maintaining their body through a drive for thinness which facilitates a valued performance of femininity, usually a performance marked by a rigid definition of perfection. Some women rely on their physical attributes in professions where they have to present themselves to the public and manage public perceptions. In other aspects of the public sphere, women are socialized to attract a man's attention and to be sexy in order to secure a husband—but not *too* sexy so as to invite (according to some) rape or other physical abuse. In fact, girls and women who deviate from emphasized femininity norms may be considered to have "no real womanhood to be violated or offended" (Coontz, 1993, p. 64), an assessment which cements the prevailing myth of women's second-class status. Although this framework for judging the female body entirely overlooks the fact that some women dress to feel good in/about themselves and to appeal to other women, the fact remains that heteronormativity pervades U.S. culture. Indeed, gender relations are historically and socially conditioned. For most, femininity and masculinity remain relational constructs—wherein the definition of either depends on the definition of the other. Most women interviewed for this book concurred with that assessment, too. However, some provided advice and suggestions for breaking the confines of the emphasized femininity model to facilitate more fluid ideas about femininity *and* masculinity for girls and women. Encouraging people to revise their expectancies of both femininity's attributes and limitations should reduce the number of violations that end up reflecting badly on girls and women. Overall, altering ways people are socialized to think about gender and its relational concepts, such as femininity, is essential. Only by examining girls' and women's embodied experiences through a social construction lens can we fully understand their lives and consider the fullest range of possibilities available on the other side of resistance to conventions established over hundreds (if not thousands) of years.

Complicating the task of defining femininity is the constant barrage of cultural messages, linguistic forms, and norms about gender and acceptable feminine behavior—as institutionalized in schools, professional sports, workplaces, and amplified by media such as the internet, television, radio, books, and magazines. Socialization often works under our radar. Girls and women may not directly be coerced to buy into popular culture's representations of emphasized femininity, yet they choose to mold their body to trends under the pressure of being chastised and marginalized if they fail to live up to idealized emphasized femininity norms. Hence, girls and women justify mediated images' representations and could be, paradoxically, contributing to their own subordination (Charlebois, 2011). Promoting open discussions and critique which bolsters critical thinking skills is essential. Adolescence, predominantly, seems to be the phase when young women succumb to mainstream culture and consequently lose their "capacity for boldness, resistance and confidence" (Harris & Dobson, 2015, p. 150) as they become acculturated into emphasized femininity norms. A counter-ideal of girl as fighter who is "assertive, usually smart, psychologically tough, physically strong" is emerging—and not just among girls considered to be delinquent or streetwise tough. These are girls who Brown (2003) suggested historically have been marginalized outside a Caucasian/White and middle-class feminine ideal but now are just as likely to be girls who perform well in school, play sports, and are likeable. So, supporting and encouraging young women to claim and to amplify their independence and critical voice is supremely important. Research that explores definitions and everyday experiences among girls and young women has decreased in recent years (Duits & van Zoonen, 2006), a pattern I sought to redress in this book with regard to how femininity is defined and lived.

Femininities scholars also must persist with recent years' trends of examining the experiences of girls and women according to their social identity intersectionalites. An inability to look beyond middle-class Caucasian/White heterosexualism stunted growth of fragmented second-wave feminism, in my view. Female gender roles across the United States may have become more egalitarian in some areas over time, but certain regions traditionally have been excluded from studies focused on women's lives. One example of this is anti-ERA holdouts, such as some southern U.S. states where traditional emphasized femininity norms have persisted across socio-economic status. Just how faith/spirituality intersects with other social identity dimensions and ways that female gender roles and norms are constructed and perpetuated by religious subcultures have far-reaching consequences, an arena rife for exploration in furthering our understanding of girls' and women's feminine identity. Moreover, physical disability generally is not understood as a context for femininity—as discussed in chapter 7, with regard to the hypersexualized images of women who use wheelchairs as projected in reality television in the United States—but it should be.

FEMININITIES AND MASCULINITIES ON A CONTINUUM

Being socialized to femininity or masculinity imposes an either/or limitation for an oppressive lifestyle and consequences that can negatively impact a person's potential and quality of life. Girls and women labeled masculine (by self or others) can experience physical and mental anguish. Ditto for boys and men labeled feminine. As discussed in chapter 7, the scholarly literature tells us there exists a *hierarchy of femininities* which includes *emphasized femininity, pariah femininity, oppositional femininity,* and *equality femininities.* Moreover, some forms of femininity are considered more valuable by media over others—such as femininity of Caucasian/White girls and women as representing an ideal for perfection. To eradicate these procrustean notions borne of an archaic framework, a more fluid continuum of femininities and masculinities (in their plural) must be considered as shaping our daily experiences. One's biologically sexed body and socially constructed gender must remain flexible, determined exclusively by the person inhabiting that body, and the outcome respected by everyone. Such a continuum embraces diversity in perspectives about how femininity and masculinity are made to mean. I concur that "biology is no more primary or real than any other aspect of lived experience" (Cornwall & Lindisfarne, 1994, p. 10). One need look no further than the life experiences of drag kings and queens—and ways these people are breaking the social rules/roles. Being a biological female does not confer femininity—and being a biological male does not confer masculinity. I am dubious that there may be a future point where social constructions shall be gender blind. However, I am hopeful that meanings about femininity and masculinity as each shapes perceptions of self and others become less rigid and that boundaries of division become more permeable for a continuum rather than an either/or framework. In practice, this shall mean abolishing lists of personality and body traits defined by gender as associated with either/or feminine or masculine. How this shall play out with regard to androgyny and transgenderism should be most informative.

One effect of such changes in ways femininities are socially constructed shall be the reform of socialization for girls and erosion of patriarchy as a governing principle for girls' and women's lives across public and private spheres. No career field shall be off limits. Girls and women may play any sport they desire. Both young and old women shall be valued—including all of those in between. Women politicians in the highest leadership positions shall be the new norm. Media stereotypes negatively representing girls and women shall become things of the past.

The *ideal* femininity or *perfection* shall be self-defined, not socially imposed. Hence, female gender role stress and conflict shall be eradicated. Consumerism and the beauty-fashion complex may rejoice due to wider options and marketing opportunities! Old rituals such as prom shall be modified and new ones shall emerge—not unlike ways LGBTQ young people have created their own forms of the high school prom. I would thus like to see the end of patriarchy and femininity as its handmaiden, turning toward a more thorough achievement of a politics of equal rights.

FEMINISM NOW AND LATER

Girls and women may resolve to resist pressures of the most popular definition of femininity (as emphasized)—and subordination as second-class citizens—as they encounter greater economic and social opportunities which afford more independence. Feminism is used to reveal among discourses the language, symbols, and images that contribute to an ideology of domination. Fifty years since second-wave feminists supported the ERA, women today strive for perfection, to be and to do it all—perfect partners, mothers, workers—and with perfect bodies. I believe in feminist scholarship's transformative potential. Like many women of my age cohort, I came to appreciate feminism later in life and did not really see its relevance when I was younger because I grew up believing that hard work would yield career achievement and that gender difference was no longer a variable. I came to learn that women still face challenges even though we were told in the 1970s and 1980s that we would not. We must remain faithful to feminism's goals of equality, opportunity, and independence for all. Postmodern feminists recognize that the body is a site where identity forming occurs and stress/conflict plays out. To date, nowhere has critical interrogation of this dynamic been more powerful than in the work of Butler (1993, 2004). In addition to having money to spend supporting themselves, girls and women in this postfeminist era must further develop their healthy skepticism and critical thinking skills to avoid uncritically buying into the yoga, cross-fit, working-out images of women who view their body as a project requiring constant maintenance—and then adorning it with the accoutrements of emphasized femininity. Buying Botox treatments, make-up, trendy shoes and handbags, jewelry, and clothes as a means to live up to some idealized youthful femininity norm without critically thinking about what they're buying into shortchanges girls' and women's political power necessary for gaining equity with boys and men in both the public and private spheres. Critiquing power relations is feminist work, necessary until women enjoy the same status at work as men and shared housekeeping and parenting at home. Postfeminist culture promotes fantasies of youthful regeneration and transformation that also speaks to a desire for change. Engaging with such goals should not come at the expense of demeaning older women and women with disabilities—for everyone ages and is only temporarily abled. These are the types of concerns that postfeminism, as an epistemological framework, promotes and encourages. Girls and women must avoid complacency, settling for status quo when the concept of femininity is used against us. The feminist spark persists when questions about power relations are ongoing and persistent.

Femininity and feminism are not binary opposites at odds with one another. In some ways, feminism had achieved the status of common sense. Yet siren songs encouraging girls and women to equate femininity with valuing and striving for "luxury lifestyling and retail pleasures . . . showplace domesticity, virtuoso parenting" (Tasker & Negra, 2007, p. 7) and fantasies of downshifting to idealized domesticity (Hollows, 2006) risk a backslide in time. Nostalgically holding up Eisenhower-era images of the blissful housewife and mother as ideal runs the risk of overlooking ways that U.S. lifestyle was coded middle-class Caucasian/White. We must resist an urge to return to some second-wave feminists' limited ethnicity/race and class vision. Adopting a feminist reflexivity—one of remaining critical of treatment and scope of opportunities for self and *all* women (including women of color and working-class women) across discourses, representations, and life experiences remains an imperative in a postfeminist or third-wave feminist context. In other ways, anti-feminist backlash has emerged among those who suggest feminism has done its job and raised levels of consciousness about women's second-class status so that gender inequalities have been abolished. Any critique that suggests women have *overstepped their limits* is proof enough that boundaries and limitations are placed on girls and women. As examined in chapter 6, legislation such as Title IX in the United States provides for equal opportunities for girls in sports—and continues to be very necessary. At the time of this writing, Title IX legislation is being celebrated as contributing to the success of girls and women winning gold at the 2016 Olympic Games in Rio. Amplifying women's voices and empowering them to embody a right to claim how their life shall transpire is central to feminist thinking. In fact, masculinity studies have been attributed to feminist values of respect, care, and interconnection—so that many feminists now use the umbrella term of *feminism* to eradicate oppression of *all* people of social identity intersectionalities including (but not limited to) age, class, culture, ethnicity, faith/spirituality, gender, physical/psychological ability, sexual orientation, and more. Resistance at the level of the everyday contributes to continued transformation of social relations for positive change. Feminism is a way of living one's life "by acting in ways that allow others to make choices, that affirm them and their perspectives, and that do not oppress and exploit" (Foss, Foss, & Griffin, 1999, p. 5).

ON *NOT* DEFINING FEMININITY BY EXCLUSION AND BY
ALLEVIATING UNEQUAL POWER RELATIONS

The idea that some naturalized hierarchical bond exists between the feminine and masculine and women and men has been long overdue for a makeover. Denying that women can be masculine, as well as feminine (and it's OK!), is akin to fears researchers have found among men who equate femininity with narcissism, exhibitionism, emasculation, a metrosexual lifestyle—and ultimately, many exhibit homophobia. Women need not exude emphasized femininity unless they want to. Categorizing some forms of femininity as *pariah* is a symptom of social constructions in need of revision. So defining femininity as the opposite of masculinity falls short in a world where all social identity dimensions and their intersectionalities must be embraced. Interviewed for this book, Lorraine, 38, African-American/Black, carefully explained how she avoids defining femininity by exclusion:

> [M]y idea of femininity, it doesn't exclude certain things. Like, a woman who fixes cars isn't *not* feminine. A woman who has, like a shaved haircut is *not* excluded from being feminine. To me, the things that exclude you from femininity are like being vulgar and coarse and ill-mannered. . . . I think that a woman can fix cars and play basketball and still be completely and utterly ladylike.

Thinking about one's femininities and masculinities on a continuum model could help to eradicate negativity associated with exclusion and Lorraine's voice offers lived experience details about how the model would play out through lived experience. The paradigm situating femininity as complementary to and inferior to masculinity has been supplanted with social justice demands for a new model, a continuum of femininities that include masculinities for women. Indeed, rejecting women who are active, aggressive, tough, competitive, intelligent, strategic, and successful in the world of sports, politics, work, and everyday life shortchanges the concept of femininities and its social construction. I concur with Charlebois (2011) in resisting emphasized femininity in advocating for egalitarian, democratic relationships among women and men.

So long as the mainstream world remains inhospitable for women and searches for means to negotiate the public and private spheres compound stressors and anxieties for women in their daily lives, there persists a need to redefine femininity as a concept that is *not* in opposition to masculinity. Unequal power relations wherein women are devalued, invisible, silenced, and made uncomfortable, must end. Women are complete human beings with lives that may include, but also exist beyond taking care of others—although that role remains important and essential among many women. Accepting that motherhood need not *completely*

define women opens the conversation for expanded definitions of masculinities, as well as non-heterosexuals' role as parents, too. Understanding
gender *inequality* as it operates in local settings begins by pondering enduring arrangements such as these which promote conflict and stress due
to unrealistic demands and violated expectancies.

Ever since hard science began legitimizing social hierarchies with men
as strong/superior and women as weak/inferior in a survival-of-the-fittest
framework, the idea that men are more evolved than women became
entrenched and legitimized. Darwin (1872) argued that human reproduction saps so much energy, leaving women with too little for any further
mental or physical development—and, therefore, subject to their emotions, passions, and child-like tendencies. In the recent past, subjecting
women's bodies to fashionable trends such as corseting and even high
heels physically limits women's mobility for the sake of measuring up to
some idealized femininity norm designed to increase a woman's value
despite her "natural" shortcomings.

Bibliography

Acker, J. (1990). Hierarchies, jobs, and bodies: a theory of gendered organizations. *Gender and Society*, 4 (2), 139–58.

Adams, N. G. (2005). Fighters and cheerleaders: Disrupting the discourse of "girl power" in the new millennium. In P. J. Bettis and N. G. Adams (Eds.), *Geographies of girlhood: Identities in-between* (pp. 101–13). New York: Routledge.

Afshar, H. (2003). Women and wars: Some trajectories towards a feminist peace. *Development in Practice*, 13(2–3), 178–88.

Anderson, S. (Producer & Director). (2013). *The punk singer* [Motion Picture]. United States: Sundance Selects.

Antunovic, D., & Hardin, M. (2013). Women bloggers: Identity and the conceptualization of sport. *New Media & Society*, 15(8), 1374–92.

Anzaldúa, G. (1987). *Borderlands/la frontera: The new mestiza*. San Francisco: Aunt Lute.

Arber, S., & Ginn J. (Eds.) (1995). *Connecting gender and ageing: A sociological approach*. Buckingham: Open University Press.

Arthurs, J. (2003). *Sex and the City* and consumer culture: Remediating postfeminist drama. *Feminist Media Studies*, 3(1), 83–98.

Aruguete, M. S., Nickleberry, L. D. & Yates, A. (2004). Acculturation, body image, and eating attitudes among Black and White college students. *North American Journal of Psychology*, 6, 393–404.

Attwood, F. (2007). Sluts and Riot Grrrls: Female identity and sexual agency. *Journal of Gender Studies*, 16(3), 233–47.

Aubrey, J. S., & Frisby, C. M. (2011). Sexual objectification in music videos: A content analysis comparing gender and genre. *Mass Communication and Society*, 14, 475–501.

Averett, P. (2009). The search for Wonder Woman. *Affilia: Journal of Women and Social Work*, 24(4), 360–68.

Bailey, C. (2002). Unpacking the mother/daughter baggage: Reassessing second- and third-wave tensions. *Women's Studies Quarterly*, 30(3/4), 138–54.

Bailey, J., Steeves, V., Burkell, J., & Regan, P. (2013). Negotiating with gender stereotypes on social networking sites: From 'bicycle face' to Facebook. *Journal of Communication Inquiry*, 37(2), 91–112.

Baird, S. (2001). *Femininity on the pitch: An ethnography of women's rugby*. Unpublished master's thesis, Bowling Green State University, Ohio.

Bandura, A. (1977). *Social learning theory*. Englewood Cliffs, NJ: Prentice Hall.

Bandura, A. (1994). Social cognitive theory of mass communication. In J. Bryant & D. Zillmann (Eds.), *Media effects: Advances in theory and research* (pp. 61–90). Hillsdale, NJ: Erlbaum.

Bandy, J., & Smith, J. (2005). Factors affecting conflict and cooperation in transnational movement networks. In J. Bandy and J. Smith (Eds.) *Coalitions across borders: Transnational protest and the neoliberal order* (pp. 231–52). New York: Rowman & Littlefield.

Banet-Weiser, S. (2012). *Authentic™: The politics of ambivalence in a brand culture*. New York: NYU Press.

Barnes, C. (2003). What a difference a decade makes: Reflections on doing "emancipatory" disability research. *Disability & Society*, 18(1), 3–17.

Baucom, D. H. (1980). Independent CPI masculinity and femininity scales: Psychological correlates and a sex-role typology. *Journal of Personality Assessment*, 44, 262–71.

Bauer, K. W., Bucchianeri, M. M., & Neumark-Sztainer, D. (2013). Mother-reported parental weight talk and adolescent girls' emotional health, weight control attempts, and disordered eating behaviors. *Journal of Eating Disorders, 1,* 1-8.

Baugh, E. J., & Barnes, A. (2015). An examination of the influence of ethnic identity and parental attachment on the body esteem of Black sorority women. *Journal of Black Studies, 46*(3), 316–29.

Baugh, E., Mullis, R., Mullis, A., Hicks, M., & Peterson, G. (2010). Ethnic identity and body image among Black and White college females. *Journal of American College Health, 59,* 105–9.

Banks, I. (2000). *Hair matters: Beauty, power, and Black women's consciousness.* New York: New York University Press.

Banner, L. (1992). *In a full flower: Aging women, power, and sexuality.* New York: Alfred A. Knopf.

Banta, M. (1977). They shall have faces, minds, and (one day) flesh: Women in late 19th-century and early 20th-century American literature. In M. Springer (Ed.), *What manner of woman: Essays on English and American life and literature* (pp. 235–70). New York: New York University Press.

Barlow, T. E., Dong, M. Y., Poiger, U. G., Ramamurthy, P., Thomas, L. M., & Weinbaum, A. E. (2005). The modern girl around the world: A research agenda and preliminary findings. *Gender & History, 17*(2), 245–94.

Barnard, M. (2001). *Fashion as communication,* 2nd ed. London: Routledge.

Barnett, B. (2013). Toward authenticity: Using feminist theory to construct journalistic narratives of maternal violence. *Feminist Media Studies, 13*(3), 505–24.

Barreto, M. Ryan, & M. Schmitt (Eds.) (2008). *The glass ceiling in the 21st century: Understanding barriers to gender equality.* Washington, D.C.: American Psychological Association.

Bartkowski, J. P. (1999). One step forward, one step back: Progressive traditionalism and the negotiation of domestic labor in evangelical families. *Gender Issues, 17,* 37–61.

Bartky, S. (1988). Foucault, femininity and the modernization of patriarchal power. In I. Diamond and L. Quimby (Eds.), *Feminism and Foucault: Reflections on resistance* (pp. 61–86). Boston: Northeastern University Press.

Bartky, S. L. (1990). *Femininity and domination: Studies in the phenomenology of oppression.* New York: Routledge.

Bartky, S. L. (2010). Foucault, femininity, and the modernization of patriarchal power. In R. Weitz (Ed.), *The politics of women's bodies,* 3rd ed. (pp. 76–97). New York: Oxford University Press.

Baumgardner, J., & Richards, A., (2004). Feminism and femininity: Or how we learned to stop worrying and love the thong. In A. Harris and M. Fine (Eds.), *All about the girl* (pp. 59–69). Routledge: London.

Baumgardner, J., & Richards, A. (2010). *Manifesta: Young women, feminism, and the future.* New York: Farrar, Strauss and Giroux.

Baur, G. (Director). (2002). *Venus boyz.* [Motion Picture]. Switzerland, United States, Germany: Clockwise Productions, ONIX Filmproduction, Teleclub AG.

Baur, N. M. (2015). Who stereotypes female candidates? Identifying individual differences in feminine stereotype reliance. *Politics, Groups, and Identities, 3*(1), 94–110.

Beck, U., & Beck-Gernsheim, E. (2001). *Individualisation: Institutionalized individualism and its consequences.* London: Sage.

Becker, P. E., & Moen, P. (2002). Scaling back: Dual-earner couples' work–family strategies. *Journal of Marriage and the Family, 61,* 995–1007.

Bederman, G. (1995). *Manliness and civilization: A cultural history of gender and race in the United States, 1880–1917.* Chicago: University of Chicago Press.

Behling, L. L. (2001). *The masculine woman in America, 1890–1935.* Chicago: University of Illinois Press.

Bell, E. L. J. E. & Nkomo, S. M. (2001). *Our separate ways: Black and White women and the struggle for professional identity.* Boston: Harvard Business School Press.

Bellafante, G. (1998). Feminism: It's all about me! *Time*, June 29, 54–60.

Bem, S. L. (1974). The measurement of psychological androgyny. *Journal of Consulting and Clinical Psychology, 42*(2), 155–62.

Bem, S. L. (1983). Gender schema theory and its implications for child development: Raising gender-aschematic children in a gender-schematic society. *Signs, 8*(4), 598–616.

Bem, S. L. (1993). *The lenses of gender—transforming the debate on sexual inequality*. New Haven: Yale University Press.

Bennett, J. (2015, August 2). I'm not mad. That's just my RBF. *New York Times*. Downloaded from, www.nytimes.com/2015/08/02/fashion/im-not-mad-thats-just-my-resting-b-face.html?smid=fb-share&_r=0.

Berenson, T. (2015, May 2). 'It was never a dress' campaign will change how you see bathroom signs. *Time*. Downloaded March 25, 2016 from, time.com/3844273/bathroom-signs-campaign/.

Berger, J. (1972). *Ways of seeing*. London: BBC and Penguin.

Best, A. L. (2000). *Prom night: Youth, schools and popular culture*. New York: Routledge.

Best, A. L. (2006). Freedom, constraint, and family responsibility: Teens and parents collaboratively negotiate around the car, class, gender, and culture. *Journal of Family Issues, 27*(1), 55–84.

Betlemidze, M. (2015). Mediatized controversies of feminist protest: FEMEN and bodies as affective events. *Women's Studies in Communication, 38,* 374–79.

Betz, N. E. (1995). Gender-related individual differences variables: New concepts, methods, and findings. In D. J. Lubinski, & R. V. Dawis (Eds.), *Assessing individual differences in human behavior: New concepts, methods, and findings* (pp. 119–43). Palo Alto, CA: Davies-African American.

Beynon, J. (2002). *Masculinities and culture*. Milton Keynes: Open University Press.

Bille, M., & Sørensen, T. F. (2007). An anthropology of luminosity: The agency of light. *Journal of Material Culture, 12*(3), 263–84.

Blanchard-Fields, F., Suhrer-Roussel, L., & Hertzog, C. (1994). A confirmatory factor analysis of the Bem Sex Role Inventory: Old questions, new answers. *Sex Roles, 30,* 423–57.

Blazina, C., & Watkins, C. E. (2000). Separation/individuation, parental attachment, and male gender conflict: Attitudes toward the feminine and the fragile masculine self. *Psychology of Men and Masculinity, 1,* 126–32.

Blithe, S. J., & Hanchey, J. N. (2015). The discursive emergence of gendered physiological discrimination in sex verification testing. *Women's Studies in Communication, 38,* 486–506.

Bobst, K. (2016, February 15). The evolving media reaction email astronauts. Mother Nature Network. Downloaded February 21, 2016 from, www.mnn.com/earth-matters/space/stories/evolving-media-reaction-female-astronauts.

Bolin, A. (1998). *Muscularity and femininity: Women bodybuilders and women's bodies in culturo-historical context: Fitness as cultural phenomenon*. New York: Waxmann.

Bolzendahl, C. I., & Myers, D. J. (2004). Feminist attitudes and support for gender equality: Opinion change in women and men, 1974-1998. *Social Forces, 83,* 759–90.

Bordo, S. (1989). The body and the reproduction of femininity. In A. Jaggar & S. Bordo (Eds.), *Gender/body/knowledge: Feminist reconstructions of being and knowing* (pp. 13033). New Brunswick, NJ: Rutgers University Press.

Bordo, S. (1995). Reading the slender body. In N. Tuana and R. Tong (Eds.), *Feminism and philosophy: Essential readings in theory, reinterpretation, and application* (pp. 467–88). Boulder, CO: Westview Press.

Bordo, S. (2000). *The male body: A new look at men in public and in private*. New York: Farrar, Straus and Giroux.

Bosson, J. K., Prewitt-Freilino, J. L., & Taylor, J. N. (2005). Role rigidity: A problem of identity misclassification? *Journal of Personality and Social Psychology, 89,* 552–65.

Bowleg, L. (2008). When Black + lesbian + woman ≠ Black lesbian woman: The methodological challenges of qualitative and quantitative intersectionality research. *Sex Roles*, 59, 312–25.

Boyle, L. (2005). Flexing the tensions of female muscularity: How female bodybuilders negotiate normative femininity in competitive bodybuilding. *Women's Studies Quarterly*, 22(1/2), 134–49.

Bradshaw, C. K. (1994). Asian and Asian American women: Historical and political considerations in psychotherapy. In L. Comas-Diaz & B. Greene (Eds.), *Women of color: Integrating ethnic and gender identities in psychotherapy* (pp. 72–113). New York: Guilford.

Braithwaite, A. (2002). The personal, the political, third-wave and post feminisms. *Feminist Theory*, 3(3), 335–44.

Brines, J. (1994). Economic dependency, gender, and the division of labor at home. *American Journal of Sociology*, 100(3), 652–88.

Broken People (Writers). (2013). Bitchy resting face. Funny or Die [webisode]. Accessed February 10, 2016 from, www.funnyordie.com/videos/d7ab80d4a5/bitchy-resting-face?_cc=__d___&_ccid=6fdf8a792309dd3b.

Brown, L. M. (2003). *Girl fighting: Betrayal and rejection among girls*. New York: New York University Press.

Brown, L. M., & Gilligan, C. (1992). *Meeting at the crossroads: Women's psychology and girls' development*. New York: Ballantine.

Brown, S. (2000). On kitsch, nostalgia, and nineties femininity. *Studies in Popular Culture*, 22(3), 39–54.

Brownmiller, S. (1984). *Femininity*. New York: Linden Press.

Brownmiller, S. (2000). Emotion. In E. Ashton-Jones, G. A. Olson, and M. G. Perry (Eds.), *The gender reader* (pp. 77–88) Needham Heights, MA: Allyn and Bacon.

Brubaker, S. J. (2007). Denied, embracing, and resisting medicalization: African American teen mothers' perceptions of formal pregnancy and childbirth care. *Gender and Society*, 21(4), 528–52.

Bruce, T., Hovden, J., & Markula, P. (Eds.). (2010). *Sportswomen at the Olympics: A global comparison of newspaper coverage*. Rotterdam, The Netherlands: Sense.

Brutsaert, H. (1999). Coeducation and gender identity formation: A comparative analysis of secondary schools in Belgium. *British Journal of Sociology of Education*, 20(3), 343–53.

Bucchianeri, M. M., Arikian, A. J., Hannan, P. J., Eisenberg, M. E., & Neumark-Sztainer, D. (2013). Body dissatisfaction from adolescence to young adulthood: Findings from a 10-year longitudinal study. *Body Image*, 10, 1–7.

Burn, S. M. (2000). Heterosexuals' use of "Fag" and "Queer" to deride one another: A contributor to heterosexism and stigma. *Journal of Homosexuality*, 40, 1–12.

Bussey, K., & Bandura, A. (1992). Self-regulatory mechanisms governing gender development, *Child Development*, 63, 1236–50.

Butler, J. (1985). Embodied identity in de Beauvoir's *The Second Sex*. Paper presented at the American Philosophical Association, Pacific Division, March 22, 1985.

Butler, J. (1990). *Gender trouble, feminism and the subversion of identity*. New York: Routledge.

Butler, J. (1993). *Bodies that matter*. London: Routledge.

Butler, J. (2004). *Undoing gender*. Albany, NY: Routledge.

Butler, M., & Paisley, W. (1980). *Women and the media*. New York: Human Sciences Press.

Buzuvis, E. E. (2012). Including transgender athletes in sex-segregated sport. In G. B. Cunningham (Ed.), *Sexual orientation and gender identity in sport: Essays from activists, coaches, and scholars* (pp. 23–34). College Station, TX: Center for Sport Management Research and Education.

Bylsma, L. M., Croon, M., Vingerhoets, A. J. J. M. & Rottenberg, J. (2011). Predictors of crying and mood change: A daily diary study. *Journal of Research in Personality*, 45, 385–92.

Cahn, S. K. (2010). From the muscle moll to the butch ballplayer: Mannishness, lesbianism, and homophobia in U.S. women's sport. In R. Weitz (Ed.), *The politics of women's bodies* (pp. 285–300). New York: Oxford University Press.

Calasanti, T, & Slevin, K. (2006). Introduction age matters. In T. M. Calasanti and K. F. Slevin (Eds.), *Age matters: Realigning feminist thinking* (pp. 1–17). New York: Routledge.

Campbell, K. K. (1998). The discursive performance of femininity: Hating Hillary. *Rhetoric & Public Affairs, 1*(1), 1–20.

Campus, D. (2013). *Women political leaders and the media.* New York: Palgrave Macmillan.

Cancain, F. M. (1987). *Love in America: Gender and self-development.* Cambridge: Cambridge University Press.

Carter, R., Silverman, W. K., & Jaccard, J. (2011). Sex variations in youth anxiety symptoms: effects of pubertal development and gender role orientation. *Journal of Clinical Child and Adolescent Psychology, 40*(5), 730–41.

Caro, J. (2016). Jane Caro: How we celebrate female sacrifice and expect women to take second place. Women's Agenda. Downloaded May 31, 2016 from, www.womensagenda.com.au/talking-about/opinions/item/7056-jane-caro-how-we-celebrate-female-sacrifice-and-expect-women-to-take-second-place#.V0zoqmEMHtl.facebook.

Carr, C. L. (2007). Where have all the tomboys gone? Women's accounts of gender in adolescence. *Sex Roles, 56,* 439–48.

Carr, D. (2002). The psychological consequences of work-family trade-offs for three cohorts of men and women. *Social Psychology Quarterly, 65*(2), 103–24.

Cejka, M. J., & Eagly, A. H. (1999). Gender-Stereotypic images of occupations correspond to the sex segregation of employment. *Personality and Social Psychology Bulletin, 25,* 413–23.

Cerulo, K. A. (1997). Identity construction: New issues, new directions. *Annual Review of Sociology, 23,* 385–409.

Chang, C. (2015). #WomenAgainstFeminism goes viral as people explain why they don't need feminism anymore. Downloaded December 28, 2015 from, www.news.com.au/lifestyle/real-life/womenagainstfeminism-goes-viral-as-people-explain-why-they-dont-need-feminism-anymore/story-fnixwvgh-1227010590106.

Channell, E. (2014). Is sextremism the new feminism? Perspectives from Pussy Riot and Femen. *Nationalities Papers, 42*(4), 611–14.

Charlebois, J. (2011). *Gender and the construction of dominant, hegemonic, and oppositional femininities.* Lanham, MD: Lexington Books.

Cheal, D. (1989). Women together: Bridal showers and gender membership. In B. J. Risman and P. Schwartz (Eds.), *Gender and intimate relationships: A microstructural approach* (pp. 87–93). Belmont, CA: Wadsworth.

Chemaly, S. (2015). 10 words every girl should learn. Downloaded January 10, 2016 from, www.filmsforaction.org/articles/10-words-every-girl-should-learn/#.VpBTB_xhxt0.facebook.

Cherniavsky, E. (2006). *The spectatorship of suffering.* London: Sage Publications.

Childs, F., & Palmer, N. (1999). *Going off: A guide for Black women who've just about had enough.* New York: St. Martin's Press.

Chng, S. C. W., & Fassnacht, D. B. (2015). Parental comments: Relationship with gender, body dissatisfaction, and disordered eating in Asian young adults. *Body Image, 16,* 93–99.

Chodorow, N. (1978). *The reproduction of mothering: Psychoanalysis and the sociology of gender.* Berkeley, CA: University of California Press.

Church of Jesus Christ of Latter-Day Saints (2004). Modest makeovers. Downloaded May 4, 2016 from, www.modestprom.com/modestmakeovers/.

Cirksena, K., & Cuklanz, L. (1992). Male is to female as ___ is to ___: A guided tour of five feminist frameworks for communication studies. In L. Rakow (Ed.), *Women making meaning: New feminist directions in communication* (pp. 18–44). New York: Routledge.

Clair, J. A., Beatty, J. E., & Maclean, T. L. (2005). Out of sight but not out of mind: Managing visible social identities in the workplace, *The Academy of Management Review*, 30(1), 78–95.

Clark, B. (2000). *Bridal showers*. Carpinteria, CA: Wilshire.

Clarke, L. H., & Griffin, M. (2007). Becoming and being gendered through the body: Older women, their mothers and body image. *Ageing & Society*, 27, 701–18.

Colligan, S. (2004). Why the intersexed shouldn't be fixed: Insights from queer theory and disability studies. In B. G. Smith and B. Hutchison (Eds.), *Gendering disability* (pp. 45–60). New Brunswick, NJ: Rutgers University Press.

Collinson, M., & Collinson, D. (1996). "It's only Dick:" The sexual harassment of women managers in insurance sales. *Work, Employment, and Society*, 10, 29–56.

Collins, P. H. (2005). *Black sexual politics: African Americans, gender and the new racism*. New York: Routledge.

Collins, P. H. (2010). Get your freak on: Sex, babies, and images of Black femininity. In R. Weitz (Ed.), *The politics of women's bodies*, 3rd ed. (pp. 143–54). New York: Oxford University Press.

Colloff, P. (2009, March 1). Sweet 15: The rise and the all-out, over-the-top, super-spectacular, bank-breaking Quinceañera. *Texas Monthly*, 140–45, 199–208.

Coltrane, S. (1989). Household labor and the routine production of gender. *Social Problems, 36*(5), 473–90.

Connell, R. W. (1987). *Gender and power*. Stanford, CA: Stanford University Press.

Connell, R. W. (1995). *Masculinities*. Berkeley: University of California Press.

Connell, R. W. (2003). Masculinities, change and conflict in global society: Thinking about the future of men's studies. *Journal of Men's Studies, 11*(3), 249–66.

Cook, E. P. (1987). Psychological androgyny: A review of the research. *The Counseling Psychologist, 15*, 471–513.

Cook, D., & Kaiser, S. (2004). Betwixt and be tween: Age ambiguity and the sexualization of the female consuming subject." *Journal of Consumer Culture, 4*(2), 203–27.

Cooky, C., Messner, M., & Hextrum, R. H. (2013). Women play sport, but not on TV: A longitudinal study of televised news media. *Communication & Sport, 1*(2), 203–30.

Coontz, S. (1993). *The way we never were: American families and the nostalgia trap*. New York: Basic Books.

Coontz, S. (2013, February 16). Why gender equality stalled. *New York Times*, p. SR-1.

Copper, B. (1988). *Over the hill: Reflections on ageism between women*. Freedom, CA: Crossing Press.

Corning, A. (2000). Assessing perceived social inequity: A relative deprivation framework. *Journal of Personality and Social Psychology, 78*(3), 463–77.

Cornwall, A., & Lindisfarne, N. (1994). *Dislocating masculinity: Comparative ethnographies*. London: Routledge.

Cowan, R. S. (1983). Two washes in the morning and the bridge party at night: the American housewife between the wars. In L. Scharf and J. M. Jensen (Eds.), *Decades of discontent: the women's movement, 1920–1940* (pp. 177–96). Westport, CT: Greenwood.

Cozens, F. W., & Stumpf, C. S. (1953). *Sports in American life*. Chicago: The University of Chicago Press.

Craig, S. (1992). Introduction: Considering men and the media. In S. Craig (Ed.), *Men, masculinity, and the media* (pp. 1–7). Newbury Park, CA: Sage.

Crandall, C., Nierman, A., & Hebl, M. (2009). Anti-fat prejudice. In T. Nelson (Ed.), *Handbook of prejudice, stereotyping, and discrimination* (pp. 469–88). New York: Psychology Press.

Cranny-Francis, A., Waring, W., Stavropoulos, P., & Kirkby, J. (2003). *Gender studies: Terms and debates*. New York: Palgrave Macmillan.

Crawford, M., & Unger, R. (2000). *Women and gender: A feminist psychology.* Boston: McGraw-Hill.Corning, A. F. (2000). Assessing perceived social inequity: A relative deprivation framework. *Journal of Personality and Social Psychology, 78*(3), 463–77.

Creedon, P. J. (1993). The challenge of re-visioning gender values. In P. J. Creedon (Ed.), *Women in mass communication* (pp. 3–3). Newbury Park, CA: Sage.

Crenshaw, K. W. (1989). Demarginalizing the intersection of race and sex: A Black feminist critique of antidiscrimination doctrine, feminist theory and antiracist politics. *University of Chicago Legal Forum 1989,* 139–67.

Crockett, R. J., Pruzinsky, T., & Persing, J. A. (2007). The influence of plastic surgery "reality TV" on cosmetic surgery patient expectations and decision making. *Plastic and Reconstructive Surgery, 120*(1), 316–24.

Cruikshank, M. (2003). *Learning to be old.* Lanham, MD: Rowman & Littlefield.

Curnalia, R. M. L., & Mermer, D. L. (2014). The ice queen melted and it won her the primary: Evidence of gender stereotypes and the double bind in news frames of Hillary Clinton's emotional moment. *Qualitative Research Reports in Communication, 15*(1), 26–32.

Currie, D. H. (1997). Decoding femininity: Advertisements and their teenage readers. *Gender & Society, 11,* 453–77.

Currie, D. (1999). *Girl talk: adolescent magazines and their readers.* Toronto: University of Toronto Press.

Czarnecki, D. (2015). Moral women, immoral technologies: How devout women negotiate gender, religion, and assisted reproductive technologies. *Gender & Society, 29*(5), 716–42.

Daniels, E. (2009). Sex object athletes and sexy aAthletes: How media representations of women athletes can impact adolescent girls and college women. *Journal of Adolescent Research, 24*(4), 399–422.

Daniels, E. A., & Wartena, H. (2011). Athlete or sex symbol: What boys think of media representations of female athletes. *Sex Roles, 65*(7/8), 566–79.

Darwin, C. (1872). *The origin of species.* New York: Bantam Dell.

Davis, F. (1992). *Fashion, culture and identity.* London: University of Chicago Press.

Davis, K. (1997). *Reshaping the female body: The dilemma of cosmetic surgery.* New York: Routledge.

Davis, S. N. (2010). Adolescent gender ideology socialization: Direct and moderating effects of fathers' beliefs. *Sociological Spectrum, 30,* 580–604.

Davis-Delano, L. R., Pollock, A., & Vose, J. E. (2009). Apologetic behavior among female athletes: A new questionnaire and initial results. *International Review for the Sociology of Sport, 22,* 131–50.

Davison, K., & Birch, L. (2001). Weight, status, parent reaction, and self-concept in five-year-old girls. *Pediatrics, 107,* 42–53.

Davies-Popelka, W. (2000). Mirror, mirror on the wall: weight, identity, and self-talk in women. In D. O. Braithwaite & J. T. Wood (Eds.), *Case studies in interpersonal communication* (pp. 52–60). Belmont, CA: Wadsworth.

Deason, G., Greenlee, J. S., & Langner, C. A. (2015). Mothers on the campaign trail: Implications of politicized motherhood for women in politics. *Politics, Groups, and Identities, 3*(1), 133–48.

de Beauvoir, S. (1968). *The Second Sex.* New York: Bantam Books.

Dejmanee, T. (2015). Nursing at the screen: Post-feminist daughters and demonized mothers on *Toddlers and Tiaras. Feminist Media Studies, 15*(3), 460–73.

de Koven, A. (1912, August). The athletic woman. *Good Housekeeping.*

De Marneffe, D. (2004). *Maternal desire: On children, love, and inner life.* New York: Little, Brown & Co.

Del Rey, P. (1978). The apologetic and women in sport. In C. Oglesby (Ed.), *Women and Sport,* (pp. 107–12). Philadelphia: Lea & Febiger.

Deleuze, G. (1986). *Foucault,* trans. S. Hand. Minneapolis, MN: University of Minnesota Press.

Denner, J., & Dunbar, N. (2004). Negotiating femininity: Power and strategies of Mexican American Girls. *Sex Roles, 50*(5/6), 301–14.

Dewar, A. (1993). Would all the generic women I sport please stand up? Challenges facing feminist sport sociology, *Quest, 45*, 211–29.

Diggs, R. C. (1999). African American and European American adolescents' perceptions of self-esteem as influenced by parent and peer communication and support environments. In T. J. Socha & R. C. Diggs (Eds.), *Communication, race, and family: Exploring communication in black, white, and biracial families* (pp. 105–46). Mahwah, NJ: Lawrence Erlbaum.

Dill, K. E., & Thill, K. P. (2007). Video game characters and the socialization of gender roles: Young people's perceptions mirror sexist media depictions. *Sex Roles, 57*(11–12), 851–64.

Dobson, A. S. (2011). Hetero-sexy representation by young women on MySpace: The politics of performing an 'objectified' self. *Outskirts*, 25 November 2011.

Dobson, A. (2014a). Performative shamelessness on young women's social network sites: Shielding the self and resisting gender melancholia. *Feminism & Psychology, 24*(1), 97–114.

Dobson, A. S. (2014b). Sexy and laddish girls: Unpacking complicity between two cultural imag(inations)es of young femininity. *Feminist Media Studies, 14*(2), 253–69.

Dolan, K. (2014). Gender stereotypes, candidate evaluations, and voting for women candidates: What really matters? *Political Research Quarterly, 67*(1), 96–107.

Doty, A. (1993). *Making things perfectly queer: Interpreting mass culture*. Minneapolis, MN: University of Minnesota Press.

Douglas, S. J. (2010). *The rise of enlightened sexism: How pop culture took us from girl power to girls gone wild*. New York: Times Books.

Dowd, A. (2011, May 25). Brooding men, smiling women seen as sexy: study. Reuters. Downloaded February 10, 2016 from, www.reuters.com/article/us-smiles-sex-idUSTRE74N7CJ20110525.

Driscoll, C. (2002). *Girls: Feminine adolescence in popular culture and cultural theory*. New York: Columbia University Press.

Duffy, B. E. (2013). *Remake, remodel: Women's magazines in the digital age*. Champaign, IL: University of Illinois Press.

Duffy, B. E. & Hund, E. (2015). Having it all on social media: Entrepreneurial femininity and self-branding among fashion bloggers. *Social Media + Society, 1*(2), 1–11.

Dufour, L. R. (2000). Sifting through tradition: The creation of Jewish feminist identities. *Journal of the Scientific Study of Religion, 39*(1), 90–106.

Duits, L., & van Zoonen, M. (2006). Headscarves and porno-chic: Disciplining girls' bodies in the European multicultural society. *European Journal of Women's Studies, 13*, 103–17.

Duke, L. (2000). Black in a blonde world: Race and girls' interpretations of the feminine ideal in teen magazines. *Journalism and Mass Communication Quarterly, 77*, 367–92.

Duke, L., & Kreshel, P. (1998). Negotiating femininity: Girls in early adolescence read teen magazines: Study of young adolescent girls' dependence on teen magazines for their definition of femininity. *Journal of Communication Inquiry, 22*, 48–71.

Dworkin, S. L. (2001). Holding back: Negotiating a glass ceiling on women's muscular strength. *Sociological Perspectives, 44*(3), 333–50.

Dworkin, S. L., & Wachs, L. F. (2009). *Body panic: Gender, health, and the selling of fitness*. New York: New York UP.

Dyer, R. (1997). *White: Essays on race and culture*. Routledge: London.

Durham, G. (2001). Adolescence, the Internet, and the politics of gender: A feminist case analysis. *Race, Gender and Class, 8*(3), 20–41.

Durham, G. (2008). *The Lolita effect: the media sexualization of young girls and what we can do about it*. New York: Overlook.

Durham, M. G. (2007). Myths of race and beauty in teen magazines: A semiotic analysis. In P. J. Creedon and J. Cramer (Eds.) *Women in mass communication*, 3rd ed. (pp. 233–45). Thousand Oaks, CA: Sage.

Eagly, A. H., & Mitchell, A. A. (2004). Social role theory of sex differences and similarities: Implications for the sociopolitical attitudes of women and men. In M. A. Paludi (Ed.), *Praeger guide to the psychology of gender* (pp. 183–206). Westport, CT: Praeger.

Eagly, A. H., & Mladinic, A. (1989). Gender stereotypes and attitudes toward women and men. *Personality and Social Psychology Bulletin, 15*(4), 543–58.

Eagly, A. H., & Wood, W. (1999). The origins of sex differences in human behavior: Evolved dispositions versus social roles. *American Psychologist, 54*, 408–23.

Edison, L. T., & Notkin, D. (2010). Guest post: Temporarily able-bodied: Useful, but not always true. Retrieved April 10, 2013, from disabledfeminists.com/2010/02/03/guest-post-temporarily-able-bodied-useful-but-not-always-true/.

Efthim, P., Kenny, M., & Mahalik, J. (2001). Gender role stress in relation to shame, guilt, and externalization. *Journal of Counseling and Development, 79*, 430–38.

Egner, J., & Maloney, P. (2015). It has no color, it has no gender, it's gender bending: Gender and sexuality fluidity and subversiveness in drag performance. *Journal of Homosexuality*, 1–29.

Ehrenreich, B., & English, D. (1978). *For her own good: 150 years of the experts' advice to women.* New York: Doubleday.

Eisenberg, E. M., Goodall, H. L. Jr., Trethewey, A. (2010). *Organizational communication: Balancing creativity and constraint,* 6th ed. Boston: Bedford/St. Martin's.

Eisler, R. M., & Skidmore, J. R. (1988). Masculine gender role stress: Scale development and com-1ponent factors in the appraisal of stressful situations. *Behavior Modification, 11*(2), 123–36.

Elsbach, K. D. (2011). Crying at work, a woman's burden. Downloaded May 8, 2016 from, gsm.ucdavis.edu/research/crying-work-womans-burden.

Enloe, C. (1993). *The morning after: Sexual politics at the end of the cold war.* Berkeley, CA: University of California Press.

Enstad, N. (1999). *Ladies of labor, girls of adventure: Working women, popular culture, and labor politics at the turn of the twentieth century.* New York: Columbia University Press.

Escobar-Lemmon, M. C., Hoekstra, V., Kang, A., & Kittilson, M. C. (2016). Just the facts? Media coverage of female and male high court appointees in five democracies. *Politics & Gender, 12*, 254–74.

Escudero-Alías, M. (2010). Shatte7-ring gender taboos in Gabriel Baur's Venus boyz. *Journal of Gender Studies, 19*(2), 16179.

Espin, O. M. (1997). *Latina realities: Essays on healing, migration, and sexuality.* Boulder, CO: Westview Press.

Ette, M. (2013). Gendered frontlines: British press coverage of women soldiers killed in Iraq. *Media, War & Conflict, 6*(3), 249–62.

Euse, E. (2016, March 21). The revolutionary history of the pantsuit. *Vice.* Downloaded May 26, 2016 from, www.vice.com/read/the-history-of-the-pantsuit-456.

Evans, C., & Thornton, M. (1991). Fashion, representation, femininity. *Feminist Review, 38*, 48–66.

Fabos, B. (2001). Forcing the fairytale: Narrative strategies in figure skating competition coverage. *Culture, Sport, Society, 4*(2), 185–212.

Fallon, M. A., & Jome, L. M. (2007). An exploration of gender-role expectations and conflict among women rugby players. *Psychology of Women Quarterly, 31*, 311–21.

Faludi, S. (1991). *Backlash: The undeclared war against American women.* New York: Doubleday.

Farrell, A. E. (2011). *Fat shame: Stigma and the fat body in American culture.* New York: New York University Press.

Fastest women in the world (1955, June 28). *Ebony.*

Favara, J. (2015). A maternal heart: Angelina Jolie, choices of maternity and hegemonic femininity in *People* magazine. *Feminist Media Studies, 15*(4), 626–42.

Feasey, R. (2009). Spray more, get more: Masculinity, television advertising, and the lynx effect. *Journal of Gender Studies, 18*(4), 357–68.

Feder-Kane, A. (2000). "A radiant smile from a lovely lady": Overdetermined femininity in "ladies" figure skating. In S. Birrell & M. G. McDonald (Eds.), *Reading sport: Critical essays on power and representation* (pp. 206-233). Boston: Northeastern University Press.

Felshin, J. (1974a). The triple option . . . for women in sport. *Quest, 21*, 36–40.

Ferber, A. L. (2007). The construction of Black masculinity: White supremacy now and then. *Journal of Sport & Social Issues, 31*(1), 11–24.

Festinger, L. (1954). A theory of social comparison processes. *Human Relations, 7*, 117–40.

Fey-Yensan, N., McCormick, L., & English, C. (2002). Body image and weight preoccupation in older women: A review. *Healthy Weight Journal, 16*, 68–71.

Fidler, M. A. (2006). *The origins and history of the all-American girls professional baseball league.* Jefferson, NC: McFarland & Company, Inc.

Fiese, B. H., & Skillmanm, G. (2000). Gender differences in family stories: Moderating influence of parent gender role and child gender. *Sex Roles, 43*(5–6), 267–83.

Fink, J. S., Kane, M. J., & LaVoi, N. M. (2014). The freedom to choose: Elite female athletes' preferred representations within endorsement opportunities. *Journal of Sport Management, 28,* 207–19.

Fink, J. S., & Kensicki, L. J. (2002). An imperceptible difference: Visual and textual constructions of femininity in *Sports Illustrated* and *Sports Illustrated for Women*. *Mass Communication & Society, 5*(3), 317–39.

Finnegan, M. (1999). *Selling suffrage: Consumer culture and votes for women.* New York: Columbia University press.

Fitzgerald, L. F., Magley, V. J., Drasgow, F., & Waldo, C. R. (1999). Measuring sexual harassment in the military: The Sexual Experiences Questionnaire (SEQ – DoD). *Military Psychology, 11*, 243–63.

Foreman, P. G. (1990). Looking back from Zora, or talking out both sides of my mouth for those who have two ears. *Black American Literature Forum, 24*(4), 649–66.

Foss, S. K. (1989). *Rhetorical criticism: Exploration and practice.* Prospect Heights, IL: Waveland Press.

Foss, K. A., Foss, S. K., & Griffin, C. L. (1999). *Feminist rhetorical theories.* Thousand Oaks, CA: Sage.

Foucault, M. (1980). *Power/knowledge: Selected interviews and other writings, 1972–1977.* New York: Random House.

Foucault, M. (1990). *The history of sexuality.* New York: Vintage.

Fox, R. L., & Lawless, J. (2011, September). "Barefoot and Pregnant, or Ready to be President? Gender, Family Roles, and Political Ambition in the 21st Century." Paper presented at the American Political Science Association Annual Meeting, Seattle, WA, September 1–4.

Franks, S. (2013). *Women and journalism.* London: I.B. Tauris.

Freud, S. (1973). New introductory lectures *on psychoanalysis.* London: Hogarth Press.

Franko, D. L., & Roehrig, J. P. (2011). African American body images. In T. Cash & L. Smolak (Eds.), *Body Image: A handbook of science, practice, and prevention* (2nd ed., pp. 221–28). New York, NY: Guilford Press.

Friedan, B. (1963). *The feminine mystique.* New York: Dell.

Friedman, E., & D'Emilio, J. (1988). *Intimate matters: A history of sexuality in America.* New York: Harper & Row.

Frohlich, R. (2004). Feminine and feminist values in communication professions: Exceptional skills and expertise or 'friendliness trap'? In M. de Bruin & K. Ross (Eds.), *Gender and newsroom cultures: Industries at work* (pp. 67–80). Cresskill, NJ: Hampton Press.

Frone, M., Russell, M., & Cooper, M. (1992). Antecedents and outcomes of work-family conflict: Testing a model of the work-family interface. *Journal of Applied Psychology, 77,* 65–75.

Fry, M. (2015, February 23). Is there something wrong? No. That's just my face. *NJBIZ.* Downloaded February 10, 2016 from, www.njbiz.com/article/20150223/NJBIZ01/302209994/is-there-something-wrong-no-thats-just-my-face.

Frye, M. (1983). *The politics of reality: Essays in feminist theory.* Trumansburg, NY: Crossing Press.

Furman, F. (1999). There are no older Venuses: Older women's responses to their aging bodies. In M. U. Walker (Ed.), *Mother time: Women, aging, and ethics* (pp. 7-22). Lanham, MD: Rowman and Littlefield.

Garland-Thomson, R. (2005). Feminist disability studies. *Signs, 30*(2), 1557–87.

Gates, G. J. (2011). How many people are lesbian, gay, bisexual and transgender? The Williams Institute, UCLA School of Law. Downloaded March 9, 2016 from, escholarship.org/uc/item/09h684x2.

Geliga-Vargas, J. A. (1999). Who is the Puerto Rican woman and how is she?: Shall Hollywood respond? In M. Meyers (Ed.), *Mediated women: Representations in popular culture* (pp. 111–32). Cresskill, NJ: Hampton Press, Inc.

George, A. (2002) Embodying identity through heterosexual sexuality: Newly married adolescent women in India. *Culture, Health & Sexuality, 4,* 207–22.

Gill, R. (2007a). Postfeminist media culture: Elements of a sensibility. *European Journal of Cultural Studies, 10*(2), 147–66.

Gillen, M. M., & Lefkowitz, E. S. (2012). Gender and racial/ethnic differences in body image development among college students. *Body Image, 9,* 126–30.

Gilman, S. (1985). Black bodies, white bodies: Toward an iconography of female sexuality in late nineteenth century art, medicine, and literature. In H. L. Gates (Ed.), *Race, writing and difference* (pp. 223–61). Chicago: University of Chicago Press.

Gilman, S. (1999). *Making the body beautiful: A cultural history of aesthetic surgery.* Princeton, NJ: Princeton University Press.

Gimlin, D. (1996). Pamela's Place: Power and negotiation in the hair salon. *Gender and Society, 10*(5), 505–26.

Givhan, R. (2007, July 20). Hillary Clinton's tentative dip into new neckline territory. *The Washington Post,* p. C01.

Givhan, R. (2015). *The battle of Versailles: The night American fashion stumbled into the spotlight and made history.* New York: Flatiron Books.

Glick, P. (1991). Trait-based and sex-based discrimination in occupational prestige, occupational salary, and hiring. *Sex Roles, 25,* 351–78.

Global Media Monitoring Project Report (2010). *Who makes the news.* Toronto, Canada: World Association for Christian Communication.

Glover, D., & Kaplan, C. (2009). *Genders,* 2nd ed. New York: Routledge.

Goffman, E. (1963). *Stigma: Notes on the management of spoiled identity.* New York: Simon & Schuster.

Goffman, E. (1976). Gender display. *Studies in the Anthropology of Visual Communication, 3,* 69–77.

Goffman, E. (1979). *Gender advertisements.* New York: Harper & Row.

Goldman, R. (1992). *Reading ads socially.* London: Routledge.

Golombok, S., & Fivush, R. (1994). *Gender development.* New York: Cambridge University Press.

Gordon, H. R. (2008). Gendered paths to teenage political participation: Parental power, civic mobility, and youth activism. *Gender & Society, 22*(1), 31–55.

Gordon, K. H., Castro, Y., Sitnikov, L., & Holm-Denoma, J. M. (2010). Cultural body shape ideals and eating disorder symptoms among White, Latina, and Black college women. *Cultural Diversity and Ethnic Minority Psychology, 16*(2), 135–43.

Gott, M., & Hinchliff, S. (2003). Sex and ageing: A gendered issue. In S. Arber, K. Davidson, and J. Ginn (Eds.), *Gender and Ageing: Changing roles and relationships* (pp. 63–78). Philadelphia, PA: Open University Press/McGraw-Hill.

Gramsci, A. (1971). *Selections from the prison notebooks of Antonio Gramsci* (Q. Hoare & G. Nowell Smith, Trans.). New York: International.

Gray, A. (2003). Enterprising femininity: New modes of work and subjectivity. *European Journal of Cultural Studies, 6*, 489–506.

Greaf, C. (2015). Drag queens and gender identity. *Journal of Gender Studies*, 1–11.

Green, R. J., & Ashmore, R. D. (1998). Taking and developing pictures in the head: Assessing the physical stereotypes of eight gender types. *Journal of Applied Social Psychology, 28*(17), 1609–36.

Green, T. S., & Alexander, A. (2000). Sheroes over the rim: A brave new women's basketball world. In T. Boyd and Kate. L. Shropshire (Eds.), *Basketball Jones: America above the rim* (pp. 176–83). New York: New York University Press.

Greenfield-Sanders, T. (Director). (2012). *About face: The supermodels then and now* [Documentary]. New York: BBC.

Greenglass, E. R. (1993). The contribution of social support to coping strategies. *Applied Psychology: An International Review, 42*, 323–40.

Greenglass, E. R. (2002). Work stress, coping, and social support: implications for women's occupational well-being. In D. L. Nelson and R. J. Burke (Eds.), *Gender, work, stress, and health* (pp. 85–96). Washington, D.C.: American Psychological Association.

Grindstaff, L., & West, E. (2006). Cheerleading and the gendered politics of sport. *Social Problems, 53*(4), 500–18.

Griffin, C. (2001). The young women are having a great time: Representations of young women and feminism. *Feminism and Psychology, 11*(2), 182–86.

Griffin, P. (1998). Opening minds, opening closet doors: Transforming women's sport. In P. Griffin (Ed.), *Strong women, deep closets: Lesbians and homophobia in sport* (pp. 207–39). Champaign, IL: Human Kinetics.

Groesz, L. M., Levine, M. P., & Murnen, S. K. (2002). The effect of experimental presentation of thin media images on body satisfaction: A meta-analytic review. *International Journal of Eating Disorders, 31*, 1–16.

Grunig, L., A., Toth, E. L., & Hon, L. C. (2001). *Women in public relations: How gender influences practice.* New York: The Guilford Press.

Gullage, A. (2014). Fat Monica, fat suits, and Friends: Exploring narratives of fatness. *Feminist Media Studies, 14*(2), 178–89.

Gullette, M. M. (1997). *Declining to decline: Cultural combat and the politics of the midlife.* Charlottesville, VA: University Press of Virginia.

Gullette, M. M. (2004). *Aged by culture.* Chicago: University of Chicago Press.

Gullette, M. M. (2011). *Agewise: Fighting the new ageism in America.* Chicago: University of Chicago Press.

Gunaratnam, Y. (2003). *Researching "race" and ethnicity: Methods, knowledge and power.* Thousand Oaks, CA: Sage.

Hagen, W. B., Arczynski, A. V., Morrow, S. L., & Hawxhurst, D. M. (2012). Lesbian, bisexual, and queer women's spirituality in feminist multicultural counseling. *Journal of LGBT Issues in Counseling, 5*, 22–236.

Halberstam, J. (1998). *Female masculinity.* Durham, NC: Duke University Press.

Hall, G. S. (1920). *Morale: The supreme standard of life and conduct.* New York: D. Appleton.

Hall, G. S. (1931). *Adolescence.* New York: Hesperides Press.

Hall, S. (2007). Plenary lecture. Presented at Cultural Studies Now Conference, University of East London. Retrieved from culturalstudiesresearch.org/page_id=12. Retrieved 12/30/15.

Hamermesh, D. S. (2011). *Beauty pays: Why attractive people are more successful.* Princeton, NJ: Princeton University Press.

Hardin, M., & Greer, J. D. (2009). The influence of gender-role socialization, media use, and sports participation on perceptions of gender-appropriate sports. *Journal of Sport Behavior, 32*(2), 207–26.

Hardin, M., & Shain, S. (2006). Feeling much smaller than you know you are: The fragmented professional identity of female sports journalists. *Critical Studies in Media Communication, 23*(4), 322–38.

Hare, B. (2015, June 3). Reality TV breeds new body ideals. Downloaded June 3, 2016 from, www.cnn.com/2010/SHOWBIZ/06/01/kardashian.body.types/index.html?iref =storysearch.

Harris, A. (2004a). Introduction. In A. Harris (Ed.), *All about the girl: Culture, power, and identity* (pp. xvii–xxv). New York: Routledge.

Harris, A. (2004b). *Future girl: Young women in the twenty-first century.* New York: Routledge.

Harris, A., & Dobson, A. S. (2015). Theorizing agency in post-girlpower times. *Continuum: Journal of Media & Cultural Studies, 29*(2), 145–56.

Harrison, K. (2003). Television viewers' ideal body proportions: The case of the curvaceously thin woman. *Sex Roles, 48,* 255–64.

Hartley, C. (2001). Letting ourselves go: Making room for the fat body in feminist scholarship. In J. E. Braziel and K. LeBesco (Eds.), *Bodies out of bounds: Fatness and transgression* (pp. 60–73). Los Angeles: University of California Press.

Hayes, D., & Lawless, J. L. (2015). A non-gendered lens? Media, voters, and female candidates in contemporary congressional elections. *Perspectives on Politics, 13*(1), 95–118.

Hebdige, D. (1988). *Hiding in the light: On images and things.* London: Routledge.

Hegarty, P., Pratto, F., & Lemieux, A. F. (2004). Heterosexist ambivalence and heterocentric norms: Drinking in intergroup discomfort. *Group Processes and Intergroup Relations, 7,* 119–30.

Heilbrun, C. G. (1988). *Writing a woman's life.* New York: Norton & Co.

Heinecken, D. (2015). So tight in the thighs, so loose in the waist: Embodying the female athlete online. *Feminist Media Studies, 15*(6), 1035–52.

Helgeson, V. S., & Taylor, S. E. (1993). Social comparisons and adjustment among cardiac patients. *Journal of Applied Social Psychology, 23,* 1171–95.

Herzberg, J. (1947). *Late city edition.* New York: Holt.

Hesford, V. (2013). *Feeling women's liberation.* Durham, NC: Duke University Press.

Hesse-Biber, S. N. (2007). *The cult of thinness,* 2nd ed. New York: Oxford University Press.

Hesse-Biber, S. N., Howling, S. A., Leavy, P., & Lovejoy, M. (2004). Racial identity and the development of body image issues among African American adolescent girls. *The Qualitative Report, 9*(1), 49–79.

Hewlett, S. A. (2007), *Off-ramps and on-ramps: Keeping talented women on the road to success.* Boston, MA: Harvard Business School Press.

Heywood, L., & Dworkin, S. L. (2003). *Built to win: The female athlete as cultural icon.* Minneapolis: University of Minnesota Press.

Highfield, R., Wiseman, R., & Jenkins, R. (2016, February 11). How your looks betray your personality. *New Scientist.* Downloaded February 14, 2016 from, www.new scientist.com/article/mg20126957-300-how-your-looks-betray-your-personality/.

Hill, J. (2015). Girls' active identities: Navigating othering discourses of femininity, bodies and physical education. *Gender and Education, 27*(6), 666–84.

Hill, S. A, & Sprague, J. (1999). Parenting in Black and white families: The interaction of gender with race and class. *Gender & Society, 13*(4), 480–502.

Hillard, E. E., Gondoli, D. M., Corning, A. F., & Morrissey, R. A. (2016). In it together: Mother talk of weight concerns moderates negative outcomes of encouragement to lose weight on daughter body dissatisfaction and disordered eating. *Body Image, 16,* 21–27.

Hinds, H., & Stacey, J. (2001). Imaging feminism, imaging femininity: The bra-burner, Diana, and the woman who kills, *Feminist Media Studies, 1*(2), 153–77.

Hochschild, A. R. (1997). *The time bind: When work becomes home and home becomes work.* New York: Metropolitan Books.

Hochschild, A., & Machung, A. (2001). Men who share 'the second shift.' In J. M. Henslin (Ed.), *Down to earth sociology: Introductory readings*, (pp. 395–409). New York: Free Press.

Hoegg, J., & Lewis, M. V. (2011). The impact of candidate appearance and advertising strategies on election results. *Journal of Marketing Research, 48*(5), 895–909.

Hoffman, R. M., Borders, L. D., & Hattie, J. A. (2000). Reconceptualizing femininity and masculinity: From gender roles to gender self-confidence. *Journal of Social Behavior and Personality, 15*(4), 475–503.

Hoffman, R. M., Hattie, J. A., & Borders, L. D. (2005). Personal definitions of masculinity and femininity as an aspect of gender self-concept. *Journal of Humanistic Counseling, Education and Development, 44*, 66–83.

Hofstede, G. (1998). *Masculinity and femininity: The taboo dimension of national cultures.* Thousand Oaks, CA: Sage.

Hollows, J. (2006). Can I go home yet? Feminism, postfeminism, and domesticity. In J. Hollows and R. Moseley (Eds.), *Feminism in popular culture* (pp. 97–118). London: Berg.

Holmlund, C. (2010). Postfeminism from A to G. *Cinema Journal, 44*(2), 116–21.

Holstein, M. B., & Minkler, M. (2003). Self, society, and the 'new gerontology'. *The Gerontologist, 43*(6), 787–96.

hooks, b. (2015). *Ain't I a woman: Black women and feminism.* New York: Routledge.

Houston, M. (1992). The politics of difference: Race, class and women's communication.

In L. Rakow (Ed.), *Women making meaning: New feminist directions in communication* (pp. 45–59). New York: Routledge.

How old's too old (2016). *Daily Mail.* Downloaded May 25, 2016 from www.dailymail.co.uk/femail/article-1210588/How-olds-old-wear-mini-New-research-shows-average-age-women-short-skirts-soared-40.html.

Hughes-Hallett, L. (1990). *Cleopatra: Histories, dreams and distortions.* London: Bloomsbury.

Hummert, M. L., Garstka, T. A., & Shaner, J. L. (1997). Stereotyping of older adults: The role of target facial cues and perceiver characteristics. *Psychology and Aging, 12*(1), 107–14.

Hunt, M. (1970, May). Up against the wall, male chauvinist pig! *Playboy*, 96.

Huovinen, A., & Weselius, H. (2015). No smiling, please, Ms. Prime minister!: Constructing a female politician on the cover of a news magazine. *Catalan Journal of Communication & Cultural Studies, 7*(1), 3–20.

Hvenegård-Lassen, K. (2013). Disturbing femininity. *Culture Unbound, 5*(12), 153–73.

The ideal woman (1926, August). *Vanity Fair*, 53.

Jackson, L. (1993). *The word woman and other related writings.* New York: Persea Books.

Jackson, S., & Goddard, S. (2015). 'I'd say 14 is too young': Pre-teen girls' negotiations of 'sexualized' media. *Continuum: Journal of Media & Cultural Studies, 29*(2), 241–52.

Jamieson, K. H. (1995). *Beyond the double bind: Women and leadership.* New York: Oxford University Press.

Janiewski, D. (1983). Sisters under their skins: Southern working women, 1880–1950. In J. V. Hawks and S. L. Skemp (Eds.), *Sex, race, and the role of women in the South* (pp. 13–35). Jackson, MS: University Press of Mississippi.

Jensen, T., & Ringrose, J. (2014). Sluts that choose vs doormat gypsies: Exploring affect in the postfeminist, visual moral economy of My Big Fat Gypsy Wedding. *Feminist Media Studies, 14*(3), 369–87.

Johnson, A. H. (2015). Beyond inclusion: Thinking toward a transfeminist methodology. In V. Demos, M. T. Segal (Eds.), *At the center: Feminism, social science and knowledge*, (pp. 21–41). Bingley, U.K.: Emerald Group Publishing Limited.

Johnson, M. S. (2011). The career girl murders: Gender, race, and crime in 1960s New York. *Women's Studies Quarterly, 39*(1/2). 244–61.

Jones, A., & Greer, J. (2011). You don't look like an athlete: The effects of feminine appearance on audience perceptions of female athletes and women's sports. *Journal of Sport Behavior, 34*(4), 358–77.

Joyce, K. & Mamo, L. (2006). Graying the cyborg: New directions in feminist analyses of aging, science, and technology. In T. M. Calasanti and K. F. Slevin (Eds.), *Age matters: Realigning feminist thinking* (pp. 99–121). New York: Routledge.

J. R. J. (2016, June 4). MILF [1]. In Urban Dictionary. Retrieved June 2016, from www.urbandictionary.com/define.php?term=milf.

Kaestner, R., & Xu, X. (2010). Title IX, girls' sports participation, and adult female physical activity and weight. *Evaluation Review, 34*(1), 52–78.

Kane, M. J., & Greendorfer, S. L. (1994). The media's role in accommodating and resisting stereotyped images of women in sport. In P. J. Creedon (Ed.), *Women, media and sport: Challenging gender values* (pp. 28–44). Thousand Oaks, CA: Sage.

Kane, M. J., & Maxwell, H. (2011). Expanding the boundaries of sport media research: Using critical theory to explore consumer responses to representations of women's sports. *Journal of Sport Management, 25*(3), 202–6.

Karraker, K. H., Vogel, D. A., & Lake, M. A. (1995). Parents' gender-stereotyped perceptions of newborns: The eye of the beholder revisited. *Sex Roles, 33*(2), 687–701.

Kasen, S., Chen, H., Sneed, J., Crawford, T., & Cohen, P. (2006). Social role and birth cohort influences on gender-linked personality traits in women: A 20-year longitudinal analysis. *Journal of Personality and Social Psychology, 91*(5), 944–58.

Kaskan, E. R., & Ho, I. K. (2014). Microaggressions and female athletes. *Sex Roles,* 1–13.

Katzmarzyk, P. T., & Davis, C. (2001). Thinness and body shape of *Playboy* I centerfolds from 1978 to 1998. *International Journal of Obesity, 25,* 590–92.

Kearney, M. C. (2015). Sparkle: Luminosity and the post-girl power media. *Continuum: Journal of Media & Cultural Studies, 29*(2), 263–73.

Keeve, D. (Director). (1995). *Unzipped* [Motion Picture]. United States: Hachette Filipacchi Films, Miramax.

Kelinske, B., Mayer, B. W., & Chen, K-L. (2001). Perceived benefits from participation in sports: A gender study. *Women in Management Review, 16*(2), 75–84.

Keller, J. (2015). Girl power's last chance? Tavi Gevinson, Feminism, and popular media culture. *Continuum: Journal of Media & Cultural Studies, 29*(2), 274–85.

Kelly, G. A. (1955). *The psychology of personal constructs.* New York: Norton.

Kenosha Evening News (Wis.) (1943, May 13), p. 8.

Kertzer, D. (1988). *Ritual, politics, and power.* New Haven, CT: Yale University Press.

Kessler, R. C., Mickelson, K. D., & Williams, D. R. (1999). The prevalence, distribution, and mental health correlates of perceived discrimination in the United States. *Journal of Health and Social Behavior, 40*(3), 208–30.

Kessler, S. (1998). *Lessons from the intersexed.* New Brunswick, NJ: Rutgers University Press.

Kilbourne, J. (1999). *Deadly persuasion: Why women and girls must fight the addictive power of advertising.* New York: Free Press.

Kilborne, J. (2010). *Killing us softly 4: Advertising's image of women.* Northampton, MA: Media Education Foundation.

Kim, K., & Sagas, M. (2014). Athletic or sexy? A comparison of female athletes and fashion models in *Sports Illustrated* swimsuit issues. *Gender Issues, 31,* 123–41.

Kim, K. K., & Shaw, H. (2008). Being a 'good' woman in Korea: the construction of female beauty and success. In K. Frith and K. Karan (Eds.), *Commercializing women: Images of Asian women in the media* (p. 33–49). Cresskill, NJ: Hampton Press, Inc.

Kimmel, M. S. (1987). Rethinking "masculinity": New directions in research. In M. S. Kimmel (Ed.), *New directions in research on men and masculinity* (pp. 9–24). Newbury Park, CA: Sage.

Kimmel, M. S. (2004). *The gendered society.* New York: Oxford University Press.

Kimmel, M. (2008). *Guyland: the perilous world where boys become men.* New York: HarperCollins.

King, N. (2006). The lengthening list of oppressions: Age relations and the feminist study of inequality. In T. M. Calasanti and K. F. Slevin (Eds.), *Age matters: Realigning feminist thinking* (pp. 47–74). New York: Routledge.

Kinser, A. E. (2010). *Motherhood and feminism*. Berkeley, CA: Seal.

Kiser, S. (2016, February 5). #TheDollEvolves: What Barbie's new body can—and cannot—do for our girls' body image. *WBUR*. Downloaded February 14, 2016 from, cognoscenti.wbur.org/2016/02/05/barbies-new-body-sarah-kiser.

Kitch. C. (2001). *The girl on the magazine cover: The origins of visual stereotypes in American mass media*. Chapel Hill, NC: University of North Carolina Press.

Kitch. C. (2003). Selling the "Boomer Babes:" *More, my generation*, and the 'new' middle age. *Journal of Magazine & New Media Research*. Online: aejmcmagazine.bsu.edu.

Kite, M. E., Deaux, K., & Haines, E. L. (2008). Gender stereotypes. In F. L. Denmark and M. A. Paludi (Eds.), *Psychology of women: A handbook of issues and theories* (2nd ed.) (pp. 205–36). Westport, CT: Praeger.

Knijnik, J. (2015). Femininities and masculinities in Brazilian women's football: Resistance and compliance. *Journal of International Women's Studies, 16*(3), 54–70.

Koenig, A. M., Eagly, A. H., Mitchell, A. A., & Ristikari, T. (2011). Are leader stereotypes masculine? A meta-analysis of three research paradigms. *Psychological Bulletin, 137*(4), 616–42.

Koivula, N. (1995). Ratings of gender appropriateness of sports participation: Effects of gender-based schematic processing. *Sex Roles, 33*(7/8), 543–57.

Kosinski, J. (1965). *The painted bird*. New York: Grove Press.

Kossek, E., & Ozeki, C. (1998). Work-family conflict, policies, and the job-life satisfaction relationship: A review and directions for organizational behavior-human resources research. *Journal of Applied Psychology, 83*, 139–49.

Krane, V., Choi, Y. P. L., Baird, S. M., Aimar, C. M., & Kauer, K. J. (2004). Living the paradox: Female athletes negotiate femininity and masculinity. *Sex Roles, 50*, 315–29.

Kreamer, A. (2011). *It's always personal: Emotion in the new workplace*. New York Random House.

Kulis, S., Marsiglia, F. F., & Hecht, M. L. (2002). Gender labels and gender identity as predictors of drug use among ethnically diverse middle school students. *Youth & Society, 33*, 442–75.

Kunzle, D. (1982). *Fashion and fetishism: A social history of the corset, tight-leasing, and other forms of body sculpture in the West*. Totowa, NJ: Rowman & Littlefield.

Lacey, J. H., & Price, C. (2004). Disturbed families, or families disturbed? *British Journal of Psychiatry, 184*, 195–96.

Ladies of little diamond (1943, June 14). *Time*, 73–74.

LaFrance, A. (2016). I analyzed a year of my reporting for gender bias (again). *The Atlantic*. Downloaded February 17, 2016 from, www.theatlantic.com/technology/archive/2016/02/gender-diversity-journalism/463023/.

LaFrance, M., Hecht, M. A., Paluck, E. (2003). The contingent smile: A meta-analysis of sex differences in smiling. *Psychological Bulletin, 129*(2), 305–34.

Lackoff, R. (1975). *Language and woman's place: Text and commentaries*. New York: Oxford University Press.

Lalik, R., & Oliver, K. L. (2005). "The Beauty Walk" as a social space for messages about the female body: Toward transformative collaboration. In P. J. Bettis and N. G. Adams (Eds.), *Geographies of girlhood: Identities in-between* (pp. 85–100). New York: Routledge.

Lareau, A. (2003). *Unequal childhoods*. Los Angeles: University of California Press.

Latner, J. D., & Wilson, R. E. (2011). Obesity and body image in adulthood. In T. Cash & L. Smolak (Eds.), *Body image: A handbook of science, practice, and prevention* (pp. 189–97). New York, NY: Guilford Press.

Laver, J. (1969). *Modesty in dress: An inquiry into the fundamentals of fashion*. Boston: Houghton Mifflin.

Laz, C. (1998). Act your age. *Sociological Forum, 13*(1), 85–113.

Lazarsfeld, P. F., Berelson, B., & Gaudet, H. (1944). *The people's choice. How the voter makes up his mind in a presidential campaign.* New York, NY: Duell, Sloan, and Pearce.

Leadbeater, B., & Way, N. (1996). *Urban girls: Resisting stereotypes, creating identities.* New York: New York University Press.

Leading feminist puts hairdo before strike. (1970, August 27). *New York Times,* p. 30.

Lee, F. R (2014, April 9). An artist demands civility on the street with grit and buckets of paste. *New York Times.* Downloaded February 12, 2016 from, www.nytimes.com/ 2014/04/10/arts/design/tatyana-fazlalizadeh-takes-her-public-art-project-to-georgia. html?smid=fb-share&_r=0.

Lenhard, K., & Pompper, D. (2015, August). *Women with disability: Sex object and supercrip stereotyping on reality television's Push Girls.* Mass Communication Division. Association for Education in Journalism & Mass Communication, San Francisco, CA.

Lenskyi, H. J. (1999).Women, sport and sexualities: Breaking the silences. In P. White & K. Young (Eds.), *Sport and gender in Canada* (pp. 170–81). Ontario, Canada: Oxford University Press.

Lenskyj, H. J. (2012). Reflections on communication and sport: On heteronormativity and gender identities. *Communication & Sport, 1*(1/2), 138–50.

Leonard, S. (2016, February 17). Which women support Hillary (and which women can't afford to). *The Nation.* Downloaded February 21, 2016 from, www.thenation. com/article/which-women-support-hillary-and-which-women-cant-afford-to/.

Levant, R. (1996). The new psychology of men. *Professional Psychology, 27,* 259–65.

Levant, R. F. 2011. Research in the psychology of men and masculinity using the gender role strain paradigm as a framework. *American Psychologist, 66,* 765–76.

Levant, R. F., & Philpot, C. (2002). Conceptualizing gender in marital and family therapy research: The gender role strain paradigm. In H. A. Liddle and D. A. Santisteban (Eds.), *Family psychology: Science-based interventions,* (301-329). Washington, DC: American Psychological Association.

Levant, R., Richmond, K., Cook, S., House, A. T., & Aupont, M. (2007). The femininity ideology scale: Factor structure, reliability, convergent and discriminant validity, and social contextual variation. *Sex Roles, 57*(5-6), 373–83.

Levine, M. & Harrison, K. (2009). Effects of media on eating disorders and body image. In J. Bryant & M. B. Oliver (Eds.), *Media effects: Advances in theory and research (3rd Edition)* (pp. 490–516). New York, NY: Routledge.

Lewis, M. I. & Butler, R. N. (1984). Why is women's lib ignoring old women? In M. Minkler and C. L. Estes, (Eds.), *Readings in the political economy of aging* (pp. 199–208). New York: Baywood.

Ligon, A. D. (2015). Striving to dress the part: Examining the absence of black women in different iterations of *Say Yes to the Dress.* In J. R. Ward (Ed.), *Real sister: Stereotypes, respectability, and Black women in reality TV* (pp. 53–67). New Brunswick, NJ: Rutgers University Press.

Linton, S. (1998). *Claiming disability: Knowledge and identity.* New York: New York University Press.

Linville, D., Stice, E., Gau, J., & O'Neil, M. (2014). Predictive effects of mother and peer influences on increases in adolescent eating disorder risk factors and symptoms: A 3-year longitudinal study. *International Journal of Eating Disorders, 44,* 745–51.

Litosseliti, L. (2006). *Gender and language: Theory and practice.* New York: Hodder and Arnold.

Long, B. C. (1989). Sex-role orientation, coping strategies, and self-efficacy of women in traditional and non traditional occupations. *Psychology of Women Quarterly, 13,* 307–24.

Lont, C. M. (1995). *Women and media: Content, careers and criticism.* Belmont, CA: Wadsworth.

Lough, N. L. (1998). Promotion of sports for girls and women: The necessity and the strategy. *The Journal of Physical Education, Recreation and Dance, 69*(5), 25–27.

Lövgren, K. (2015). Comfortable and leisurely: Old women on style and dress. *Journal of Women & Aging,* 1–14.

Luhaorg, H., & Zivian, M. T. (1995). Gender role conflict: The interaction of gender, gender role, and occupation. *Sex Roles, 33*(9/10), 607–20.

Lunsford, S. (2005). Seeking a rhetoric of the rhetoric of disabilities. *Rhetoric Review, 24*(3), 330–33.

Lynxwiler, J., & Wilson, M. (1988). The code of the new Southern belle: Generating typifications to structure social interaction. In C. M. Dillman (Ed.), *Southern women* (pp. 113–25). New York: Hemisphere Publishing Corporation.

MacDonald, B. (1983). *Look me in the eye: Old women, aging and ageism.* San Francisco, CA: Spinsters, Ink.

MacInnes, J. (1998). *The end of masculinity.* Buckingham/Philadelphia: Open University Press.

Mackay, S., & Dallaire, C. (2013). Skirtboard net—A narrative: Young women creating their own skateboarding representations. *International Review for the Sociology of Sport, 48*(2), 171–95.

MacKinnon, K. (2003). *Representing men: Maleness and masculinity in the media.* New York: Oxford University Press Inc.

Madden, W. C. (1997). *The women of the all-American girls professional baseball league: A biographical dictionary.* Jefferson, NC: McFarland & Company, Inc.

Maira, S. (2002). *Desis in the house: Indian American youth culture in New York City.* Philadelphia, PA: Temple University.

Markula, P. (Ed.) (2009). *Olympic women and the media: International perspectives.* New York, NY: Palgrave Macmillan.

Marmion, S., & Lundberg-Love, P. (2004). Learning masculinity and femininity: Gender socialization from parents and peers across the life span. In M. A. Paludi (Ed.), *Praeger guide to the psychology of gender* (pp. 1–26). Westport, CT: Praeger.

Marsh, M. (1990). *Suburban lives.* New Brunswick, NJ: Rutgers University Press.

Marshall, B. L., & Katz, S. (2006). From androgyny to androgens: Re-sexing the aging body. In T. M. Calasanti and K. F. Slevin (Eds.), *Age matters: Realigning feminist thinking* (pp. 75–97). New York: Routledge.

Marshall, J. (1984). *Women managers: Travelers in a male world.* Chichester, U.K.: Wiley.

Martin, J. L. (2010). Anticipating infertility: Egg freezing, genetic preservation, and risk. *Gender & Society, 24,* 526–45.

Martin, P. Y. (2003). "Said and done" versus "saying and doing:" Gendering practices, Practicing gender at work. *Gender and Society, 17*(3), 342–66.

Mason, D. L. (2007). Bewitched, bedeviled, and left behind: Women and mass communication in a world of faith. In P. J. Creedon and J. Cramer (Eds.) *Women in mass communication,* 3rd ed. (pp. 177–90). Thousand Oaks, CA: Sage.

Matthews, G. (1987). *Just a housewife: The rise and fall of domesticity in America.* New York: Oxford University Press.

Mayo Clinic Staff (2016, January 16). Depression in women: Understanding the gender gap. Downloaded February 10, 2016 from, www.mayoclinic.org/diseases-conditions/depression/in-depth/depression/art-20047725.

McBride, A. B. (1990). Mental health effects of women's multiple roles. *American Psychologist, 45,* 381–84.

McCracken, E. (1993). *Decoding women's magazines: From* Mademoiselle *to* Ms. London: Macmillan.

McHale, S. M., Crouter, A. C., & Whiteman, S. D. (2003). The family contexts of gender development in childhood and adolescence. *Social Development, 12,* 125–48.

McKinley, N. M. (2006). The development and cultural contexts of objectified body consciousness: A longitudinal analysis of two cohorts of women. *Developmental Psychology, 42,* 679–87.

McMullin, J. A. & Berger, E. D. (2006). Gendered ageism/age(ed) sexism: The case of unemployed older workers. In T. M. Calasanti and K. F. Slevin (Eds.), *Age matters: Realigning feminist thinking* (pp. 201–23). New York: Routledge.

McPherson, T. (2003). *Reconstructing Dixie: Race, gender and nostalgia in the imagined South.* Durham, NC: Duke University Press.

McPherson, T. (2000). Who's got next? Gender, race, and the mediation of the WNBA. In T. Boyd and Kate. L. Shropshire (Eds.), *Basketball Jones: America above the rim* (pp. 184–97). New York: New York University Press.

McRobbie, A. (1978). Working class girls and the culture of femininity. In Women's Studies Group Centre for Contemporary Cultural Studies University of Birmingham (Eds.), *Women take issue: Aspects of women's subordination,* (pp. 96–108). London: Hutchinson of London.

McRobbie, A. (1991). *Feminism and youth culture: From Jackie to Just Seventeen.* Basingstoke, U.K.: Macmillan.

McRobbie, A. (1998). *British fashion design: Rag trade or image industry.* Boca Raton, FL: Taylor & Francis.

McRobbie, A. (2000). *Feminism and youth culture.* London: Macmillan.

McRobbie, A. (2004a). Notes on *What Not To Wear* and post-feminist symbolic violence. In L. Adkins and B. Skeggs (Eds.), *Feminism after Bourdieu* (pp. 99–109). Oxford: Blackwell.

McRobbie, A. (2004b). Post-feminism and popular culture. *Feminist Media Studies, 4*(3), 255–64.

McRobbie, A. (2007). Postfeminism and popular culture: Bridget Jones and the new gender regime. In Y. Tasker and D. Negra (Eds.), *Interrogating postfeminism: Gender and the politics of popular culture (console-ing passions)* (pp. 27–39). Durham, NC: Duke University Press.

McRobbie, A. (2009). *The aftermath of feminism: Gender, culture and social change.* Thousand Oaks, CA: Sage.

Meadows, R., & Davidson, K. (2006). Maintaining manliness in later life: Hegemonic masculinities and emphasized femininities. In T. M. Calasanti and K. F. Slevin (Eds.), *Age matters: Realigning feminist thinking* (pp. 295–312). New York: Routledge.

Merskin, D. (2005). Making an about-face: Jammer girls and the World Wide Web. In S. R. Mazzarella (Ed.), *Girl wide web: Girls, the Internet, and the negotiation of identity* (pp. 51–67).

Messerschmidt, J. W. (2004). *Flesh and blood: Adolescent gender diversity and violence.* Lanham, MD: Rowman and Littlefield.

Messerschmidt, J. W. (2011). The struggle for heterofeminine recognition: Bullying, embodiment, and reactive sexual offending by adolescent girls. Feminist Criminology, *6*(3), 203–33.

Metcalfe, B. A. (1989). What motivates managers: an investigation by gender and sector of employment. *Public Administration, 67,* 95–108.

Meyerowitz, J. (1993). Beyond the feminine mystique: a reassessment of postwar mass culture, 1946-1958. *Journal of American History, 79,* 1455–82.

Milkie, M. A. (2002). Contested images of femininity: An analysis of cultural gatekeepers' struggles with the 'real girl' critique. *Gender and society,* 16(6), 839–59.

Mlotek, H. (2016, February 26). When did the red carpet become prom? *New York Times Magazine.* Downloaded March 5, 2016 from, www.nytimes.com/2016/02/26/magazine/when-did-the-red-carpet-become-prom.html?_r=0.

Montemurro, B. (2002). You go 'cause you have to: The bridal shower as a ritual of obligation. *Symbolic Interaction, 25*(1), 67–92.

Mooney, G. (1937). The benefits and dangers of athletics for the high school girl. Department of Physical Training for Women Records (Health Ed. folder), Box 3R251. Barker Texas History Center, University of Texas, Austin.

Moseley, R. (2002). Glamorous witchcraft: Gender and magic in teen film and television. *Screen, 43*(4), 403–22.

Nash, M., & Grant, R. (2015). Twenty-something Girls v. thirty-something Sex and the City women. *Feminist Media Studies, 15*(6), 976–91.

Naugler, D. (2010). Oh, sure they're nice, but are they real?: Greeting cards and the normalizing of cosmetic surgical intervention in practices of feminine embodiment. *Resources for Feminist Research, 33*(3/4), 119–35, 208.

Nelson, D. L., & Burke, R. J. (2002). A framework for examining gender, work stress, and health. In D. L. Nelson and R. J. Burke (Eds.), *Gender, work, stress, and health* (pp. 3–14). Washington, D.C.: American Psychological Association.

"No Sam Brown Belts, Says Mrs. Roosevelt" (1941, July). *New York Times Magazine,* 6.

Noble, D. (2000). Ragga music: Dis/respecting Black women and dis/reputable sexualities. In B. Hesse (Ed.), *Un/settled multiculturalisms: Diasporas, entanglements, transruptions* (pp. 148–69). London: Zed Books.

Nussbaum, J. F., Pecchioni, L. L., Robinson, J. D., & Thompson, T. L. (2000). *Communication and aging,* 2nd ed. Mahwah, NJ: Lawrence Erlbaum Associates, Inc., Publishers.

Odland, S. B. (2009). On a salable motherhood, ambivalent domesticity: The construction of maternal identity in *Ladies Home Journal* in 1946. *Journal of Communication Inquiry, 34* (1), 61–84.

Olson, E. (2007, September 2). Catching the bouquet, in a dress you bought online. Downloaded September 2, 2007 from, www.nytimes.com/2007/09/02/business/yourmoney/02dresses.html?pagewanted=1&th&emc=th.

Olympic boxing body considers skirts for female competitors. (2011, November 4). Associated Press. Downloaded March 3, 2016 from, www.foxnews.com/sports/2011/11/04/olympic-boxing-body-considersskirts-for-women-competitors/.

O'Brien Hallstein, D. L. O. (2011). She gives birth, she's wearing a bikini: Mobilizing the postpregnant celebrity mom body to manage the post-second wave crisis in femininity. *Women's Studies in Communication, 34,* 111–38.

Ogle, J., & Damhorst, M. (1999). Dress for success in the popular press. In K. P. Johnson, S. J. Lennon, K. P. Johnson, & S. J. Lennon (Eds.), *Appearance and power* (pp. 79–101). New York, NY: Berg.

O'Neil, J. M. (1981). Male sex-role conflict, sexism, and masculinity: Implications for men, women, and the counseling psychologist. *The Counseling Psychologist, 9,* 61–80.

O'Neil, J. M. (1990). Assessing men's gender role conflict. In D. Moore & F. Leafgren (Eds.), *Men in conflict: Problem solving strategies and interventions* (pp. 23–38). Alexandria, VA: American Association for Counseling and Development.

O'Neil, J. M. (2008). Summarizing 25 years of research on men's gender role conflict using the gender role conflict scale: New research paradigms and clinical implications. *The Counseling Psychologist, 36,* 358–445

O'Neil, J. M., Good, G. E., & Holmes, S. (1995). Fifteen years of theory and research on men's gender role conflict: New paradigms for empirical research. In R. Levant & W. Pollack (Eds.), *The new psychology of men* (pp. 164–206). New York: Basic Books.

O'Neill, D. , Savigny, H., & Cann, V. (2015). Women politicians in the UK press: Not seen and not heard? *Feminist Media Studies, 16*(2), 293–307.

O'Reilly, A. (2010). Outlaw(ing) motherhood: A theory and politic of maternal empowerment for the 21st century. In A. O'Reilly (Ed.), *21st century motherhood: Experience, identity, policy, and agency* (pp. 366–80). New York: Columbia University.

Orenstein, P. (2011). *Cinderella ate my daughter: Dispatches from the front lines of the new girlie-girl culture.* New York: Harper.

Orloff, A. S., & Shiff, T. (2016). Feminism/s in power: Rethinking gender equality after the second wave. *Political Power and Social Theory, 30,* 109–34.

Overstreet, N. M., Quinn, D. M., & Agocha, V. B. (2010). Beyond thinness: The influence of a curvaceous body ideal on body dissatisfaction in Black and White women. *Sex Roles, 63,* 91–103.

Padavic, I., & Butterfield, J. (2011). Mothers, fathers, and mathers: Negotiating a lesbian co-parental identity. *Gender and Society, 25*(2), 176–96.

Padavic, I., & Reskin, B. (1990). Men's behavior and women's interest in blue-collar jobs. *Social Problems, 374,* 613–28.

Paik, , A., Sanchagrin, K. J., & Heimer, K. (2016). Broken promises: Abstinence pledging and sexual reproductive health. *Journal of Marriage and Family, 78*(2), 546–61.

Parameswaran, R. (2004). Global queens, national celebrities: Tales of feminine triumph in post-liberalization India. *Critical Studies in Media Communication, 21*(4), 346–70.

Parker, S., Nichter, M., Nichter, M., Vuckovic, N., Sims, C. & Ritenbaugh, C. (1995). Body image and weight concerns among African American and white adolescent females: Differences that make a difference. *Human Organization, 54,* 103–14.

Patierra, A. C. (2015). Cuban girls and visual media: Bodies and practices of (still-) socialist consumerism. *Continuum: Journal of Media & Cultural Studies, 29*(2), 194–204.

Pay inequity in athletics (2016). Women's Sports Foundation. Downloaded June 11 from, www.womenssportsfoundation.org/home/research/articles-and-reports/equity-issues/pay-inequity.

Peake, A., & Harris, K. L. (2002). Young adults' attitudes toward multiple role planning: The influence of gender, career traditionality, and marriage plans. *Journal of Vocational Behavior, 60,* 405–21.

Penington, B. A., & Turner, L. H. (2004). The function of talk in African American and European American mother-adolescent daughter dyads. In P. M. Buzzanell, H. Sterk, & L. H. Turner (Eds.), *Gender in applied communication contexts* (pp. 275–94). Thousand Oaks, CA: Sage.

Perkins, T. E. (1979). Rethinking stereotypes. In M. Barrett, P. Corrigan, A. Kuhn, and J. Wolff (Eds.) *Ideology and cultural production* (pp. 135–59). New York: St. Martin's.

Perloff, R. M. (2002). The third-person effect. *Media effects: Advances in theory and research, 2,* 489–506.

Person, E. S. (1999). *The sexual century*: Yale University Press.

Pham, M-H. T. (2012, January 17). If the clothes fit: A feminist takes on fashion. *Ms.* Downloaded May 26, 2016 from, msmagazine.com/blog/2012/01/17/if-the-clothes-fit-a-feminist-takes-on-fashion/.

Pham, M-H. T. (2013). Susie Bubble is a sign of the times: The embodiment of success in the Web 2.0 economy. *Feminist Media Studies, 13*(2), 245–67.

Phillips, A. P., & Dipboye, R. L. (1989). Correlational tests of predictions from a process model of the interview. *Journal of Applied Psychology, 74,* 41–52.

Picariello, M. L., Greenberg, D. N., & Pillemer, D. B. (1990). Children's sex-related stereotyping of colors. *Child Development, 61,* 1453–60.

Pike, K. M., Rodin, J. (1991). Mothers, daughters, and disordered eating. *Journal of Abnormal Psychology, 100,* 198–204.

Pingree, S., Hawkins, R. P., Butler, M., & Paisley, W. (1976). A scale for sexism. *Journal of Communication, 26,* 193–200.

Pinhas, L., Weaver, H., Bryden, P., Ghabbour, N., & Toner, B. (2002). Gender-role conflict and suicidal behaviour in adolescent girls. *The Canadian Journal of Psychiatry, 47*(5), 473–76.

Piper, A., & Jeanso, R. (2016). Women write about family, men write about war. *New Republic.* Downloaded April 9, 2016 from, newrepublic.com/article/132531/women-write-family-men-write-war?utm_content=buffer6d188&utm_medium=social&utm_source=Twitter.com&utm_campaign=buffer.

Pipher, M. (1995). *Reviving Ophelia: Saving the selves of adolescent girls.* New York: Ballantine.

Pitt, R. N. (2010). 'Still looking for my Jonathan': Gay Black men's management of religious and sexual identity conflict. *Journal of Homosexuality, 57,* 39–53.

Plant, R. J. (2010). *Mom: The transformation of motherhood in modern America.* Chicago: University of Chicago Press.

Pleck, J. H. (1995). The gender role strain paradigm: An update. In R. F. Levant & W. S. Pollack (Eds.), *A new psychology of men* (pp. 11-32). New York: Basic Books.

Pompper, D. (2007). The gender-ethnicity construct in public relations organizations: Using feminist standpoint theory to discover Latinas' realities. *The Howard Journal of Communications, 18*(4), 291–311.

Pompper, D. (2010). Masculinities, the metrosexual, and media images: Across dimensions of age and ethnicity. *Sex Roles: A Journal of Research, 63*(9), 682–96.

Pompper, D. (2011). Fifty years later: Mid-career women of color against the glass ceiling in communications organizations. *Journal of Organizational Change Management, 24*(4), 464–86.

Pompper, D. (2012). On social capital and diversity in a feminized industry: Further developing a theory of internal public relations. *Journal of Public Relations Research, 24*(1), 86–103.

Pompper, D. (2014a). *Practical and theoretical implications of successfully doing difference in organizations*. Bingley, UK: Emerald Group Publishing Limited.

Pompper, D. (2014b). Female Tunisian revolutionaries, leadership, and social (dis)order in global news production. *Mass Communication & Society, 17*(4), 1–22.

Pompper, D., & Crandall, K. (2014). The erotic-chaste dialectic and the new southern belle code at the high school prom: Feminine gender role stress across ethnic and socio-economic factors. *The Journal of Popular Culture, 47*(5), 937–51.

Pompper, D., & Jung, T. (2016, August). *Permeable public-private sphere boundaries: A survey of work-home life balance among public relations, communication management and strategic communication practitioners*. Public Relations Division. Association for Education in Journalism & Mass Communication, Minneapolis, MN.

Pompper, D., & Koenig, J. (2004). Cross-cultural-generational perceptions of ideal body image: Hispanic women & magazine standards. *Journalism & Mass Communication Quarterly, 81*(1), 89–107.

Pompper, D., Soto, J., & Piel, L. (2007). Male body image and magazine standards: Considering dimensions of age and ethnicity. *Journalism & Mass Communication Quarterly, 84*(3), 525–45.

Powell, G. N., & Greenhaus, J. H. (2010). Sex, gender, and the work-to-family interface: Exploring negative and positive interdependencies. *Academy of Management Journal, 53*(3), 513–34.

Puri, L. (2016). Gender equality is everyone's business. U.N. Women. Downloaded June 26, 2016 from, www.unwomen.org/en/news/stories/2016/6/lakshmi-puri-speech-at-forbes-powerful-women-summit.

Pyke, K., & Dang, T. (2003). FOB and whitewashed: Intra-ethnic identities and internalized oppression among second generation Asian Americans. *Qualitative Sociology, 26*, 147–72.

Pyke, K. D., & Johnson, D. L. (2003). Asian American women and radicalized femininities: 'Doing' gender across cultural worlds. *Gender and Society, 17*(1), 33–53.

Quach, T. (2008). Femininity and sexual agency among young unmarried women in Hanoi. Culture, *Health & Sexuality, 10*, S151-S161.

Rakow, L. (1989). From the feminization of public relations to the promise of feminism. In E. L. Toth & C. G. Cline (Eds.), *Beyond the velvet ghetto* (pp. 287–98). San Francisco: IABC Research Foundation.

Rakow, L. F., & Wackwitz, L. A. (2004). Representation in feminist communication theory. In L. A. Rakow & L. A. Wackwitz (Eds.), *Feminist communication theory: Selections in context* (pp. 171–1186). Thousand Oaks, CA: Sage.

Ray, R. E. (2006). The personal as political: The legacy of Betty Friedan. In T. M. Calasanti and K. F. Slevin (Eds.), *Age matters: Realigning feminist thinking* (pp. 21–45). New York: Routledge.

Readdy, T., Cardinal, B. J., & Watkins, P. L. (2013). Muscle dysmorphia, gender role stress, and sociocultural influences. *Research Quarterly for Exercise and Sport, 82*(2), 310–19.

Reilly, M. (2016). Meet the women going on the back of the $10 bill. Downloaded August 14, 2016 from www.huffingtonpost.com/entry/women-10-bill_us_5718f5fbe4b024dae4f14601?post_id=1142445275813017_1142445302479681#_=_.

Return of curves, (1927, July). *Woman Citizen*, 29.

Reynolds, J. (2008). *Single woman: A discursive investigation*. New York: Routledge.

Richards, J., Wilson, S., & Woodhead, L. (Eds.). (1999). *Diana: The making of a media saint*. London: I. B. Taurus and Co Ltd.

Richmond, K., Levant, R., Smalley, B., & Cook, S. (2015). The femininity ideology scale (FIS): Dimensions and its relationship to anxiety and feminine gender role stress. *Women & Health, 55*(3), 263–79.

Ringrose, J. (2006). A new universal mean girl: Examining the discursive construction andsocial regulation of a new feminine pathology. *Feminism & Psychology, 16*(4), 405–24.

Ringrose, J. (2013). *Postfeminist education? Girls and the sexual politics of schooling*. London: Routledge.

Ringrose, J., & Harvey, L. (2015). Boobs, back-off, six packs and bits: Mediated body parts, gendered reward, and sexual shame in teens' sexting images. *Continuum: Journal of Media & Cultural Studies, 29*(2), 205–17.

Rivière, J. (1929/1986). Womanliness as masquerade. In V. Burgin, J. Donald and C. Kaplan (Eds.), *Formations of fantasy* (pp. 35–44). London: Routledge.

Robertson, J. M., Johnson, A. L., Benton, S. L., Janey, B. A., Carbral, J., & Woodford, J. A. (2002). What's in a picture? Comparing gender constructs of younger and older adults. *The Journal of Men's Studies, 11*(1), 1-27.

Robison, L. (2009). Bodies, Southern nostalgia, and the construction of Whiteness in *Divine Secrets of the Ya-Ya Sisterhood*. *The Journal of Popular Culture, 42*(6), 1115–33.

Robnett, B. (1997). *How long, how long? African-American women in the struggle for civil rights*. New York: Oxford University Press.

Rochlen, A., & Mahalik, J. R. (2004). Women's perceptions of male partner's gender role Conflict as predictors of psychological well-being and relationship satisfaction. *Psychology of Men and Masculinity, 5*, 147–57.

Rodgers, R., Faure, K., & Chabrol, H. (2009). Gender differences in parental influences on adolescent body dissatisfaction and disordered eating. *Sex Roles, 61*, 837–49.

Rolnik, A. M., Engeln-Maddox, R., & Miller, S. A. (2010). Here's looking at you: Self-objectification, body image disturbance, and sorority rush. *Sex Roles, 63*, 6–17.

Rosdahl, J. (2014). The myth of femininity in the sport of bodysculpting. *Social Alternatives, 33*(2), 36–42.

Rose, T. (1994). *Black noise: Rap music and Black culture in contemporary America*. Hanover, N.H.: Wesleyan University Press.

Rosie the riveter (2016). A&E Television Networks, LLC. Downloaded April 10, 2016 from, www.history.com/topics/world-war-ii/rosie-the-riveter.

Rossie, A. (2015). Moving beyond 'Am I pretty or ugly?': Disciplining girls through YouTube feedback. *Continuum: Journal of Media & Cultural Studies, 29*(2), 230–40.

Roth, A., & Basow, S. A. (2004). Femininity, sports and feminism: Developing a theory of physical liberation. *Journal of Sport & Social Issues, 28*, 245–65.

Rouse, F. (1989). *Understanding fashion*. Oxford: BSP Professional Books.

Rowbotham, S. (1974). *Hidden from history*, 2nd ed. London: Pluto Press.

Rubchak, M. (2012). Seeing pink: Searching for gender justice through opposition in Ukraine. *European Journal of Women's Studies, 19*(1), 55–72.

Rubenstein, S., & Caballero, B. (2000). Is this America and undernourished role model? *JAMA, 283*, 1569.

Rubin, J. (2008). Obama finance chieftan slams Palin parenting. Commentary Magazine, September 6. Downloaded May 26, 2016 from, www.commentarymagazine.com/2008/09/06/obama-finance-chieftan-slams-palin-parenting/.

Ruddick, S. (1995). *Maternal thinking: Toward a politics of peace*, 2nd ed. Boston: Beacon.

Ruddick, S. (1999). Virtues and age. In M. U. Walker (Ed.), *Mother time: Women, aging and ethics* (pp. 45–60). Lanham, MD: Rowman and Littlefield.

Rudman, L. A., Greenwald, A. G., & McGhee, D. E. (2001). Implicit self-concept and evaluative implicit gender stereotypes: Self and ingroup share desirable traits. *Personality and Social Psychology Bulletin, 27*(9), 1164–78.

Russell, K. (2002). *Women's participation motivation in rugby, cricket, and netball: Body satisfaction and self identity.* Unpublished doctoral dissertation, Coventry University, Coventry, U.K.

Sahadi, J. (2016). Yes, men earn more than women. *CNN Money.* Downloaded August 10, 2016 from money.cnn.com/2016/03/23/pf/gender-pay-gap/.

Salvatore, J., & Marecek, J. (2010). Gender in the gym: Evaluation concerns as barriers to women's weight lifting. *Sex Roles, 63,* 556–67.

Sanghvi, M., & Hodges, N. (2015). Marketing the female politician: An exploration of gender and appearance. *Journal of Marketing Management, 31*(15–16). 1676–94.

Scharrer, E. (2004).Virtual violence: Gender and aggression in video game advertisements. *Mass Communication and Society, 7,* 393–412.

Scharrer, E. (2012). Television and gender roles: Cultivating conceptions of self and other. In M. Morgan, J. Shanahan, & N. Signorielli (Eds.), *Living with television now: Advances in cultivation theory and research.* New York, NY: Peter Lang.

Schippers, M. (2007). Recovering the feminine other: Masculinity, femininity, and gender hegemony. *Theory & Society, 36*(1), 85–102.

Scott, J-A. (2015). Almost passing: A performance analysis of personal narratives of physically disabled femininity. *Women's Studies in Communication, 38,* 227–49.

Scott, W. (2016). Julianna Margulies: It's a wonderful time for women in television. *Parade.* Downloaded February 6, 2016 from, parade.com/349072/walterscott/julianna-margulies-its-a-wonderful-time-for-women-in-television/#.VrYnSwOuuEQ.facebook.

Serano, J. (2013). *Excluded: Making feminist and queer movements more inclusive.* Berkeley, CA: Seal Press.

Shakib, S. (2003). Female basketball participation: Negotiating the conflation of peer status and gender status from childhood through puberty. *American Behavioral Scientist, 46,* 1405–22.

Shor, E., van de Rijt, A., Miltsov, A., Kulkarni, V., & Skiena, S. (2015). A paper ceiling: Explaining the persistent underrepresentation of women in printed news. *American Sociological Review, 80*(5), 960–84.

Simon, R. (2007, July 24). Edwards is mad and won't take it anymore. Politico. Downloaded May 29, 2016 from, www.politico.com/story/2007/07/edwards-is-mad-and-wont-take-it-anymore-005081.

Schacht, S. P. (2004). Beyond the boundaries of the classroom: Teaching about gender and sexuality at a drag show. *Journal of Homosexuality, 46*(3-4), 225–40.

Schippers, M. (2007). Recovering the feminine other: masculinity, femininity, and gender hegemony. *Theory and Society, 36,* 85–102.

Schroeder, J. E., & Zwick, D. (2004). Mirrors of masculinity: Representation and identity in advertising images. *Consumption, Markets and Culture, 7*(1), 21–52.

Scott, W. (2014, October 24). Julianna Margulies: 'It's a wonderful time for women in television.' *Parade.* Retrieved February 6, 2016, from parade.condenast.com/349072/walterscott/julianna-margulies-its-a-wonderful-timefor-women-in-television/.

Sefton, A. A. (1937). Must women in sports look beautiful? *Journal of Health and Physical Education, 8,* 481.

Sefton, A. A. (1941). *The women's division national amateur athletic Federation: Sixteen years of progress in athletics for girls and women, 1923–1939.* California: Stanford University Press.

Sherman, L. (2010). Google wants to be more fashionable. Fashionista.com. Downloaded May 1, 2016 from, fashionista.com/2010/07/google-wants-to-be-more-fashionable/.

Sherrill, R. (1970, September 20). That equal rights amendment—what, exactly, does it mean?, *New York Times Magazine,* 26.

Shome, R. (2014). *Diana and beyond: White femininity, national identity, and contemporary media culture.* Chicago: University of Illinois Press.

Siegel, J. M. (2009). Thank you Sarah Palin, for reminding us: It's not about the clothes. *Virginia Journal of Social Policy & the Law, 17*(1), 144–79.

Silva, J. M. (2008). A new generation of women? How female ROTC cadets negotiate the tension between masculine military culture and traditional femininity. *Social Forces, 87*(2), 937–60.

Silverstein, B., Carpman, S., Perlick, D. & Perdue, L. (1990). Nontraditional sex-role aspirations, gender identity conflict and disordered eating among college women. *Sex Roles, 23*(11), 687–95.

Sinkman, E. (2013). *The psychology of beauty: Creation of a beautiful self.* New York: Jason Aronson.

Six, B., & Eckes, T. (1991). A closer look at the complex structure of gender stereotypes. *Sex Roles, 24*(1/2), 57–71.

Slevin, K. F. (2006). The embodied experiences of old lesbians. In T. M. Calasanti and K. F. Slevin (Eds.), *Age matters: Realigning feminist thinking* (pp. 247–68). New York: Routledge.

Smith, D. E. (1990). *Text, facts, and femininity: Exploring the relations of ruling.* London: Routledge.

Smith, S. (2015). *Women and socialism: Class, race, and capital.* Chicago: Haymarket Books.

Smith, S. L., & Donnerstein, E. (1998). Harmful effects of exposure to media violence: Learning of aggression, emotional desensitization, and fear. In R. G. Green and E. Donnerstein (Eds.), *Human aggression: Theories, research, and implication for social policy* (pp. 167–202). San Diego, CA: Academic Press, Inc.

Sojourner Truth's "Ain't I woman?" (2016). Nolo. Downloaded June 24, 2016 from, www.nolo.com/legal-encyclopedia/content/truth-woman-speech.html.

Solnit, R. (2015). *Men explain things to me,* 2nd ed. Chicago: Haymarket Books.

Solórzano, D. G, Ceja, M., & Yosso, T. (2000). Critical race theory, racial microaggressions, and campus racial climate: The experiences of African American college students. *Journal of Negro Education, 69,* 60–73.

Sotirin, P. (2004). Consuming breasts: Our breasts, our selves. In D. Grant, C. Hardy, C. Oswick, N. Phillips, & L. Putnam (Eds.), *The handbook of organizational discourse* (pp. 123–45). Thousand Oaks, CA: Sage.

Spar, D. L (2013). *Wonder women: Sex, power, and the quest for perfection.* New York: Picador.

Spence, J. T., & Buckner, C. (2000). Instrumental and expressive traits, trait stereotypes, and sexist attitudes: What do they signify? *Psychology of Women Quarterly, 24,* 44–62.

Springgay, S., & Freedman, D. (2010). Breasted bodies and pedagogies of excess: Towards a materialist theory of becoming mother. In B. Schultz, J. Sandlin, and J. Burdick (Eds.), *Public pedagogy: Education and learning beyond,* (pp. 351–65). New York, NY: Routledge.

Sprowl, J. P. (1993). Commentary. In C. Berryman-Fink, D. Ballard-Reisch, and L. H. Newman (Eds.), *Communication and sex-role socialization* (pp. 201–7). New York: Garland Publishing, Inc.

Stacey, J. (1994). *Stargazing: Hollywood cinema and female spectorship.* London: Routledge.

Steers, F. (1932, October 7). Spirit. *Amateur Athlete.*

Steinmetz, K. (2014, May 29). America's transition. *Time,* 38–46.

Stern, B. B. (2003). Masculinism(s) and the male image: What does it mean to be a man? In T. Reichert and J. Lambiase (Eds.), *Sex in advertising: Perspectives on the erotic appeal* (pp. 215–28). Mahwah, NJ: Lawrence Erlbaum Associates, Publishers.

Stevenson, B. (2010). Beyond the classroom: Using Title IX to measure the return to high school sports. *The Review of Economics and Statistics, 92*(2), 284–301.

Stewart, H. M. (2004). " Señioritas and Princesses: The Quinceañera as a context for female development." Diss. The Institute for Clinical Social Work.

Still, J. (2003). (Re)presenting masculinities: Introduction to *Men's Bodies. Paragraph: Journal of Modern Critical Theory, 26*(1–2), 1–16.

Stoller, E. P., & Gibson, R. C. (2000). Different worlds in aging: Gender, race and class. In E. P. Stoller and R. C. Gibson (Eds.), *Worlds of difference: Inequality in the aging experience*, 3rd ed., pp. 1–15). Thousand Oaks, CA: Pine Forge Press.

Strings, S., & Bui, L. T. (2013). She is not acting, she is. *Feminist Media Studies, 14*(5), 822–36.

Sue, D. W., Bucceri, J. M., Lin, A. I., Nadal, K. L., & Torino, G. C. (2007). Racial microaggressions and the Asian American experience. *Cultural Diversity & Ethnic Minority Psychology, 13*, 72–81.

Sue, D. W., Capodilupo, C. M., & Holder, A. M. B. (2008). Racial microaggressions in the life experience of Black Americans. *Professional Psychology: Research and Practice, 39*, 329–36.

Sue, D. W., Capodilupo, C. M., Torino, G. C., Bucceri, J. M., Holder, A. M. B., Nadal, K. L., (2007). Racial microaggressions in everyday life: Implications for clinical practice. *American Psychologist, 62*, 271–86.

Susong, L. (2016). Why the wedding industry needs a feminist analysis. Downloaded July 21, 2016 from motto.time.com/4410312/wedding-industry-feminism/.

Svetkey, B. (1998, July 17). Spice Girls tour divorce. *Entertainment Weekly*. Downloaded April 10, 2016 from, www.ew.com/article/1998/07/17/spice-girls-tour-divorce.

Tavris, C. (1992). *The mismeasure of women*. New York: Simon & Schuster.

Tasker, Y., & Negra, D. (2007). Introduction: Feminist politics and postfeminist culture. In Y. Tasker & D. Negra (Eds.), *Interrogating postfeminism* (pp. 1–26). Durham, NC: Duke University Press.

Twenge, J. (1997). Changes in masculine and feminine traits over time: A meta-analysis. *Sex Roles, 36*, 305–25.

Taylor, L. (2012, August 9) Olympic sexism from NBC. The Washington Post. Downloaded March 3, 2016 from, www.washingtonpost.com/blogs/postpartisan/post/olympic-sexism-from-nbc/2012/08/09/af930be0-e24c-11e1-98e7-89d659f9c106_blog.html.

Taylor, J. M., Gilligan, C., & Sullivan, A. M. (1995). *Between voice and silence*. Cambridge, MA: Harvard University Press.

Taylor, R., & Chatters, L. (1991). Religious life. In J. S. Jackson (Ed.), *Life in Black America* (pp. 105–23). Newbury Park, CA: Sage.

Taylor, V., & Rupp, L. J. (2005). When the girls are men: Negotiating gender and sexual dynamics in a study of drag queens. *Signs, 30*(4), 2115–39.

Tenenbaum, H. R., Hill, D. B., Joseph, N., & Roche, E. (2010). It's a boy because he's painting a picture: Age differences in children's conventional and unconventional gender schemas. *British Journal of Psychology, 101*, p. 137–54.

The henpecked house. (1970, August 12). *New York Times*, p. 40.

The lifetime wage gap, state by state. (2016). National Women's Law Center. Downloaded August 15, 2016 from, nwlc.org/resources/the-lifetime-wage-gap-state-by-state/.

Thiel-Stern, S. (2014). *From the dance hall to Facebook: Teen girls, mass media, and moral panic in the United States, 1905–2010*. Boston: University of Massachusetts Press.

Thomas, G. S. (2010). Are black fashion bloggers being ignored? Clutch Magazine Online. Downloaded May 1, 2016 from, clutchmagonline.com/newsgossipinfo/are-black-fashion-bloggers-being-ignored/.

Thomas, T., & Stehling, M. (2016). The communicative construction of FEMEN: Naked protest in self-mediation and German media discourse. *Feminist Media Studies, 16*(1), 86–100.

Thompson, A. K., (2008). 'You can't do gender in a riot': Violence and post-representational politics. *Berkeley Journal of Sociology, 52*, 24–49.

Thompson, J. K., & Stice, E. (2001). Thin-ideal internalization: Mounting evidence for a new risk factor for body-image disturbance and eating psychology. *Current Directions in Psychological Science, 10*, 181–83.

Thorne, B. (1982). Feminist rethinking of the family: An overview. In B. Thorne and M. Yalom (Eds.) *Rethinking the family: Some feminist questions* (pp. 12–15). New York: Longman.

Thornton, A., Alwin, D. F., & Camburn, D. (1983). Causes and consequences of sex-role attitudes and attitude change. *American Sociological Review, 48,* 211–27.

Thornton, J. E. (2002). Myths of aging or ageist stereotypes. *Educational Gerontology, 28,* 301–12.

Thumim, N. (2012). *Self-representation and digital culture.* New York, NY: Palgrave Macmillan.

Tiggemann, M. (2004). Body image across the adult life span: Stability and change. *Body Image, 1,* 29–41.

Tincknell, E. (2011). Scourging the abject body: Ten years younger and fragmented femininity under neoliberalism. In R. Gill and C. Scharff (Eds.), *New femininities: Postfeminism, neoliberalism, and subjectivity,* (pp. 83–95). New York: Palgrave Macmillan.

Tolman, D. L., Impett, E. A., Tracy, A. J., & Michael, A. (2006). Looking good, sounding good: Femininity ideology and adolescent girls' mental health. *Psychology of Women Quarterly, 30,* 85–95.

Tong, R. (2009). *Feminist thought: A more comprehensive introduction* (3rd ed.) Boulder, CO: Westview.

Tonn, M. B. (1996). Militant motherhood: Labor's Mary Harris 'Mother' Jones," *Quarterly Journal of Speech, 82,* 1–21.

Torres, J. B. (1998). Masculinity and gender roles among Puerto Rican men: Machismo on the U.S. mainland. *American Journal of Orthopsychiatry, 68,* 16–26.

Tracy, J. L., & Beall, A. (2011). Nice guys finish last: The impact of emotion expressions on sexual attraction. *Emotion, 11,* 1379–87.

Traister, R. (2016a). *All the single ladies: Unmarried women and the rise of an independent nation.* New York: Simon and Schuster.

Traister, R. (2016b). Hillary Clinton vs. herself. *New York.* Downloaded May 31, 2016 from, nymag.com/daily/intelligencer/2016/05/hillary-clinton-candidacy.html?mid=fb-share-di.

Traister, R. (2010). *Big girls don't cry: The election that changed everything for American women.* New York: Free Press.

Traustadottir, R. (1990). Obstacles to equality: The double discrimination of women with disabilities. *Journal of Leisurability, 19*(2), 4–9.

Trethewey, A. (2000). Revisioning control: A feminist critique of disciplined bodies. In P. Buzzanell, (Ed.), *Rethinking organizational and managerial communication from feminist perspectives* (pp. 107–27). Thousand Oaks, CA: Sage.

Trolan, E. (2013). The impact of the media on gender inequality within sport. *Procedia Social and Behavioral Sciences, 91,* 215–27.

Tsuji, A. (2016, June 7). Serena Williams wants equal pay for women in sports. *USA Today.* Downloaded June 24, 2016 from, ftw.usatoday.com/2016/06/serena-williams-equal-pay-women-sports-tennis-glamour-cover-interview.

Tuana, N. (1993). *The less noble sex: Scientific, religious, and philosophical conceptions of women's nature.* Bloomington, IN: Indiana University Press.

Turkle, S. (2011). *Alone together: Why we expect more from technology and the less from each other.* New York: Basic Books.

Turner, V. (1995). *The ritual process: Structure and anti-structure.* New York: Aldine de Gruyter.

U.N. Women (2016). *Progress of the world's women 2015–2016.* New York.

U.S. Department of Labor (1995). *Good for business: Making full use of the nation's human capital.* Washington, D.C.: Government Printing Office.

Ussher, J. (1991). *Women's madness: Misogyny or mental illness?* London: Harvester Wheatsheaf.

Ussher, J. (1997). *Fantasies of femininity: Reframing the boundaries of sex.* New Brunswick, NJ: Rutgers University Press.

Valian, V. (1989). *Why so slow? The advancement of women.* Cambridge, MA: The MIT Press.

van Zoonen, L. (1994). *Feminist media studies.* Thousand Oaks, CA: Sage.

van Zoonen, L. (2006). The personal, the political and the popular: A woman's guide to celebrity politics. *European Journal of Cultural Studies, 9*(3), 287–301.

Vinciguerra, T. (2011, August 28). Glittering rage. *New York Times,* p. SR-6.

Wackwitz, L. A., & Rakow, L. F. (2007). Got theory? In P. J. Creedon and J. Cramer (Eds.) *Women in mass communication,* 3rd ed. (pp. 257–71). Thousand Oaks, CA: Sage.

Wajcman, J. (1998). *Managing like a man: Women and men in corporate management.* University Park, PA: The Pennsylvania State University Press.

Waldman, K. (2013). Why does everyone expect women to smile all the time? *Slate.* Downloaded February 2, 2016 from, www.slate.com/articles/double_x/doublex/2013/06/bitchy_resting_face_and_female_niceness_why_do_women_have_to_smile_more.html?wpsrc=sh_all_dt_tw_top.

Walker, A. (1992, January/February). Becoming the third wave. *Ms.,* 39–41.

Walkerdine, V. (1997). *Daddy's girl: Young girls and popular culture.* Cambridge, MA: Harvard University Press.

Wallis, C. (1989). Onward women. *Time,* December 4, 80–89.

Walston, M. (2016). 1972, civil rights, Shirley Chisholm, U.S. president, women's liberation. Downloaded June 24, 2016 from, markwalston.com/2012/04/25/shirley-chisholm-runs-for-president/.

Walter, H., & Gottwald, L. (Producers). (2016). *Ain't your mama* [video] Available from msmagazine.com/blog/2016/05/06/j-lo-shows-off-her-fierce-feminist-side-in-new-video/.

Ward, E. G. (2005). Homophobia, hypermasculinity and the US black church. *Culture, Health & Sexuality, 7*(5), 493–504.

Wärn, K. E. (2012). *The Swedish fashion bible from 1867 to the present.* Stockholm, Sweden: Bonnier fakta.

Warner, J. (2010, October 29). The new momism. *New York Times.* Downloaded May 26, 2016 from, www.nytimes.com/2010/10/31/magazine/31FOB-wwln-t.html.

Watzlawik, M. (2009). Instructing femininity and masculinity: methodological potentials and limitations. *Integrative Psychological and Behavioral Science, 43,* 126–37.

Weedon, C. (1997). *Feminist practice and poststructuralist theory* (2nd ed.). Malden, MA: Blackwell.

Weekes, D. (2002). Get your freak on: How Black girls sexualize identity. *Sex Education, 2*(3), 251–62.

Weinstock, M. (2015, June 24). LEGO adds more women in science to its lineup. *Scientific American.* Downloaded June 4, 2016 from, blogs.scientificamerican.com/voices/lego-adds-more-women-in-science-to-its-lineup/.

Weitz, R. (2010). A history of women's bodies. In R. Weitz (Ed.), *The politics of women's bodies,* 3rd ed. (pp. 3–12). New York: Oxford University Press.

Wellington,E. (2015, July 22). Mirror, mirror: Recognizing beauty in the female athletic body. *Philly.com.* Downloaded July 23, 2015 from, www.philly.com/philly/columnists/elizabeth_wellington/20150722_Mirror__Mirror__Mirror__Mirror__Strong__successful_____masculine_.html.

Welter, B. (1966). The cult of true womanhood, 1820-1860. *American Quarterly, 18,* 152.

West, C., & Zimmerman, D. (1987). Doing gender. *Gender & Society, 1,* 125–51.

Westerberg, K. (2001). History and conflicting themes in a gender creating culture. *Mind, Culture, and Activity, 8*(3), 231–49.

Westman, J. C. (1991). Juvenile ageism: Unrecognized prejudice and discrimination against the young. *Child Psychiatry and Human Development, 21,* 237–56.

Whittier, N. E. (1995). *Feminist generations: The persistence of the radical women's movement.* Philadelphia: Temple University Press.

Willis, J., & Todorov, A. (2007) First impressions: Making up your mind after a 100-ms exposure to a face. *Psychological Science, 17*(7), 592–98.

Wilson, D. B., Musham, C., & McLellan, M. S. (2004). From mothers to daughters: Transgenerational food and diet communication in an underserved group. *Journal of Cultural Diversity*, 11(1), 12–17.

Wolf, N. (1991). *The beauty myth: How images of beauty are used against women*. New York: Morrow.

Wolfram, H-J, Mohr, G., & Borchert, J. (2009). Gender roles self-concept, gender-role conflict, and well-being in male primary school teachers. *Sex Roles*, 60, 114–27.

Wollstonecraft, M. (1792/1983). Vindication of the rights of woman. In M. B. Mahowald (Ed.), *Philosophy of woman: An anthology of classic and current concepts*, 2nd ed. (pp. 203–20). Indianapolis, IN: Hackett.

Woo, D. (2000). *Glass ceilings and Asian Americans: The new face of workplace barriers*. Walnut Creek, CA: Altamira Press.

Wood, J., & Fixmer-Oraiz, N. (2015). *Gendered lives: Communication, gender, & culture*, 12th ed. Belmont, CA: Thomson Wadsworth.

Woodward, K. (1995). Tribute to the older woman: psychoanalysis, feminism, and ageism. In M. Featherstone and a Wernick (Eds.), *Images of aging: Cultural representations of later life* (pp. 79–96). New York: Routledge.

Wray, M. (2006). *Not quite white: White trash and the boundaries of whiteness*. Durham, N.C.: Duke University Press.

Wylie, M. (1964). *Career girl, watch your step!* New York: Dodd Mead.

Yarm, M. (2012). *Everybody loves our town: An oral history of grunge*. New York: Three Rivers Press.

Young, I. M. (1990). *Throwing like a girl and other essays in feminist philosophy and social theory*. Bloomington, IN: Indiana University Press.

Young, I. M. (2010). Breasted experience: The look and the feeling. In R. Weitz (Ed.), *The politics of women's bodies*, 3rd ed. (pp. 179–91). New York: Oxford University Press.

Yount, K. R. (1991). Ladies, flirts, and tomboys: Strategies for managing sexual harassment in an underground coal mine. *Journal of Contemporary Ethnography*, 19, 396–422.

Zalta, A. K., & Chambless, D. L. (2012). Understanding gender differences in anxiety: The mediating effects of instrumentality and mastery. *Psychology of Women Quarterly* 36(4), 488–99.

Zamarripa, M. X., Wampold, B. E., & Gregory, E. (2003). Male gender role conflict, depression, and anxiety: Clarification and generalizability to women. *Journal of Counseling Psychology*, 50(3), 333–38.

Zeisler, A. (2016). *We were feminists once: From Riot Grrrl to Cover Girl, the buying and selling of a political movement*. New York: Public Affairs.

Zhang, L., & Haller, B. (2013). Consuming images: How mass media impact the identity of people with disabilities. *Communication Quarterly*, 61(3), 333–39.

Zuberi, T. & Bonilla-Silva, E. (Eds.). (2008). *White logic, white methods: Racism and methodology*. Lanham, MD: Rowman & Littlefield Publishers.

Index

AAGPBL. *See* All-American Girls Professional Baseball League

AAU. *See* Amateur Athletic Union

About Face: The Supermodels Then and Now, 195–196, 204

acculturative stress, 43

adolescence: body image during puberty, 29–30, 40–41; female gender role stress/conflict in, 57–61; gender expectations in, 40–41; girls' safety and, 58–59, 193; media and, 88; sexting in, 61

adolescent femininity, 88–89

advertising campaigns: consumer capitalism and, 86; in magazines, 87, 88; in media, 75, 86–93; sex in, 86–87; stereotyping by, 86–87

African-American/Black masculinity, 129

African-American/Black women, 15, 29; beauty culture industry and, 161–163; femininity of, 68–69, 161–163; hypersexuality and, 161, 162–163; invincible Black woman syndrome, 143; in magazines, 68; media on, 69; stereotyping of, 68

age: beauty culture industry and media shaming of older women, 201–204; beauty culture industry and youth, 78, 197–200; body image and, 196; cosmetic surgery and, 100, 197–198, 199, 202; discussion on, 205; emphasized femininity relating to, 190–191, 192–195; ethnicity and, 197; femininity, across age cohorts, 37; feminism relating to, 191–192; girls and young women socialized to emphasized femininity, 192–195; health, femininities, and, xviii, 189–205; magazines on, 201–203,

204; mother-daughter relationship and, 192; older women, power, and femininity, 195–201; political activism relating to, 217–218; popular culture, youth, and empowerment, 89; socialization and, 189; socio-economic class and, 197; workplace relating to, 197

ageism, 191, 217

All-American Girls Professional Baseball League (AAGPBL), 126–128, 128

Alley, Kirstie, 46

Amateur Athletic Union (AAU), 126

androgyny: femininity and, 21; in magazines, 21; in workplace, 107

anxiety: emphasized femininity and, 86–93; from female gender role stress/conflict, 54, 55–56, 61. *See also* Gender Role Stress/Conflict paradigm

appropriate femininity, 133

Aristotle, 14–15

Asian/Asian-American women, 157–160

athletics. *See* sports and athletics

Babylonian Code of Hammurabi, 14

baby showers, 76–77, 99–100

baseball, 126–128

basketball, 128

bathroom signs, 7

beauty culture industry: African-American/Black women and, 161–163; cosmetic surgery and, 100, 197–198, 199, 202; ethnicity and, 81–82; hairstyles and, 80; mannequins in, 78; older women shamed by, 201–204; salons in, 80; social acceptance and, 79–80;

standard for perfection and, 77–82; thinness and, 77–79; *What not to Wear* and, 47; youth and, 78, 197–200

beauty maintenance, 4–5, 53; popular culture on, 60–61

beauty pageants: for children, 97–99; Miss America Pageant, 12, 83, 97

beauty products, 78, 79–80, 198–199

Beauvoir, Simone de, 224

benchmarking behaviors, 29, 47

Bikini Kill, 20, 85

binary dualism, 2–3

biological sex-role socialization model, 172–173

biological theory, 6

Bitchy Resting Face (BRF), 177–178

body: femininity and body shape/size, 149–150; science, sports, and, 139

bodybuilding, 136

body image: age and, 196; child bearing and, 40, 100–101, 114–116; ideal femininities and, 27–28; media and, 29, 47; during puberty, 29–30, 40–41

body projects, 7

body weight: beauty culture industry and thinness, 77–79; college experience and thinness, 49–50; cult of thinness, 7; ethnicity, thinness, and, 42–45; family and, 42–45; fat shaming, 78–79; food and, 44–45; media on, 46

body work, 114–115

boxing, 135

brassiere: fashion and, 83; training bra, 29

breasts: dress and, 34, 159; ethnicity and, 30–31; hiding, 29–30; ideal femininities and, 29–31, 34; in magazines, 31; in media, 31; in sexting, 61; training bra and, 29

BRF. *See* Bitchy Resting Face

bricolage, 172

Bridget Jones's Diary, 22, 32

bullying, 71

career. *See* workplace

career girls, 118–119

cheerleading, 130–132

chick flicks, 89–90

child bearing: body image and, 40, 100–101, 114–116; body work after, 114–115

child beauty pageants, 97–99

Chisholm, Shirley, 207, 221–222, 223

Civil Rights Act, 103–104; Title IX, 125–132

Civil Rights and Economic Opportunity Act, 103

Clinton, Hillary Rodham, 207–208, 211–212, 222–224

college experience: ethnicity and, 49–50; ideal femininities and, 49–50; peer group acceptance in, 66; thinness and, 49–50

commodity feminism, 41–42, 215

consumer capitalism, 86

consumer culture, 18

consumerism, 48, 78

consumerist misrepresentations, xvii–xviii, 75–77; beauty culture industry and standard for perfection, 77–82; discussion on, 101; emphasized femininity across media platforms, 86–93; by fashion industry and femininity trends, 82–86; femininity framed through rituals, 93–101

coping behaviors, 167; for female athletes, 137, 138

corsets, 31, 33

cosmetic surgery: age and, 197–198, 199, 202; as rituals, 100

Cox, Courteney, 46

crisis of masculinity, 56–57

cult of thinness, 7

culture: consumer, 18; drag queen and king, 181–183; gender roles relating to, 53; multiculturalism and, 157; postfeminist, 77, 215. *See also* beauty culture industry; popular culture

culture jamming, 48

Darwin, Charles, 15, 228

data collection and analysis, ix–xii

Diana (princess), 23, 81–82

discrepancy strain, 55

dolls, 80–81
domesticity, 4–5; female gender role stress/conflict on, 72–73; gender roles and, 11; ideal femininities and, 35–36; media on, 48; unpaid work at home, 108–109, 110
drag queen and king culture, 181–183
dress, 65–67, 76; breasts and, 34, 159; hijab and, 153–154; in politics, 222–224; stereotyping according to, 41–42, 229; in workplace, 113–114

eating disorders, 45
eldercare, 109
emotion: smiling and, 63, 177–178; in workplace, 112–113
emphasized femininity, 9–11, 54, 176, 177; age relating to, 190–191, 192–195; anxiety and, 86–93; drag queen and king culture for, 181–183; girls and young women socialized to, 192–195; in media, 86–93; sports and, 133; under-emphasized femininity and, 190
empowerment: through *girl power* movements, 18–21, 84–86, 215–216; popular culture, youth, and, 89; in *Sex and the City*, 90
equality femininity, 10, 209
Equal Pay Act, 103
Equal Rights Amendment (ERA), 15–16, 169, 219–220
erotic-chaste dialectic, 60, 126
ethnicity: age and, 197; beauty culture industry and, 81–82; body weight, thinness, and, 42–45; breasts and, 30–31; college experience and, 49–50; female gender role stress/conflict and, 67–70; femininity relating to, 45–46, 156–163; politics relating to, 212–213; socio-economic class and, 165, 166–167; sports and athletics and, 132–133. *See also specific ethnic groups*
exclusion, 237–238

family: body weight, thinness, and, 42–45; girls, women, femininity, and, 39–45; mother-daughter relationship, 39–40, 42–45, 192
fantasies, 75
fashion: brassiere and, 83; consumerist misrepresentations and femininity trends in, 82–86; corsets and, 31, 33; feminists and, 84–85; *girl power* movements and, 84–86; guns and, 83–84; ideal femininities and, 32–34; masculinity and, 83; modesty and, 60; pink in, 92–93; popular feminism and, 215–216; tailored suits in, 83, 84, 222, 229. *See also* beauty culture industry; dress
fashion-beauty complex, 76
fashion magazines, 82. *See also* magazines
Fat Actress, 46
fat shaming, 78–79
female athletes: celebrity, 137, 138, 142–145; coping behaviors for, 137, 138; media representations of, 139–142. *See also* sports and athletics
female gender knowledge, 192–193
female gender role demands, 57–61
female gender roles, 11–14. *See also* gender roles
female gender role stress/conflict, xvii; in adolescence, 57–61; "Am I feminine enough?," 61–67; anxiety from, 54, 55–56, 61; discussion on, 73; on domesticity, 72–73; ethnicity and, 67–70; femininity and, 53–57; GRS/C paradigm and, 55–57; intra-gender competition and femininity, 70–72; media and, 58, 64; private/public spheres dichotomy and, 72–73; protectionism and, 58–59; social identity intersectionalities and, 67–70, 148; in social institutions, 65–67; struggling with female gender role demands, 57–61; as theoretical foundations, xii–xiii; in workplace, 73
Female Gender Role Stress Scale (FGRSS), 56
FEMEN, 218–219
feminine masculinities, 171–172; sexuality and, xviii

The Feminine Mystique (Friedan), 13, 62, 113, 191–192

femininities, xvi; age, health, and, xviii, 189–205; on continuum, 234; hierarchy of, 147, 176; masculine, xviii, 171–172, 179, 210; non-heteronormative, 150–152; oppositional, 11, 65, 71, 150–152; pariah, 10, 150–152; politics and, xviii, 207–225; subordinate, 176; in workplace, xviii, 103–121. *See also* ideal femininities

femininity: adolescent, 88; of African-American/Black women, 68–69, 161–163; across age cohorts, 37; "Am I feminine enough?," 61–67; androgyny and, 21; appropriate, 133; of Asian/Asian-American women, 157–160; backlash effects of femininity expectancies, 16–18; body shape/size and, 149–150; concept of, xvii; defining, 1–6, 36–39, 58, 229, 237–238; discussion on, 25; equality, 10, 209; ethnicity relating to, 45–46, 156–163; female gender roles and, 11–14; female gender role stress/conflict and, 53–57; framing as purity, innocence, and unattainable, 93–101; Freud on, 13–14, 174; gender construction of, 2–3; *girlie-girl*, 18–21, 41, 193; girls, family, women, and, 39–45; GRS/C, sports, and, 132–139; GRS/C paradigm and, 55–57, 230–231; heteronormativity and, 4–5, 179–181; historical perspectives on, 14–16; intersectionality shaping, xviii; intra-gender competition and, 70–72; of Latinas, 69–70, 160; leadership and, 64–65; male fear of, 56–57; masculinity relating to, 2–4, 7–8; non-cisgendered people and, 152–153; older women, power, and, 195–201; paraphernalia of, 6, 229; physical disability, 164–165; power relations and, 3–4, 8–11, 195–201, 237–238; preppy, 71; rhetoric of, 22–23, 228; through rituals, 93–101;

sexuality and, 172–177; socialization and, 231–233; socio-economic class and, 165–167; subversive, 182–183; symbols of, 22–23, 228; undefining, 58; in Victorian society, 15, 165; women held back through, 14–16; women's rights and, 14–16. *See also* emphasized femininity

Femininity Ideology Scale (FIS), 56

femininity-inspired microaggressions, 177–178

femininity trends, in fashion industry, 82–86

feminism, 84–85; age relating to, 191–192; backlash against, 62, 88, 168–169; commodity, 41–42, 215; first-wave, 216, 220; generational differences among popular and third-wave feminism, 215–216; now and later, 235–237; in politics, 88; second-wave, 62, 150, 215–216, 220; social identity intersectionalities and, 150, 168–169; term use for, xvi; third-wave, 84–85. *See also* postfeminism

feminists: fashion and, 84–85; in media, 64; in popular culture, 17; poststructuralist, 8

feminist theory, xiii

FGRSS. *See* Female Gender Role Stress Scale

figure skating, 142

film medium, 89–90. *See also specific films*

first-wave feminism, 216, 220

FIS. *See* Femininity Ideology Scale

fitness, 194–195. *See also* sports and athletics

food, 44–45

football, 135

Foucault, Michel, 8

Freud, Sigmund, 13–14, 174

Friedan, Betty, 80; *The Feminine Mystique*, 13, 62, 113, 191–192

Friends, 46

gender: Foucault on, 8; sex distinguished from, 6–8; use of term, xvi

gender construction, 2–3
gender discrimination: gendered
    physiological discrimination, 139; in
    politics, 213–214; in schools,
    130–132
gender double bind, 221–224
gendered physiological discrimination,
    139
gender expectations, 40–41
gender identity, 172
gender roles: culture relating to, 53;
    domesticity and, 11; female, 11–14;
    power relations and, 53–54;
    stereotyping associated with, 5,
    9–10, 180–181
gender role strain, 55, 194
Gender Role Stress/Conflict (GRS/C)
    paradigm: emergence of, 55;
    femininity and, 55–57, 230–231; on
    masculinity, 180; sports, femininity,
    and, 132–139. *See also* female gender
    role stress/conflict
gender socialization practices, 54–55
gender variance, 8
Gibson, Charles Dana, 45
Gibson Girl, 45
girlie-girl femininity, 18–21, 41, 193
girl power movements, 18–21, 215–216;
    fashion and, 84–86
girls: activism by, 217–219; career,
    118–119; family, women, femininity,
    and, 39–45; safety for, 58–59, 193;
    socialized to emphasized
    femininity, 192–195; Title IX and
    school sports for, 129–132. *See also*
    adolescence
glitter bombing, 93
Great Depression, 15, 129
GRS/C paradigm. *See* Gender Role
    Stress/Conflict paradigm
guns, 83–84

hairstyles, 80
Hanna, Kathleen, 20–21, 84
health: age, femininities, and, xviii,
    189–205; discussion on, 205; eating
    disorders and, 45; fitness and,
    194–195
hegemonic masculinity, 9–10, 54

heteronormativity: femininity and, 4–5,
    179–181; masculinity and, 180; as
    social control, 179–181; stereotyping
    of, 180–181
hierarchy of femininities, 147, 176
hijab, 153–154
homophobia, 57
hormone replacement therapy (HRT),
    200
hypersexuality: African-American/
    Black women and, 161, 162–163; in
    popular culture, 59–60

ideal femininities, xvii; body image
    and, 27–28; breasts and, 29–31, 34;
    college experience and, 49–50;
    defining, 36–39; discussion on,
    50–51; domesticity and, 35–36;
    fashion and, 32–34; girls, women,
    family, and femininity, 39–45; in
    magazines, 32–34; media and,
    31–34, 45–49; motherhood relating
    to, 35–36; narcissism and, 34–35; in
    new millennium, 36–39; social
    comparisons on ideal feminine
    woman, 28–36; stereotyping
    according to dress, 41–42, 229;
    thinness, body weight, and
    ethnicity, 42–45; words/phrases
    associated with, 36–39, 37, 174–175
identity: gender, 172; male, 175–176.
    See also social identity
    intersectionalities
individualism, 88
Industrial Revolution, 15
innocence, 93–101
intersectionality: femininity shaped by,
    xviii; as theoretical foundations, xv.
    See also social identity
    intersectionalities
intra-gender competition: femininity
    and, 70–72; stereotyping of, 70; in
    workplace, 72
invincible Black woman syndrome, 143

journalism, 117–118, 219–224. *See also*
    media

Kardashians, 91, 114–115, 198

Kelly, Grace (princess), 23
Knowles, Beyoncé, 29

language, 16–17, 227; speech dominance and, 112; word choices and, xvi; words/phrases associated with ideal femininities, 36–39, 37, 174–175
Latinas: femininity of, 69–70, 160; *marianismo* for, 160; *Quinceañera* ritual for, 93, 94, 160. *See also* ethnicity
leadership: femininity and, 64–65; in politics, 211, 220–222; in workplace, 106
A League of Their Own, 127–128
lesbianism, 150–152, 179; labeling of, 64; media on, 64
Lopez, Jennifer, 104–105
Love, Courtney, 20–21
luminosity, 91–92

magazines, 12, 148–149; advertising campaigns in, 87, 88; African-American/Black women in, 68; on age, 201–203, 204; androgyny in, 21; breasts in, 31; fashion, 82; ideal femininities in, 32–34; motherhood in, 48; *Playboy* magazine, 13, 220; *Sports Illustrated* swimsuit issue, 140–141
male fear, of femininity, 56–57
male identity, 175–176
mannequins, 78
Manuel, Simone, 140
Marciano, Paul, 32–34
marginalization, 10
marianismo, 160
The Mary Tyler Moore Show, 107
masculine femininities, 171–172, 179, 210; sexuality and, xviii
masculinities, xvi; on continuum, 234; feminine, xviii, 171–172
masculinity: African-American/Black, 129; crisis of, 56–57; drag queen and king culture and, 181–183; fashion and, 83; femininity relating to, 2–4, 7–8; GRS/C paradigm on, 180; hegemonic, 9–10, 54;

heteronormativity and, 180; male identity and, 175–176; studies on, 227; theory on, 86; traditional, 57
media, 12, 229; adolescence and, 88; advertising campaigns in, 75, 86–93; on African-American/Black women, 69; benchmarking behaviors by, 29, 47; body image and, 29, 47; on body weight, 46; breasts in, 31; consumerism and, 48, 76; on domesticity, 48; emphasized femininity in, 86–93; on ERA, 220; fantasies and, 75; female gender role stress/conflict and, 58, 64; feminists in, 64; ideal femininities and, 31–34, 45–49; journalism and, 117–118, 219–224; on lesbianism, 64; on military women, 185; on motherhood, 48; older women shamed by, 201–204; on rituals, 76–77; sexuality in, 32; social, 61, 88, 177–178; social learning from, 48; sports industry and female athlete representation by, 139–142; stereotyping by, 76–77; *Toddlers and Tiaras* and, 97–99; Walt Disney films and, 46–47, 91–92; on women in politics, 219–224; workplace and, 117–119. *See also* magazines; popular culture; *specific films*
metrosexualism, 57, 180
microaggressions, 177–178
MILF acronym, 115–116
military, 183–185
Miss America Pageant, 12, 83, 97–99
modesty, 60
mother-daughter relationship, 39–40; age and, 192; body weight, thinness, and, 42–45
motherhood: baby showers and, 76–77, 99–100; body work in, 114–115; child bearing and body image, 40, 100–101, 114–116; ideal femininities relating to, 35–36; in magazines, 48; media on, 48; MILF acronym and, 115–116; new momism, 114–116; parental stereotyping, 41; politicized, 214, 225; pregnancy, sex, and sports, 125–126; support for

mothers, 111; in workplace, 114–116
motorcycles, 136
multiculturalism, 157
muscle molls, 125
Myers, Michelle, 157, 158

narcissism, 34–35
new momism, 114–116
non-cisgendered people, 152–153
non-heteronormative femininities, 150–152
norms, 16–18
nostalgia, 6, 90

Obama, Michelle, 212–213
occupations. *See* workplace
older women: beauty culture industry and media shaming of, 201–204; power, femininity, and, 195–201. *See also* age
Olympic Game events, 124, 139, 139–140, 142–144
O'Neil, James M., 57
oppositional femininities, 11, 65, 71, 150–152
The Origin of the Species (Darwin), 15

paid-work environment, 111–114
Palin, Sarah, 214, 222
Paltrow, Gwyneth, 92
paraphernalia of femininity, 6, 229
parental stereotyping, 41
pariah femininities, 10, 150–152
patriarchal ideology, 11
patriarchy, 88, 107, 173
peer group acceptance, 66
peer pressure, 64; bullying and, 71
perfection, standard for, 77–82
physical disability, 164–165
pink, 92–93
Playboy magazine, 13, 220
political activism: age relating to, 217–218; girls' and women's activism and women's issues, 217–219; social movements and, 15–16
politicized motherhood, 214, 225
politics: backlash against women politicians, 209–210; Chisholm in,

207, 221–222, 223; Clinton in, 207–208, 211–212, 222–224; discussion on, 224–225; dress in, 222–224; ethnicity relating to, 212–213; femininities and, xviii, 207–225; feminism in, 88; gender discrimination in, 213–214; gender double bind and, 221–224; generational differences among popular and third-wave feminism, 215–216; leadership in, 211, 220–222; media, on women in, 219–224; Obama in, 212–213; Palin in, 214, 222; private/public spheres dichotomy and, 11; sexuality and, 212; stereotyping women in, 208–214
popular culture, 12; on beauty maintenance, 60–61; *Bridget Jones's Diary* and, 22, 32; chick flicks and, 89–90; *About Face: The Supermodels Then and Now* and, 195–196, 204; female celebrity athletes in, 142–145; feminists in, 17; film medium and, 89–90; *Friends* and, 46; hypersexuality in, 59–60; luminosity, sparklefication, and, 91–92; rhetoric on, 22; *Say Yes to the Dress* and, 32; *Sex and the City* and, 22, 32, 90; *Spice Girls* and, 19, 20; workplace relating to, 114–116; youth, empowerment, and, 89
popular feminism, 215–216
porn stars, 64
postfeminism, 17–18, 76, 215–216
postfeminist culture, 77, 215
postfeminist thinking, 87–88
poststructuralist feminists, 8
power relations: femininity and, 3–4, 8–11, 195–201, 237–238; gender roles and, 53–54; marginalization and, 10; older women, femininity, and, 195–201; popular culture, youth, and empowerment, 89. *See also* empowerment
pregnancy, 125–126. *See also* child bearing; motherhood
preppy femininity, 71
Princess Diana, 23, 81–82

Princess Grace Kelly, 23
private/public spheres dichotomy: female gender role stress/conflict and, 72–73; politics and, 11; in workplace, 107–113
prom, 96–97
protectionism, 58–59, 193
puberty, 29–30, 40–41. *See also* adolescence
purity: balls, 93–95; framing femininity as, 93–101
Pussy Riot, 218–219

Quinceañera ritual, 93, 94, 160

racism, 69
religion, 153–156
Reserve Officers' Training Corps (ROTC), 184
rhetoric: of femininity, 22–23, 228; on popular culture, 22
rhetorical criticism, xiii–xv
riotgrrl movement, 18–21, 85–86
rituals: baby showers, 76–77, 99–100, 100; cosmetic surgery as, 100; femininity through, 93–101; media on, 76–77; prom, 96–97; purity balls, 93–95; *Quinceañera*, 93, 94, 160; weddings, 32, 76–77, 95–96, 99–100
"Rosie the Riveter," 23, 24
ROTC. *See* Reserve Officers' Training Corps
rugby, 135

safety, 58–59, 193
salons, 80
sandwich generation, 109
Say Yes to the Dress, 32
school: gender discrimination in, 130–132; sports for girls and Title IX, 129–132. *See also* college experience
science, 139
second-wave feminism, 62, 150, 215–216, 220
sex: in advertising campaigns, 86–87; biological sex-role socialization model, 172–173; gender distinguished from, 6–8; pregnancy,

sports, and, 125–126
Sex and the City, 22, 32; empowerment in, 90
sexism, 54, 69
sexting, 61
sexual deviation, 10
sexual harassment, 106
sexuality: erotic-chaste dialectic and, 60, 126; feminine masculinities and, xviii; femininity and, 172–177; masculine femininities and, xviii; in media, 32; metrosexualism, 57, 180; politics and, 212; sports and athletics relating to, 134–135; stereotyping and, 180; in Victorian society, 150
smiling, 63, 177–178
Soccer Girl Problems, 137–139
social acceptance, 79–80
social cognitive theory, 39
social comparisons, 28–36
social comparison theory, xiii, xiv–xv
social constructionism, xiii, xiv
social control, 179–181
social expectations, 134–137
social identity intersectionalities, xviii, 147–149; discussion on, 170; ethnicity and femininity, 45–46, 156–163; female gender role stress/conflict and, 67–70, 148; femininity and body shape/size, 149–150; feminism and, 150, 168–169; non-cisgendered people and femininity, 152–153; non-heteronormative, pariah, and oppositional femininities and, 150–152; physical disability and femininity, 164–165; religion and spirituality, 153–156, 154; socio-economic class and femininity, 165–167
social institutions, 65–67
socialization: age and, 189; biological sex-role socialization model, 172–173; femininity and, 231–233; gender socialization practices, 54–55; of girls and young women, to emphasized femininity, 192–195; theory, 39
social learning, 66; from media, 48

social media, 61, 177–178; Twitter hashtag, #WomenAgainstFeminism, 88. *See also* media

social movements: political activism and, 15–16; stereotyping and, 41

social norms, 16–18

social roles, 4

socio-economic class: age and, 197; ethnicity and, 165, 166–167; femininity and, 165–167

softness, 174–175

sparklefication, 91–92

speech dominance, 112

Spice Girls, 19, 20

spirituality, 153–156, 154

sports and athletics, xviii; AAGPBL and baseball, 126–128; AAU, 126; basketball, 128; bodybuilding, 136; boxing, 135; cheerleading, 130–132; coping behaviors for female athletes, 137, 138; discussion on, 145–146; emphasized femininity and, 133; ethnicity and, 132–133; female celebrity athletes, 137, 138, 142–145; figure skating, 142; fitness, 194–195; football, 135; GRS/C, femininity, and, 132–139; media and sports industry, 139–142; Olympic Game events, 124, 139, 139–140, 142–144; professional women's sports, birth of, 126–129; rugby, 135; school sports for girls and Title IX, 129–132; science, body, and, 139; sex, pregnancy, and, 125–126; sexuality relating to, 134–135; Soccer Girl Problems, 137–139; social expectations surrounding femininity and, 134–137; sport typing in, 124, 130, 141; tennis, 137, 138, 143–144; before and after Title IX, 125–132; tomboys and, 126–127, 142–145; Zumba, 134

Sports Illustrated swimsuit issue, 140–141

sport typing, 124, 130, 141

stereotyping, 4; by advertising campaigns, 86–87; of African-American/Black women, 68; by

dress, 41–42, 229; gender roles associated with, 5, 9–10, 180–181; of heteronormativity, 180–181; of intra-gender competition, 70; by media, 76–77; parental, 41; in politics, 208–214; sexuality and, 180; social movements and, 41

strength, 174–175

subordinate femininities, 176

subversive femininity, 182–183

suicide, 59

superwoman myth, 143

symbols: on bathroom signs, 7; of femininity, 22–23, 228

tailored suits, 83, 84, 222, 229

10 Years Younger, 47

tennis, 137, 138, 143–144

theoretical foundations: female gender role stress/conflict as, xii–xiii; feminist theory as, xiii; intersectionality as, xv; rhetorical criticism as, xiii–xv; social comparison theory as, xiii, xiv–xv; social constructionism as, xiii, xiv

thinness: beauty culture industry and, 77–79; body weight, ethnicity, and, 42–45; college experience and, 49–50; cult of, 7; family and, 42–45. *See also* body weight

third-wave feminism, 84–85, 215–216

Title IX: school sports for girls and, 129–132; sports and athletics before, 125–132

Toddlers and Tiaras, 97–99

tomboys, 126–127; female celebrity athletes and, 142–145; labeling of, 144–145

toys, 80–81

traditional female gender roles, 11–14

traditional masculinity, 57

training bra, 29

Twitter hashtag, #WomenAgainstFeminism, 88

unattainable femininity, 93–101

undefining femininity, 58

under-emphasized femininity, 190

unfeminine, 63–64

unpaid work, at home, 108–109, 110

victim-blaming, 63
Victorian society: femininity in, 15, 165; sexuality in, 150
violence, 63, 124

wage gap, 104
Walker, Alice, 84
Walt Disney films, 46–47, 91–92
We Can Do It! campaign, 23, 24
weddings, 76–77, 95–96, 99–100; *Say Yes to the Dress* and, 32
What not to Wear, 47
Williams, Serena, 137, 138, 143
women: femininity holding women back, 14–16; girls, family, femininity, and, 39–45; ideal feminine woman, 28–36; intergenerational differences in, 10; in military, 183–185, 186; use of term, xvi. *See also* older women; *specific subjects*
women's rights, 207–208; activism and women's issues, 217–219; Equal Pay Act for, 120; ERA on, 15–16, 169, 219–220; femininity and, 14–16
women's suffrage movement, 207, 210, 211
Wonder Woman, 80–81
word choices, xvi
words/phrases, associated with ideal femininities, 36–39, 174–175

workplace, 64; age relating to, 197; androgyny in, 107; career girls, 118–119; discussion on, 120–121; dress in, 113–114; emotion in, 112–113; Equal Pay Act relating to, 120; female gender role stress/ conflict in, 73; femininities in, xviii, 103–121; inequitable and inhospitable, 104–107; intra-gender competition in, 72; leadership in, 106; media and, 117–119; motherhood in, 114–116; new momism and, 114–116; occupations historically unavailable to women, 116; occupations with gender imbalance, 119–120; paid-work environment, 111–114; popular culture relating to, 114–116; private/ public spheres dichotomy and division of labor in, 107–113; sexual harassment in, 106; unpaid work, at home, 108–109, 110; wage gap in, 104
World War I, 184
World War II, 23, 184, 186

youth: beauty culture industry and, 78, 197–200; popular culture, empowerment, and, 89. *See also* adolescence; age

Zumba, 134

About the Author

Donnalyn Pompper, PhD, is a tenured Full Professor working in the School of Media & Communication at Temple University in Philadelphia, where she teaches and researches about power as it plays out in social identity (e.g., age, ethnicity/race, gender, sexual orientation), in organizations, and in media representations. Overall, her research provides routes for enabling people, globally, to enjoy equality and respect at work and in ways their social identity groups are represented across mass media platforms. She is an award-wining and internationally recognized scholar who has written *Corporate Social Responsibility, Sustainability, and Public Relations: Negotiating Multiple Complex Challenges* (2015, Routledge), *Practical and Theoretical Implications of Successfully Doing Difference in Organizations* (2014, Emerald Publishing), and co-edited *Representing Resistance: Media, Civil Disobedience & the Global Justice Movement* (2003, Praeger) with Andy Opel. Pompper also has published extensively in academic journals such as *Sex Roles: A Journal of Research, Mass Communication & Society, Journal of Applied Communication Research, Journal of Public Relations Research*, and many other peer-reviewed academic journals. She may be contacted at dpompper@temple.edu.